Financial Aspects of Marketing

The Marketing Series is one of the most comprehensive collections of textbooks in marketing and sales available from the UK today.

Published by Heinemann Professional Publishing on behalf of the Chartered Institute of Marketing, the series has been specifically designed, developed and progressively updated over a number of years to support students studying for the Institute's certificate and diploma qualifications. The scope of the subjects covered by the series, however, means that it is of equal value to anyone studying other further or higher business and/or marketing related qualifications.

HEINEMANN
ON BEHALF OF
THE CHARTERED
INSTITUTE OF MARKETING
THE
MARKETING SERIES
CIM

Formed in 1911, the Chartered Institute of Marketing is now the largest professional marketing management body in Europe with over 22,000 members and 25,000 students located worldwide. Its primary objectives are focused on the development of awareness and understanding of marketing throughout UK industry and commerce and in the raising of standards of professionalism in the education, training and practice of this key business discipline.

Other titles in the series

Financial Aspects of Marketing

Keith Ward

Published on behalf of the
Chartered Institute of Marketing

Heinemann Professional Publishing

Heinemann Professional Publishing Ltd
Halley Court, Jordan Hill, Oxford OX2 8EJ

OXFORD   LONDON   MELBOURNE   AUCKLAND   SINGAPORE
IBADAN   NAIROBI   GABORONE   KINGSTON

First published 1989
Reprinted 1990 (twice)

British Library Cataloguing in Publication Data
Ward, Keith
Financial aspects of marketing.
I. Title   II. Institute of Marketing
658.1'55

ISBN 0 434 92221 8

Photoset by Wilmaset, Birkenhead, Wirral
Printed in Great Britain by
Redwood Press Limited, Melksham, Wiltshire

Contents

Preface

The objective of this book is to create a degree of financial literacy among marketing managers and other managers in marketing-led businesses. Thus the book is not designed to train bookkeepers or to prepare the reader for a career as an accountant but to explain and illustrate all the financial techniques which are relevant to marketing decisions and business in general.

In order to achieve this the structure of the book is designed around the practical role of finance and accounting in business with a section on each stage of the continual process of 'analysis, planning and control'. The last part of the book is given over to examples relating to each element of the marketing mix and to marketing strategy. This aims to demonstrate how the techniques are applied within the marketing area, and to reinforce the emphasis of the book on the role of finance as an aid to decision-making not as an historic scorekeeper.

The emphasis on marketing issues throughout means that the book covers the new, completely revised syllabus of the Chartered Institute of Marketing paper in Financial and Management Accounting and should therefore be of help to students preparing for this examination. I am grateful to Professor Richard Wilson, Senior Examiner in this area for the Chartered Institute of Marketing, for his very detailed comments on the drafts of the book.

No assumption has been made regarding previous knowledge of the subject and so, wherever possible, financial terms are defined when they are first used. To assist in cross-referencing the pages of these definitions are given in the index, if the reference is not included in the detailed list of contents.

I would like to thank the Burton Group plc for permission to use their figures but the views expressed and relationships calculated are, as in all the company examples including those whose strategies are examined, completely my responsibility. I also want to thank my secretary, Sheila

Hart, who (with able assistance from her colleagues, Chris Williams and Marjorie Dawe) typed the several versions of the manuscript, and my wife, Angela, and children, Samantha and Robert, for putting up with me while I was writing this book.

I hope that you, the reader, feel that the effort has been worthwhile but I would like to offer a word of encouragement. The subject may, at first, appear daunting but, if accountants can understand it, it cannot be that difficult!

Keith Ward
Cranfield

PART ONE

INTRODUCTION AND OVERVIEW

1

Accounting as 'the common business language'

All businesses need to record the financial details of their external trading transactions (for example, sales and purchases) so that they at least know who owes them money and what money they owe – this is also useful at a personal level but is normally on a much simplified scale. However, this very detailed level of 'accounting for the business' is only one aspect of financial involvement in business management and is not the main area of emphasis for this book. In any commercial operation there is a continual need to make decisions. This consequently requires converting a multitude of totally different resources into some common system of measurement or currency so that meaningful comparisons between alternatives can be made and, therefore, sound decisions taken.

In the production environment of a car manufacturing company, for example, it is impossible to compare meaningfully tonnes of steel, numbers of machines including robots, hours of labour, etc. without converting each to an equivalent monetary value. This conversion enables the potential benefits of reducing the amount of steel or labour by increasing the level of automation to be properly evaluated. The requirement for this financial analysis is equally great in all businesses and all areas of business, not least the marketing area. For example, it may be possible to organize the sales activity for a particular fast-moving consumer goods (fmcg) company in a number of ways. These could range from having a directly employed salaried field sales force, through employing a mainly office-based telephone selling operation supported by part-time field merchandisers, to using a third party specialist sales company paid on a commission basis only. If a sensible comparison of these alternatives is to be made, the financial costs and benefits of each should be compared. Thus a common language can be established by converting business issues and decisions to their financial consequences. It should be noted immediately that, as is clear from the sales force question, obtaining the necessary financial information may not be easy and will often require the use of considerable managerial judgement. Frequently it will call for an assessment of an alternative which has not been tried before and therefore no past financial information exists. This process of using accounting as 'the common business language' is logical since a major business objective is normally to earn a satisfactory financial return for the owners of the business. This highlights three fundamentally important issues: it is vital that the right alternatives are being considered, and that these alternatives are compared against a consistent base by carrying out the financial analysis properly, and that financial control is possible when the decision is implemented.

The importance of this financial analysis to business decisions is so great that it cannot be left to the financial managers and accountants, because they may be unaware either of all the possible alternatives or of the full consequences of each alternative. This is particularly true in the critical area of marketing decisions where a complex interrelated series of alternatives will often be available and where the full consequences require a very good understanding of the particular marketing relationships. It must also be emphasized that the company only normally records what *has* happened on a historical basis whereas decisions clearly affect the future, and hence the relevant financial information will normally be forward-looking.

Financial involvement in marketing

A sensible analysis of these past events may provide a good basis for planning the future. If this process is enhanced by monitoring how well plans are being achieved and making changes where appropriate, then a sound basis of financial control can be established. This process is clearly continuous as decisions taken affect plans and so on. This book concentrates on the following three phases of financial involvement in marketing:

1 financial analysis to establish the basis for planning;
2 financial planning to set objectives and decide how to achieve them;
3 financial control to monitor the outcome of decisions and the achievement of objectives including corrective action where necessary.

In a well-managed company these three phases of financial involvement in marketing should be integrated into the overall marketing activities of the business, in a similar way to the classical four Ps of the marketing mix (product, price, promotion, place; illustrated in Figure 1.1).

It may be helpful to consider these financial aspects in the context of a

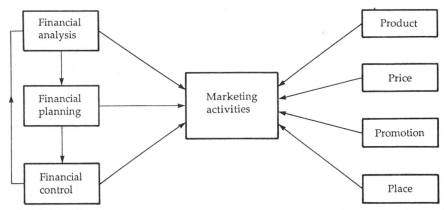

Figure 1.1 *Financial involvement in marketing*

proposal to start a new marketing company. A marketing consultant developed a new concept of using savings stamps as a way of building consumer loyalty, in a variation of the 'Green Shield stamp' idea. These savings stamps were to be given away on an exclusive basis by selected retailers to their customers but, instead of saving the stamps to redeem against a catalogue of products, the stamps would be redeemed through ABTA (Association of British Travel Agents) as partial payment for any holiday provided by 'participating' tour operators.

The attractions of the concept were many, but before launching the idea it was necessary to produce a financial plan to evaluate the viability of the business. In order to do this, the marketing consultant approached an operations management expert who also introduced a financial consultant, and together they constructed a detailed 5-year plan for the proposed business. This had to consider all the costs of operating the business (expenses), including purchasing the stamps and savings books, distributing them to retailers, collecting the redeemed books from travel agents, advertising and promoting the scheme, and administering the whole system. The plan also had to establish where the business obtained its sales revenue (income) from as, in this particular business, there is not one simple source of sales revenue (such as the sale of goods from a retail shop).

This 'holiday stamps' business had several potential sources of income which were needed to pay the operating expenses and also provide a reasonable level of profits (profit is the excess of sales revenue over the expenses incurred in the business and is considered in detail in Chapter 3) for the ultimate owners of the company. One source of income was a commission charged to the retailers when they purchased the stamps (prior to giving them away to their customers), but if the retailers could be made to pay for the stamps when purchased a second sizeable source of income would become available. There would be a considerable time delay between the stamps being received by the retailer and being redeemed at the travel agent; the retailer had to pass the stamps to their customers, who then had to accumulate them into full savings books, and use the full books as partial payment when booking a holiday (an annual event for many families). The company could have these funds deposited in a bank account throughout this period and thus earn considerable interest income before having to repay these funds as the stamps were redeemed. This valuable benefit caused by the impact of the timing of cash flows (that is, the receipt of cash into or the payment of cash out of the business) is of vital importance to many other businesses in other industry sectors and will be frequently referred to throughout the book.

The savers would frequently refer to their savings books both while filling them and when taking them to the travel agent for redemption. This could provide a third source of income through the sale of advertising space in the savings books both to participating retailers and tour operators. If advertising was to be sold a more glossy presentation would be needed for the books and this would increase their cost. Therefore it was important to ensure that the advertising revenue generated would exceed the extra costs incurred in improving the quality of the savings books.

A fourth potential source of income would have been through the non-redemption of many of the savings stamps sold to retailers and given by them to the customers. Some retail customers would lose them, not save them, or simply forget to redeem them; but the Trading Stamps Act provides for very strict controls to safeguard the public against 'stamp companies' not having adequate funds retained to meet all outstanding obligations for trading stamps issued by them. Thus legislative restrictions on potential sources of income must be taken into account.

These various potential sources of sales revenue, and their significantly differing time-frames, illustrate the complexities involved in trying to develop a valid financial evaluation of a deceptively simple potential business idea. A more detailed examination of a more standard new business should clarify these principles.

New business – example of financial involvement

George Taylor was made redundant from his job as a salesman for a toiletries company and has been selling some 'end-of-range' products, bought from his old employer, to small local retailers. He believes he could be successful if he opened his own business as a small retailer specializing in chemist-type products. He needs to collect a great deal of information if he is to produce a business plan to assess the potential success of this venture. A first decision is whether he buys an existing retailing business in his chosen field or starts a new business from scratch. In looking at existing businesses he needs to carry out financial analysis of their trading results and their assets (an asset is anything which has value and is owned by the business, such as buildings or stock held for resale) to determine whether they are worth the purchase price. This is complicated as their values (what it is worth paying for the businesses) will be determined not by their past results which he can analyse but by their expected future results. He then needs to compare the best purchase alternative with the potential of starting his own business. In this case less concrete material exists for analysis as there is no specific financial history to examine. By using his knowledge of the industry and any existing retail business that he is considering buying, he can build up a financial picture of his proposed business and the factors critical to its success or failure.

He has to decide on the way he wishes to develop his business and this will be particularly true in the area of the marketing mix or four Ps (see Figure 1.1). The location and size of the shop is vitally important in terms of generating customer flow, but the better sites will logically command higher prices and he has to balance the extra costs against the extra sales revenue he will generate. In fact he is not only interested in the sales revenue he can generate but in the profits he can make out of the extra sales revenue. Another decision relates to whether he tries to buy the shop (which creates an asset of the business) or rents it, which may be dictated by the funds he has available.

Having selected a potential site he has to consider the product range which he will carry. Will he generate enough customers if he only sells toiletries or does he need to sell other products such as fancy goods or possibly confectionery? This part of the analysis will include what other retailers there are in the vicinity, but the wider the range of products stocked the greater the amount of funds he will tie up in the business and the total funds available may again be a constraint.

He also needs to decide on his pricing policy as this will affect the level of his sales. He could decide to take a relatively small mark-up over his purchase cost (that is, sell for only slightly more than his buying-in price which would produce a low gross margin) and hope to sell a high volume, or he could accept a lower level of sales but at a higher margin. His financial analysis should consider the likely impact on sales levels of these differing pricing strategies, and this will again be affected by the level and style of competition in his chosen area.

Another important decision relates to the type and scale of promotional activity he plans to undertake which could consist of local advertising, selective low prices on certain product lines for limited periods, or some form of consumer loyalty bonus (such as savings stamps). The relative financial costs and benefits of each of these have to be analysed before sensible decisions can be reached.

This is merely the tip of the iceberg as far as the financial analysis George needs to undertake before he can develop a business plan for his new venture. It is also becoming evident that he is in danger of never finishing the analysis and hence never actually starting the new business. There is therefore a need for a cost/benefit analysis on the financial information which is considered before taking the decision to start in business. A cost/benefit analysis, in this context, compares the cost incurred in obtaining the information with the financial evaluation of the benefit which will be received by having the particular information. The benefit may be received through removing or reducing a risk associated with the project by having the additional piece of analytical information. The nature of each decision will dictate its importance in terms of:

1   *how easy it is to change the decision once taken* – it is difficult to change the physical location of the shop if it turns out to be in the wrong place; and
2   *the relative amount of funds involved* – it may be disastrous initially to buy a large stock of a very expensive product line in case it does not sell well.

The most critical items deserve the most careful financial analysis and this is true for all businesses at all stages of development. It is sometimes easy to generate too much financial data on relatively unimportant matters which confuses rather than clarifies the issues and this becomes more of a hindrance than a help to the decision process. The later sections of the book deal with techniques relevant to each of George's key decisions as well as how to identify which decisions are the most important.

After carrying out a sensible level of financial analysis and deciding on a particular location for his *first* shop (after all, every large business has to start somewhere), George now needs to produce a financial plan. A prerequisite for this is that he has a good idea of what he wants the business to achieve; does he want to build a retail empire or just earn a reasonable living and play golf regularly? The objectives set for a business will determine the way in which the business should try to develop and the appropriate type of marketing strategy. If George wants to expand rapidly he may want to go for a low price and high volume position. This may create pressures on the amount of cash he can take out of the business in this early period, as he will need to replace stock very quickly, as well as employ more staff, and possibly invest in a second shop. Thus the financial involvement in marketing/business decisions can be broken down into even more detailed phases, but which build up into a continuous process of analysis, planning and control (Figure 1.2).

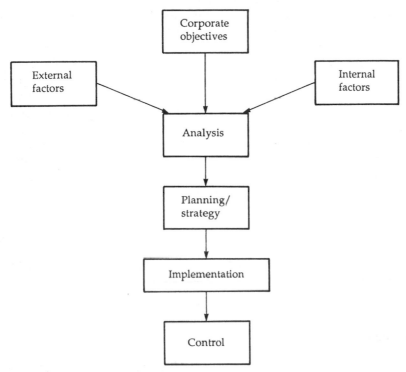

Figure 1.2 *Enlarged view of financial involvement in marketing*

George needs to do this financial planning from two complementary but different aspects. In starting this business he will be looking for a good return (that is, profit) on the funds and effort he is investing in the shop, and he will compare this forecast return with his present level of income from his business selling to other retailers. He may be willing to accept a lower level in the near future in order to build the new business in anticipation of higher profits later, or he may demand a higher level of income immediately to compensate for the increased risk he is under-taking in the new venture. He evaluates this forecast return by compari-son to the alternative opportunities available to him which is the only sensible approach to all financial decisions. If he wants to expand rapidly he may decide not to take all of this return out of the business but to reinvest it to make the business grow – buy a wider range of stock or open another shop, etc. The return or profit produced by the business may therefore not be available to be withdrawn by George in cash, and this difference between profit and cash is of fundamental importance and is considered at length in Chapter 3. Businesses do not have to cease trading just because they make an accounting loss, but they do if they run out of cash.

There are innumerable examples of businesses which have run out of cash although in accounting terms they were actually making a profit. Thus it is vital that George plans the funding requirements (that is, the cash and available credit needed) of his business very carefully and ensures that he has adequate available funds before he starts. He needs funds to buy the shop and a van (if needed), and to pay for any fixtures and fittings, etc. as well as to buy stock to sell. This is all required to be spent before he can open for business and receive cash from customers. If he is starting from scratch or changing the positioning of an existing business (for example, moving to a discount price strategy) he will also need to invest (spend) funds in marketing (for example, promotional effort) to communicate to potential customers and it may take some time for sales levels to build to a level which cover the running costs of the shop. All of these items have to be included in the funds flow forecast to assess the total needed before the business becomes self-funding, in other words, does not require any extra funds to be injected to meet payments made. If George does not have enough personal funds and cannot raise the balance by either borrowing it or getting other people to buy a share in the ownership of his business, it would be unwise to start the business as he is likely to lose most of his investment. He may be able to reduce the amount of cash needed by changing the way he does business; he could rent the shop, which reduces the initial payment needed but increases the cash outflow every month or quarter to pay the rent. Also he could decide to buy goods only from suppliers who will sell to him on credit so that he delays the timing of the payment for the goods, hopefully until he has generated the necessary cash by selling some of the stock. These suppliers may charge him higher prices as a consequence which may mean he can earn less on the sale of these goods, but he has reduced the total need for *cash* in the business by introducing another type of funds, that is, credit made available to the business. He needs to compare the value to him of this saving in his funds tied up in the business with the reduction in margin he would get on his sale. It may be cheaper to borrow more funds from the bank (in other words, use an alternative source of available credit) and pay cash to his suppliers immediately.

Another important factor in his plan is how it is affected by different levels of trading activity. George will use his financial analysis to produce his best estimate of the financial outcome of his plans. Unfortunately the only certain thing about financial plans is that they will be wrong because they depend on so many unknown, uncertain and, in some respects, uncontrollable variables. Some of the expenses of the business are not really unknown or variable, and their differing nature will have an important impact on the business if actual levels of activity are significantly away from those on which the plan is based. If George rents the shop and hires two people to work for him, he will have taken on a number of costs which he will have to pay whatever level of sales revenue he is able to generate. In fact quite a lot of his costs will be relatively constant as they are incurred just by opening for business, rather than taking cash through the tills. Rent and rates, lighting and heating, wages, etc. will not alter unless the level of activity changes dramatically (for example, if he is extremely busy, he may need to hire temporary or part-time staff to cope with the peak periods) or he changes the method of doing business (by deciding to stay open later in the evenings for example), but some of the costs (most clearly the cost of the actual goods sold) will change directly with the level of sales. This difference between costs which are constant and those that change with activity is very important. If George's business does not generate the forecast sales revenues but he still has to pay for a high proportion of his forecast costs he will use up more cash than anticipated. Unless there is an adequate buffer allowed for this eventuality he may have to stop trading for lack of cash even though in the long term the prospects for his business may be good (this is normally described as being 'undercapitalized' or 'overtrading'). Within the marketing area these different impacts can be illustrated through different forms of promotional expenditure which are very different in the ways that their costs alter. The cost of advertising is determined by the decision as to the media time or space taken and not directly by the resulting sales levels; whereas the total cost of a price reduction per unit of product sold changes according to the actual sales level achieved. The significance of this and the appropriate control mechanisms for each type of expenditure are considered in Parts Three and Four.

George Taylor actually started his business by buying the freehold of a small shop in a local high street and borrowed the additional funds required from his bank. Once up and running he needs to keep tight controls on how the business is performing and this is where his plan continues to be of great value. If the plan is properly broken down it should be possible to compare it to actual achievements and examine the reasons for any significant differences. The critical reason for doing this is to enable decisions to be taken both where things are going wrong, thus trying to avoid major disasters, and where new opportunities are identified which were not forecast in the plan but can be exploited if changes are made quickly. Most business is conducted in a very dynamic, rapidly changing environment, so therefore good financial control systems allow for this by helping to make adjustments to strategies so that the overall objectives are adhered to. George will have to make adjustments to selling prices on lines which are not selling well and may change his level of advertising once he gets an idea of the impact it is having, but in each case he should try to evaluate the impact that the changes will have on the business. He could, of course, do this by redoing the en'.ire plan and comparing the forecast result before and after the change, but this would be totally impractical for the multitude of decisions needed in any business. Fortunately this is unnecessary because many of the business items will be unaffected by any particular change; therefore they will appear in the original plan and in the revised version at exactly the same level. Consequently the impact of any decision can be assessed by looking only at what changes as a result of the decision and ignoring the vast majority of items which stay the same. If George considers increasing his advertising expenditure in the local newspaper this will hopefully increase the level of sales revenue achieved as a consequence. Increased sales revenues will mean increased costs for the products sold but they are unlikely to increase the cost of lighting and heating the shop, etc. and thus the justification for the higher spend on advertising is the difference between the extra sales revenues and the costs of the additional goods sold. By concentrating on the changes to the business resulting from specific decisions a good effective financial control system for assisting decision-making can be achieved, and this is considered in detail in Part Four.

We shall leave George to build his business for a while but return at various stages in the book to see how he is getting on.

Specific issues of financial involvement in marketing

We have already highlighted that there is a need for financial involvement in business, including marketing, at the various stages of analysis, planning and control and that this process is continuous because the control process leads to changes in the plan, and so on. There are several particular problems associated with accounting for marketing and it is important to illustrate the more important ones before getting too involved in the subject.

In order to prepare financial information, whether plans or actual financial statements, it is necessary to define a time period, such as a month or a year. This makes it possible to look at cash flows or profits for these periods and to draw conclusions from them regarding the success, viability, etc. of the business. With many forms of marketing activity there can be a quite considerable time lag between the expenditure taking place (that is, the cash leaving the business) and the benefit being seen. This lag effect, for example with advertising, can quite easily mean that the expenditure takes place in one accounting period but the benefit is received in a subsequent accounting period (Figure 1.3). This complication should not be allowed to affect the way in which the financial decision is taken, because it is important that all the costs and benefits should be compared but it means that more sophisticated financial techniques may be needed to ensure that the correct financial analysis is carried out – these are explained in detail in Part Three. It also means that there may be an apparent distortion in published financial statements, that is sets of financial accounts, if exceptionally high levels of expenditure take place in one specific time period (for example, when a major new product launch takes place).

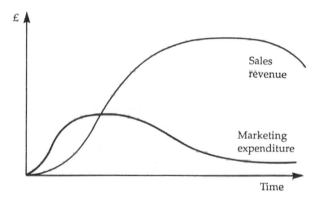

Figure 1.3   *Relation of product life cycle and marketing activity*

It is also well understood within marketing that all goods and services (throughout the book the description 'product' will be used for both goods and services where the argument applies equally to both) follow a life cycle pattern and that sales are by no means level throughout this cycle, at first growing rapidly before the maturity phase which is followed by a period of decline. This means that the financial return from any product will automatically vary over its life cycle due to the changing sales levels (as shown in Figure 1.3), but this is often exacerbated by the impact of marketing expenditure. Not only is much marketing activity paid for in advance of the resulting sales achievements but the relative level of marketing support is normally highest in the early years of any product life cycle as the market and the particular product franchise are developed. Thus in the early growth phase marketing expenditure may exceed the level of return being achieved from current sales, and this should be recouped against the higher sales in the future which require less marketing support. There is therefore a further difference between the concept of short-term return and the longer-term return over the complete product life cycle. As published financial statements are produced at least annually, which is a relatively short time period in relation to product lives, this can create significant distortion in these reported results and could confuse the decision-making process unless the true position is fully understood. The true position can be seen by analysing the financial return over the whole period of the product life cycle (in some cases many years). This should be done by the business through its decision-making process, which should not be distorted by the emphasis on an arbitrary one year time frame.

A further area of complication is related to these different timings between marketing activities and their resultant financial consequences. In many industries, most notably capital goods industries, there may be a long time delay between a sales order being obtained by a company and the order being fulfilled by delivering the end product to the customer in a satisfactory working condition (for example, a ship or a power station). This means that the specific marketing effort which is primarily directed at 'order getting' may not be spent in the same accounting period as that in which the 'order is filled' and therefore again adjustments may be needed to reflect the true position. The accounting treatment of these issues is considered in detail in Part Two, but some basic principles regarding the financial implications will be established now.

Companies exist primarily to earn a satisfactory financial return for their shareholders and this is achieved by making sales at prices which more than offset the costs incurred in satisfying the sale requirements. Thus to make this financial return (that is, profit) a sale must first take place and this is not the same as either receiving an order or producing goods for possible sale at some time in the future. Order-getting is a prime objective of much sales and marketing activity and if these activities are to be kept under proper financial control, then their relative success must be recorded and evaluated. An order only becomes a sale if the product is delivered to the potential customer who placed the order and is accepted by the customer as being in compliance with that order. Therefore, although 'accounting for' (recording the transactions and analysing the information) order-getting is important to control the effectiveness of activities designed to produce orders, it would be inaccurate for a business to assume that it has made a profit simply because it has received an order.

The satisfying of orders (order-filling) will determine whether the business makes a real profit on the orders received, as this will take into account all the costs needed to provide the specified product to the customer. Some of these costs may not be incurred until a considerable time after the transaction appears to have finished, but this does not alter the need for an estimate (known in accounting terminology as a 'provision') to be included if order-filling is to be properly financially evaluated. This process of 'accounting for' order filling must be separated from the normal manufacturing activities which may not necessarily be directed at satisfying any specific orders. Manufacturing output could be added to existing stock levels and held by the company to await future orders. These future orders could then be filled very quickly by utilizing previously produced goods (it is normally difficult to stockpile services prior to orders being received, and for services the time-gap between order-getting and order-filling is in many cases quite short).

An example from the car manufacturing industry may make these differences clearer. The marketing activities of car manufacturers are focused on obtaining orders for their particular vehicles from customers, who may be end consumers (users of the cars) or intermediaries (car dealers, who sell the product on to their own customers). This order-getting activity may concentrate on one particular model of car if the company has previously manufactured too many and has a large physical stockpile of finished cars. In this case the orders received can be satisfied very quickly by delivering some of the already finished cars to the customers, thus completing the sale transaction and enabling the company to account for the fulfilled order. If the company wants to know if the sale made a profit or a loss, then it has to include all the costs incurred at all the stages in the transaction. This includes getting the order, manufacturing the car and fulfilling the order by delivering it to the customer and providing for the post-sales service specified in the sales contract (for instance, a one or three year post-sales warranty where any defects are repaired without charging the customer). If the overall time period involved is so considerable, this complicates the accounting process and, if the car manufacturer produces over one million cars each year, it is impossible to identify the costs involved in any specific order and subsequent sale transaction, so that transactions have to be grouped into time periods (accounting periods).

The modern marketing trend in the car industry is to provide an increasing range of options and styles to try to suit the wishes of individual customers and this changes the process. Customers now place their orders for very precisely defined vehicles, and the detailed specification may make their car unique. Until the order is received, the manufacturer cannot produce the complete vehicle; although many of the components can be held in part-assembled form. Thus the 'order-getting' process now controls the final manufacturing timetable and the order is 'filled' by the particular car being produced for the customer. In this case it becomes theoretically more possible to identify the costs involved in producing the specific car for a particular order; but most of these 'unique' cars are still produced in batches because the vast majority of the vehicle is standard and fitting the 'unique' red seat trims instead of blue involves exactly the same manufacturing process.

These different and changing ways of doing business illustrate some of the complexity of recording transactions in a sensible and meaningful way. If orders are received well in advance of the goods being produced and delivered to the customer, it will be very important for the company to know the quantity, value, composition and trend of its outstanding orders. This will provide a major input into its financial planning process and thus the information must be properly recorded and analysed. If this is not done and information is only gained when the order is filled, the company may maintain or even expand its production capacity when the trend in incoming orders indicated a downward trend (or vice versa). Thus 'accounting for order-getting' is vitally important, and also assists in evaluating the effectiveness of marketing activities.

As manufacturing levels of activity may bear little resemblance to current incoming order levels or sales levels, particularly in seasonal businesses, it is also important to record and reflect the costs of manufacturing. If these activities are properly accounted for so that costs incurred are identified with the goods produced, it becomes possible to match these costs of goods produced with the order which they are used to fill; thereby producing a sale for the company. This accounting concept of 'matching' costs to the activity which causes the cost to be incurred is fundamental and will be explained in depth in Part Two. This includes the idea of estimating costs which will have to be paid for in the future because of making a sale now (for example, the warranty costs on the car). However in some cases order-getting costs may be spent well in advance of the resultant order being fulfilled, and this means that the marketing costs may fall into a different time period from the resultant sale. The company must make decisions based on all the available information even if the time lags are considerable, and the published financial presentation (discussed below) is confusing.

Organizational structure issues

What is obviously needed is a close level of communication and cooperation between the marketing function and the accountants/financial managers, so that both areas understand the full implications of specific decisions and ensure that the correct relevant financial information is supplied and used appropriately. Unfortunately, this has often not been the case in many organizations and may be caused, at least partly, by the organizational structures that exist in businesses, particularly in the finance and accounting areas. The role of finance and accounting within a company can be split into several parts which include the historic recording (accounting) function of financially based events (financial accounting) and the more forward-looking decision support role which encompasses analysis, planning and control (management accounting). Marketing needs to have good communication links into both areas, as it must ensure that all its transactions are properly recorded as well as having good financial decision making support. A third subdivision is normally into corporate finance (sometimes referred to as treasury or financial management) which is concerned with ensuring that adequate funds are available in the most appropriate form to enable the business to pursue its objectives. Normally the funding implications of marketing plans are included in the financial plans produced in the managerial accounting area, and the financing impact of subsequent changes should be highlighted by the financial control system operated in the same area. It is also sensible and normal to set up internal control systems which ensure that the detailed financial recording of transactions is done automatically according to clearly established rules (known as accounting policies and procedures).

Figure 1.4 summarizes the major business areas of involvement for the three subdivisions of finance and accounting and where each area has a need for interaction with marketing. Financial accounting must ensure that transactions stemming from marketing activities are accurately recorded, but if clearly established rules have been agreed the problem areas and consequent need for interaction should be limited. Financial management must be aware of any changes in the funding requirements caused by marketing activities but, as indicated above, the funding implications will normally be produced as an integral part of the financial analysis, planning and control operated within the management accounting area. This indicates that the main interaction with marketing is required by the management accounting area. Often the senior management emphasis within the finance and accounting organization is on the more externally focused areas and the communication may take place with the wrong people, who do not necessarily understand the particular problems and requirements of the marketing area, or at the wrong level of management. Some companies have recognized the need for closer involvement by financial managers in the main functional areas of the business and have now created a role for someone called a 'marketing accountant'. Merely changing someone's job title does not solve the problem, but if it reflects the direct involvement of a skilled financial person in the marketing analysis, planning and control process then it must be seen as a very positive move.

It is perhaps salutary to remember that the production and engineering areas of most businesses have been served by specialized financial people (cost accountants) for many years, and yet the financial needs of marketing generally have been less well supported. Some companies have attempted to concentrate the focus of their marketing accountant by making the individual report into the marketing management team, whereas in most organizations the accountants will, whatever area of the business they are specializing in, report into their own professional area, ultimately to the financial director/chief financial officer. If the most important financial involvement in marketing is properly understood, it becomes clear that the principal financial skills involved are those of analysis and interpretation, not of historical or external financial reporting nor of raising funds from stock markets or the company's bankers. Therefore many aspects of a traditional accounting training have limited relevance to the requirements of a 'marketing accountant', and that training includes very scant background in marketing and its particular requirements. In many companies it may be more sensible to take a numerically skilled marketing manager and provide training in the financial analysis and interpretation techniques which are required for the financial support role envisaged than to transfer a fully but irrelevantly trained accountant into the marketing area on a short-term basis.

Such a marketing based manager would logically see a long-term career in the marketing side of the business, whereas for most accountants a role as marketing accountant or anywhere in the marketing area is merely a temporary transfer away from their mainstream area of involvement. Their personal career prospects will be much more influenced by the senior managers in the accounting area of the business, as they will control the senior financial management and accounting positions in other areas of the company. Unfortunately, if an accountant is put in this position of working within the marketing area, whether formally reporting into marketing managers or not, it is quite possible that there will be an element of mistrust from the marketing managers towards this potential 'spy in the camp'. The long-term career dependence on senior colleagues in their own professional area can certainly create tension and suspicion when marketing and financial managers are in conflict regarding future levels of marketing expenditure. Any such problems can greatly weaken the effectiveness of management decision-making, because effort is diverted away from achieving the corporate objectives and the benefit of creating a marketing management team which includes the required financial skills is largely destroyed. Whatever the exact reporting relationship it is essential that a good close

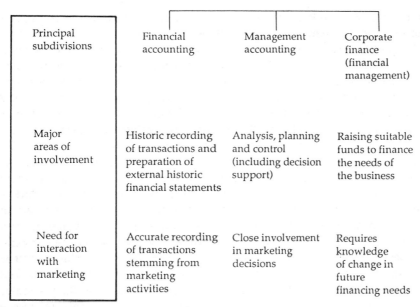

Principal subdivisions	Financial accounting	Management accounting	Corporate finance (financial management)
Major areas of involvement	Historic recording of transactions and preparation of external historic financial statements	Analysis, planning and control (including decision support)	Raising suitable funds to finance the needs of the business
Need for interaction with marketing	Accurate recording of transactions stemming from marketing activities	Close involvement in marketing decisions	Requires knowledge of change in future financing needs

Figure 1.4 *Finance and accounting functions*

working involvement is established between the marketing function and the financial support activity. It should also be emphasized that the financial involvement is that of supporting marketing management not of controlling or dictating to marketing. In some companies there is a tendency for the financial area's ownership and understanding of the common business language (accounting) to grant it seemingly excessive power to achieve dominance over other areas. If the marketing strategy is wrong or poorly implemented the best financial control/analytical system in the world will not make it right but it can highlight the problem in time for the *marketing function* to make corrective changes where necessary.

Published financial statements: external financial reporting

Financial and management accounting can be distinguished in terms of the relative emphasis of financial accounting on the past and of management accounting on the present/future, but this distinction can also be taken a stage further. The emphasis of managerial accounting, and hence of this book, is on providing information for use within the business by the management team. In most sizeable organizations there is a separation between this management role and the ownership of the business. In the case of a publicly quoted company (that is, a company whose shares are quoted on a stock exchange, so that the 'public' can easily buy shares in the company, and consequently become 'part owners' of the company), ownership may be widely spread amongst a mixture of large investment institutions (such as life assurance companies and pension funds) and individual investors. Most large companies are now managed, on behalf of these owners, by boards of directors who themselves own only a small fraction of the company. This split largely developed as a result of the increasingly large requirements for finance caused by the more complex businesses following the Industrial Revolution, and this led to the development of the limited liability company. It is unreasonable to expect any outsider to a business (that is, someone not involved on a day-to-day basis) to unconditionally guarantee an unlimited proportion of their personal wealth to the needs of the business; but the increasing scale of business required the bringing together of many of these investors in order to finance one new business. Thus the limited company was conceived as a separate legal entity into which investors can put a specific amount of funds by buying shares in the company. As they may not be involved in the management of the company, the only funds they have risked are those subscribed for their shares and their liability is consequently limited. If a limited company is not set up and the business gets into financial trouble the owners are potentially liable to the *full extent of all their personal wealth* to pay all liabilities due to outsiders. This is clearly something for all new businesses, such as our retailer George Taylor, to consider carefully.

The separation of ownership and management in limited liability companies has led to the creation of a complex set of laws which control how companies have to be controlled and which are supposed to safeguard the interests of the owners, so that the managers cannot abuse the power they have through the day-to-day control of the company.

In this situation of the owners delegating the responsibility for managing their company to a separate employed group of people, it is not surprising that there are rules regarding how these managers tell their owners (shareholders) what has happened in the business. All companies must publish a set of financial statements for each year (in cases where companies are quoted on a stock exchange there has to be some information published quarterly or half-yearly) so that the shareholders can see how their business has performed. These published financial statements are of interest to many other groups of people as well as the shareholders and this influences not only what is legally required to be included but also the attitude of the managers to what they should include. (The details contained in a set of published financial statements are examined in Part Two.)

Existing or prospective shareholders are interested in the past performance of their company but, like the management, they are even more interested in the prospects/plans for the future. In many ways, the board of directors would like to communicate their ideas and strategies to the owners, particularly if they are very good; but, unfortunately, this is not a private, closed set of documents as can be the case with management accounts where access can be tightly controlled. Published financial statements are available to anyone who takes the trouble to obtain them as they have to be sent to the Registrar of Companies who places them on a publicly available register which is open to the public, subject to the payment of a small fee. Therefore this published financial information will be examined carefully by competitors, suppliers and customers to try to gain a competitive advantage. This general availability precludes the inclusion of any specific information regarding the future, or even with respect to particular segments of the business, which could be harmful to the company. Thus the emphasis is purely historical in terms of explaining to the shareholders what happened in the previous account- ing period. It is now generally accepted that, for a publicly quoted company, the market price per share (the price at which one share can be bought or sold on the stock exchange) is an important measure of financial success (not least by making the owners more wealthy if it increases) and published financial statements constitute the major corporate communication to all potential shareholders and their advisers (stock market analysts and investment fund managers, etc.). Therefore most companies now treat their published financial statements as a major part of their 'corporate marketing effort' and issue very glossy, carefully produced booklets in which the actual financial statements form a very small part. This is very often enhanced as a communications exercise by a series of presentations to important shareholders and advisers to explain the results in more detail, thus trying to confirm how strong and successful the company is.

Interestingly if the company is made to look too successful its suppliers, including its work-force, and customers may feel that *their* relative share of the benefit of trading together is inadequate and use these very good financial results against the company at the next opportunity. If they have a strong negotiating position they may use the financial success of the company to prove its ability to pay increased wages, or higher prices for supplies and customers may complain that any proposed price increases cannot be justified in view of the current financial results. This has certainly been true of some major recent wage claims by the more sophisticated union negotiators and has affected price increases of major public utility companies.

In most companies not all the required funds will have been put in by the shareholders, as some will probably have been borrowed on a long- term basis from a bank or other lender and in most cases supplies will have been bought on a credit or delayed payment basis rather than on immediate payment terms. These outside organizations will be interested in their prospects of being paid at their due date, which may be next month or not for 25 years, and therefore will look at the financial strength of the company (that is, its ability to meet its financial obligations as they fall due, even if the performance of the business suffers a downturn). The most relevant indicator in this area is the strength of the cash flow, as a lack of cash is what would stop the company paying its obligations as they fall due. Therefore people awaiting payment by a company will put priority on different financial measures of strength and success, than those who are the owners of the company. The ways in which all these groups of outsiders analyse published financial statements are considered in Part Two, and these different groups of interested people are summarized in Figure 1.5.

Published financial statements therefore are very different to the internally produced financial reports, even if the numbers included may be the same. It may be useful to consider these differences in more detail, as the later parts of the book deal almost exclusively with the internal financial aspects.

Published financial statements versus internal management information

The differences discussed in the text are summarized in Table 1.1. Internal financial information is produced to assist in the analysis, planning and control of the business and thus the investigation of the past is only done to assist in controlling the future. Externally published financial statements are often produced to meet the minimum legal requirements of the current relevant Companies Act (for example, 1985 for UK companies), but even when used as a communication exercise they are still principally used to explain the past. As the business environment changes quickly and decisions may be needed correspondingly quickly internal financial reports are normally produced far more frequently than the legally required annual external statements. If internal reports are to help managers to control their areas of the business then their frequency should be dictated by the relevant decision timescale, which will vary by area of the business and by the type of expenditure in that area. Most companies are unfortunately not yet very selective in how they produce this information and prepare a full set of internal financial statements every month, even if they do not need all this information with this degree of frequency.

If appropriate decisions are to be taken in the light of this information, then speed of preparation is important and, if necessary, some approxi-

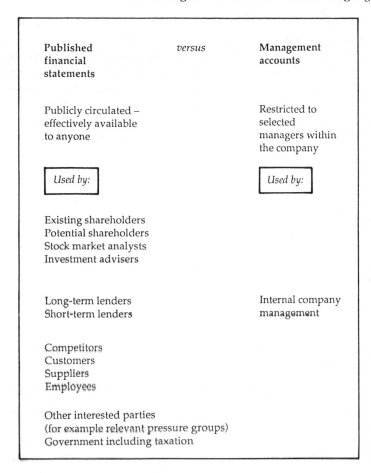

Figure 1.5 *Users of financial statements*

mations and estimates may be used to reduce the time delay. With published financial statements this is not the case because these documents will be subjected to rigorous scrutiny over a longer period (monthly internal reports will after all be superseded one month later), and consequently a much greater emphasis is put on getting the detail right, even if it delays the publication slightly. Also the published financial statements are subjected to an examination by external, professionally qualified accountants (the auditors) who verify that the published figures are not misleading (their report has to state that they show a 'true and fair view' which is a technical phrase, rather than indicating the absolute 'truth' of the published figures, such as the profit for the period) and this process adds to the time delay before publication can

Table 1.1   *Comparison of financial information sources*

Management financial information	versus	Published financial statements
Internal	Distribution	External
Present/future	Emphasis	Past
Control	Principal use	Explanation
Monthly	Normal frequency	Annual
Fast but approximate	Time scale	Slow but accurate
Not prescribed individualized	Format	Standard/legal and professional constraints
Business split into parts/ divisions as appropriate	Analysis/ presentation	Each legal entity
Different information for different levels	Content	One level of summary information
Money or physical	Unit	Money

take place. This means that external financial statements are published some time after the end of the accounting period to which they relate.

Published financial statements are all produced in a very similar format which is constrained by legal and professional requirements, whereas the form of internal reports is at the total discretion of the company's management as they are the only group entitled to receive the reports. As the issues facing different companies are so varied it is sensible that the presentation of internal financial information should be tailored to suit each particular company.

Published financial statements are produced for the company as a whole, whereas for most large companies (particularly those with diversified interests) the various parts (operating divisions with different products or in different market segments) of the business will require their own internal financial information. Indeed there are many different ways in which businesses can be organized, depending on the particular marketing strategy pursued, and the particular structure selected will determine the way in which the management's regular financial reports are produced. For example, the business could be segmented according to markets and customer grouping, or geographically, or by product groupings according to the prevailing technology, or functionally so that all sales and marketing activities are grouped together with manufacturing possibly split on a different (say technology) basis. The issues determining the most appropriate structure are considered in Part Four, but whatever formal organization is set up for a business the relevant financial information for any particular decision must be capable of being presented and this may cut across the group's operational structure of divisions, etc. The legal framework of limited companies, which may be the result of the historical growth and acquisition of the group, may not match the operational structure and may be largely irrelevant to the internal decision-making process.

For any complex large company it is also clear that senior managers need very summarized, selective information on the performance and future plans of individual sections of the business if they are to avoid being buried under a mountain of financial information. Other managers need detailed information on their particular areas of responsibility and thus appropriate levels of information can be supplied to the different layers of management to satisfy their individual requirements. Internally to a business this is sensible and very common, but it is considered completely unacceptable to do the same with externally published financial statements. Everyone outside the company must receive the same financial information and, because of the problem of lack of confidentiality mentioned earlier, everyone gets summarized overall historic information.

Accounting, as the common business language which makes very different resources comparable, is normally done in money terms. Thus published financial statements are produced in money terms, which should make the results of one company easier to compare with any other at any point in time. However, money is a poor unit of measurement as inflation reduces its real value over time and makes comparison of this year's results with those of previous years more difficult. Even relatively low rates of inflation can create significant distortion over five or ten years, and adjustments need to be made if comparisons over time are to be meaningful. (A 7.5 per cent annual rate of inflation over ten years leads to a doubling in the average level of prices. Unless profits have increased accordingly, in other words doubled, they have reduced in real terms.)

Even more importantly sudden significant changes in relative price levels can render absolute money values in plans meaningless when compared to the actual results achieved, which will have been affected by the unforecast changes in relative price levels. Therefore for internal financial planning and control an absolute measure of money value alone is not adequate, as the relative values will be vital for financial decisions. Many areas of management control hinge on the relationship between inputs and outputs rather than pure price measurements and it may be more sensible to focus some detailed controls on these more physical relationships with only overall regard to the financial result in absolute terms. If this is forgotten, the marketing department of a car company could find itself trying to advertise a four-door car with only three doors because suddenly steel prices go up 25 per cent. A sudden change in raw material prices will only affect the company if it is unable to pass on the increase to its customers. The decision it should be considering is whether it can recover the cost increase by raising its prices and if not what other alternatives are available. The techniques for using physical relationships rather than money alone are dealt with in Part Three.

Important concepts for internal financial involvements in marketing

The issue of engineering type relationships mentioned above – so called because of the measurable level of outputs for any specified level of inputs and vice versa – is by no means restricted to the production environment and has many applications in marketing, including within service businesses. The use of a physical measure, rather than just a monetary value, can help to focus management's attention on the areas where it can actually take actions which will have a beneficial impact on the business. If the price of media advertising suddenly increases substantially, the obvious reaction of reducing the number of 'opportunities to see' within a particular campaign so as to stay within budget may totally remove any benefit from the activity, because 'the share of voice' becomes too small to register at all. A more logical reaction is to question whether the increased level of required expenditure for the planned campaign is still financially justified and to consider what alternative ways there may be of achieving the same objectives in a more cost-effective manner. By doing this, marketing is exercising managerial discretion rather than rigidly adhering to a monetary budget which was based on a now wrong assumption regarding advertising media costs.

Suddenly changing external costs are unfortunately a fact of life for most businesses and they can dramatically affect the financial return achieved by the company. Therefore the financial control system used must take account of their impact as soon as the company becomes aware of the change. To ignore a major change in the external environment because it is not allowed for in the current financial plan is ludicrous, and this illustrates the need for timely monitoring and updating of financial plans. The fact that such an external change is not controllable by anyone within the company needs to be incorporated within the financial reporting system. Most companies have some form of financial performance measurement for managers so that the manager is motivated to try to achieve what the company as a whole is trying to achieve. It is very important that any such managerial performance measurement only includes changes from agreed financial plans over which the manager has some degree of control. If large uncontrollable changes are included when judging the manager's performance the likely result will be a high level of demotivation towards the control system, if not the company. A large external change may significantly affect the economic performance of the company as a whole, but this impact should be separated from assessing the manager's exercise of control over his own area.

As far as possible these sudden external shocks should be kept to a minimum and this is achieved by the best possible analysis of both internal company matters and important external factors affecting the business. The planning process is therefore based on the best information available at the time, but if this proves incorrect it is essential to have a fast method of responding to the new environment in which the company finds itself. So we come back to the three-stage financial process: analysis, planning, and control. We will now consider each in depth.

PART TWO

ANALYSIS

2

Establishing the
start point

Key issues

Before starting out on any journey, it is common sense to establish where
you are starting from and whether you have a bicycle, car or aeroplane to
travel in. It is ludicrous to set corporate objectives and prepare business
plans in a vacuum. Without reference points indicating the existing state
of the business and the external environment it has to deal with, we
could start our journey heading in completely the wrong direction. What
is needed is a process of information gathering and then analysis of that
information to establish what resources we currently have, how they
have been utilized and how they compare to what it is likely we will
need. If there appears to be a significant gap between what we have and
what we need, we must either acquire extra resources or modify our
objectives to something more practical.

   This concentration on financial analysis as a basis for planning helps to
focus attention on what type of information is needed and how it should
be analysed. In essence the aim is to establish where the business is and
how it got there, because a good understanding of past achievements
and present positioning is the best possible base for planning for the
future. The role of financial analysis is not therefore principally that of
decision-making but of identifying weaknesses and problems, highlighting opportunities and in general raising questions which must be
answered before irreversible decisions are taken.

SWOT analysis

A good technique for starting the process is what is normally referred to
as a SWOT analysis. SWOT stands for strengths, weaknesses, opportunities and threats and forces the business to consider what it is good at

compared to its competition and also where it has relative deficiencies, that is, it is a detailed internal analysis of the company. It also requires a close examination of what is happening in its external environment which is affecting or could affect the business operations in either a favourable or detrimental way. The financial impact of many of these factors will not be easily quantifiable and it may require the exercise of considerable management judgement in order to decide whether any issue is really a strength or weakness, etc. at the particular point in time.

It is important that the lists compiled are not unmanageably long and filled with relatively trivial issues. This is achieved by ranking the items under each heading so that the most important receive the greatest attention in the planning process. The objectives are simple and obvious: build on the strengths and eliminate or reduce the weaknesses, exploit the opportunities and avert the threats wherever possible. This may be very easy to say but is much more difficult to do; the analytical process is a major help in identifying what the critical areas of the business are. It is also essential that each area is considered in the relative context of competition and the environment, as being *good* at marketing may not be enough for success if all your competitors are *better* at it than you are. Fundamental to the usefulness of this approach is a willingness by the managers to admit that there are weaknesses in, and threats to, their business. The presentation of the summarized results in the form of the simple matrix illustrated in Figure 2.1 is a useful way of highlighting whether there is a lack of balance in the analysis, for example a long list of strengths without any corresponding weaknesses should at the very least lead to the inclusion of potential complacency or arrogance as weaknesses and would require consideration of the threat of a new entrant or other external change destroying the existing success.

	Favourable	Unfavourable
Internal	Strengths	Weaknesses
External	Opportunities	Threats

Figure 2.1   *SWOT analysis*

A very successful marketing consultancy company would certainly have included its team of consumer promotions consultants as a major strength since they had developed an excellent reputation in the market and a substantial client base which gave them continual repeat business. What they did not recognize was the threat to their high level of success which suddenly materialized when the whole of this management team left to start their own company. In a very short period the major clients had followed the team to their new business.

Example of a SWOT analysis

If we consider the SWOT analysis which might have been prepared for a well-established leading branded biscuit manufacturer, the relevant issues may become clearer. The company's key strengths are likely to include strong brand franchises developed over many years and it may have built up a good national sales force with very full distribution through major retailers on a direct basis and access to the smaller outlets through a national network of wholesalers. It should have developed good manufacturing skills if it has been in the industry for many years and the sheer scale of production facility required may deter new entrants from coming into the industry. The idea of a barrier to entry will also be achieved by the branding of the products as any new company would be forced to spend very heavily on marketing support over a long period to develop a comparable product positioning. (A barrier to entry can be anything which is likely to deter new entrants from coming into the industry.)

The weaknesses for such a company are also significant and include a dependence upon retailers for access to the end consumer. Thus no matter how good the advertising is at creating awareness and demand for the product, the company's ability to make it available to the consumer through this indirect channel of distribution is critical. The current high level of distribution may be under pressure as the industry is very mature, having being around for a long time, and in total the market is not growing. This is likely to create heavy competitive pressure among the existing manufacturers, who have all sunk substantial funds into their production plants. This competitive pressure may reduce price levels, or require increased marketing support in other forms, all of which will reduce profit margins. If total sales of the product range are static, the retailers may wish to reallocate their shelf space to products where sales are increasing, and this further increases competitive pressure as companies fight to retain their access to the consumer. With static sales and pressure on profits it may not be possible to spend the level of marketing expenditure required to maintain the brand at its present level of market share and this would obviously reduce a principal strength of the company.

In Chapter 1 the concept of the product life cycle was applied and in this industry the product has clearly reached the maturity phase of stable sales and is in danger of moving into the declining sales of the saturation phase. A high level of dependence on one product range is a clear weakness for any company as its success can be dramatically affected by any change in the market for that product (that is, any external threat can cause a greater degree of damage), but for a company whose only product range is in the later stages of its product life cycle the situation is even more critical.

Boston matrix

A neat way of diagrammatically illustrating this is by using the Boston matrix, named after the Boston Consulting Group which developed the technique. This matrix, illustrated in Figure 2.2, can be drawn in various ways depending on the key areas of attention but the normal logic is to compare market attractiveness (normally referenced by rate of growth of the market, as a rapidly growing market is more attractive to a company than a static or declining one) to the company's strength in that market (relative market share is the usual measure of company strength). For any company, the most logical new product strategy is to launch new products in possibly new, but anyway rapidly growing attractive markets, which could be specific segments of large mature markets. Consequently many products start their life cycle in the top right-hand box of the matrix (that is, in a highly attractive market but with no established company strength; there could be none for this new product but possibly the company had no established position from previous products in this market either). There follows a period of very high marketing support both to build the company strength through developing market share and to maintain the high rate of market growth which made the new product launch so attractive in the first place.

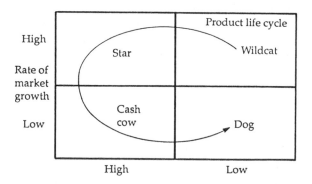

Figure 2.2   *Boston matrix*

Thus marketing expenditure (this means the funds spent on all types of marketing support for the product) may well exceed the return generated by sales of the product until the market share reaches a reasonable level. If this critical mass is attained while the market is still attractive the company has a very successful product and will normally want to maximize its long-term potential by continuing to spend heavily on the development of the market as well as maintaining or increasing market share. Therefore this may not be a period where the product generates vast profits for the company, because a high level of marketing support may be sensible to prevent competitors stealing share in the market and to ensure that the total market realizes its full potential. The product life cycle indicates that eventually the rate of market growth will slow as maturity is reached and inevitably this is followed by saturation and decline. It is important that the company changes its marketing strategy at this stage in a product's development because expenditure now which is still attempting to expand the market will produce a very poor financial return, whereas marketing activity designed to increase the market share for the product at the expense of competitors may be financially worthwhile. It is sensible to use this period of high company strength in a mature market to produce high profits and cash flow, where the income generated by sales is not all spent on activities focused on market development. However, the company's market share should still be safeguarded until the market becomes so unattractive that even this is not worthwhile. If the company can no longer financially justify marketing activities to maintain market share, product sales will normally decline rapidly and become very unattractive, representing low share in a no growth market. It is at this point that the business needs to consider when and how it kills the product, which will normally be when the product starts incurring real losses (that is, where it costs more to keep the product on sale than it would cost to close it down).

It is essential that the analysis process plots each product (and subsets of products where relevant) through this cycle because the appropriate marketing strategy must be applied to maximize the company's success. The technique has been popularized by the use of short emotive descriptions (as illustrated in Figure 2.2) for each of the boxes but the critical analytical requirement is for information indicating the need for a change in the type or level of marketing activity.

Cash generation form of matrix

An alternative form of presentation of the matrix is also illustrated in Figure 2.3 to indicate the cash flow expectations of each segment. This shows how important it is that product strategies not only follow the flow of the product life cycle but that the products spend the appropriate period of time in each segment. For example, if a product does not stay as a cash generator for long enough it may not recoup the earlier funds expended on marketing, etc. in its development, and the company may have inadequate cash flow to finance the launch and development of the next generation of products. In some companies this can be a problem as the immediate reaction of marketing to a reduction in the rate of growth in sales may be to increase marketing support to restore the previous high growth levels. If the market has moved into maturity this may be a futile but very expensive gesture, and the analysis highlighting the current position becomes vital for sensible planning.

		Relative market share — High		Relative market share — Low	

Rate of market growth	**High**	Cash generation
		Cash Use:
		  Market development
		  Share development
		  Net cash flow
			High
			
			High
			High
			0
				Cash generation
				Cash use:
				  Market development
				  Share development
				  Net cash flow
					Low
					
					High
					High
					–

	Low	Cash generation
		Cash Use:
		  Market development
		  Share development
		  Net cash flow
			High
			
			Low
			Med
			+
				Cash generation
				Cash use:
				  Market development
				  Share development
				  Net cash flow
					Low
					
					Low
					Low
					0

Relative market share

Figure 2.3   *Boston matrix cash flow indicator*

This changing profile of cash generation during the product life cycle is important and illustrates a fundamental issue of business decision-making. Companies spend funds on research and development into new products in the belief that the resulting new products can be successfully sold in their marketplace. If a new product results from this expenditure, the company will probably have to spend still more funds to buy or construct buildings, machinery, computers, etc. to enable production of the goods or provision of the service to take place. Even more funds will need to be spent on launching the product into the market, before any proceeds from sales are received. The company is 'investing' considerable funds in the new product, and can only recover this investment from sales of the product over its life cycle. An investment can therefore, in this context, be defined as the expenditure of funds in advance of the financial benefits which are expected to be generated as a direct result of the expenditure, and where the expenditure is financially justified by the value of the expected future benefits. If this investment is high in the development and launch phase of the product life cycle, it is very important that the product remains a cash generator, during its maturity phase, in order to repay the high initial expenditure.

Shareholders make a similar form of investment when they buy shares in a company because their expenditure on the shares (measured by the market price paid) is based on an assumption of receiving a flow of income from the company (dividends paid to them, by the company) and receiving a payment from a new shareholder when they sell their shares. The investment in any business can thus be represented as a two-stage process with shareholders investing in the business enterprise (the company) by buying shares and the enterprise investing in particular projects (new products, etc.) Both types of investment are based on the expectation of future results which may or may not be proved to be correct! The flowchart representation of this two-stage process is shown in Figure 2.4.

Example conclusion

By applying this technique to our biscuit company example, as summarized in Figure 2.5, it is clear that, in this mature market, significant marketing support can only be justified to sustain or increase market share. In the severely competitive environment any significant gain in share at the expense of a competitor is likely to create an early aggressive response and the gain may well be shortlived. The financial analysis should therefore indicate the results of past marketing activities and the time-scale and severity of competitive reaction as this will greatly assist in predicting the likely outcome of future proposed activities (that is, planning future strategy).

The external factors affecting this company are also likely to be significant and a number of threats can be identified. The increasing buying power of the major retailers is eroding the branding strength of many manufacturers and this is obviously greater in a mature, already intensely competitive industry where levels of marketing support are under pressure. The development of private retailer brands (own-label) is another element in this major threat to the established branded companies in the biscuit industry. The high level of existing investment in manufacturing capacity was identified as a strength as it represented a barrier to entry. However, if new technological advances with either cost or scale of operation advantages are achieved, this can pose a significant threat because it may be difficult for a large well-established company to

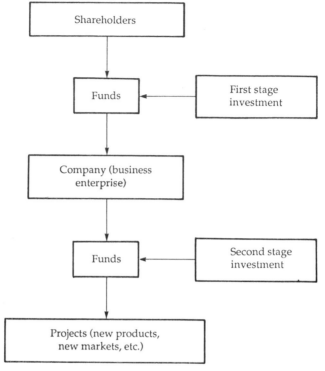

Figure 2.4   *Investment process*
The second stage investment by the company can be regarded as the
reinvestment 'internally' by the company of the funds provided by the
'external' financial markets (shareholders and other sources of funds)

respond as quickly as new entrants who have not made any previous
large expenditures on existing and now outdated manufacturing processes. Although the market as a whole may be static, there will be
different segments experiencing very different conditions including
some parts which may be growing rapidly. The danger is that new
entrants, including retailers and others selling direct to the consumer,
will aim for the growth segments, which further squeezes the potential
for our mainstream company. Another problem is that biscuits, like
many food products, are a low value item compared to their physical bulk
(compared with razor blades, for example). Therefore, if distribution
costs increase faster than the potential for price rises in food products
generally, profits (the difference between sales revenues and expenses)
inevitably will be reduced. In the particular situation of our industry,
competitive pressure may force biscuit price rises to be less than general
food price movements and the downward pressure on profits is

	Strengths	Weaknesses
Internal	Strong brands	Dependent on retailers
	National sales force	Static market
	Full distribution	Mature product
	Manufacturing expertise	Heavy competitive pressure
	High cost of entry to newcomers	Reducing profitability
		Potential loss of branding
		Dependent on one product range
	Opportunities	Threats
External	Good historic financial record	Change in customer buying power
	Possible available finance for new investment	Own label development
	Strong position in market	New technologies
	Diversify into related growth products	New focused entrants
		Distribution costs significant
		Lower current financial returns
		Leading to lack of new investment

Figure 2.5 *Potential SWOT analysis for a leading branded biscuit company*

increased still further. Similar arguments can be put forward for some of the other major cost items, such as packaging. A consequence of the present position the company is in is that, compared to the previous years of more rapid and profitable growth, the cash generated by the business will be relatively poor. If so there is a real danger that the new expenditures required to address the existing problems and develop new products, etc. will not be forthcoming and the company will decline at an increasing rate.

The major opportunities available revolve around the established position of the company and the financial strength built up during the growth period of the market. As long as the business is still closely in touch with the new developments in products and manufacturing technology, which it should be as a leading branded manufacturer, it is in the best position to respond to new trends as they arise. It should also have funds available to invest in these new developments, or to diversify into other more attractive markets where its proven marketing skills may give it a competitive advantage (for example, other food products). Whether the potential of these investments in new business areas is classified as an opportunity by the shareholders will be determined by the credibility of the management and their perceived ability to plan and deliver consistent results. If the shareholders believe that they have allowed the present market to decline too far while following the wrong strategy, it is unlikely that they will want to invest new funds in the business, compared to their other financial investment alternatives.

Problems of financial analysis

This example shows that financial analysis has to provide a comparison of the specific business over time and of the business against others, most importantly competitors and other trading partners. For some companies this raises an immediate problem of obtaining financial information on these other companies. The primary source of financial information on other companies is the set of published financial statements which will certainly be publicly available as mentioned in Chapter 1. If the particular competitor is part of a very large diversified group which only publishes an overall set of financial statements as it is legally allowed to do, the overall group information obtained may be relatively unhelpful. This forces our analysing company to use other sources wherever possible but complicates the process of external comparison considerably. Even where companies in an industry are more similarly structured, the level of detailed information published is restricted as the competitors realize that voluntary public disclosure may be used against them. The overall financial performances which are available can be contrasted and this at least puts the absolute results of the company into a more meaningful context. It is also important to put the industry performance into a broader context as well, by comparing it to the general business and economic environment and to the financial performances of supplying industries and, where relevant, customers. Making a smaller loss than the competition may be a good relative performance in the industry concerned but, if the economy is growing strongly and most other sectors are financially very healthy, shareholders may not wish to reinvest too heavily in the loss-making business.

Here again the analysis should look at this relative performance over time so that we can understand how the industry got where it is. These losses in an economic boom could be caused by being in the decline phase of the product life cycle or by having just launched a new product when losses are expected. It is also important to understand how the performance of an industry is affected by different levels of general economic activity and to try to identify particular items (often known as key financial parameters) which will indicate what the prospects for the future are. (For many years the demand for new cars has been felt to be a good indicator of short-term overall economic prospects and this has led various governments to try to affect this demand by such devices as hire purchase controls).

The most detailed aspect of financial analysis is the internal assessment of the business, but the impact of the external factors (previous opportunities and threats which actually occurred) must be included so that meaningful trends are revealed. As there is a mass of data available internally in any organization (including the individual recording of each financial transaction) the rationale for carrying out the financial analysis must be carefully highlighted. A prime objective is to identify where the existing resources are being allocated (that is, where the effort is being directed) and what level of financial return is being achieved from these resources (that is, how effective is this effort). This should indicate where bottlenecks and constraints exist which are dissipating efforts elsewhere in the business and also whether there is a balanced allocation of resources throughout the operation. If massive effort is being put into generating demand for a new product (that is, good or service), but the resources dedicated to ensuring that this demand can be satisfied (for example, setting up the distribution channels) are inadequate, most of the investment in (that is, expenditure on) advertising will be wasted. Many companies have relatively few constraints which are of vital importance and the financial analysis must identify these so that their effective utilization is maximized. These vitally important constraints which can influence the overall success or failure of the whole business are often described as 'key constraints' or 'limiting factors', as they limit the ability of the business to achieve more financial success. Analysis over time will also reveal how these limiting factors change which means that the business must review the balance of resources regularly. The lack of distribution channels may be redressed by the company and as the marketing activity takes effect it may be that access to customers is no longer constraining the business. In the rapid growth period of the product life cycle it is quite often that the capacity to produce the product lags behind the growth in demand and this becomes *the* key limiting factor. When this has been the case, many companies have overcompensated by increasing capacity to cope with future expected demand, extrapolated at existing growth rates. Unfortunately, unless the analysis is good enough to focus on the phases of growth, this vastly increased capacity can come on-stream just as the growth curve flattens out, resulting in unnecessary and underutilized capacity.

This again indicates that relative indicators (for example, year-on-year sales growth) are as important as absolute levels, but undue concentration on relative levels may create problems. If a services company multiplies its branches one year from five to 50 it has to have the financing for 45 new branches. The following year to maintain the same relative tenfold growth rate and expand to 500 branches will require financing for 450 new branches. This may be the same relative increase in cash needs but it is a considerably larger absolute amount of cash, which may not be available. In this case availability of funds to finance this growth may be a critical resource constraint and force the company to modify its plans. Financial analysis therefore has to differentiate between the profit generated from the performance of the business and the financial strength of the business which is disclosed by its present cash levels and readily available access to funds. No apology is made in this book for the continual emphasis placed on this difference between the accounting return shown by profit and loss accounts and the cash flow position of the business.

The cash flow analysis also needs to consider the different time periods in which the company needs available finance. Businesses need cash to pay outstanding bills in the short-term and the liquidity position at present and in the past should be analysed carefully. The type of industry and the particular way of doing business can significantly affect the amount of funds which need to be tied up in this area, but a shortage of cash in the short term can seriously affect the company's ability to trade effectively. Our retailer, George Taylor, needs cash to buy stock, pay the wages and operating expenses before he can expect to sell goods to customers. If he has a short-term cash problem he may not be able to replace his stock and this will mean sales will be lower and hence his profitability will be reduced. Indeed, inadequate short-term cash availability can destroy a business by eventually making it run out altogether. However, if George wants to expand by buying another shop, which would also increase the stock level needed, or by getting a bigger van to collect stock, or by acquiring a computerized checkout system he will need more cash than if he just wants to continue trading at the existing level. This long-term cash flow requirement to replace or increase assets raises the question of the solvency or viability of the business and its ability to fund growth. If the existing level of trading is producing a steady net level of cash inflows, this can be reinvested (that is, spent within the business) to enable the business to grow and the rate of cash generation could be the key constraint to this growth. The company could accelerate its growth rate by injecting more cash than that produced by the current business; this would involve either obtaining more funds from the owners or borrowing from a bank or other lender.

If more cash is raised on a long-term basis the expanded business must be capable of supporting this additional finance over the same long-term period by increasing the return generated and sustaining this increased level, as it would be nonsense to invest more funds in a business and get only the same or less profit back.

As soon as we start considering returns over long periods we hit the problem that values over time are distorted by inflation. This is true of all absolute financial measures including sales values; if a company's sales increase in value by 10 per cent per year when inflation is causing the price levels to increase at 15 per cent, the company's sales are getting smaller in volume terms. If sales volumes were being maintained over time the sales values would be increasing by the level of price rises and when this is not being achieved, it indicates a decline in sales volumes or 'real' sales levels. Over several years even relatively low rates of inflation can distort the apparent trends in absolute numbers quite significantly. Hence care must be taken to distinguish between the real financial indicators and nominal returns which have not been adjusted for the impact of inflation. Real financial indicators are those adjusted for the distorting effects of inflation, whereas nominal figures include inflation and have not been adjusted. Thus in our simple sales example the nominal level of increase in sales values is 10 per cent, even though it includes a price increase of 15 per cent. Adjusting this nominal level of increase for the impact of the inflationary rise in prices shows that real sales values (that is, reflecting what is happening to sales volumes between the 2 years) are actually declining. The simplest way of dealing with this in financial analysis terms is to work in relative measures within the separate years. Thus instead of comparing absolute sales levels or absolute profits from year to year, the level of profit per £ of sales (known as the profit margin) in each year could be compared and this would give a guide to the true trend in the profitability of the business. Ratios are also used to compare performance levels across time within companies, but comparisons using similar ratio calculations need to be made with other comparable companies and other industries to analyse whether inflation is having the same impact on all businesses.

When analysing cash flows, and some aspects of profit performance, over time even more care needs to be exercised as inflation can show its effects in different ways. The obvious impact of inflation on cash is that it reduces its purchasing power as price levels rise. However, if the cash has been borrowed from a bank, the amount repaid after, say, 25 years is the same absolute amount as was borrowed (that is a 25-year £30 000 endowment mortgage is repaid to the bank as £30 000 at the end of the period). This would appear to mean that borrowing in a period of high inflation is a good idea as the relative value has reduced dramatically when it is repaid. The banking industry would have gone out of business a long time ago if this was true but they compensate for the impact of inflation through the annual rate of interest charged on the loan, not by increasing the amount due for ultimate repayment. This way of accounting and charging for inflation creates an added complication when analysing the financial position of a business, as the way in which funds have been raised can distort various aspects of the published financial statements.

The detailed implications of all these issues and the techniques for carrying out the necessary financial analysis are considered in Chapters 3, 4 and 5 before we consider how this analysis is used in planning and then controlling the business.

Financial statements

Overview of chapter

In this chapter we consider the normal set of financial statements produced and published externally by a company. A set of published financial statements comprises:

1 a *profit and loss account*; also known as the *income statement*;
2 a *balance sheet*; also known as the *position statement*; and
3 a *source and application of funds statement* also known as the *funds flow statement*.

Each of these documents is prepared for a different purpose, and shows different aspects of the financial position and performance of the company. The documents are not therefore contradictory but complementary and together form an integrated set, which can be used to analyse the business financially.

Preparing a set of financial statements requires the exercise of considerable judgement and many accounting rules and conventions have been developed to try to limit the available choices so as to make financial statements comparable among different companies and over time. Some of these rules have been made into legal requirements, but the main impact of the law is in regard to the disclosure and publication of financial information by companies rather than the detailed preparation of that information. The accounting profession has set up its own self-regulating body which develops general accounting standards which set out rules and conventions that have to be followed in preparing externally published financial statements. In the United Kingdom these are published as *statements of standard accounting practice* (SSAPs) and there are also some *international accounting standards* (IASs), which cover the major areas of accounting judgement. These SSAPs and IASs have to allow for the vast range in size, scope and complexity of the companies which will have to apply the rules and, consequently, there is still a considerable degree of judgement and interpretation which has to be left to the company's discretion.

Some of these judgements are illustrated in the body of the chapter. At the end of the chapter is an example for the reader's use in practising applying the techniques by preparing a full set of financial statements. A fully worked answer with explanations is included to assist the understanding of the construction of these key accounting documents.

Introduction

We have already mentioned the terms profit and cash flow, and highlighted that both are important but that the concepts are different. In this chapter we consider each in detail which will make the differences much clearer as well as demonstrating how the preparation of a balance sheet, at a point in time, can help in reconciling these differences. A balance sheet, also known as a position statement, shows a snapshot of the financial position of the business as at the last day of each accounting period, and includes all the assets, as already defined, and liabilities (which are costs which have not yet been paid for by the business) which exist at the date of the balance sheet.

Businesses are formed with the primary objective of making an economically acceptable return for the effort (that is, the resources) employed. One part of the return is measured by accounting for the trading activity of a business and this is done through the profit and loss account (also known as the income statement). Almost all businesses require cash or other sources of funds to acquire the resources needed and to pay for the efforts used. It is intended that eventually more cash will be received from sales to customers but it may be a very long time before all the initial cash is recouped. In reality this may never happen, as when the cash is generated it is immediately reinvested in making the business grow. The cash flows of the business are therefore very important as sufficient cash must be generated to pay amounts owing as they fall due. The difference between profit as disclosed through the profit and loss account and cash would be reduced if all sales and purchases were paid for immediately as the cash flows would more closely correspond to the trading activities of the business. This indicates that the main difference is simply one of timing; we assess profit on the basis of trading activity but cash flow relates to the physical movements of funds (modern banking means that most business payments do not involve physical cash but the electronic transfer of funds from one bank account to another – thus cash flow statements are not restricted to physical movements of cash). In the normally published source and application of funds statement a broader definition is used which defines 'net liquid funds' as including other short-term items as well as cash, and this is considered in detail later in this chapter.

Profit vs. Cash
Both are important but they are different

Profit or loss?

As the movements in cash balances will be affected by any payments or receipts which take place, including the proceeds of the sale of shares and the repayment of loans, which are financing activities of the business and not part of trading activities, the cash balance is not an adequate measure of the results of trading in any period. Any definition of accounting profit should, therefore, try to indicate how the business is performing and this cannot be done merely by reference to the movement in cash balances. Successful trading for any business consists of generating sales revenue which exceeds the expenses incurred in achieving the sales. Therefore the profit or loss for any period can be established by measuring the sales revenue achieved in the period and deducting the expenses attributable to the same period, as shown below, provided, of course, that appropriate definitions for both sales and expenses can be agreed.

$$\frac{\text{Profit}}{\text{for a period}} = \frac{\text{Sales Revenue}}{\text{for the period}} - \frac{\text{Expenses}}{\text{for the period}}$$

(A loss is incurred when expenses exceed sales revenues.)

Sales revenue

Even the simple question of when is a sale a sale can, from the accounting viewpoint in many businesses, require some judgement to be exercised. This requires that rules are established (accounting policies) so that a consistent approach is adopted by the particular business. Any sales transaction consists of many parts which may occur in slightly different sequences; the customer places an order with the company, the company manufactures the goods or provides the service, the goods are physically delivered to the customer or the service is performed for the customer, the customer is charged for the goods or service by being sent an invoice, the customer accepts that the order has been properly fulfilled and agrees to pay, and the payment is received from the customer. In some cases many of these aspects take place at the same time, as in the example of supermarket retailing where the customer orders the goods by self-selection, pays for them at the checkout where they are given an invoice and receipt, and receives physical delivery by taking their goods out of the shop. This sale clearly takes place at the checkout where the legal ownership of the goods changes from the supermarket to the customer. The sale would still 'happen' at the checkout even if the customer 'paid' by using a cheque or credit card (where receipt of cash by the retailer is delayed slightly), or bought on credit granted by the retailer (where cash receipt is further delayed).

At the other extreme is the situation of a major long-term contract for a large office building or a tailormade computer system, where the customer places an order and the seller then starts work on the project. The customer may well make payments during the period of the contract (called stage payments) including an initial deposit to finance the work, but the question of legal ownership during the contract period will depend on the specific contractual agreement. The total project will be finally accepted when everything is finished, but even this signing-off procedure normally allows the customer to retain a small percentage of the price in case any subsequent problems are discovered during the usual warranty period. When and how this sale is included from an accounting viewpoint will depend on the particular accounting policies implemented by the company, but the objective is to record the activity of the company during any accounting period. An accounting period is any period of time for which a set of financial statements is prepared and can therefore be a day, a month, a year or for the full period of the long term contract. All companies are legally required to produce and publish an annual set of financial statements but for internal management control purposes both shorter and longer accounting periods are very common. Therefore all the sales value should not be included when the order is obtained; although marketing may argue that the sales revenue has been achieved by winning the order, the accounting convention is to recognize sales revenue as the order is fulfilled, not won. Neither will the sales value be determined by the amount of cash received from the customer in any accounting period. If a customer is allowed to buy on credit so that cash is received sometime after the sale takes place, the sales *activity* will still be recorded in the profit and loss account. Even if a deposit is received in advance, this does not mean that this amount can be treated as a sale unless a corresponding proportion of the work has been carried out in the period: again the timing of the sale and the receipt of cash can differ. In the case of major contracts, which go on for longer than the particular accounting period (remember, external published financial statements are normally produced for a year whereas internal management accounts are produced more frequently, for example, monthly) it is necessary for the company to decide on an accounting procedure as to how much, if any, of the contract is to be taken as sales revenue in each period. It could take the extreme views that either all of it will be taken when the contract is started or none of it will be taken until the work is finished and the customer is satisfied, but neither of these would reflect the activity level in the business. Also, for many companies, this would result in massive fluctuations in sales revenue levels from year to year based on the value of contracts which were started or finished in the year.

The sensible approach is to take the appropriate proportion of the contract value relative to the work actually carried out in the period; and this is what most companies do. This introduces an element of managerial judgement as in a complex project it may not be obvious exactly what proportion of the work has been completed or how much there is still to do. As it is important that the financial analysis is meaningful over a number of years this judgement must be exercised in a consistent way, so that the sales revenue in each accounting period matches the level of business activity. This application of consistency over time is a fundamental concept of accounting and is applied to all accounting judgements, not merely those relating to sales revenues. The sales revenue for any accounting period can therefore be defined, for all businesses, as the financial value of the sales activities in the accounting period, whether or not these sales activities are paid for in the accounting period – as summarized below:

Sales revenue =Financial value of sales transactions in the period,
for a period   whether or not paid for in the period; that is, it is
             activity based

Timing of sales is normally when legal title in the goods/service passes to the customer. This is normally taken when the goods are despatched or delivered to customers or the services are performed for the customer.

Expenses
Once the basis of arriving at the sales revenue has been determined, the appropriate level of expenses for the same accounting period must be established to produce the profit or loss for the period. As we are interested in the profit and loss account reflecting the relative success of the trading of the business it is important that all the relevant costs incurred in achieving the sales are reflected in the same period. A business should therefore 'match' costs incurred to the accounting period in which the related sales are achieved. Again this means ignoring whether these costs have been paid for in cash or not and relates to usage and activity rather than physical payment.

The question of when costs incurred by the business should be matched against sales is largely answered by considering the nature of the costs themselves. Under our matching principle costs should be accounted as an expense in the same period as the relevant sales revenue which led to the costs being incurred. For a retailer a major cost is the cost of the goods sold (COGS) whereas for a manufacturer this could be broken up into raw materials, wages, energy, etc. Other more general expenditure including some marketing activities is on items which are more related to specific time periods than to specific sales transactions; rent and rates, and wages for the retailer's employees are examples of these *period costs*. As it is very difficult to associate this type of cost with particular sales revenues, period costs are often treated as an expense in the specific accounting period to which they relate – this may still differ from the period in which they are paid for.

Accounting terminology differentiates between 'expenditure' which is the amount spent and 'expense' which is the amount matched against sales revenues in any periodic profit and loss account. Expenditure therefore relates to the acts of buying or committing cash (incurring the cost), whereas expense is concerned with the using up of the resources through business activity (consuming the expenditure). The accounting jargon for expenses being included in the profit and loss account is that the costs have been 'written off'.

Some of these costs will require judgement to be exercised because the exact expense is not known at the end of the accounting period and will only be accurately ascertained in the future. A good example of this is warranty costs which are incurred by a company having to repair products free of charge during the post-sales guarantee period. These repair expenses, although spent after the sale, are clearly incurred as a direct result of the sale and must be accounted for in the same period as the sales revenue before an accounting profit can be arrived at. Therefore an estimate of these outstanding warranty costs must be made and set against the sales of the period – the accounting jargon for this is 'to set up a provision for' future warranty costs – even though the cash outflow has not yet taken place.

This logic of 'providing for' expenses which will be paid for in future accounting periods is applied to all areas of the business including bringing in salespersons' commissions if paid in arrears and estimating retrospective sales discounts to be allowed to customers depending on their sales levels in a specified period.

There are also costs paid for in advance of the resulting sales being achieved, for example, advertising. The principle of matching these to the period when sales are made would require the costs to be carried forward. If a major new product is launched near the end of one accounting period, the benefits of the high launch marketing support cost should be felt in the next accounting period when, *hopefully*, high sales will be achieved. The description 'hopefully' indicates the risk that no extra sales will result from this marketing expenditure and it is therefore 'prudent' not to carry forward expenditure where the benefit is doubtful. This concept of preparing financial statements on a prudent basis is fundamental to the preparation of externally published financial statements and tries to avoid businesses showing an unrealistically good profit in one accounting period, which is subsequently shown to be based on false assumptions about the future value of current expenditure. Consequently most companies tend to 'write off' in their current profit and loss account all their marketing expenditure as they cannot be sure of the future benefit that will be realized from particular activities. Although this may be 'prudent' in accounting terms it is often completely unrealistic in economic terms and can cause a major distortion in the externally published profit. For internal decision-making, it is very important that the company does not confuse itself by using these unrealistically 'prudent' assessments of trading profit.

It would be absurd to argue that there will be any future benefit from some marketing expenditure – for example, where considerable effort and cost has been put into winning a major contract but the company knows it has been awarded to a competitor. Any expenditure which is known to have no further value to the business must be treated as an expense of the current accounting period. There are other time-related expenditure items which will have a reasonably certain future benefit, and where the expenditure has simply been incurred in advance of the consumption of the benefit, such as prepayment of insurance premiums or the purchase of a piece of equipment which has long term value to the business. For these items matching is important and can be achieved by spreading the cost proportionately on a time basis, whereas if the benefit is less certain the solution is less straightforward. This leaves us with two types of expense: those costs incurred in achieving the sales revenue included in the same period and identified through the matching process, *plus* any costs incurred (expenditure) which cannot be considered as having any future value to the business by matching against future sales. Timing of payment for these costs is irrelevant.

Expenses = All costs incurred in achieving the sales revenue
for a   for the period
period   *plus*

Any costs incurred which cannot be directly
attributed to future periods' sales

This conflict between the accounting concept of 'prudence' (writing off expenditure as incurred) and 'matching' (carrying forward until the benefit of expenditure is realized through sales) can create complications in accounting for marketing. As has already been mentioned, marketing expenditure often exceeds the profit produced from sales in the early part of the product life cycle and if this is written off or 'expensed' as it is incurred the period's profit and loss account will show a loss. However, it is this early level of marketing support which will enable the product to earn substantial profits in the later years of the product life cycle, when the proportion of sales revenue spent on marketing will decline substantially. If a company has a broad range of products which are at different stages in their product life cycles, it will be able to show a consistent level of profit as products with very high levels of marketing activity are balanced by more mature, more highly profitable products. New or rapid growth companies may have a majority of their product portfolio in the early phases which require very high relative degrees of marketing expenditure and, under the prudence concept of accounting, this will result in low profits or even losses being reported in their published financial statements. Alternatively a company with products which are all in the mature phase of their lives and which can justify lower marketing support will show higher levels of profits, even though this company has very limited prospects for the future as the next phase for its main products is to go into the saturation phase and so decline in sales and profits. It is important to analyse properly the financial position of a company so that the reasons for the current levels are understood, as without this information the prospects for future profits cannot be forecast. One original application of the Boston matrix was to focus attention on the need for a balanced portfolio of products so that the mature products produced profits which could offset the marketing investment being made in the new potential stars of the future.

Expense or asset?

Although not acceptable for external published financial statements where the prudence concept must be applied, it is essential for internal decision-making that companies consider marketing expenditure on new growth products as an investment (as defined in Chapter 2) which will generate profits for a number of years if the product is successful. This is considered in more detail later in the book but basically the argument is that the company is creating a marketing asset (for example, a brand franchise or a major distribution network) which is no different from the other assets held by the business. Where expenditure is incurred which has benefits over a number of periods the matching principle takes the total cost and spreads it fairly across the accounting periods which benefit from the expenditure. For example, a computer software company may buy computers, not to sell on to its customers but to allow its systems development staff to work effectively and produce computer systems which it will then sell. These computers are fixed assets in that they will not directly be turned into cash as sales revenue but will be used in the company to produce profits over several accounting periods, in the same way as George Taylor owns and uses a freehold shop and a van in his retail business, and a car or biscuit manufacturer uses a lot of plant and machinery. In accounting terms an asset is anything which has future value to the business and will therefore have a benefit to a future period by helping to improve profits, possibly by reducing the need for expenditure in that period. It is therefore a resource owned by the business which has not been consumed by the current activity. Accounting statements differentiate between assets which will be used up by being turned directly into cash in the near future, such as stock and outstanding debtors ('current assets'), and those which will be retained for all or most of their useful lives ('fixed assets' of the business). What is a current asset to one company may be a fixed asset to its customer, for example, the van bought by George Taylor and which is a fixed asset to him, would have been a current asset (a stock item) to the motor manufacturer who built it and to the dealer who sold it to George, as shown in Figure 3.1.

	Motor manufacturer and dealer	Retailer (George Taylor)
Fixed assets*		
Land and buildings		Freehold shop
Plant and machinery	Manufacturing plant	(one van)
Net fixed assets	_____	_____
*Current assets***		
Stock of goods for resale	(including one van)	
Debtors		
Cash	_____	_____
Total current assets	_____	_____
less Current liabilities		
Trade creditors		
Tax		
Bank overdraft		
Total current liabilities	_____	_____
Net current assets	_____	_____
Total assets less current liabilities		
less Creditors:		
Amounts falling due after more than one year	_____	_____
	══════	══════

*Fixed assets will be retained and used in the business (for example, George Taylor's van).

**Current assets will be turned into cash by the trading activity of the business (for example, the motor manufacturer's van prior to selling it to George Taylor).

Figure 3.1   *Specimen balance sheets (net assets portions only)*

An *asset* is anything which has future value to the business, i.e. beyond the current accounting period.

A *fixed asset* is something which will be used in the business for all or most of its useful life. The cost of using the asset (its reduction in value) will be expensed over this useful life through each period's profit and loss account.

A *current asset* is a shorter term asset (less than 12 months) which will normally be consumed by the business or turned into cash through the trading operations of the business (for example, stocks of goods which will be sold to customers).

If the matching of consumption of the asset to the benefits obtained from it is to be as accurate as possible it is important that the correct period of time is used to write off the cost. This is the period of usefulness of the asset (known as its 'economic life'), but unfortunately for most fixed assets this cannot be decided with certainty and requires the exercise of managerial judgement as illustrated later in this section.

As well as the period of usefulness of the fixed asset the company also has to estimate the total reduction in value over this period. Many fixed assets may have a quite considerable value remaining at the end of their useful lives as assets of any particular business. Therefore the proportion of the original cost which is written off in the profit and loss account should allow for this balance. The residual value of the fixed asset, as the remaining unused balance at the end of its economic life is known, should be used to reduce the cost of consumption which is matched against the benefit obtained from the use of the fixed asset. Residual values are often important in assessing the depreciation cost of motor vehicles as many companies dispose of salesforce cars, for example, when they still have considerable 'trade-in values' (that is, residual values).

Depreciation
Depreciation expense is the accounting expense in the profit and loss account caused by the using up of the cost of a fixed asset over its economic life, and is part of the matching process. As the fixed asset is used up its *accounting* value is reduced and this reduction is reflected in the balance sheet.

Example 1
A company purchases ten new cars for the salesforce for £8000 each and intends to keep the cars for three years before replacing them with new cars. In view of the high mileage which the members of the salesforce will drive during the three years, the company estimates that the cars will

have residual values (trade-in values at the end of three years) of £2000 each.

The company will therefore suffer a cost of using the cars equal to the drop in value (cost less residual value) of £6000 per car over the three years. The simplest method of matching this cost involves proportioning the £6000 per car equally over the three years which gives a depreciation expense of £2000 per car per year, or £20 000 per year in total for the ten cars.

This annual depreciation expense is heavily dependent on the residual value estimate made by the company, because if they had forecast that each car would be worth £5000 at the end of three years the annual depreciation expense would be £1000 per car or £10 000 per year in total (cost of £80 000 less residual value of £50 000, giving a total expense of £30 000 for the three years, or £10 000 per year).

As with all forecasts, particularly those made for three years ahead, there is a high probability of this residual value estimate being inaccurate, and the cars will actually realize a different value to that forecast on their eventual sale by the company. This sale will generate a gain or loss on disposal which must be recorded in the accounting statements appropriately, as a non-trading item.

Balance sheets

	Year 1	Year 2	Year 3	Year 4
Fixed assets				(Asset sold at beginning of year 4)
(4)				
Motor vehicles at cost	£80 000	£80 000	£80 000	–
less Accumulated depreciation	£20 000	£40 000	£60 000	–
Net book value	£60 000	£40 000	£20 000	–

Profit and loss accounts

	Year 1	Year 2	Year 3	Year 4
Depreciation expense	£20 000	£20 000	£20 000	–

Figure 3.2   *Balance sheets and profit and loss accounts (extracts only)*

It may be helpful to illustrate how the normal transactions would be reflected within extracts of the appropriate accounting statements, and this is shown in Figure 3.2. The profit and loss accounts will include the annual depreciation expense which reflects the using-up of the value of the fixed assets (the cars) within the business. This reduction in value of the asset must also be reflected in the balance sheet as the future value of the asset is being consumed by the business, and assets must not be stated in the balance sheet at more than their future value to the business. This is done by classifying the initial expenditure on the cars as a fixed asset (£80 000) since the cars are intended to be retained and used in the business. As this cost is consumed, the value is reduced by the same amount as is shown in the profit and loss account as the depreciation expense (this is logical because the profit and loss account is reflecting the consumption of the asset). The presentation is made clearer if the balance sheet continues to show the original cost of the fixed assets so that both the scale of the original investment is easily identifiable throughout the asset life and the proportion of the assets which have been used up is revealed. This requires the fixed asset to be shown at cost less the cumulative amount of depreciation expense which has been written off through the profit and loss account. This balance is known as 'accumulated depreciation' and the undepreciated portion of the cost (that is, cost less accumulated depreciation) is described as the 'net book value' of the fixed asset.

When the fixed assets (cars) are sold at the beginning of year 4 the whole of the asset record (cost, accumulated depreciation and net book value) is removed from the face of the balance sheet as the asset is no longer part of the business. If the sale proceeds differ from the remaining net book value (£20 000), the company has made a gain or loss on disposal, but this should not be regarded as a normal trading gain or loss. The company is not in the business of buying and selling cars, but simply because it uses cars within its business it occasionally has to sell the cars it owns and buy new ones. Thus the gain or loss on disposal should be classified in the profit and loss account as a 'non-trading' item, which enables any reader of the financial statements to understand the operating results of the company without these distortions. In reality the gain or loss on disposal is caused by the depreciation expense being misstated while the fixed asset was in use within the business, and if gains or losses are very large the operating results of the previous accounting periods may have suffered distortions due to the depreciation expense being wrong.

For some types of companies this can be a large problem and lead to some misunderstanding of their financial performance by outside observers (for example, investment analysts). One such industry is the holiday tour operating industry where some of the larger companies (for example, Thomson and ILG which owns Intasun) also own their own airlines (Britannia and Air Europe, respectively). Estimating the residual value of the aeroplanes at the projected date of disposal is no easy task. If the planes are bought new (as in Air Europe's case) the difference between actual residual value and net book value on the balance sheet at the time of disposal can be considerable. If the accounting policy on depreciation is prudent, the company may well show regular large gains on disposal of aeroplanes which are classified as non-trading income on the profit and loss account, as is the case for ILG in recent years. The excessive depreciation expense which is generating these gains on disposal is classified as normal trading activity and hence reduces trading profit. The comparison with other companies in the industry may also be complicated if competitors follow different strategies, such as buying older secondhand aeroplanes and keeping them longer, so that the planes will have much lower residual values on eventual disposal. Any likely error in forecasting these much lower residual values will have substantially smaller impacts on the published financial statemeents of the companies concerned.

Having considered examples of the impact of residual values in detail, we need to return to the question of the economic life of the fixed asset. In the case of the salesforce cars, the company may remove the potential for error by deciding that all cars will be changed after three years, and the error is then centred on the estimate of residual value at the end of the fixed economic life. Some companies, however, change company cars when they have done a specified mileage (such as 60 000 miles; 96 500 km) on the basis that a very high mileage car will have a very low residual value and the total overall costs incurred for that car will become very high as a consequence. If this policy is adopted the estimates of both the economic life and the residual value become subject to error, and the depreciation expense figure used is very judgemental. Other factors can also have a significant impact on economic lives of fixed assets. With the increasing pace of technological change the economic life of many fixed assets is being reduced and this can have a material affect on reported profits.

Example 2
The computers acquired by our previously mentioned software company for (say) £200 000 may last between two and five years and the choice of economic life rests with the company. If the company decides on five years as the period over which it thinks it will receive benefit from these fixed assets it will show as an expense in its profit and loss account for each of the next five years an appropriate proportion of the £200 000 cost. The simplest and most common method of depreciating (writing-off) a fixed asset is to charge the cost evenly over the economic life and this would result in a depreciation expense each year of £40 000 (£200 000 divided by five years), assuming a nil residual value for the computers, and the impact of these expenses is shown as option 1 in Figure 3.3. This expense reduces the profits achieved in each of those years but no cash

changes hands as a consequence of this accounting entry. The cash outflow to buy the computers probably occurred at the time of their acquisition but this cash payment is not the best way to reflect their impact on the trading activity of the business. Another timing difference between profits and cash has been created by this accounting cost known as depreciation.

Option 1: five year life

Balance sheets (extracts)

	Year 1	Year 2	Year 3	Year 4	Year 5
Fixed assets					
Computers at cost	£200 000	£200 000	£200 000	£200 000	£200 000
less Accumulated depreciation	40 000	80 000	120 000	160 000	200 000
Net book value	£160 000	£120 000	£ 80 000	£ 40 000	–

Profit and loss accounts (extracts)

	Year 1	Year 2	Year 3	Year 4	Year 5	Total
Depreciation expense	40 000	40 000	40 000	40 000	40 000	200 000

Option 2: two year life (assuming computers are actually retained for full five years as in option 1)

Balance sheets (extracts)

	Year 1	Year 2	Year 3	Year 4	Year 5
Fixed assets					
Computers at cost	£200 000	£200 000	£200 000	£200 000	£200 000
less Accumulated depreciation	100 000	200 000	200 000	200 000	200 000
Net book value	£100 000	–	–	–	–

Profit and loss accounts (extracts)

	Year 1	Year 2	Year 3	Year 4	Year 5	Total
Depreciation expense	£100 000	100 000	–	–	–	£200 000

Figure 3.3   *Depreciation: Example 2 – computers*

Should our software company take the more aggressive view of the life of these computers and believe that they will only last for two years before they have to be replaced, the annual expense for depreciation in those two years will be £100 000. Thus by exercising their judgement in a different way there is a £60 000 (£100 000–£40 000) per annum reduction in profit reported in the first two years, but this is balanced in the longer term as the company choosing five years would still have to charge depreciation of £40 000 per year in years three, four and five, as can be seen by comparing options 1 and 2 in Figure 3.3. Again it is important to register that there will be no change in the cash flow of the business as a direct effect of these different accounting treatments, but it will affect the timing of reported profits.

It would be potentially harmful if this accounting judgement regarding the estimate of the economic life of the computers made any difference to the company's decision as to when they changed to new hardware. This should be controlled by the actual timing of the changes in technology, which were being forecast in the different estimates of economic life. If the computers are changed after two years and the existing machines have almost nil residual value at this time, the option 2 choice (as shown in Figure 3.3) with its two-year economic life has accurately reflected the actual events and requires no adjustment. However option 1 with a five-year life still shows a net book value for the computer at the end of year 2 of £120 000 and this would give rise to a substantial 'loss on disposal' entry in the profit and loss account for the accounting period when the computers are sold.

Should the computers last five years before being scrapped, option 1 would accurately reflect the actual events and need no adjustment. No adjustment *can* be made to option 2 because all the fixed asset has been written-off in the first two years. The profit and loss accounts in years three, four and five of option 2 cannot reflect any accounting cost for the use of the computers which are generating benefits. These benefits *are* reflected in those profit and loss accounts through the sales revenues created by using the computers, thus leading to distortion of the financial results in each of the five years through the inaccurate estimation of economic life.

Another area of accounting for depreciation exists where alternative treatments are used and this in regard to the way in which the reduction in asset value is spread over the economic life. The simplest method, which has been used in the earlier examples, is to spread the total reduction in asset value *evenly* over the economic life of the asset. This is known as the straight-line method of accounting for depreciation and is very common, not least because of its ease of computation. However, most fixed assets do not reduce in market value (that is, realizable value at any point in time) on a straight-line, or even, basis. The early periods of ownership often see dramatic declines in the market values of assets relative to the later periods of the economic life – motor cars are a clear example of this rapid early decline in resale value. It is not essential that companies reflect the exact decline in market value of each fixed asset in each accounting period as fixed assets are, by definition, retained and used in the business. The precise market value at a point in time may not reflect the future value to the business of the fixed asset. Many companies continue to use the straight-line depreciation method even though it gives rise to differences between net book value of the fixed asset and the resale value of the asset in the early years of use. The net book value, which is included in the balance sheet, of fixed assets reflects the future value *to* the business and the balance sheet does not try *to value* the business at a point in time.

However, if the fixed asset is not retained for its expected economic life but is sold earlier, the disposal proceeds received may be lower than the net book value of the asset under straight line depreciation. This will result in the company suffering a 'loss on disposal', as in the example of the computers, and this will affect the profit and loss account in the period of disposal, albeit as a non-trading item. If a faster, i.e. more accelerated, method of depreciating the fixed asset had been used, under which relatively more depreciation expense is charged in the early periods of use, the net book value could have more accurately repre-sented the disposal proceeds of the asset, and no gain or loss on disposal would have arisen. In order for the correct total amount of reduction in value to be shown as depreciation over the economic life of the fixed asset, this accelerated method must have a higher depreciation expense in the early periods of use and a lower level of depreciation expense in the later years when compared to the straight-line method.

The most commonly used method of accelerated depreciation is known as the 'reducing balance' method (also known as declining balance), under which a constant annual percentage rate of depreciation is applied to the reducing balance (that is, net book value) of the fixed asset. Two examples comparing the impact of this 'reducing balance' method and the straight-line depreciation calculation will highlight the differences.

Example 3

Our software company could decide to depreciate its computers over five years, but to allow for the risk of their being scrapped after only two or three years by using an accelerated method of depreciation. Under the straight-line method the depreciation expense was a constant £40 000 per year, as shown in Figure 3.3, but under the reducing balance method the annual depreciation expense reduces over the economic life of the asset. In order to write-off the £200 000 cost over the five-year expected life at a constant annual percentage of the remaining balance, an annual percent-age rate of considerably greater than the 20 per cent rate used under straight-line depreciation is required. (Mathematically it is impossible to reduce a value to exactly zero using a constant percentage of a reducing balance, but for accounting purposes a sufficiently accurate approxima-tion can be obtained.) The actual constant percentage required in this example is around 65 per cent per year and this gives the depreciation expense figures and net book values shown in Table 3.1.

Table 3.1 *Comparing methods of depreciation: example 3*

		Straight line depreciation		Reducing balance depreciation
Cost of asset		£200 000		£200 000
Year 1 depreciation expense				
	(@ 20% on cost)	40 000	(@ 65% on reducing balance)	130 000
Net book value at end year 1		£160 000		£70 000
Year 2 depreciation expense (@ 20%)		40 000	(@ 65%)	45 500
Net book value at end year 2		£120 000		£24 500
Year 3 depreciation expense (@ 20%)		40 000	(@ 65%)	15 925
Net book value at end year 3		£80 000		£ 8 575
Year 4 depreciation expense (@ 20%)		40 000	(@ 65%)	5 575
Net book value at end year 4		£40 000		£3 000
Year 5 depreciation expense (@ 20%)		40 000	(@ approximately 65%)	3 000
Net book value at end year 5		—		—

As can be seen from Table 3.1 the reducing balance method gives dramatically changing levels of annual depreciation expense. In year 1 the expense is significantly greater than the constant £40 000 per year expense given by the straight-line method and the depreciation expense then reduces rapidly so that for years three, four and five the expense is very much lower than under the alternative system. Both methods depreciate the total cost of £200 000 over the economic life of five years, but the different timing of the depreciation expenses in the annual profit and loss accounts will have a significant impact on the reported profits for the company (in year one, the gross impact is a change of £90 000). Again it is important to note that there is no effect on the cash flow of the business due to a change in depreciation policy between straight-line and reducing balance methods – accounting profits may be moved between accounting periods but cash flow is not affected by depreciation policies.

It is also significant to realize that the impact of having to scrap the computers after two years is dramatically reduced under reducing balance depreciation. If the computers had nil residual values at the end of year two the company would have a large loss on disposal of £120 000 under straight-line depreciation, whereas under the reducing balance method this loss on disposal would be reduced to £24 500 because of the much higher depreciation expense charged to the profit and loss account in year one. Reducing balance method of depreciation is regarded as a prudent accounting policy for companies with a high risk of rapid technological obsolescence and consequent volatility in fixed asset economic lives.

Example 4
If we were to apply reducing balance depreciation to our salesforce cars in example 1, the annual depreciation expenses would also be increased in the early years and reduced in the later years, as shown in Table 3.2. (The impact is less spectacular than the previous example because of the higher relative residual value of the asset at the end of its economic life.)

Table 3.2   *Comparing methods of depreciation: Example 4*

	Straight line depreciation		Reducing balance depreciation
Cost of assets	£80 000		£80 000
Year 1 depreciation expense (@ 25%)	20 000	@ 37% of	29 600
Net book value at end year 1 on cost)	£60 000	the reducing	£50 400
Year 2 depreciation expense (@ 25%)	20 000	balance	18 648
Net book value at end year 2	£40 000		31 752
Year 3 depreciation expense (@ 25%)	20 000		11 752
Net book value at end year 3 = Residual value of cars	£20 000		£20 000

The higher depreciation expense in year one under the reducing balance method means that the consequently lower net book value at the end of year one may more closely approximate the resale value of the cars at the end of year one. This more prudent depreciation policy, which reduces accounting profits in the early years of using the fixed assets, may be attractive to companies who are not sure how long they will in fact keep these fixed assets in use within the business. If the fixed assets will be kept for a fixed period or for the full economic life, the closer representation of market values in each balance sheet will be less important to the company, and straight-line depreciation can be justified as more evenly matching the using up of the asset value within the business. It must be remembered that the aim of depreciation is to match this using up of the asset within the business and not to make the net book value of fixed assets approximate market value at each balance sheet date. The balance sheet is *not* a valuation statement of the business at a point in time.

There are safeguards established to try to ensure that companies do not produce ridiculous financial results by taking absurd accounting policies for their fixed assets. This is done by making companies publish their accounting policies in regard to depreciating fixed assets and by having their published annual financial statements examined by qualified independent accountants (the auditors) who have to accept the appropriateness of the accounting policies.

Several other areas of accounting require the exercise of considerable managerial judgements (for example, accounting for research and development, accounting for long-term contracts, accounting for foreign exchange). Companies are required to disclose how they exercised these judgements by stating, in their published external set of financial statements, what their accounting policies are in any of these areas, particularly if they have a significant impact on their financial results. The auditors are required to consider the appropriateness of all these accounting policies in the particular circumstances of the company. The auditors have to prepare an audit report on the published financial statements and this audit report is included as part of the published documents. If they believe that any of the accounting policies adopted by the company are unacceptable in the specific circumstances they must state this in their report and indicate what impact their proposed change to the current accounting policy would have on the published financial statements. Wherever managerial judgement is involved there are likely to be substantial differences of opinion, even among experts in the same industry, and thus similar companies have significant differences in accounting policies, particularly with regard to depreciation. Consequently financial analysis comparisons among companies need to allow for the impact of any differences in accounting policy.

It is frequently difficult to do this with any great degree of accuracy because the public disclosure on accounting policies may be very broad and general, thus restricting specific adjustments which would make companies with different policies more directly comparable. For example, the accounting policy on depreciation may be stated as, 'the company provides depreciation so as to write-off the reduction in value in fixed assets over their economic lives which range from three years to 50 years on a straight-line or reducing balance basis as appropriate'. Other information which has to be disclosed regarding the classification of the fixed assets will help a little to clarify the position, but it may not be possible to carry out a complete and detailed comparison because of the differing accounting policies selected by the different companies.

Exercise of judgement

Selection of depreciation policy is not the only area where the exercise of judgement in preparing financial statements can affect the reported level of profits, but none of these accounting policy decisions can alter the physical movements of cash in and out of the business. Many financial analysts use cash flows in the short term and use profits only in the longer term, as it is possible to move expenses or even sales, and hence profit, from one accounting period to another, but it is impossible to change the overall total profit which has been made in the long term. Whether the computers in examples 2 and 3 are given a two- or five-year life the total cost will have to be depreciated against the profits of the overall period and hence these profits will be reduced by the cost of £200 000 over the economic life of the asset.

Any decision regarding the size of a provision for an expense which will be incurred after the end of the current accounting period gives rise to the possibility of different profit levels being reported if the necessary judgements can be exercised in varying ways. In most companies sales are made on credit so that customers are given an agreed period in which to pay for their purchases. Some companies use this credit policy as part of their marketing strategy, by giving extended credit or offering a discount to customers who pay earlier than required. There is obviously a risk that some of these customers will not pay because they have gone into liquidation or disappeared, etc. If this happens after the end of the accounting period the seller will already have taken the profit on the sale in their financial statements based on the premise of matching sales to activity and not to cash flow. If a company wishes to show a properly matched profit or loss for the period it may want to provide against a proportion of its outstanding customers not paying and so it will set up a provision for doubtful debts in its profit and loss account. (Any outstanding debts which will definitely *not* be collected will be written off in the profit and loss account and the specific balance will not be shown on the balance sheet as an asset.)

The impact will be to reduce the reported profit for the period but again this accounting provision will not affect the cash balances held by the company. It is obviously a matter of judgement as to how large the provision should be, but logically the level can be gauged by reference to the past experience regarding bad debts suffered – this use of historic financial analysis to set provisions is very common and probably would be the basis for setting the level of the provision for warranty costs in a previous example.

Example – provision for doubtful debt

A mail order company has historically suffered a level of non-paying customers of 3 per cent of its annual credit sales. In this case it would be sensible for the company to allow for this cost in the period in which the sales are made, rather than waiting for the particular customers to fail to pay and writing-off a specific bad debt in a subsequent accounting period. Such a write-off would reduce the profit of the wrong trading period, because it is the act of selling on credit which causes the bad debt to be incurred as a cost. If credit sales in the accounting period are £10 million, a provision for doubtful debts of £300 000 would be shown as an expense of the period. When specific customers included in the sales of £10 million failed to pay, the cost would not show as an expense of the subsequent period but would be offset against the provision of £300 000 created specifically for that eventuality. Only if bad debts eventually proved to be more than £300 000 out of that period's sales would the actual bad debts incurred, in excess of those provided for, need to affect subsequent accounting periods' trading results adversely. Should the provision subsequently prove to be excessive, the unrequired balance can be released and this would reduce future expenses and hence improve subsequent profits.

Thus if the company forecasts incorrectly by making the provision greater or smaller than the costs actually incurred in the future, the net balance will be shown in the profit and loss accounts of those subsequent periods.

Stockholding and valuation of stock

Another marketing decision which can affect profits without altering cash flows to the same extent is the area of holding stock for subsequent sale to customers. Almost all companies have to hold some level of stocks so that they can respond to customer demands and maintain a reasonable flow of work through their organization. Some manufacturing companies implement a policy of being able to respond to customer orders very quickly and this will require holding high stocks of finished goods. It may also necessitate physically locating those finished goods close to the customer, by having a number of regional warehouses rather than one central warehouse near their own production facilities. These companies therefore incur higher costs of manufacturing, storing and distributing to their warehouses before they have anything that can be regarded as a sale – in other words, more of their current costs are being spent on sales which will happen in the following accounting period. The ultimately prudent approach would be to expense all these costs as they are incurred, but this would breach any attempt to match profits to sales activity levels. As long as there is a high probability that the goods concerned will be sold in subsequent accounting periods, the costs incurred now, which improve the value of the goods, can be carried forward and matched against the relevant sales. This only includes expenditure which can be shown to be improving the value of the goods and therefore excludes general expenses of running the company (period costs). Profits are realized at the point of selling not manufacturing or relocating the products and therefore only costs can be included in valuing *stocks* held at the end of each accounting period and any profit expected on the sale must be excluded. The prudence concept means that if it is likely that the stock will have to be sold at less than its cost, the prospective loss must be allowed for in the current period, as illustrated below.

Valuation of stock (inventory)

(Stock and work-in-progress are valued at the lower of cost and net realizable value. Cost includes all expenditure incurred in bringing the stock to its present condition and location. Net realizable value is the current market value of the stock minus any expenses which would have to be incurred in realizing this market value.)

In financial statements we do not anticipate profits but we do provide immediately against forecast losses. Thus if we hold a stock of gold jewellery at the end of our financial year and the price of gold has gone up, thereby allowing us to raise our prices and increase our profits, there would be no adjustment in this period and the higher profits would be shown *next* year when the stock is actually sold. If the price of gold had fallen dramatically so that our stock would have to be sold for less than we paid for it, we would reduce its value by making a provision in *this* year's profit and loss account. A 'similar' provision would be required for obsolete stock which can happen in high technology and fashion goods industries, when changes in the market make it impossible to sell old stock except below the cost. For accounting purposes all stock is valued at the lower of cost and net realizable value (what it could be sold for) which forces companies to adhere to this prudent policy of recognizing losses early but deferring profits until realized. In many cases defining this cost of stock is by no means an easy task. In any large business there will be a vast number of transactions in each accounting period but the accounting rules say that the cost of bringing the stock held at the end of the period to its present condition and location should be assessed. This should include all the elements which have increased its value to the business. In a manufacturing company this will include purchase cost of raw materials, labour costs, depreciation of machinery used in its manufacture and the energy costs of running the machine as well as manufacturing expenses including some of the rent of the factory and any distribution costs incurred in moving and storing the items.

Our computer systems company will have stock in the form of work-in-progress on some of its large contracts and its value will include labour costs, computer machine time in developing the system (this will include some depreciation of the computer used) and a proportion of other company expenses. Neither company should include any of its marketing expenditure in its stock value as this is directed at achieving sales, and under the prudence concept this will normally be expensed in the period when it is incurred rather than being carried forward. A substantial area of judgement is needed in deciding how much of the more general expenses should be attributed to the stock on hand and how much goes against this period's sales. The exercise of this judgement can affect quite significantly the profit reported in this period; although as usual a corresponding balancing effect will be felt in the subsequent period and obviously this judgement has no impact on the cash flow which is only changed by physical cash movements. Hence a marketing decision to build up or reduce stocks at the end of an accounting period because of forecast or planned activity early in the next period can change this period's profit by altering the level of expenditure carried forward in stock value.

Other changes in the marketing mix can also affect the timing of profit because of the way in which marketing expenditure is written off in published financial statements in the period when it is incurred. Thus if a company switches from a strategy of high advertising expenditure (which will be expensed in advance of the resulting sales being achieved) to one of price discounting or of heavy promotional support at the point of sale the cost of marketing will be felt at the time the sale is made and not in the previous period. Using an external sales force paid entirely on commission should enable the company to match its sales expenses exactly to its sales revenues, whereas by employing its own sales force on a salary basis the costs will be written off as they are incurred. If there is a substantial lead time in obtaining orders from new customers this could affect the timing of profit. These and many other examples of the financial impact of marketing decisions are considered in more detail in Part Five; however the ability of judgements to move profit from one accounting period to another highlights the fact that decisions should be based on the more objective and immovable measures of cash flow. These accounting problems affect published financial statements because of the prudence concept, but it is very important that management accounting information is based on more sensible and more decision-oriented principles.

Before leaving the profit and loss account to consider the funds statement, it may be helpful to show as in Figure 3.4 a full profit and loss account as published by a large software company, so that the elements mentioned can be seen in context. (The same set of financial statements will be used to illustrate the other accounting documents later in the chapter and commentary on the figures is delayed until all the documents have been illustrated.)

XYZ plc: profit and loss account for the year ended 30 April 1987*

	£000	£000
Sales revenue		78 785
Operating expenses:		
Product expenses	15 570	
Staff employment expenses	39 114	
Depreciation expense	2 577	
Other operating expenses	16 204	73 465
Operating profit		5 320
Interest income		505
Profit on ordinary activities before taxation		5 825
Taxation on profit on ordinary activities		2189
Profit on ordinary activities after taxation		3 636
Dividends		666
Retained profit for the year		2 970

*As previously defined in this chapter, this profit and loss account shows the sales revenue of the accounting period from which the expenses attributable to that period are deducted. These expenses include taxation on profits. This leaves the accounting profits for the period which can either be distributed to the shareholders as dividends or retained/reinvested in the business to help the business grow and produce increased profits in the future.

Figure 3.4

Funds flow statements

A funds flow statement (also known as a *funds statement*) is prepared to reflect the movements in funds for the same accounting periods for which the profit and loss account shows the financial results of the trading activity. It is important that these two accounting documents are prepared for the same time period as they each illustrate significant but different aspects of the company's financial position, and reconciling these timing differences is only practical if the basis of presentation is common. Several timing differences between expenditure being incurred and the accounting expense being written off have already been illustrated but the funds flow statement includes an even more comprehensive picture of the financial affairs of any business. 'Funds' means purchasing power (that is, cash plus credit) and covers financing and trading because this purchasing power can be made operational through working capital movements as well as cash. Working capital is the net investment made by the business in short-term (current) assets, such as stock and debtors, and short-term liabilities, such as trade creditors, and is discussed in detail later in the chapter when the balance sheet is examined fully.

A more descriptive title is the source and application of funds statement for the period and this indicates that the objective is basically twofold – to explain where the funds came from and where they went to; this is illustrated in the funds statement in Figure 3.5 for our software company, discussed in the appendix to this chapter. It then attempts to analyse whether the business is sensibly financing its activities, by considering the appropriateness of the sources of finance in relation to the uses to which the funds are put. Very early in the book it was stated that businesses typically fail because they run out of cash not because they report accounting losses, and therefore ensuring that any business is soundly financed is very important. It is also important to remember that although we produce a funds flow statement *for a period* the business actually needs cash at a *point in time*. Therefore the adequacy of the cash balance at the end of the period is important but it is also essential that the business has adequate funds for any seasonal peaks or abnormal requirements that may be experienced during the period. New product launches can tie up substantial amounts of cash in new fixed assets, pre-launch marketing and stocks before any cash is recovered from sales. It is perfectly reasonable to consider that profit is made over a period rather than at any point in time, and it is true that cash is also generated over the accounting period, but there is this fundamental difference that cash is also required at a point in time if all the company's financial obligations are to be met. There is an adage in corporate finance that the only time you cannot raise any money is when you really need it, as you must, by definition, be a bad credit risk – this emphasizes the need for adequate finance to be available in advance.

The potential sources of finance for any company are quite simple – initially funds can be raised by selling ownership in the company (issuing shares in exchange for cash) or funds can be borrowed from a bank or similar organization in exchange for a promise to repay the principal and to pay interest on the outstanding balance. Once a company has been trading successfully for a while it is hoped that more cash will be produced from the business than is used in operating the business and therefore these surplus funds can be used in the business. There are two complications; we have already seen that profit is not necessarily produced in the form of cash and not all of this profit necessarily will be retained in the company. The owners of the business may wish or need to receive some level of cash return on their investment (as they would if they had put their funds on deposit in a bank) and for a company this is achieved by paying a proportion of the profits out as dividends to the

**XYZ plc: source and application of funds statement for the year ended
30 April 1987***

	£000
Sources of funds	
Arising from trading:	
Profit on activities	5825
aad Back trading items not resulting in funds movement	
Depreciation	2577
Funds from operations	8402
plus Proceeds of sales of fixed assets	116
	8518
New shares issued	513
New borrowings in period	94
Total sources	9125
Applications of funds	
Purchase of fixed assets	8650
Repayment of loans	59
Payment of dividends	449
Payment of taxation	1018
	10 176
Net sources/(application) of funds	(1051)
Increase/(decrease) in working capital	
Stock (contracts in progress)	3229
Debtors	7321
Creditors (an increase represents less tied up)	(4924)
	5626
Increase/(decrease) in net liquid funds	
Bank balances and short-term deposits	(6677)
	(1051)

*This source and application of funds statement shows that the company produced £8.4 million from its trading operations in the year, which was increased by the proceeds of selling some fixed assets and some new shares, as well as borrowing some more funds on a long-term basis (none of these other sources can be regarded as part of the trading operations). However, despite generating funds of over £9 million the company spent more than £10 million, most going on the purchase of new fixed assets.

As applications were greater than sources, the company used up part of its existing stockpile of funds and the bottom section shows in detail how this was done. Bank balances and short-term deposits (that is, effectively cash) decreased by £6.67 million because extra funds were tied up in debtors (increase of £7.3 million) and stocks (increase of £3.2 million). Creditors (that is, payments outstanding to suppliers) also increased and this reduced the total amount of extra funds tied up in working capital, but not by enough to remove the significant fall in cash balances.

Figure 3.5

shareholders. Dividends are paid out in cash and therefore reduce the funds which can be reinvested in the business. The payment of dividends represents a permanent reduction in the potential reinvestment that can be available to the business.

The funds so raised are used by businesses to acquire assets needed for their operations and as has already been mentioned these assets can be divided into long term (fixed assets) and relatively short term (current assets). Although these short-term assets are individually turned into cash within 12 months this does not mean that the investment is no longer required as, if the business is to continue trading in the same way, more current assets will be continually replacing those turned into cash. Let us consider the flow of money in the case of our retailer, George Taylor. He invests some funds on a long-term basis by purchasing the freehold of his shop, buying a van and purchasing some second-hand fixtures and fittings and a till.

These represent his fixed assets and these funds will be tied up in the business until either surplus cash is produced from operations or the assets (for example, the freehold of the shop) are sold. He also has to invest in shorter-term assets such as stock to sell in the shop and he will have to pay some costs annually in advance, such as road tax and insurance on the van, insurance on the premises and stock, and the rates on the premises. As he makes sales he will need to replace the stocks sold if he wants to stay in business and so he still has this cash invested in his business. With regard to the prepayments (that is, the operating costs paid in advance of their use within the business) he will use up the expenditure during the year (and this will show as expenses in his profit and loss account) but he will not have to pay out any more cash until the beginning of the next financial year. This cash investment is therefore fluctuating, whereas the stock investment is relatively constant, and if George wants to expand the scale of his business he may need to inject more cash to increase the stocks held by the business. So far we have assumed that George pays cash for his purchases but he may be able to buy on credit which will reduce the cash he has to tie up in current assets.

In the same way as buying something which is not used up in the accounting period creates an *asset*, buying something which is not paid for within the accounting period creates a *liability* (a liability is any amount of cash owed to anybody by the business). Accounting also differentiates between short-term (current) liabilities payable within 12 months and longer-term liabilities payable later than this. Long-term liabilities tend to be restricted in most businesses to bank (or similar) borrowings (excluding overdrafts and short-term loans) and possibly some outstanding tax balances, which are not purchases but represent unpaid obligations of the company and hence are included as liabilities. It could be argued that if bank borrowing is a liability then so is the cash paid in by the owners of the company to buy their shares but as there is no legal obligation to repay any funds put in by ordinary shareholders this is not how it is classified in published financial statements, being shown separately as a source of capital. In this context 'capital' represents the funds invested in the company by the owners and can result from an active investment through the subscription of funds in exchange for shares issued by the company or a more passive investment where the company retained some or all of the funds produced by the operations of the company for reinvestment in the business. This can be illustrated by considering the shareholders' funds section of the balance sheet (the net assets section, that is, the fixed and current assets less the current and long-term liabilities, was illustrated in Figure 3.1) as shown below (extract only):

Share capital and reserves
Issued and called up share capital	X
Share premium account	X
Profit and loss account	X
Total shareholders' funds	X

'Issued and called up share capital' shows the number of shares which have been issued (that is, sold) by the company to the shareholders multiplied by their nominal or par value. All shares legally have to have a par value (which is often 25 pence for companies quoted on the Stock Exchange, but can be any amount, such as £1, 10p or 1p) which simply reflects the value stated on the share certificate, but does not indicate the current market value of the share. This par value does not necessarily even bear any resemblance to the price at which the shares were issued by the company, and this will be particularly true when a company issues additional shares after several years of successful trading which have resulted in a significant increase in the market value of the shares. The company will issue the new shares at the highest possible price in order to raise the maximum funds to invest in the business, and this is likely to represent a substantial premium over the par value. The issued share capital line on the balance sheet is only increased by the par value of the new shares issued and the balance of the proceeds from the new issue (representing this premium price) is shown as the appropriately named 'share premium account'. This means that the issued share capital line is always the par value of the shares multiplied by the number of shares in issue, but the full amount of the funds received by the company in exchange for shares issued is reflected within shareholders' funds on the balance sheet.

Shareholders also invest in the company by leaving in the company profits which could be taken out as dividends. Dividends must be seen in two ways: first, they are an appropriation of profits, which reduces the profits available for reinvestment in the business; second, they are paid out to the shareholders in cash, and thus represent a use of funds by the business. Therefore, in order to pay dividends a company needs both profits, from which the appropriation can be made, and available funds, out of which the dividend is paid. The level of dividends paid by a company depends on the level recommended by the directors of the company and the payment has to be approved by the shareholders at the annual general meeting (AGM) of the company. These reinvested profits (sometimes described as retained earnings) can accumulate over time to very substantial amounts (often far in excess of the share capital balance) if the company trades successfully and reinvests a high proportion of the profits. The cumulative balance is shown on the balance sheet classified normally as profit and loss account or described as 'distributable reserves', which reflects the fact that legally this amount could be distributed to shareholders as dividends. The total of the owner's capital injected and retained is shown as 'total shareholders' funds' and normally forms one half of the balance sheet which can be contrasted with the 'assets' half as shown in Figure 3.1.

Current liabilities include amounts owing to trade suppliers, and any other unpaid bills (for example, income tax is deducted from employee's wages and salaries before payment to the employees, but the tax deducted is paid to the government by employers one month in arrears and the unpaid balance features as a current liability), and this ability to delay payment by taking credit reduces the cash invested in the business. These outstanding unpaid suppliers are known as *creditors*. Most businesses not only buy on credit but also sell on credit and this creates a delay between making the sale (when the activity is recorded) and receiving the cash from the customer. This increases the amount of cash tied up in the working of the business by adding a new category of current assets called *debtors*. The net amount of cash required to finance the activity of the company is therefore shown by the total of current assets (stock, prepayments and debtors) less the amount which can be delayed by using current liabilities (creditors). Not surprisingly since this net amount finances the working of the business it is often referred to as the 'working capital'. As part of it at least can also be regarded as a constant flow (stock is bought on credit and then is sold to create debtors, who eventually pay cash, some of which is used to pay creditors, and so the process continues) this net investment is also known as 'circulating capital' (or 'finance merry-go-round') and is illustrated in Figure 3.6.

We now have quite a sophisticated way of classifying the total amount of funds invested in the business by analysing the fixed assets and the

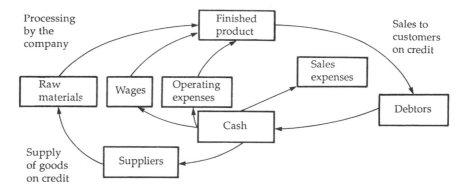

Note:
Cash goes out to pay wages, suppliers and operating and sales expenses, before hopefully more cash is received from customers following a sale. The 'operating cash cycle' of the business is defined as the number of days between the cash leaving the business to pay for goods and services and it being received back from customers as a result of those specific goods and services being sold. This operating cycle period indicates the growth in financing needed for additional working capital if sales levels increase

Figure 3.6   *Cash circulation process*

various elements of working capital. However, any sensible financial analysis is also interested in how the cash requirements of the business changed over time and therefore the periodic statements of sources and uses of funds will show the changes or flows of cash within the period rather than concentrating on the absolute balances at the period end (these are shown by the third accounting statement – the balance sheet). The uses of cash in the period will be analysed between investment in new fixed assets of different types and any increases in working capital requirements. It is of considerable interest whether any increased investments are caused by expansion of the scale of operations (such as George Taylor buying another shop) or because the company is trading less efficiently (such as needing more working capital by holding higher levels of stocks or taking longer to collect cash from outstanding debtors). Analysing whether the increased funds are invested on a short-term or long-term basis is also important because this will affect the appropriate source which should be used to finance the increased need. It is sensible to match the time-scale of cash needs by raising funds on a similar time-scale as it is very inappropriate to raise long-term or permanent finance for a temporary need such as to support increased marketing activity or a seasonal peak in the level of stocks held by the business.

As already noted, increased funds can be made available by asking shareholders to inject more cash, by increasing borrowings, by selling some fixed assets, or by retaining some of the cash generated by profitable trading. Hopefully, successful operations will be a major source of funds to the business, but certain adjustments are needed to the profit revealed in the profit and loss account to show the cash produced from trading. In arriving at accounting profits, sales revenues are included irrespective of whether the sales proceeds have been received or are still outstanding as debtors. Expenses are included whether suppliers have been paid for goods and services used or not (with any outstanding unpaid balances included in the balance sheet as creditors). Suppliers paid in advance for items not used in the period are similarly excluded but this requires the prepayments to be classified as an asset on the balance sheet. All of these timing differences can be and are normally included separately in the funds flow statement by analysing the changes in outstanding debtors, etc. at the end of the period compared to those outstanding at the beginning. If customers owe more cash at the end of the period than they did at the beginning it is clear that the business has effectively increased the funds tied up in financing debtors. Similarly if higher stocks are held at the end of the period than at the beginning, more funds have been invested during the period in financing stocks of goods for resale. However, if the company has over the period increased the amount of cash it owes to creditors then it has effectively reduced the cash tied up in working capital by using suppliers' cash flows rather than its own (for example, by not paying for the increased stock levels). The accounting terminology can sometimes make this confusing and the American terms are more descriptive; debtors are called *receivables* and creditors are called *payables*, which makes it much clearer how the cash will subsequently move.

One timing difference cannot be included other than by adjusting profit and this is in regard to depreciation. Depreciation expense has already been defined as the accounting expense of writing-off the cost of fixed assets so as to match their use against the benefits received but this does not represent any cash outflow to the business. Therefore the cash generated from trading is greater than the profit reported in the profit and loss account by the level of any depreciation expense included therein. The source of funds (cash generated) from operations can be shown as profit plus depreciation, as long as the other timing differences in working capital are included separately in the funds flow statement. To balance this presentation on depreciation it is necessary to show the actual funds used to purchase new or replacement fixed assets as a cash outflow from the business, as previously mentioned. The detailed forms of presentation of funds flow statements in published financial statements vary, depending on the particular items that the companies wish to highlight or disguise, but they will normally list the various sources of funds and then show how these were used in the period as shown in Figure 3.5. Any net difference between the sources generated and these applications shows in an equivalent adjustment of working capital, with any resulting net change not accounted for in working capital being revealed in a movement of cash and bank balances held by the company – if more cash comes in than goes out, cash held by the company increases, and vice versa.

Balance sheet

We have now established methods of producing a financial report on the trading activities of the business (the profit and loss account) and an analysis of the funds movements within the business (the funds flow statement). We have also highlighted the differences in preparing these financial statements and how both emphasize changes over the accounting period rather than the position of the business at any particular point in time. It would be very useful if a third financial statement was produced which reconciled the differences between profit generation and cash flow and showed the financial position of the business at a point in time. This is what the balance sheet prepared at the end of each accounting period does.

The balance sheet is a snapshot of the financial position at a particular point in time (midnight on the last day of the accounting period) which shows all the assets and liabilities of the business at that instant. As has been shown, assets and liabilities are created by the timing differences which occur between cash flows and the accounting activity being reflected through the profit and loss account. Balance sheets are the reconciliation documents which make published financial statements into a fully integrated set. This reconciliation is done at a point in time and thus includes the cumulative differences between profit and cash since the business started, not just those reflected in this period's financial statements. All balances are also therefore cumulative including retained profits which show the total which have been left in the company over time, and which have accumulated to the total retained profit at the particular balance sheet date.

One common misconception is that a balance sheet is a valuation statement for the business, which is very far from the truth. A balance sheet is normally prepared on the assumption that the business will continue trading in a similar manner to the present; in other words, that it is a 'going concern'. Thus fixed assets will continue to be used in the business, stocks will be sold in the normal course of trading and customers will pay off their outstanding balances, whereas if the business was really being valued it could be worth more by breaking it into bits and selling off the assets (for example, the land and buildings). Some assets, most notably the brand franchises which are not normally included in the balance sheet, may be worth considerably more on break-up than as a 'going concern' but the presumption of a balance sheet is that the business will continue. This idea of the business as a going concern is important to the use of the balance sheet as an indicator of the company's ability to grow or survive problems in the future, because it shows the assets of the company in the context of their usefulness to the business and the future payments and their relative timing needed to discharge the liabilities. We must remember that an asset must have future value to the business, but assets can only be included at their cost or there is a danger of counting profits before they are realized by sales. Hence stocks, debtors, etc. are simply the timing differences between their cash flow impacts and their profit and loss account representation and fixed assets are shown at the unused proportion of their cost. A fixed asset is created on the balance sheet by expenditure which has long-term benefits and therefore is not expensed immediately; however, the periodic depreciation expense reflects the reduction in value of the asset by its effective consumption within the business. The unexpired value at any time is the original cost less the accumulated depreciation balance expensed up to that time. Fixed assets, therefore, are shown on the balance sheet at this 'net' book value which reduces over the economic life of the asset.

In some cases showing fixed assets at this depreciated net book value, that is less than their original cost, may distort the balance sheet reader's understanding of the company's financial position. This can be true in the case of assets which appreciate in value (most frequently land and buildings) during the period of ownership, because this increase in value can often be significant and has effectively also increased the value of the owners' investment in the business. In order to reflect this increased value of investment, the fixed asset can be revalued and shown in the balance sheet at its restated value, with an equal and corresponding increase being shown on the other side of the balance sheet, as part of shareholders' funds, so as to maintain the balance sheet's balance. This revaluation surplus (the difference between the original value and the new restated value) is classified separately on the face of the balance sheet, and is not added to accumulated profits (the revaluation surplus is not included in the period's profit and loss account as it cannot be regarded as a profit and does not arise from trading). It is not regarded as being available for distribution to shareholders by way of dividends until the revalued asset has been sold, because until then no funds have been generated from the revaluation to enable the dividend to be paid (revaluation surpluses are consequently classified as 'capital reserves'). When a fixed asset has been revalued, the restated value is used as the basis for future depreciation calculations; even though the asset (for example, building) may be revalued again in a few years' time (this is logical because the building can still be regarded as being used up in the sense that its remaining economic life is getting shorter, notwithstanding that its value is increasing).

The balance sheet is segmented according to the lifespan of the items, as shown in Figure 3.7, for our software company, so that fixed assets are separated from shorter time-scale current assets which are logically grouped with current liabilities. By deducting current liabilities from current assets, the investment in working capital (now normally described as 'net current assets') at the end of the period is highlighted. The total of fixed assets and net current assets gives the total funds invested in the business on a medium-term basis but this does not indicate where the financing comes from. It is important to separate out cash borrowed (which is a legal liability of the company) from funds put in or left in by the owners and this is done by deducting non-current (more than 12 months to date of repayment) liabilities from the total assets less current liabilities figure, leaving a net balance invested by the owners of the business. The accounting convention is that share capital (cash injected) and cumulative retained profits (funds left in) are shown as the balancing item on the other half of the balance sheet, but it is the first commandment of accounting that the balance sheet must balance. Upon reflection this must happen because all the cash put into the business has either been used up (reflected in the profit and loss account, the balance of which is included in the balance sheet) or still exists as an asset on the balance sheet. Any items used but not paid for will be included on the balance sheet as a liability and therefore it is possible to trace any transaction through to its impact in the financial statements. It is useful to do this as shown in Table 3.3 because the integrated nature of the set of financial statements is revealed and it shows how any change in presentation would affect the results of the company.

For example, collecting cash from an outstanding debtor would not affect the profit for the period but would increase the funds received and alter the balance sheet (by reducing debtors and increasing cash balances). On the other hand, if it was decided that this debtor was unlikely to pay, and a provision for bad debts was needed, then this would reduce profit but not affect the cash balance held by the company. The balance sheet would be affected by reducing current assets in the form of debtors by the amount of the provision and also by reducing accumulated profit (because this period's profit is reduced) by the same amount. The balance sheet will still balance in both cases as the

XYZ plc: balance sheet as at 30 April 1987

	£000	£000
Fixed assets		7 662
Current assets		
Contracts in progress (stock)	6 687	
Debtors	25 594	
Cash at bank	7 680	
	39 961	
Creditors: Amounts falling due within one year	20 679	
Net current assets		19 282
Total assets less current liabilities		26 944
Creditors: Amounts falling due after more than one year		1 826
		25 118
Capital and reserves		
Called-up share capital		3 700
Share premium account		16 000
Profit and loss account		5 418
Shareholders' funds		25 118

Figure 3.7

adjustments are self-balancing (this is the logic of double-entry book-keeping!) because the cash and bank balance and the balance of the profit and loss account are included in the balance sheet.

The value added statement

The full set of financial statements provides a very full picture of the recent performance and financial status of the business but there can be several complications when we try to compare one company with another one even in the same industry. There are many different strategies that can be used in any particular market and they may have significantly different impacts on the financial statements. If we take an example of two companies selling petrol through retail service stations principally to private motorists, at first sight we would expect them to achieve similar returns on similar types of assets used in the business. However, if one company owns oil fields in the North Sea, refines its own crude oil into petrol and controls the distribution channel to the petrol station, whereas the other company simply buys the finished product by the tanker load from the cheapest wholesaler it becomes

Table 3.3   *Integrated nature of financial statements*

Transaction to be presented in accounting documents	Profit and loss account	Cash flow (as represented by cash, bank and credit balance; net liquid funds)	Balance sheets (excluding cash balance and profit and loss account balance)
(1) Purchase on credit of items consumed in period	√ (expense)	x (not paid for)	√ (creditor created)
(2) Payment for item (1) in subsequent period	x (no trading activity)	√ (payment made)	√ (creditor removed)
(3) Sale to customer on credit	√ (sales revenue)	x (cash not received)	√ (debtor created)
(4) Payment received from customer in (3)	x (no trading activity)	√ (cash received)	√ (debtor removed)
(5) Sale for cash	√	√	x (no reconciliation needed)
(6) Purchase of fixed asset for cash	x (no trading activity)	√ (payment made)	√ (asset created)
(7) Depreciation of fixed asset	√ (trading expense)	x (no cash movement)	√ (reduction in asset value)
(8) Provision for doubtful debt	√ (trading expense)	x (no cash movement)	√ (reduction in asset value)

√ = item reflected
x = item has no impact

obvious that the real businesses are not so directly comparable. The more vertically integrated company (the one finding the oil and processing it) will have a much greater value of assets employed in its business (this is normally described as being more 'capital intensive') and will need to earn higher profits to compensate for this greater investment. The other company can afford to make lower profits as its asset base will be lower but a very large proportion of its costs are outside its control being represented by the purchase cost of the petrol. Like any other retailer, this service company does not alter the product very much and only adds value by storing the product and presenting it to customers in more manageable quantities (normally referred to as 'breaking bulk'). This concept of 'adding value' is not the same as profit because it differentiates the *internal* processes carried out by the company from the *externally* purchased goods and services. Therefore the fully integrated oil company adds much greater value through processing and distributing the product than can be achieved by the service station operator. Out of the value added, the company has to pay for all its internally created costs, wages often being the greatest element but depreciation of machinery can also be very significant, with the balance left over being profit.

Value added does not replace profit as a measure of return on activity but it does help to focus attention on the proportion of internal activity which is available to the business as profit. This can be a very useful way of comparing the relative success of different strategies. Thus our integrated oil company should examine what proportion of its value added it earns as profit compared to the service station operator who generates less value added but could make more or less profit relative to the effort put into (or value added by) the business. Most value added statements analyse the internal value added into its various major applications such as wages, taxes paid to government, depreciation and profit, as illustrated in Figure 3.8 for our software company.

XYZ plc: value added statement (for year ended 30 April 1987)

		£000
Sales revenue		78 785
Other income: interest income		505
		79 290
less Bought-in goods and services		31 774
Value added		47 516
Disposal of value added		
Salaries and wages paid to employees		39 114
Taxes paid to government		2189
Providers of capital: dividends		666
		41 969
Reinvestment in the business		
depreciation	2577	
profit retained	2970	5547
		47 516

Figure 3.8

Profit is normally further analysed into the part paid out as dividends and that part retained to make the business grow. This retained part of profits is then often added to the depreciation expense to show the total of the funds reinvested in the business. The proportion that this represents of the value added can indicate the level of growth which can be expected in the future. Another way of presenting the value added statement is to show the 'application of sales revenue' where the objective is to split the sales revenue into its major elements of bought-in goods and services and the various internal components of the business.

Value added

$$\text{Value added} = \begin{array}{c} \text{Sales revenue} \\ \text{for the period} \end{array} - \begin{array}{c} \text{Bought-in goods and services} \\ \text{for the period} \end{array}$$

Whereas it is normally true that the higher the profit the better, as long as the investment needed remains the same, it is not always true that increasing the value added will increase the profit. Therefore simply trying to maximize the value added is not a foolproof strategy. A change from employing a direct sales force to buying in sales support from an external company will reduce the value added but if the external service is more cost-effective profits may be improved. Similarly, selling through distributors rather than direct to end consumers will reduce value added but could improve profitability. Alternatively, ceasing to manufacture all the company's products and buying some in will again reduce value added, but if cheaper sources of supply are obtained profits may increase. The overall impact of any change in marketing strategy needs to be considered and not just the effect on value added. Value added analysis is a common and useful additional piece of the financial jigsaw puzzle, but it needs careful consideration before it can be fitted properly into place.

We have now included all the published financial statements for our illustrative software company (Figures 3.4 and 3.5 and 3.7) and a few comments on the table and figures may be helpful. (A detailed analysis is not considered appropriate at this stage as the techniques for doing this are the subject of the next chapter.)

The profit and loss account (Figure 3.4) reveals a profitable trading period for the company, and a high proportion of these profits have been retained in the business for reinvestment in growth. The need for this retention of profits is revealed by the source and application of funds statement (Figure 3.5) which shows that, despite generating substantial funds from its trading operations, the cash balances of the business reduced significantly in the period. This was caused by a large investment in fixed assets and additional working capital, which should indicate increasing levels of activity for the business.

The decrease in cash balances might be a cause for concern but the balance sheet (Figure 3.7) at the end of the period shows that the company still has sizeable cash deposits, which will enable it to pay its creditors as they fall due for payment. The total shareholders' funds show that shares have been issued at substantial premiums to their par value (the large amount of share premium shown) and that the retained profits are relatively small compared to the capital directly injected by the shareholders. This is likely to indicate a relatively new and rapidly growing company, given the successful trading period and the high retained profits for the period.

The value added statement (see Figure 3.8) shows a high level of internally generated value, which is mainly created by the salaries and wages paid to employees.

Summary

A set of financial statements for any period comprises three integrated documents:

1 a *profit and loss account* which shows the results of the trading activity for the period, but is subject to a number of management judgements;
2 a *funds flow statement* which analyses the physical movements of funds in and out of the business in the period;
3 a *balance sheet* which gives a snapshot of the financial position at the end of the period and reconciles the differences between the profit and loss account and the funds flow statement on a cumulative basis.

These financial statements follow four overriding accounting concepts:

1 the matching principle which prescribes that expenses are matched against the sales activity which benefits from them;
2 the prudence concept which states that only items with relatively certain future benefit to the business can be carried forward to future periods and all other costs should be written off as an expense in the current period;
3 the idea of consistency which means that the same accounting policies should be applied each year, so as to avoid distorting the results in any year – if the policy is changed the effect of the change should be clearly disclosed;
4 the going-concern concept which assumes that the business will continue in its present form and not be split up which may significantly change the value of the assets.

Exercises

Before considering how to analyse this set of financial statements in the next chapter, readers should complete the worked example which follows (as the appendix) and check their answers against those provided. The answers are provided with a full explanatory text of potential treatments and the judgements required, and should be read through, even if the exercise is completed correctly.

Appendix: worked example

Paul Cook: wholesaler and distributor extraordinary

Paul Cook decides to start up in business as a wholesaler and distributor of office supplies including computer equipment. He has personal cash resources available of £20 000 (having recently received an inheritance), and an elderly aunt has offered him a personal interest-free loan of £30 000 to get him started. The loan would be repayable at some unspecified time in the future when the business can afford it. In addition he has arranged an overdraft facility at his bank of up to £25 000, but the overdraft must be repaid within two years of the business starting.

Suitable warehouse storage and showroom premises are found at an inclusive cost (that is rent and rates, etc.) of £12 000 per annum payable quarterly in advance. Warehouse expenses for lighting and heating, etc. are estimated to cost £200 per month payable quarterly in arrears. He needs a van to both deliver sales and collect purchases and he can lease a suitable vehicle for £200 per month payable quarterly in advance. In addition the leasing company require a £1200 initial deposit which is repayable to Paul at the end of the three-year lease. The road fund tax and insurance of £200 per annum is payable in advance, and the vehicle running costs of £300 per month are payable monthly in arrears.

The other necessary equipment (fork lift trucks, etc.) can also be leased at a cost of £2000 per annum payable six monthly in advance.

He believes he can eventually generate sales of £50 000 per month, but initially sales are forecast to be £20 000 in month one (a detailed monthly sales forecast is set out in Table 3.A1 below). However, to achieve this he needs to work on an average gross profit margin on sales (excess of selling price over buying-in cost) of 10% and also to extend 30 days' credit to his customers. Paul also plans to spend £700 per month on local press advertising for the first six months. After this period, he plans to reduce this level to £300 per month. All this expenditure will be payable in the month when the advertising takes place.

Table 3.A1

Month	1 £	2 £	3 £	4 £	5 £	6 £	Total £
Sales forecasts	20 000	30 000	40 000	45 000	50 000	50 000	235 000
Purchases forecasts	25 000	35 000	45 000	55 000	56 000	55 500	271 500

Credit terms of 30 days have been arranged with suppliers but Paul feels that he needs to build up a comprehensive range of stock during the first six months. He therefore plans initally to buy considerably in excess of his forecast sales levels. His buying plan is also set out in Table 3.A1.

Excluding his own requirements for living expenses which he feels he can temporarily limit to £600 per month for the first year, his wage bill is expected to be £1200 per month.

At the end of the first six months trading Paul Cook expects to have £60 000 worth of stock left (valuing the stock at purchase cost).

Questions

1 Prepare a *cash flow forecast* for the first six months, assuming that the overdraft limit is used to offset any overall negative cash balances. Items should be included when cash movements are actually expected to take place.

2 Prepare a *profit and loss account* for the first six months, using the format given in Figure 3.A1, remembering that this should be related to trading activity and not to the timing of cash movements.

3 Prepare a *balance sheet*, using the format given in Figure 3.A2, as at the end of the first six months to reconcile the differences between the cash flow forecast and the profit and loss account.

(Check your answers with those at the back of the worked example on pages 87–100 and read the commentary before doing question 4 for which answers are supplied, but no commentary.)

4 Assuming that sales continue at £50 000 per month for the second six months but that purchases only replace goods sold (so that the stock level remains at £60 000 at the end of the first 12 months), and that all other expenses are constant (except where previously mentioned), prepare a cash flow and profit and loss account for the *second* six months (*not* the first year as a whole), and a balance sheet as at the end of 12 months' trading.

Introduction

It is only by practising the accounting principles discussed in this chapter that full understanding will be gained. However, the first examples tried

Paul Cook
Profit and loss account for first six months

	£	£
Sales revenue		
Opening stock	*nil*	
add Purchases	___	
Subtotal		
less Closing stock		
Cost of goods sold	===	
Gross margin on sales (10%)		£___
less Operating expenses:		
Rent and rates		
Van lease expenses		
Road fund tax and insurance		
Vehicle running expenses		
Other equipment leasing		
Advertising		
Wages		
Warehouse expenses		
Total operating expenses	===	£___
Profit (loss) for the period		£
less Owner's drawings for the period		___
Retained earnings at end of period		£___

Figure 3.A1   *Proposed profit and loss account format*

inevitably seem complicated and the answers, even when given, far from clear. Consequently this complete example has been worked through in great detail so that you should be able to follow each element of the answer.

Where relevant the text also generalizes from this particular example to draw out other similar points which should prove useful. Therefore it is recommended that you read the *whole* of the text rather than just referring to any elements where errors were made.

As stated in the body of the chapter, these three accounting documents are the only major ones which need to be considered. If they are understood any company's accounts can be properly analysed.

At this stage taxation on profits, value added tax, and interest payable on the overdraft have been ignored, as they complicate the numerical computations but add little to the underlying understanding of the accounting principles.

Other minor elements (such as deductions from wages being paid out at different times) have also been ignored as they do not affect the practical relevance of this example.

Paul Cook
Balance sheet as at the end of first six months

	£	£	£
Fixed assets (net of depreciation)			
Current assets			
Stock			
Debtors			
Prepayments			
Cash			
Total current assets		£	
less Current liabilities			
Trade creditors			
Unpaid expenses			
Bank overdraft			
Total current liabilities		£	
Net current assets			£
Net assets			£
Paul Cook capital account			
Profit and loss account			
less Owner's drawings in period			
Total owner's capital			
Loan account			
Capital employed			£

Figure 3.A2   *Proposed balance sheet format*

Notes and explanation: First six months

Cash flow forecast
This is shown in Figure 3.A3.

General
1 In a cash flow statement we are only concerned with the physical timing of movements of cash. Therefore the timing of the trading *activity* can be *ignored* and the transaction is reflected in the cash flow when the cash is received or paid out.
2 We are equally not concerned with what sort of transaction the cash movement relates to. Thus paying in of long-term capital and loan funds can be added to the receipts from sales. Equally cash paid out to buy fixed assets would be added to purchases of stocks or payments of wages.

Cash in

Own capital and aunt's loan
Although it is not all needed in month one it is easiest to assume that all

Paul Cook
Cash flow forecast: first six months

Month	1	2	3	4	5	6	Total
Cash in							
Own capital	20 000						20 000
Aunt's loan	30 000						30 000
Sales income	–	20 000	30 000	40 000	45 000	50 000	185 000
Total in (1)	50 000	20 000	30 000	40 000	45 000	50 000	235 000
Cash out							
Purchases	–	25 000	35 000	45 000	55 000	56 000	216 000
Rent and rates	3000	–	–	3000	–	–	6000
Warehouse	–	–	600	–	–	600	1200
Van lease	1800	–	–	600	–	–	2400
Road fund tax and insurance	200	–	–	–	–	–	200
Vehicle running	–	300	300	300	300	300	1500
Other equipment lease	1000	–	–	–	–	–	1000
Advertising	700	700	700	700	700	700	4200
Wages (employees)	1200	1200	1200	1200	1200	1200	7200
Own drawings	600	600	600	600	600	600	3600
Total out (2)	8500	27 800	38 400	51 400	57 800	59 400	243 300
Movement in month ((1)–(2))	41 500	(7800)	(8400)	(11 400)	(12 800)	(9400)	–
Balance brought forward	–	41 500	33 700	25 300	13 900	1100	–
Balance carried forward	41 500	33 700	25 300	13 900	1100	(8300)	(8300)

Figure 3.A3 *Worked example: answers*

the cash is injected when the business starts. If there was interest payable on the loan then the cash would only be put into the business as it was needed, so as to minimize the interest payable. Thus the bank overdraft (which, of course, does bear interest) is only used after all the non-interest-bearing funds have been used up.

Sales income
In order to generate the sales levels forecasted Paul felt it necessary to give 30 days' credit to his customers. This meant that, although sales were made in month one, no cash was received into the business until month two. While this policy of credit sales is continued there will always be the same time-lag between the sale being made and the cash being received. Therefore the business has effectively made a *permanent* investment of cash which is tied up in debtors. This is in spite of the

short-term nature (30 days) of any single transaction. This area of credit sales also represents one of the highest risk areas in forecasting. Not only does the business have the usual problem of predicting future sales revenues, but it also has to estimate how long, in reality, its customers will take to pay. Paul is being relatively optimistic in assuming that his customers will, on average, pay on time. A more conservative assumption would be to defer the cash receipt of sales until 45 days or 60 days after the transaction. This would clearly have a dramatic impact on the cash tied up in the business!

It is also important to remember that this level of cash tied up in debtors fluctuates in line with the level of sales activity of the business. If sales increase, more cash will be tied up in debtors; if generating cash is critical to the short-term survival of the business this may require lower sales in this short-term, which is contrary to what many businesses strive to do. However, trading at a level of activity which cannot be properly financed by the funds available (which is known as 'overtrading') to the business can mean the total failure of the business if it causes it to run out of cash as it grows. This is a common cause of business failures in the first few months of trading — the business becomes a victim of its own success!!

Cash out

Purchases
In exactly the same way as cash received from sales is lagged so is the cash paid out for purchases because of the credit period granted by suppliers. Therefore no cash is paid out in month one and all payments are made one month after the goods are bought.

However, a further complication is caused by Paul's need to build up stocks of goods for future sales. Cash is required to pay for these purchases whether they are sold next month or next year. Therefore the build up to £60 000 of stock on hand at the end of the six months is expensive in terms of tying up cash even though the stock has not been sold. Many businesses (particularly retailers of fast-moving consumer goods) will try to minimize the cash tied up in stocks by restricting stocks held to the credit period granted by their suppliers. Paul is using some of his own available capital to finance the level of stock which he thinks is necessary for his business.

As with debtors this net cash invested in stock (that is, stock level minus trade creditors) is a long-term investment in the business, because although each item may be sold and paid for relatively quickly, it will normally be replaced. Therefore only a change in the method or level of trading will dramatically affect the size of the required cash investment.

Rent and rates
The annual charge of £12 000 is payable quarterly in advance and thus £3000 is paid out in months one, four, seven and ten. Here again the payment and usage are out of step but this time the payment is made before the usage takes place.

Warehouse expenses
The £200 per month expense is paid after the event on a quarterly basis, so £600 leaves the business in months three, six, nine and twelve. (It is possible to argue that the payments would in fact be made at the beginning of months four, seven, ten and thirteen rather than the ends of the preceding months). This highlights one of the problems of preparing cash flow forecasts by month or any particular period. Cash flows are not normally even and regular throughout a month and, in particular, certain payments have to be made on a *specific day* rather than sometime in a particular month. Therefore if the cash flow is critical at any particular period then a more detailed cash flow forecast may be necessary.

   It must be remembered, however, that these are only forecasts and trying to estimate whether customers will pay you on a Monday or a Tuesday may be a trifle overcomplicated. A more sensible approach is to analyse the payments to see whether sufficient payments can be delayed until your customers *have* paid you!

Van lease
The £1200 deposit is obviously a cash payment even though the benefit will not be received until it is repaid by the leasing company at the end of the lease. There is also the normal quarterly payment of £600 made in months one, four, seven and ten.

Road fund tax and insurance
The whole payment for the year is made in advance in month one.

Vehicle running
Although paid monthly, the payments are made after the event, so no cash is paid out in month one and month two's payment relates to the activity in month one. Consequently the payment in month six relates to activity in month five and there is one month's activity unpaid at the end of the period.

Other equipment leasing
Payable half yearly in advance means that £1000 is paid out in months one and seven.

Advertising
This is paid for as it is used, so a monthly payment of £700 is made for the first six months.

Wages and own drawings
Wages are normally paid either weekly or monthly and may (if weekly) be complicated by being paid one week in arrears. The simplest assumption is that the cash is paid out in the relevant month. Paul Cook's own drawings are also paid out in the relevant month. If he had formed a limited company, he would have to pay himself a salary which would be classified as an operating expense of the company.

General points
Different assumptions and interpretations regarding specific payments and receipts can always be made. It is therefore important when preparing any cash flow forecast that the relevant assumptions are clearly stated to avoid confusion.

The presentation at the bottom of the cash flow forecast shows the overall impact of the individual items on the cash flow of the business. The 'movement in month' line is simply the net inflow or outflow for that month, calculated by deducting the total cash out from the total cash in.

'Balance brought forward' is clearly nil at the beginning of month one as it represents the cash available to the business at the start of any particular month. It is also, therefore, equal to the closing balance at the end of the previous month which is given by the total shown as 'balance carried forward'. This is calculated from the balance brought forward plus or minus the net movement in the month.

The results
The cash flow forecast shows that the £50 000 of initial capital (the owner's funds and the loan) has been more than used up by the end of the six-month period. Indeed £8300 of the overdraft facility has had to be utilized. If the figures are examined more closely it becomes clear that this is caused by the delay in receiving cash from customers and the payment for supplies which were higher than the level of sales in the period. Although cash from sales was not all received in the period the operating expenses of the business were, on the whole, fully paid for and this increased the drain on the cash flow of the business.

This highlights the essential nature of the cash flow forecast because if Paul had not arranged the overdraft facility in advance the business could have failed for lack of cash in month six. Without such a forecast no business can be confident of having the right level of financial resources available at any given time. Obviously running out of cash is absolutely

disastrous but having too much cash, idly lying around, can be excessively expensive as well. The business has to assess the cost of having idle
cash resources by calculating what alternative use could be made of these
funds, for example, by putting the cash on deposit at a bank so as to earn
interest. This idea of comparing the financial return which could be
achieved from alternative courses of action is fundamental to financial
decision-making and is known as the opportunity cost concept, this is
considered in detail in Chapter 6.

Having established the cash position for the first six months it is
important that the trading performance of the business is also assessed so
that Paul can decide if investing all these funds in the business is
financially worthwhile. This can be done by preparing the profit and loss
account for the period and then any profit earned can be put into a
relative context by assessing this profit against the type of investments
required as disclosed by the balance sheet, prepared at the end of the
period.

Profit and loss account
This is shown in Figure 3.A4.

General
1   In the profit and loss account we are concerned with activities carried
    out by the business and the question of physical cash movements
    does not arise. Thus sales generated by the business in the specified
    period are included whether the cash is received or not. All the items
    used by the business to generate those sales are also included
    whether paid for in the period or not. However, items paid for in the
    period but not used up in the period are carried forward to a future
    period (provided, of course, that they have some future value to the
    business).
2   As this profit and loss account is being prepared for a six-month
    period we require sales and expenses for six months only.

Sales revenue
Sales are forecast to be made in each of the six months and the total sales
value is simply the total of the individual months (that is, £235 000). The
fact that not all this cash will be received is irrelevant, and the
reconciliation will appear on the balance sheet as debtors.

Cost of goods sold
We are interested in the cost of those goods *sold*, not those goods
purchased or paid for in the period. Consequently we need to match

Paul Cook
Profit and loss account for first six months

	£	£
Sales revenue	–	235 000
Opening stock		
Purchases	271 500	
	271 500	
less Closing stock	60 000	
Cost of goods sold		211 500
Gross profit margin on sales (10%)		£23 500
less Operating expenses:		
Rent and rates	6000	
Van lease expenses	1200	
Van road fund tax and insurance	100	
Vehicle running expenses	1800	
Other equipment leasing	1000	
Advertising	4200	
Wages	7200	
Warehouse expenses	1200	
Total operating expenses		22 700
Profit (loss) for the period		£800
less Owner's drawings for the period		3600
Retained earnings at end of period		£(2800)

Figure 3.A4 *Worked example: answers*

sales and remove stock levels from the calculation. This is very straight-forward as, in this case, it is the same as the control required for physical stocks. As this is the first period of trading, there are no opening stocks, whereas in the second six months the opening stock will, of course, be equal to the closing stock at the end of the first six months. Goods are to be delivered in each of the six months, and we can ignore the dates of payment for these goods as it is the physical activity of delivery which is important. Therefore the goods physically purchased by the business in the first six months total £271 500.

However not all of those goods will be sold in this period as we know that Paul expects to have stock left at the end of the period worth £60 000. This stock can be sold in future periods and is thus an asset of the business. Therefore we should not treat it as having been consumed in the first six months. If we reduce our purchases figure by this level of closing stock, we should have the cost of those goods actually used up (that is, sold) in the period. This gives a cost of goods sold figure of £211 500.

Gross margin on sales
This is simply the difference between the sales revenue and the cost of goods sold – in this example £23 500. Out of this, the business must pay for all the other operating expenses incurred in achieving the sales levels forecast before a profit or loss can be established.

In most businesses the level of gross margin relative to sales revenue is fairly well known and is normally closely monitored to see whether the business is trading satisfactorily. In Paul's case, he forecasts a 10 per cent gross margin on sales and this provides a good check on the profit and loss account figures.

Operating expenses
For all the operating expenses six months' activity has taken place and therefore this level of expense should be reflected in the profit and loss account, irrespective of how much has been paid for.

In most cases the amount paid for is, in fact, equal to the amount used up in the period, although if a profit and loss account were to be drawn up for one month or four months, etc., this would definitely not be so. However, with regard to the van lease a deposit is payable in addition to the monthly cost of leasing. Only the monthly leasing expense is to be charged to the profit and loss account.

Also the road fund tax and insurance payment of £200 relates to a full year, and only six months' worth will be used up in the relevant period. Therefore the expense in the profit and loss account will be £100 only.

Conversely the vehicle running expenses are paid in arrears and thus only five payments are forecast to be made in the period. The van will be used throughout the six months and therefore the expense for the whole period should be included in the activity-based profit and loss account, that is £1800.

As a minor matter of presentation, in this type of business which is not a limited company (Paul is commencing trading as a sole trader) it is normal practice to regard owners' drawings as part of the profit of the business rather than an expense as ordinary wages obviously are. In the case of a limited company the directors (whether the owners or not) will normally be paid a salary for the work they do and this salary is classed as an expense in the profit and loss account.

Profit for the period
Having deducted all the operating expenses (excluding Paul's drawings) from the gross margin the profit for the six-month period is left.

Although small, £800, the business is forecasting a profit for its first six months of trading and this must be encouraging. This is particularly true when the rate of growth in sales over the period is allowed for, and the steady level of operating expenses over the same period is considered. If sales remain at £50 000 per month for the second six months, the profits should increase significantly unless operating expenses are allowed to rise as well.

In many growing businesses it is important to consider carefully whether the profit achieved in any particular period is properly representative of the ongoing level of profit which should be achieved. In order to judge Paul's business it is clearly necessary to prepare a profit and loss account for the next six months so that a more steady and representative level of sales can be considered.

However, before doing this, it is important to complete the set of documents for the first six months and to try to reconcile the two apparently conflicting stories represented so far.

Paul's business has available cash of £50 000 as it starts, and yet at the end of only six months he has to borrow £8300 from the bank. However, he appears to have made a profit of £800 in the same period. Hopefully this illustrates the difference between profit and cash. He is spending the cash in the business, but in doing so he is creating assets which will have value to the business in the future. Preparing the balance sheet at the end of the period should reveal where this cash has gone and why the profit earned is not reflected in more cash than he started with.

Balance sheet
This is shown in Figure 3.A5.

General
1   The balance sheet is prepared at a moment in time rather than for a period. It must be considered, therefore, as a fleeting representation of the business and is probably best regarded as a reconciliation between the profit and loss account and the cash flow statement.
2   In this example we are trying to explain how a business can apparently spend £58 300 and yet show a profit of £800 over a six-month period.

Fixed assets
In order to minimize the cash outflow Paul has leased, on a short-term basis, all the equipment, etc. needed for his business. Consequently he does not own or have any real financial interest in any fixed assets. Obviously if he had bought the van he could have included it on the balance sheet, but would possibly have run out of cash completely.

Current assets
Current assets will, within 12 months normally, be turned back into cash but are temporarily tied up so that the business can function. They

Paul Cook
Balance sheet as at the end of first six months

	£	£	£
Fixed assets			
Current assets			
Stock	60 000		
Debtors	50 000		
Prepayments	1300		
Cash	–		
Total current assets		111 300	
less Current liabilities			
Trade creditors	55 500		
Accrued expenses	300		
Bank overdraft	8300		
Total current liabilities		64 100	
Net current assets			47 200
Net assets			47 200
Paul Cook capital account			20 000
Profit and loss account	800		
less Owner's drawings in period	3600		(2800)
Owner's capital			17 200
Loan account			30 000
Capital employed			£47 200

Figure 3.A5   *Worked example: answers*

comprise two major categories: goods or services bought before they need to be used in the business; and items used in the business which have not yet been paid for by customers.

In the first category the major item is likely to be stock on hand, and debtors will be the principal component of the second category.

However, in order to value these items it is helpful to compare the cash flow figures to those in the profit and loss account. As previously discussed on pages 78–80 any transaction should feature in two out of the three accounting statements (profit and loss account, balance sheet and cash flow), and an asset is created if something is bought but not used up in the period.

The simplest start point for preparing a balance sheet can, therefore, be to check out the cash flow items against the profit and loss items. If an item is paid for or received (that is, in the cash flow) and used up or consumed (that is, in the profit and loss account) then it will not feature on the balance sheet.

However, if sales income received (£185 000) is compared to sales revenue in the period (£235 000) a difference is immediately apparent. This difference is caused by the delay in payment by customers and represents £50 000 of sales made in month six but not yet paid for. This £50 000 thus features on the balance sheet as outstanding debtors (receivables) and the cash is expected the following month.

Similarly, the payments made for the van lease (£2400) and road fund tax and insurance (£200) do not equal the amounts shown as expenses in the profit and loss account (£1200 and £100 respectively). The differences (£1200 and £100) represent payments made in advance by the business and are assets, because in future either the cash will be repaid or the specific asset can be used without any further payment being made (for example, the van can be driven for a further six months with no further payment for tax and insurance).

Another form of payment in advance relates to stock on hand, which represents items bought but not used in the period. However, we are interested not just in items paid for as per the cash flow but all items shown as purchases which are still on hand. Consequently most businesses conduct physical stock counts and valuations at the end of their accounting periods to ascertain accurately the level of stock on hand. In our example we are told that this is forecast to be £60 000 and this is included on the balance sheet. This item is still included on two accounting statements as it was the figure used to reduce purchases in preparing the profit and loss account.

Current liabilities
Current liabilities are items which will require payments to be made, normally within 12 months, because they have been used up before being paid for.

The major element is caused by buying on credit, and if the purchases figure in the profit and loss account (£271 500) is compared to the payments for purchases in the cash flow forecast (£216 000), it becomes clear that £55 500 remains unpaid at the end of the period. This represents goods purchased in month six which are not due for payment until month seven under the payment terms agreed by the suppliers.

A similar smaller balance is revealed by comparing vehicle running payments (£1500) with the vehicle running expense in the profit and loss account (£1800). Thus £300 will have to be paid in the following month because payments are made in arrears. This item is shown on the balance sheet under 'accrued expenses', which is a common heading for unpaid expenses brought in under the matching concept but not yet billed to the company by the supplier. If the good or service has been billed (that is, invoiced) by the supplier it will normally be included as 'trade creditors'.

The remaining current liability in this example may at first seem slightly unusual but it does, in fact, conform to the previously stated rules. Because more net cash has been paid out than was originally available, Paul has had to borrow, on a short-term basis, from the bank. Consequently he will have to pay out cash in the future to repay the loan – he has effectively used up the bank's cash without paying for it. The overdraft is not shown as an expense in the profit and loss account because the items paid for by using the extra cash are expenses of the business. The overdraft shows on the cash flow forecast and as a current liability on the balance sheet. (It is arguable that the overdraft could be classified as a long-term liability if it will not be repaid within 12 months. Almost all companies show overdrafts as current liabilities as overdrafts are repayable on demand by the bank. If the company is using overdraft financing to fund long-term uses of cash in the business, this indicates a risk of it not being able to repay the overdraft if this is suddenly demanded by the bank. Thus the sources and uses of funds are not suitably matched.)

Net working capital (net current assets)
This simply shows the net investment made by the business in assets which it intends to turn into cash. It is given by deducting total current liabilities from total current assets. It is an important comparative measure for businesses because it gives a more relevant assessment of the necessary investment in 'short-term' assets than current assets alone. If, for example, a business carries high stocks this would show on the balance sheet as high current assets. However, if these stocks are bought on extended credit from the suppliers, there would be a correspondingly high level of trade creditors included in current liabilities. The net working capital would offset the two balances and reflect the true investment which requires financing by the business.

In Paul's business it is clear that a large part of the stock level is, indeed, financed by the level of trade creditors and the major element requiring financing by the business is the level of outstanding debtors.

Net assets
Net assets represents one half of the balance sheet and shows what has been done with the funds made available to the business. If more funds are injected into the business or profits made and retained in the business then the total of net assets should increase.

In our example it equals net working capital as there is no investment yet in fixed assets.

Capital employed
This is the total of the other half of the business and indicates where the funds came from that have been turned into the net assets.

As previously discussed there are three primary sources of finance for any business: the owners can put their own funds into the business; the owners can inject cash into the business, or they can leave in the business some of the profits made by trading; and they can borrow funds on a long-term basis. In our example Paul has done all of these to some extent.

Owner's capital

Paul put in £20 000 of his own funds when the business started – this was shown as cash into the business but, since the capital has not been used up or sold in the period, it did not directly feature in the profit and loss account. Therefore under our rule it must show up on the balance sheet. It is 'a sort of liability' of the business as it has received cash without doing anything for it. However the owner does receive 'ownership' in exchange for his investment, and owner's capital account (which would be 'share capital' in a limited company) is normally separated from other long-term liabilities and grouped together under 'total owner's capital' or 'shareholders' funds'.

The other source of owner's capital is any profits left in the business. In our example Paul made a profit of £800 but drew out £3600 in the period. In fact, therefore, he reduced his capital account by £2800 in the period to a net total of £17 200. As a sole trader he can introduce and withdraw funds from the business without any of the formalities required of a limited company.

In the case of a limited company, the initial capital is invested in the form of the share capital of the company and this cannot be withdrawn while the company continues in existence. However, the owners of the company can withdraw funds in two major ways. They can pay themselves a salary for working in the company which is shown as an expense in the profit and loss account and thus reduces the profit. Alternatively a dividend can be paid to all the shareholders out of the profits made by the company. It is essential that the company makes profits before a dividend can be paid, though salaries can be paid even if the company is making losses (but the company needs to have cash to pay the salaries!)

Loan account

The aunt's loan is clearly a liability of the business as it is to be repaid 'at some unspecified time in the future', which is most unlikely to be within the next 12 months. It is therefore classified as part of the capital employed in the business, and added to the total of owner's capital.

As the loan is repaid the balance remaining will reduce, and only the outstanding balance is included on the balance sheet.

The end product

The completed balance sheet shows where the funds came from (capital employed) and how these funds were invested (net assets) and reconciles the differences between the high cash usage in the period and the small profit made from trading.

Clearly no single accounting statement can give a true picture of the business; each statement looks at a different facet of the same business but, by using the integrated set of three statements, a good financial understanding of the business can be gained.

Answers only: Second six months

These are shown in Figures 3.A6, 3.A7 and 3.A8.

Paul Cook
Cash flow forecasts: second six months

Month	7	8	9	10	11	12	Total
Cash in							
Sales income	50 000	50 000	50 000	50 000	50 000	50 000	300 000
Total in (1)	50 000	50 000	50 000	50 000	50 000	50 000	300 000
Cash out							
Purchases	55 500	45 000	45 000	45 000	45 000	45 000	280 500
Rent and rates	3000	–	–	3000	–	–	6000
Warehouse	–	–	600	–	–	600	1200
Van lease	600	–	–	600	–	–	1200
Road fund tax and insurance	–	–	–	–	–	–	–
Vehicle running	300	300	300	300	300	300	1800
Other equipment lease	1000	–	–	–	–	–	1000
Advertising	300	300	300	300	300	300	1800
Wages (employees)	1200	1200	1200	1200	1200	1200	7200
Own drawings	600	600	600	600	600	600	3600
Total out (2)	62 500	47 400	48 000	51 000	47 400	48 000	304 300
Movement in month ((1)–(2))	(12 500)	2600	2000	(1000)	2600	2000	(4300)
Balance brought forward	(8300)	(20 800)	(18 200)	(16 200)	(17 200)	(14 600)	(8300)
Balance carried forward	(20 800)	(18 200)	(16 200)	(17 200)	(14 600)	(12 600)	(12 600)

Figure 3.A6   *Worked example: answers*

Paul Cook
Profit and loss account for second six months
(not whole of first year)

	£	£
Sales revenue		300 000
Opening stock	60 000	
add Purchases	270 000	
	330 000	
less Closing stock	60 000	
Cost of goods sold		270 000
Gross profit margin on sales (10%)		30 000
less Operating expenses:		
Rent and rates	6000	
Van lease	1200	
Road fund tax and insurance	100	
Vehicle running	1800	
Other equipment leasing	1000	
Advertising	1800	
Wages	7200	
Warehouse expenses	1200	
Total operating expenses		20 300
Profit (loss) for the period		£9700
less Owner's drawings for the period		3600
Retained earnings at end of period		6100
add Retained earnings brought forward		(2800)
Retained earnings at end of period		£3300

Figure 3.A7   *Worked example: answers*

Paul Cook
Balance sheet as at the end of second six months

	£	£	£
Fixed assets			
Current assets			
Stock	60 000		
Debtors	50 000		
Prepayments	1200		
Cash	–		
Total current assets		111 200	
less Current liabilities			
Trade creditors	45 500		
Unpaid expenses	300		
Bank overdraft	12 600		
Total current liabilities		57 900	
Net current assets			53 300
Net assets			£53 300
Paul Cook capital account			20 000
Balance on retained profits brought			
forward		(2800)	
Retained profits in period	9700		
less Owner's drawings in period	3600	6100	3300
Owner's capital			23 300
Loan account			30 000
Capital employed			£53 300

Figure 3.A8   *Worked example: answers*

4

Interpretation

Introduction

The full integrated set of financial statements (namely the balance sheet, profit and loss account, and source and application of funds statement), which are published externally and normally produced internally for management control purposes, contain the basis for a very extensive financial analysis of the current position of the business. We have already seen that a number of managerial judgements are required in their preparation and that it is important to place the published results into their proper context. For example, knowing that a business made a profit of £5 million last year does not enable us to decide whether this was a good or bad achievement. If it related to the business recently started by George Taylor the result is clearly incredible; but if the results were for a leading multinational company which previously had reported annual profits consistently in excess of £100 million it represents a major disaster for the business.

Therefore it is essential to place the absolute figures into the relative context of previous years and current expectations as well as comparing these figures externally (that is, by looking outwards and forwards). In the absence of information from the particular company, these current expectations may have to be based on the published financial statements of competitors or similarly structured businesses or on general economic indicators applied to past results. Financial comparisons, whether internal or external, are even more meaningful when ratios are used to relate the absolute values to other appropriate elements in the business or outside standards. Using trends over time in these ratios also puts the financial position into a proper context, indicating whether the position is improving or deteriorating. A set of published financial statements contains detailed figures for only the current and previous years but normally a summary set of figures is included covering the past five or ten years. (Even if these are not included the past years' financial statements are publicly available and so a good historical financial record can be built up for any company.) This longer-term view must be analysed carefully to ensure that no major changes have occurred in the composition or strategy of the company and that the accounting policies have been consistently applied.

Before we can consider, in detail, what financial analysis should be carried out, we need to understand the purpose behind the analysis because there is a vast range of information available and a mass of potential ratios and trends to evaluate. As discussed in Chapter 1, a wide range of people, both from inside and outside the business, will be interested in the financial position of the company but from varying perspectives. While most people are interested in the profit performance of the company, in some cases this will be the sole focus for the financial analysis and there will be an attempt to understand in detail how and why the particular financial results were achieved. The profits as shown by the profit and loss account need to be placed in the context of the level of investment required to achieve this particular level of profit. Thus profitability, which can be defined as the profit achieved per £ of investment, is a relevant measure of financial performance. For others, performance is only one area of interest in the financial position and greater emphasis may be put on the current financial strength of the business which requires analysis of the balance sheet and cash flow rather than just profitability. The financial strength of the business is reflected in its ability to meet its financial commitments as they fall due and this can be measured by the liquidity of the net assets. A liquid asset can be defined as cash or an asset which can be quickly and easily turned into cash. Liquidity measures the short-term ability of a business to meet its liabilities, and this requires the use of these liquid assets which can be turned into cash at very short notice should this prove necessary. A business also needs to have the ability to meet its liabilities in the longer term and this is defined as the 'solvency' of the business. Another group of analysts will be trying to value the business or possibly partial ownership of the company (for example, one share) and they will be concerned with comparative financial performance and future prospects as well as financial strength. This third group will be particularly interested in how the method of financing chosen by the company has affected the financial return achieved by the owners, and therefore will want to analyse the capital structure of the company. The capital structure of a company shows the relative proportions and types of shareholders' funds and debt which have been employed to finance the net assets used in the business. We can therefore distinguish three groups of financial ratios, one or more of which may be of significance to anyone analysing a company: these concentrate on financial performance (profitability); financial strength (liquidity); and financial structure (gearing and valuation) and we will consider each in turn.

Overview

However, there are also common elements to any financial analysis which help to put the overall company position into context before the analysts concentrate on their particular area of interest. This analytical process is diagrammatically represented in Figure 4.1. If this overview stage is ignored then the detailed analysis may lead to false conclusions because the relationships were examined out of context. A sensible start point is to derive some general financial performance and status ratios for comparable companies or for the industrial category as a whole and to compare these to the company under scrutiny. It is often useful to include a company regarded as a market leader in the industry as its financial position can provide a good reference point for analysing relative strengths and weaknesses. This helps to place the company financially against the competition and this financial ranking should be compared with other perceptions created by indicators such as market share and strength in the marketplace. For most industries it is also possible to obtain other companies' results in ratio form. (A commercial service publishing such comparative results is provided by Inter Company Comparisons Ltd, Jordan and Sons Surveys Ltd and other more specialized organizations.) Also many trade federations carry out performance comparisons within their industry and publish the outcomes on an anonymous basis to enable members to see how they rank against other companies in the industry. It is important to compare against businesses in the same or similar industries as the level of profitability achieved and the necessary financial strength revealed by the balance sheet ratios vary dramatically from industry to industry, but for large conglomerate companies this is far from easy. In modern published financial statements some information has to be disclosed on sales revenue and profit by different industrial categories and geographical areas, as shown in Figure 4.2.

This may not only enable a more sensible comparison to be made with other businesses, but could also highlight risks regarding dependence on any particular industry or areas of the world with potential volatility in future profitability or cash flow (some countries have stopped foreign companies taking their profits out of the country).

This first stage financial analysis should include a review of the funds statement to see whether the business is being sensibly financed. If long-term uses of cash (for example, the purchase of long economic life fixed assets) are being funded by short-term sources of finance (for example,

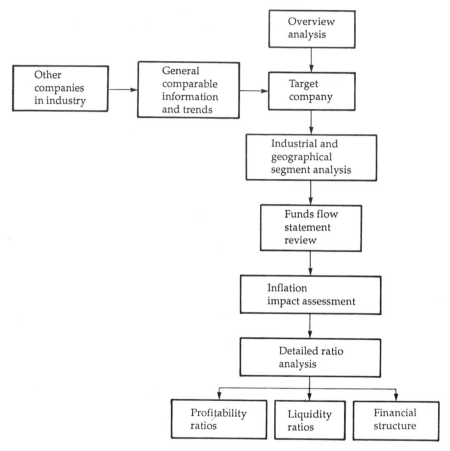

Figure 4.1   *Financial analysis process*

overdraft borrowing), the company may run into cash flow problems in the future. The funds statement also highlights the cash generated from trading operations and this is a good measure of the ability of the company to fund growth, as well as to pay its existing obligations. This overview may include an inflation-adjusted review of the financial performance over time to see how the business is doing in real terms. The numbers included in the annual financial statements have to be adjusted to a common basis – often current money values are used by multiplying the actual figures published in the past by the appropriate retail price index (RPI) movement to bring the historic items to current equivalent values as illustrated in Figure 4.3.

This will show whether sales revenues and profits have increased excluding inflation but it may still not indicate whether sales volumes are

Hanson plc and subsidiaries: published financial statements for the year ended 30 September 1987: Sales turnover and profit by class of business and geographical location*

1987	1986		1987	1986
£ million			£ million	
Profit on ordinary activities			*Sales turnover*	
United Kingdom				
207	94	Consumer	3370	1614
73	623	Building products	246	2398
85	49	Industrial	387	310
42	22	Food	623	269
407	227		4626	2432
United States				
44	42	Consumer	528	530
74	53	Building products	500	423
81	78	Industrial	620	522
21	14	Food	408	339
220	187		2056	1814
627	414	Total	6682	4246

*This information is extracted from note 1 of the Hanson published financial statements which actually gives more information, including the figures in US dollars.

Figure 4.2

up or down because prices may have risen more or less than general inflation. Care, therefore, needs to be exercised in adjusting the figures by using specific inflation indices wherever possible rather than general RPI measures of inflation to ensure that greater comparability is achieved rather than greater confusion. For example, if a comparison of real share price movements over time was being done for any company by adjusting for inflation, it might also be useful to monitor what had happened in real terms over the same period to some general measure of share prices, for example, the Financial Times All-Share Index.

Financial performance ratios

In most cases, the overview financial analysis will require more detailed information on the financial performance of the company and in particular on the methods employed in earning the return achieved. Any sensible measure of financial performance compares profit to the investment required to generate that profit and this immediately requires some careful clarification of the terms being used. In any profit and loss account profit can be measured at several different points and it is

1987 Financial statements	£ million	1988 Financial statements
1750	Sales revenue	1800
1600	Total expenses	1635
150	Profit on ordinary activities	165

It appears that both sales revenues and profit have increased in 1988 over 1987, but if the 1987 figures are restated at 1988 values by multiplying by the increase in the retail price index (RPI) in the 12 months period (say 5%) the picture is changed somewhat and a more realistic comparison can be made.

1987 Base data		1987 Restated figures	1988 Figures
1750	Sales revenue	1837.5	1800
1600	Total expenses	1680.0	1635
150	Profit on ordinary activities	157.5	165

This has indicated that, in inflation adjusted terms, sales revenues have declined but profits have increased due to a greater relative fall in total expenses.

Figure 4.3   *Extracts of a hypothetical profit and loss account*

important, in any analysis, to use the appropriate measure of profit and to ensure that all comparisons are done at the same level of profit. As can be seen from the published profit and loss account for the Burton Group plc illustrated in Figure 4.4 there may be six levels of profit referred to by a company. Gross profit can itself have many interpretations in different businesses, but normally it is calculated by deducting the costs which are directly identifiable with the goods or services sold from the sales revenue for the period. The period costs (that is, those incurred by reference to time rather than due to levels of product or service being sold) are then deducted from the gross profit to give 'profit on ordinary activities before interest and taxation' which may be loosely described as 'trading profit'. This horrendous-looking heading is quite straightforward when broken down; 'on ordinary activities' is included to show that the profit is made by trading and not by some other accounting adjustment. If the company sold off some of its fixed assets (say land and buildings) for more than they were included in the balance sheet, the company has made a profit on the sale. Unless the company is in the business of selling land and buildings, this one-off profit could distort the financial results for the year and should not be treated as normal profit. It should, therefore, be excluded from 'profit on ordinary activities' to make it clear that the financial performance of the company cannot continually be supported by sales of fixed assets, and it should be classified as a 'non-trading' item as indicated in Chapter 3.

Equally if the period under consideration contained some abnormal costs which were not part of the normal trading activities of the business these would be excluded when arriving at 'profit from ordinary activities'. For example, if a downturn in general sales levels or problems in the sales of one product led to the decision to close a factory or major sales division of the company, the specific costs of closure including redundancy costs would be regarded as outside the normal trading activities of the business. These items are shown separately lower down the profit and loss account as 'extraordinary items', which can include all non-recurring financial events outside the ordinary business transactions undertaken by the company. Obviously these 'extraordinary items' are ignored when an analyst is looking for the trend of financial performance, but will be included in the funds statement if they result in any movements in funds into or out of the company (for example, some of the costs of closing a factory such as redundancy costs for employees will result in cash payments, and the sale of land and buildings will normally result in a substantial cash inflow into the business).

Profit on ordinary activities is first stated 'before interest and tax' to give the overall return on the operations from the business without regard to how the company has raised the necessary finance. If borrowed funds (debt) have been used there will be an interest cost incurred as the charge by the lender for using their funds; and this interest expense will be shown as a reduction in the net profit made by the business. Borrowing will have reduced the investment required from the owners (shareholders) and therefore paying interest may enable the shareholders to get a higher return on the lower level of funds committed.

Companies and other businesses pay taxes on their profits after deducting all the allowable expenses (which include all the normal costs of generating the sales revenue and interest on cash borrowed for use in the business) and so before any profit is available to the owners, taxation must be deducted from the 'profit on ordinary activities after interest' level of profit.

Any items previously excluded as 'extraordinary' are now included as a net of tax adjustment to give the overall net 'profit for the financial year'. All of this profit is owned by the shareholders in the company but part only may be distributed as dividends, which they receive in cash. The rest is retained by the company and reinvested to make the business grow so that future years' profits increase. As mentioned, dividends represent a distribution of profits to the shareholders, but they are paid out in cash. Therefore in order to declare and pay dividends, a company

The Burton Group plc and subsidiaries: published consolidated profit and loss account (for the financial year ended 29 August 1987)

	£ million	
Sales revenue	1338.6	
less Cost of Sales	(1098.3)	
Gross profit	240.3	(1)
less Other expenses	40.2	
Profit on ordinary activities before interest and taxation	200.1	(2)
less Interest	(16.7)	
Profit on ordinary activities before taxation	183.4	(3)
less Taxation	(64.1)	
Profit on ordinary activities after taxation	119.3	(4)
add (less) Extraordinary items (after taxation)	6.9	
Profit for the financial year	126.2	(5)
less Dividends	(39.7)	
Retained profits for the year	86.5	(6)

(*Note*   For clarity of presentation a few minor figures have been amalgamated under other headings)

Figure 4.4

must have produced profits (that is, have traded profitably) and have cash which is not required to finance the continuing trading activity of the company.

Return on shareholders' funds
Different levels of profits are relevant to different types of analysis and thus for a detailed review of financial performance the focus of attention should be specified. If the analysis is from the point of view of the shareholders in the company, they will be interested principally in the profit which is available to them, and which is likely to be produced on a regular basis. This is the net profit on ordinary activities after taxation (normally abbreviated to net profit after tax or PAT), irrespective of how much has been paid out as dividends. This profit after tax can be related to the shareholders' investment in the company. The normal basis for the shareholders' investment is the previously illustrated balance sheet total of shareholders' funds (that is, share capital plus reserves), which can be extracted from the published balance sheet of the Burton Group plc (Figure 4.5) but it must be remembered that the balance sheet is not a valuation statement of the business.

(Therefore this return cannot be compared directly to investing cash in

**The Burton Group plc and subsidiaries: consolidated balance sheet
at 29 August 1987**

	£ million	£ million
Fixed assets		
Tangible assets		683.0
Investments		139.5
		822.5
Current assets		
Stocks	208.9	
Debtors	79.4	
Properties held for resale	40.6	
Investments	7.7	
Bank balances and cash	19.9	
Total current assets	356.5	
less Current liabilities		
Bank loans and overdraft	18.9	
Trade creditors	162.7	
Other creditors	67.3	
Lease obligations	6.3	
Taxation	35.7	
Accruals	23.8	
Proposed dividend	28.7	
	343.4	
Net current assets		13.1
Total assets less current liabilities		835.6
less Creditors (due after more than one year)		233.5
Provisions for liabilities and charges		64.2
Minority Interests		14.7
		523.2
Capital and reserves		
Called-up share capital		276.0
Share premium account		0.7
Revaluation reserve		30.1
Retained Earnings (profit and loss account)		216.4
Shareholders' funds		523.2

(Note   For clarity and ease of presentation a few minor items have been added together
or reclassified)

Figure 4.5

other investments such as a bank deposit or building society account. A more direct way of comparing the investor's return with such an alternative investment is by calculating the profit earned by each share in the company and this ratio, known as earnings per share, is considered in the valuation section of this chapter, page 130.) This relationship, *return on shareholders' funds* (or *return on equity* as it is often called), can be compared to the levels generated by other companies, particularly within the industry.

$$\text{Return on shareholders funds:} = \frac{\text{Net profit after tax}}{\text{Shareholders' funds}} \times 100\%$$

The ratio, like many others, is normally expressed as an *annual* percentage, and the resulting ratio for the Burton Group plc is shown below.

Return on shareholders' funds for the Burton Group plc

$$\text{ROSF} = \frac{\text{Net profit after tax}}{\text{Shareholders' funds}} \times 100\% = \frac{119.3}{523.2} \times 100\% = 22.8\%$$

It is important to ensure that all return measurements are expressed in annual equivalents as otherwise the comparison of the percentages becomes confusing. As financial results are often expressed for periods shorter than a year, any such published profit figures must be annualized.

Shareholders will look for a good return on shareholders' funds with an increase over time as a sign of a good company to have invested in. Any new investor is really buying the prospect of future profits and therefore the level of return made now and in the past is regarded as an indicator of the future returns which can be achieved. As has already been shown the position of products in their life cycle can affect this significantly because a very high current return on shareholders' funds may not be sustained in the future if the major products are near the end of their life cycles. Investors also require a return to compensate them for the risks that they run and therefore the higher the risk involved in a business the greater the return required by the shareholders. This is shown graphically in Figure 4.6.

Even for a totally risk-free investment investors require some level of financial return as compensation for giving up the ability to use their cash immediately for personal consumption. In an inflationary period, investors also require a return because their funds will lose purchasing power if consumption is delayed by making the investment. On top of these overall returns, investors need a specific return relating to the perceived risk of the particular investment. One clear sign of risk associated with financial performance is a high degree of volatility in annual profit levels,

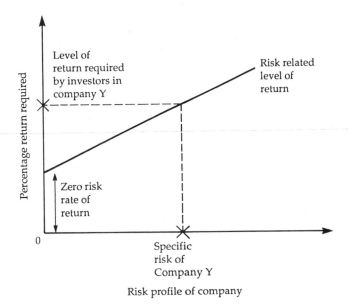

Figure 4.6   *Risk and return relationship*

particularly if this volatility is caused by very few external factors. The trend in return on shareholders' funds is therefore very important and if there are violent fluctuations, shareholders will demand a higher average level of return to compensate. The worldwide motor car industry has a recent history of making very high profits and then making incredible losses for two to three years, before returning to very high profits again. The high losses were caused by a decline in the size of the major markets caused by the sudden oil price increase and the ensuing recessions. Despite the return to high profits there is still a perceived risk of the industry being dramatically affected by any new external shock. The recession followed by the large oil price reductions created similar problems for the oil companies themselves and reduced their returns on shareholders' funds substantially. In several parts of the computer industry very high levels of competition, caused by too many suppliers with shortening product life cycles and dramatically reducing real prices, have also affected levels of return for many companies. These factors should have affected the particular industry relatively evenly but the impacts on individual companies were far from even. Identifying companies with the ability to weather adverse conditions as well as exploit opportunities when they arise is a major aim of financial analysis, and the ratios used should link into the SWOT analysis discussed in Chapter 2.

Return on capital employed (ROCE)

The return on shareholders' funds does not necessarily measure the return on all the assets utilized by the business as the assets can be financed by borrowed funds (debt) as well. To some extent, the operating performance should be separated from the way in which the business is financed and the return on all the assets used is a good indicator of overall financial performance. The normal way of doing this is to add together shareholders' funds and long or medium term debt (loans with more than one year to repayment) and this total is often described as total capital employed. Some companies which use overdraft borrowing as a continual source of funding for the business (for example, BP and BAA) include these borrowings as part of their total debt for the purposes of this calculation, even though the borrowings are technically repayable within 12 months. Capital employed, for most companies, is equal to the total assets minus the current liabilities of the company and these are often referred to as the 'net assets employed in the company' (refer to the restated summarized balance sheet in Figure 4.7 for clarification and remember that the balance sheet must balance). If we are going to include debt (at least that with more than one year to repayment) as part of the investment calculation, it is logical to adjust the return part of the equation. We have already mentioned that interest is paid on borrowings and therefore we should take profit before the appropriate portion of interest (interest is payable on *all* loans outstanding during the accounting period but, if some short-term borrowings are excluded from capital employed, the interest on this short-term borrowing should be excluded as well).

Net fixed assets		X
Current assets	X	
less current liabilities	X	
Net current assets		X
Total assets less current liabilities (net assets)		X
Shareholders' funds		X
Long-term debt		X
Capital employed		X

Note   In the balance sheet illustrated in Chapter 3 and in Table 4.4, long-term debt was deducted from the assets portion of the balance sheet and this form of presentation is most common in published financial statements.

Figure 4.7   *Summarized restated balance sheet*

It is often argued that taxation on profit is distorted by various government inspired fiscal strategies to the point that the particular level of tax charged in any year does not bear any direct relationship to the financial performance of the business. A good example is where taxation rates are successively reduced year by year from 52% through 50%, 45% and 40% to 35% so that the after-tax profit of a company will appear to have improved each year even if the before-tax levels have been static for five years. As a consequence it is quite common practice to calculate overall return measures on a 'before-tax' basis, but it is very important to compare like with like, and not muddle comparisons of pre-tax profits or returns with post-tax levels. Although common practice in financial analysis, it must be remembered that taxation of profits is a fact of commercial life and it is therefore dangerous to calculate measures of return which bear no relationship to economic reality and the ability of the company to produce a financial return for its owners.

However, at the before-tax level an overall business return measure can be calculated as follows:

$$\text{Return on capital employed (ROCE)} = \frac{\text{Profit before interest and tax}}{\text{Capital employed}} \times 100\%$$

(Where capital employed = shareholders' funds + long-term debt)

The relationship between ROCE and return on equity is considered under financial status ratios later in this chapter (page 178).

In order to illustrate the calculation of these ratios the illustrated financial statements of the Burton Group plc shown in Figures 4.4 and 4.5 will be used, wherever appropriate, throughout the remainder of this chapter. Readers should ensure that they are aware of where within the financial statements the particular figures used come from. Thus the ROCE ratio is shown separately below, but for future ratios the numbers are included when the ratio is defined, and are simply given as illustrative examples.

Return on capital employed (ROCE): The Burton Group plc

$$\text{ROCE} = \frac{\text{Profit before interest and tax}}{\text{Capital employed}} \times 100\%$$

$$= \frac{£200.1 \text{ million}}{£835.6 \text{ million}} \times 100\% = 23.9\%$$

(Capital employed has been taken as being equal to total assets *less* current liabilities. The total of shareholders' funds plus long-term debt may be slightly different due to the possible inclusion or exclusion of 'provisions for liabilities and charges'. This item is frequently treated as part of shareholders' funds, but it is more important that it is treated consistently so that meaningful trends can be analysed and interpreted.)

Since capital employed is equal in value to the net assets part of the balance sheet it is possible to substitute net assets for capital employed (see below) in the ratio and still have exactly the same relationship:

Return on capital employed (ROCE) = Return on net assets

$$= \frac{\text{Profit before interest and tax (PBIT)}}{\text{Net assets}} \times 100\%$$

[where net assets = fixed assets + current assets − current liabilities]

The arithmetic shown below enables the overall ratio to be further analysed into much more detail which is very helpful. Knowing that a company made a return on capital employed of 20 per cent is interesting, but it is much more relevant to understand the strategy that was used and why the return achieved differed from other companies in the industry.

Return on net assets – analysed

By some simple arithmetic it is possible to break the ratio into two parts:

$$\text{Return on net assets (RONA)} = \frac{\text{PBIT}}{\text{Sales revenue}} \times \frac{\text{Sales revenue}}{\text{Net assets}} \times 100\%$$

$$= \text{Profit margin} \times \text{Net asset turnover ratio} \times 100\%$$

Illustrative calculation

$$\text{RONA} = \frac{200.1 \text{ million}}{1338.6 \text{ million}} \times \frac{1338.6 \text{ million}}{835.6 \text{ million}} \times 100\%$$

$$= 14.9\% \times 1.6 \times 100\% = 23.9\%$$

The return on net assets (capital employed) can now be seen to be controlled by the relative performance of two relationships; how much profit the company makes per £ of sales revenue; and how much investment in net assets is required to generate the sales revenue achieved. This indicates that a company can make any particular level of return on capital employed using many different strategies. There are very significant differences between industries, but there are also large variations caused by alternative marketing strategies within the same industry. If a business has a target ROCE of, say, 30 per cent it could achieve this in a variety of ways as shown in Table 4.1. Thus the greater the investment needed for any given level of sales revenue the higher the profit margin that is required to earn any target level of ROCE.

The fixed assets required in different industries range from very large sophisticated plant and machinery, including computer-controlled equipment for a manufacturer of complex products (such as motor cars and steel, normally referred to as having high capital intensity) to almost nothing at all for some service industries. A high absolute value of the

Table 4.1 *Return on capital employed (ROCE): different strategies to achieve one level of return*

ROCE	= Profit margin	× Net asset turnover ratio	Comments
30%	= 30%	× 1	Very high profit margin with
30%	= 15%	× 2	high asset investment
30%	= 10%	× 3	Reasonable profit margin and medium asset turnover ratio
30%	= 5%	× 6	Low profit margin and relies
30%	= 2%	× 15	on fast asset turnover to achieve target ROCE

fixed assets need not dramatically reduce the net asset turnover ratio because the unit sales value may be correspondingly high (as for cars). Therefore, provided the volume produced is high, the asset turnover ratio may be quite acceptable. Equally the level of net current assets needed ranges from nil to a very high absolute value where stocks of raw materials, work-in-progress and finished goods are all held and where customers take a long time to pay but where limited financing is available from suppliers. If a whisky producer wishes to sell a premium 12 years' old product, the stock will have been maturing for this length of time and the distiller needs a good profit margin to compensate for the capital tied up in these stocks. The marketing strategy employed must take into account the potential to obtain a high net profit margin to compensate for the overall investment required relative to the sales achieved.

Some specialist high technology manufacturing industries may be able to achieve a high net profit margin of around 30 per cent but for other companies, such as supermarkets, the pricing policy needed to obtain this level would make them completely uncompetitive. The level of profit margin achievable is normally related to the value added by the business. A supermarket retailer may have to accept a relatively low net profit margin as the 'value added', by his part in the process is smaller than other parts of the business chain, and a wholesaler possibly adds even less value with a consequent need to accept still lower profit margins. If profit margins are constrained the investment in net assets must be reduced to achieve a comparable ROCE. For a supermarket retailer it may be possible to manage the assets and liabilities so that the net asset turnover ratio is over ten times per year which enables an ROCE of 30 per cent to be earned with a net profit margin of only 3 per cent. This will depend on the particular way of running the business including the fundamental decision regarding whether to own the freehold of the shops or to rent them. Consideration of the balance sheet for a retailer or wholesaler will show the main fixed assets required are land and buildings (if owned) and fixtures and fittings for the shops including any computer equipment. In the case of The Burton Group plc properties total £460.4 million out of total tangible fixed assets of £683 million. The net working capital will consist of stocks held for resale and debtors, if sales are made on credit, but the capital required will be reduced if purchases are made on credit so that outstanding creditors are shown on the balance sheet (net current assets in Figure 4.5 are only £13.1 million but stocks held are £208.9 million).

If our retailing strategy is to go for the lowest practical investment base to keep the asset turnover ratio as high as possible, this can be done by renting the premises and selling only for cash which eliminates the need to finance debtors. We need to have stocks on the shelves to sell but if we run a tight system of inventory control and take the maximum period of credit available from suppliers we can minimize the net investment in working capital. Some very large supermarket chains have developed this to the point where outstanding creditors exceed the total of all current assets including stocks and debtors. This means that there is *negative* working capital in the business (that is, either part of the fixed assets are being financed with suppliers' money or the supermarket is able to invest the cash generated from selling stocks which it has not yet paid for, and earn interest on these funds). Ratios for considering each element of the balance sheet are considered shortly, but first we need to consider what factors affect the level of profit margin.

Marketing strategies

A marketing strategy of differentiating goods or services from others in the market may enable a company to earn greater profit margins than their competitors by maintaining higher prices. The higher marketing expenses associated with this differentiation will be charged against profit and this will reduce profit margins. Therefore the price differential gained must be greater than the increased marketing support required, if net profit margins are to be increased. The alternative way for a company to get a better than normal profit margin is by having a lower cost base than any of its competitors. This cost advantage means that it can sell at the same or even slightly lower prices but still show a higher profit per £ of sales. It is possible for a company to specialize in certain segments of a total market, and by doing so achieve either a cost advantage or a particular differentiation which enables it to show higher profit margins than competition. The cost advantage could be due to concentrating on a localized region and the differentiation achieved by offering specialized services which are particularly appropriate to one group of customers, who are prepared to pay extra for this level of service. These alternative strategies are developed in great detail by Michael E. Porter in two books*

Alternative types of strategy

Industry wide	Low cost	Differentiation
Focused	Focus/niche	

It is important that any user of financial information understands what strategy is being implemented by a company as it can be misleading to compare directly the ratios achieved by two companies implementing very different strategies in the same industry. It can be more useful to compare the relative ratios achieved by companies in different industries which use similar marketing positions. This technique has been very fully developed, particularly in the United States, by the PIMS studies (profit impact of market strategies) which have financial analyses on over 3000 companies in various industries that can be used as a base for comparison. Uses of PIMS data are considered in Chapter 5.

If a company does not have an obvious competitive advantage against its competition it may try to gain one by selecting a policy of lower pricing than normal. This will reduce its profit margin but it may obtain a higher level of sales due to its lower prices and the improved net asset turnover ratio may produce a better overall ROCE. The impact of this policy depends on the price elasticity of demand in this market and the value of the additional investment needed by the increased level of activity – the cost/volume/profit relationship is considered in Part Three. The change in investment is revealed by the financial analysis of the net asset turnover ratio over time and by breaking it down into its component elements.

Net asset turnover ratio

It is possible to calculate an asset turnover ratio for each of the significant elements in any company's balance sheet and the relative importance of each shows where most analytical effort should be allocated:

$$\text{Net asset turnover} = \frac{\text{Sales revenue}}{\text{Net assets}}$$

$$= \frac{\text{Sales revenue}}{\text{Fixed assets} + \text{current assets} - \text{current liabilities}}$$

Illustrative calculation:

$$\text{Net asset turnover ratio} = \frac{1338.6 \text{ million}}{822.5 \text{ million} + 356.5 \text{ million} - 343.4 \text{ million}} = 1.6$$

Competitive Strategy, 1980, Free Press; *Competitive Advantage*, 1985, Free Press.

Fixed asset turnover ratio

$$\text{Fixed asset turnover ratio} = \frac{\text{Sales}}{\text{Net fixed assets}}$$

With all components of asset turnover ratios the particular industry and strategy being followed have an important impact but the most noticeable impact will be in the area of fixed assets. One retailer could decide to own its shops, as the Burton Group plc have done, and so have to place substantial fixed assets on the balance sheet, or it could rent the properties and have a significantly higher fixed assets turnover ratio – it is difficult to argue that the turnover of the retailer will increase because the company owns its shops. Although it should have to provide depreciation on the buildings, by owning the shops the company does not have to pay rent which increases the profit margin by reducing the operating expenses and there is a net gain in profit margin. If the business is averagely profitable, the net gain in profit margin from ownership is sufficient to maintain the ROCE at the levels it would achieve if the shops were rented due to the decreased asset turnover ratio caused by the high increase in fixed assets.

Example: alternative fixed asset strategies for the Burton Group plc
The group has two headings of fixed assets in its balance sheet as shown in Figure 4.5, and the investments shown at £139.5 million represent shares owned in other companies where the group does not exercise overall control. These investments generated an income of £44.2 million in 1986–87 which represents the group's share of the profits earned by these other companies. This was included in trading profit by reducing the other expenses deducted from the gross profit.

As investments are a completely different category of fixed asset which do not affect the sales revenue of the group we are ignoring them in calculating the fixed asset turnover ratio. (This illustrates some of the practical complexities of carrying out financial analysis on large groups of companies.)

1 Using only the tangible fixed assets of the group, the fixed asset turnover ratio can be calculated as:

$$\text{Fixed asset turnover ratio} = \frac{\text{Sales revenue}}{\text{Fixed assets}} = \frac{1338.6 \text{ million}}{683.0 \text{ million}} = 1.96 \text{ times}$$

2 However, if the group did not own their properties but rented them the fixed assets would be reduced by £460.5 million to a new total of £222.6 million and the ratio could be recalculated as:

$$\text{Fixed asset turnover ratio} = \frac{\text{Sales revenue}}{\text{Adjusted fixed assets}} = \frac{1338.6 \text{ million}}{222.6 \text{ million}} = 6.01 \text{ times}$$

This highlights the impact which a strategy of owning property can have on the performance ratios of a business. This impact must be considered against the following other points:

1 If the properties were not owned the profit margin would be reduced by the rentals on the properties occupied by the business, so that the improvement in ROCE would be less than implied by this adjustment;

2 By owning properties the group gains the potential of capital gains through the revaluation of the properties over time – the group had a revaluation reserve on its balance sheet at 31 August 1987 of £30.1 million representing this increase in value over cost.

Therefore, the business cannot be judged solely on ROCE because it now owns freehold land and buildings which may appreciate in value over time. This raises a problem of how we can incorporate such an asset properly in the financial statements when the balance sheet only includes assets at cost and profits can only be made by sales. As mentioned in Chapter 3, it is possible to revalue fixed assets which have increased in value so that the balance sheet shows a more realistic view of the position of the company. The increase in value is not treated as a profit on trading, and is not included in the profit and loss account, but is included directly as part of shareholders' funds on the balance sheet – normally being separately shown and described appropriately as 'reserve on revaluation' as shown for the Burton Group plc in Figure 4.5. Unfortunately revaluing the property above its original cost means that the net assets of the business are increased still further and thus ROCE is further depressed, although the value of the business may have increased. It is clear that this kind of adjustment makes analysis of returns over time very difficult and can also complicate the comparison between companies in the same industry if they have different strategies regarding ownership of fixed assets. (Many large supermarket chains also now have substantial fixed assets in land and buildings.)

Another example of this can be taken from shipping companies or airlines. Some companies own their ships or aeroplanes and hence they are included as fixed assets on the balance sheets. Other companies choose to rent these items on a short-term (single journey) or long-term (lease contract) basis which gives them the right to use the assets but does not give them ownership. Hence in some cases they do not include them as fixed assets on their balance sheets which can considerably alter the apparent ROCE being achieved. Considerable care needs to be taken to take account of what is referred to, for obvious reasons, as 'off balance sheet financing'.

The possible level of vertical integration of a business has already been mentioned and this can substantially affect fixed asset turnover ratios. If one company subcontracts all its manufacturing and concentrates on marketing and distribution, it will not need to invest in the same level of fixed assets relative to its turnover. However, part of the overall profit will now have to be passed to the manufacturers and so the profit margin is lower but the fixed asset turnover ratio is higher. The key question is what happens to the overall ROCE, but this is not always fully understood by companies. Some businesses started as marketing organizations but have expanded their successful operations into manufacturing their own product range, perhaps on the basis that their suppliers were making a profit at their expense. They may increase the absolute value of total profits but the increased investment in fixed assets may significantly reduce the more relevant return on net assets.

Several other factors affect the fixed asset turnover ratio and although examples are given in more detail in Part Five the key points are noted here. Fixed assets are included in the balance sheet at their unused cost and the depreciation expense is deducted from the balance each year. Over its economic life, the net book value of any fixed asset on the balance sheet declines considerably. Also in most industries the cost of a new fixed asset will be greater than the cost of one purchased several years ago. Thus older assets start with a lower cost and this lower cost has been greatly depreciated over time. Therefore the company with old nearly worn out fixed assets may show the highest net fixed asset turnover ratio of any company in its industry, although the inefficiency of these assets may decrease its profit margins.

The value of fixed assets held by a business is affected by the intensity with which it uses those assets. If the company works 24 hours per day, seven days per week and almost 52 weeks per year (stopping only for major maintenance) it will need less fixed assets than a competitive company working only 40 hours per week, 46 weeks per year but producing the same output. There will normally be increased costs of working (shift premiums, etc.) associated with this strategy which reduce profit margins to offset the advantage. In some industries it will be the normal way of working so that the cross-company comparisons are on the same basis. However, many companies have changed their ways of working over several years and therefore the trend in asset turnover ratio may reflect these changes in basis rather than more or less efficient performance. This question of length of working also illustrates another issue regarding interpretation of the fixed asset turnover ratio. If a company is running its machines for every hour available or using every square metre of office or shop space, it cannot cope with any growth in sales volumes without investing in new fixed assets. The turnover ratio is therefore at its current maximum, but the company with spare capacity could expand its sales level without increasing the investment base and this may highlight opportunities for the company. It must be noted that this physical information on fixed assets is normally not available from published financial statements.

Stock turnover ratio

$$\frac{\text{Stock turnover}}{\text{ratio}} = \frac{\text{Cost of goods sold}}{\text{stock}}$$

Illustrative calculation:

$$\text{Stock turnover ratio} = \frac{\text{Cost of goods sold}}{\text{Stock}} = \frac{1098.3 \text{ million}}{208.9 \text{ million}} = 5.26 \text{ times}$$

(*Note*   The cost of sales figure has been used even though this includes some costs which will not be included in the stock valuation as no specific analysis is provided of the costs of goods sold. This is a normal problem of financial analysis and using cost of sales provides a much more meaningful ratio than is obtained by using sales revenue.)

As stock is valued at cost it is necessary to compare stocks to cost of goods sold, if an accurate figure is available. It is vital to use the same basis of calculation for all the financial analysis on stocks, and *not* to switch between sales and cost of goods sold from year to year or company to company.

Stock levels can be substantially affected if the marketing strategy of the company sets maximum periods to fulfil a customer's order, or extends the range of products sold which increases the stock holding requirement. Therefore the stock turnover ratio cannot be considered in isolation as lower stock turnover may be compensated by higher profit margins. Where the financial analysis is relying on external *annual* financial statements there is the problem of taking a snapshot view of stocks at the balance sheet date. This creates a major problem when sales are highly seasonal as in the case of a Christmas cracker company or a fireworks business, where the timing of the year end could affect the stock levels significantly. It should not affect the trend over time of the ratio but would complicate the analysis across companies with different balance sheet dates. If internal regular information is available the seasonality problem can be smoothed out by using some form of monthly average or comparing stock build-ups and rundowns over several seasonal cycles.

Stocks may be deliberately increased not because of seasonal demand, but due to impending promotional efforts or new product launches. If these cross the end of the accounting period the very high stocks will be seen in the balance sheet but the reason may not be apparent until the new marketing activity occurs in the following period. It is important to remember that, for many companies, there is a very high financial cost in physically holding stocks in terms of storage, handling and losses, so that the turnover ratio is not the only financial analysis necessary. It may be worthwhile spending extra on marketing activity to stimulate demand if stock levels are building up and stockholding costs are high. Stockholding costs can be spent throughout the organization as when the company owns its own warehouses, which will be included as a fixed asset, and the total costs should be considered in the decision, as illustrated in Chapter 15.

The stock turnover ratio may appear very good if the company is less vertically integrated than others in the industry by, for example, buying all the products rather than manufacturing. Again the higher turnover ratio is at least partially offset by the lower profit margin which is normally achieved in this situation.

Many companies, particularly wholesalers and retailers, are quite happy to hold high stocks as it gives the opportunity to generate higher sales revenues provided that they do not have to tie up their own funds. In other words, the net funds tied up in stocks are more important than the gross level of stocks held.

Creditor (payables) turnover ratio

$$\text{Creditor turnover ratio} = \frac{\text{Purchases on credit}}{\text{Creditors (payables)}}$$

This is now commonly presented as creditor days outstanding which is calculated as shown below:

$$\text{Creditor days} = \frac{\text{Creditors}}{\text{Purchases on credit}} \times 365$$

As already discussed most business is transacted on a credit basis and consequently companies have not paid for all the items which appear as stocks on their balance sheets. They show the unpaid bills as trade creditors and this reduces the finance tied up in stocks. There used to be a philosophy in financial management (still prevalent in some companies) that this creditor financing should be extended as far as possible. This was on the logic that the funds obtained by not paying creditors were free, whereas if cash was borrowed from the bank to pay these suppliers interest was charged by the bank. It is illogical to believe that suppliers are willing and able to finance your business by allowing excessive credit to be taken. They will have to recover their financing costs through their price levels, and this will mean higher prices and lower profit margins as a consequence. When customers have much greater negotiating power through size, etc. it may be possible for them to extend their payment period and force the suppliers to recover the cost from their other less powerful customers.

The net investment in stocks-creditors is of particular significance in certain industries such as retailing, and this can be monitored as 'net days of stock' or as an absolute value (for the Burton Group this is £46.2 million, that is, £208.9 million − £162.7 million).

As all businesses produce financial statements, if one company has a creditor another company has an equal debtor, that is, company X owes company Y money, and this features in both companies' balance sheets but on opposite sides. Therefore if creditor financing is important so is debtor collection because the longer it takes to collect cash from customers the greater is the investment needed to operate the business.

Debtor (receivables) turnover ratio

$$\text{Debtor turnover ratio} = \frac{\text{Sales on credit}}{\text{Debtors}}$$

(*Note:* As most of the Burton group's sales are made for cash, and the level of sales on credit is not disclosed, this ratio has not been calculated.)

This is also often shown as debtor days outstanding which expresses the ratio in terms of the number of days sales which are still outstanding as debtors, as shown below. Normally a lower figure for this form of the ratio is considered an improvement in debtor collection.

$$\text{Debtor days outstanding} = \text{Debtors} \times \frac{365}{\text{Sales on credit}}$$

The overall credit policy can be seen as part of the marketing strategy and should be decided in relation to the normal levels for the industry. Selling on credit is essential in most industries but the period of credit given should be linked to the risks associated with providing goods or services before payment is received, and to the return (profit margin) achieved from accepting such a risk. It may be that the risk of non-payment should be avoided and therefore a good strategy could be to sell at lower prices but to demand cash before or at the time of sale. Alternatively the risk of non-payment may be considered fairly small for the industry and one way of differentiating the company from competitors could be to offer a longer period of credit or even phased payments. If the company has to finance the sale for longer, it will need more investment and this reduction in return is reflected in a decreased debtor turnover ratio.

These policies can be used selectively as in the case of trying to smooth out highly seasonal sales, when selling on extended credit during the low sales period may tempt new customers to buy or bring forward other purchases. Effectively a discount is being offered on the selling price, but it affects the asset turnover ratio rather than, as normally, reducing the profit margin. It should by now be clear that a fairly detailed understanding is needed of the accounting policies and strategies employed by a company if a good financial analysis is to be carried out. The particular return on capital employed achieved is affected by both profit margin and asset turnover ratios, but these are often interrelated. It is therefore necessary to consider the overall impact on the financial performance to understand what is really happening to the business.

Deciding on a very strict credit policy can reduce the total sales revenue achieved by the business although the total profits earned may increase but this is a different managerial role to the implementation of the selected policy. Setting individual credit limits for customers and establishing detailed procedures for collecting payments when due is a specialist financial management role whatever overall type of credit policy is selected and is very important to maintaining the financial strength of the business. High levels of financial performance are very desirable but they should not be achieved in the short term at the cost of destroying the financial strength of the business in the longer term by unsound financing strategies. Consequently financial analysis of the short-term and long-term financial strength of the business is important.

Financial status ratios

If an outsider is considering lending cash directly to a company by way of a loan or indirectly by trading on credit, the ability of the business to pay the cash when due is of paramount importance. Financial status ratios are designed to indicate whether this is likely to happen or not, and look at both the short-term ability to pay and the longer-term funding of the business.

Solvency ratios

Solvency ratios are a way of considering how the company is being financed in the longer term. They compare the amount of borrowed funds used in the business with the level of shareholders' funds and are commonly expressed in one of the two ways shown below.

$$\text{Gearing ratio} = \frac{\text{Long-term debt}}{\text{Shareholders' funds} + \text{long term debt}} \times 100\%$$

$$\text{Debt to equity ratio} = \frac{\text{Long-term debt}}{\text{Shareholders' funds}}$$

Illustrative calculations:

$$\text{Gearing ratio} = \frac{\text{LTD}}{\text{Shareholders' funds} + \text{LTD}} \times 100\%$$

$$= \frac{233.5 \text{ million}}{523.2 \text{ million} + 233.5 \text{ million}} \times 100\% = 30.9\%$$

(*Note* Creditors due after more than one year have been used as the measure of long-term debt.)

As shown these ratios express the same relationship in slightly different ways so that a gearing ratio of 50% is equivalent to a debt:equity ratio of 1:1. The debt:equity ratio shows clearly the value of shareholders' funds per £ of debt in the company, whereas the gearing ratio highlights the proportion of the long-term funding which is provided by debt.

As borrowed funds typically receive a rate of interest which is specified and fixed no matter how profitable the business is (the profit after tax being owned by the shareholders), the lender is unwilling to advance too much of the funds needed. The proportion that can be borrowed depends on the perception of the risk of non-repayment, which is closely linked to the volatility of cash flows from the business. This can also be expressed by reference to the proportion of profits which are used to pay interest expenses on the borrowed funds. If the proportion of debt financing used is high interest costs will absorb a great proportion of profit before interest. This indicates that a downturn in profitability could leave the lender at risk for both the interest and the principal on the loan, and this is illustrated in the example below. This risk is shown by calculating the interest cover ratio which indicates the amount by which operating profits can fall before the interest costs put the company into a loss-making position.

$$\text{Interest cover} = \frac{\text{Profit before interest and tax}}{\text{Interest}}$$

Illustrative calculation:

$$\text{Interest cover} = \frac{\text{PBIT}}{\text{Interest}} = \frac{200.1 \text{ million}}{16.7 \text{ million}} = 12.0 \text{ times}$$

(*Note* This indicates that profits can decline quite dramatically before interest payment will turn the company into a loss maker.)

Interest cover will logically fall as the level of gearing rises in any business assuming profits are constant. Therefore the trend of the two relationships must be considered together, which is how banks do their financial analysis. Lenders set a desired maximum gearing ratio for different types of business based on the industry and the size of the company, where the ratio reflects the acceptable risk to them for the return being obtained in the form of interest rate. If a company wishes to borrow beyond the normal maximum, the lender will increase the rate of interest charged to compensate for the increased risk. There is still a maximum borrowing level as eventually the risk level will become unacceptable to lenders, and the increasing return demanded by the lenders makes the increased borrowing unattractive to shareholders. The lenders also look for ways in which they can get their funds back if the company does not trade as successfully as everyone plans. If the future cash flow is inadequate to repay the loan, lenders can use their security (guarantees of repayment) to take possession of and sell assets of the company to get their funds back. This means that banks are more willing to lend to businesses with assets which can easily be sold for high values even when trading is going very badly (for example, land and buildings).

The lender sets his maximum lending level but the company has to decide how much debt financing it wants to use. Borrowing funds can restrict the way the company can operate as the bank or other lender will include terms in the loan agreement to safeguard its position. It also increases the risk of failure because interest and capital repayments have to be paid when due, whether the business is trading profitably and generating enough cash or not. If only funding from shareholders (equity) was used and the business was not doing well, it could reduce or even suspend dividend payments to conserve cash if necessary. Therefore our normal logic has to be applied, a company should only increase its financing risk if, by doing so, it increases the return sufficiently to compensate. This can be achieved if the cost of borrowing money (that is, the interest rate) is lower than the overall return made by the business (given by the return on capital employed, ROCE). In this case using borrowed funds can increase the return obtained by the owners of the company. An example may make this clearer – the numbers have been taken at the extreme for illustrative purposes but this is a well-used way of getting rich.

A would-be millionaire identifies a potential new product investment requiring £100 000 which will generate a forecast pre-tax return of 22 per cent (£22 000) per year. Our entrepreneur realizes that at 22 per cent it will take a long time to become a millionaire and so sets a target return of 50 per cent on personal capital invested. If a lender is willing to provide £80 000 to finance the project at (say) 15 per cent interest per year, the target of 50% is achieved as shown below.

Use of gearing to increase shareholders' returns

Total project	– £100 000 invested at 22% yields	£22 000
Borrowed funds	– £80 000 *lent* at 15% *costs*	£12 000
Leaving an *equity*	– £20 000 which receives the profit	£10 000
investment of	after interest but before tax	

A £10 000 profit on a £20 000 investment represents a 50 per cent return for the owners compared to only a 15 per cent return to the bank lending the funds, but this is how borrowed funds should be used in a company – as a multiplier for the return obtained by the equity investment. Borrowing funds at 15 per cent to invest in a business which is only earning 10 per cent on that money is clearly financially nonsense; and yet some companies seem to do it! This is not true of the Burton Group plc as can be seen if the calculation is done for them. On an approximate calculation, which is all that it is possible to do, their average interest rate is around 8 per cent before tax. These borrowed funds are used in a business which is generating a ROCE of 23.9 per cent, so that using debt enhances the return received by the shareholders in the group.

Although the bank in our example is getting a far lower return it is also taking a lower risk than our entrepreneur. If the new product returns less than 22 per cent the bank will still demand interest of £12 000 and any shortfall will be borne by the entrepreneur. Also any lender will have sought security for the loan and, if the cash flow is less than forecast, will be repaid in full before the entrepreneur gets back any of the £20 000 invested.

Liquidity ratios

The long-term financing of the company needs to be on a sound basis which requires borrowing facilities to be used sensibly but the short-term financial position can cause immediate problems if this is not managed properly. If suppliers become worried about a company's ability to pay for goods already delivered they can, and do, withdraw credit sale facilities at a moment's notice and refuse to deliver to the company until all outstanding balances are paid. In the normal operating cycle, illustrated as Figure 3.6 in Chapter 3, the business will turn stocks or work-in-progress into debtors and then into cash and use this cash to pay the expenses incurred as necessary (taking account of creditor financing as available). The objective of the liquidity ratios is to indicate this relationship between the levels of current assets and current liabilities for the operation of the business and to show the trend over time rather than the absolute value at one particular moment. Liquidity ratios obviously share the problems associated with current assets and liabilities of balance sheet distortions caused by seasonality, etc., but the trend in liquidity should still be indicative of changes in financial strength.

$$\text{Current ratio} = \frac{\text{Current assets}}{\text{Current liabilities}}$$

Illustrative calculation:

$$\text{Current ratio} = \frac{\text{Current assets}}{\text{Current liabilities}} = \frac{356.5 \text{ million}}{343.4 \text{ million}} = 1.04$$

From the previous discussion on working capital it should be clear that the ratios for different industries will vary tremendously, depending on the operating cycle involved. The current ratio, shown above, will be affected by the way the business is operated and therefore the impact of changes in strategy is much more interesting than the absolute level. A decrease in the ratio may indicate potential liquidity problems but it is commonly felt that the current ratio is too broad an indicator of the problem. Current assets and current liabilities are aggregate totals and it is necessary to look at the constituent parts in order to draw meaningful conclusions regarding the liquidity of a company. Stock and work-in-progress is included as a current asset and can be a major determinant in the value of the current ratio but it may not be possible to turn stock into cash very quickly if there is a liquidity crisis. A tighter test of liquidity is to exclude stock and to use the *acid test ratio* (also known as the quick assets ratio). This compares only debtors, cash and marketable securities with current liabilities, and is illustrated below.

$$\text{Acid test ratio} = \frac{\text{Debtors} + \text{cash} + \text{marketable securities}}{\text{Current liabilities}}$$

Illustrative calculation:

$$\text{Acid test ratio} = \frac{79.4 \text{ million} + 19.9 \text{ million} + 7.7 \text{ million}}{343.4 \text{ million}}$$

$$= \frac{107.0 \text{ million}}{343.4 \text{ million}}$$

$$= 31.2\%$$

It therefore indicates how much of the current obligations could be paid without making any more sales. Not all of the current liabilities may be payable immediately or even in the next three months (a current liability will be payable within 12 months) and this is a very strict test of liquidity which should be interpreted carefully. (For example, the Burton Group plc correctly includes as current liabilities its outstanding taxation but this will be paid on a known specific date and is probably only payable nine months after the date of the balance sheet.) Again, a downward trend may indicate forthcoming problems and the comparison with similar businesses can also be useful.

Valuation ratios

The above indicators of financial strength are of interest to anyone considering investing in a company but the main determinant will be the prospects for future profits and returns from the investment. A share-holder can obtain a return by receiving a dividend from the company or the profits made can be retained by the company to make the business grow. If this is done the prospects for future profits are improved and the shareholder should see an increase in the value of the shares held (a capital gain could be made by selling the shares at a profit). This is of greatest significance to shareholders in publicly quoted companies where values of their shares are adjusted very quickly but the same financial logic is applied to all companies.

The main basis of share valuation should ignore the question of dividends and concentrate on the profits earned by the company, whether paid out or retained. We have already examined the return on shareholders' funds (ROSF) which compares profit after tax with the balance sheet statement of the owners' investment in the business. However, the balance sheet is not a valuation statement and normally the share price will bear no relationship to the apparent value derived from a balance sheet. Anyone owning one share in a company is entitled to a proportionate share in the profits after tax based not on the balance sheet but on the number of shares in the company. This measure of profit per share gives a good indication of financial performance over time, provided it is adjusted for inflation, as it removes any distortion caused by changes in the number of shares in existence. The relationship is normally described as 'earnings per share' and is very simply calculated as shown below.

$$\text{Earnings per share} = \frac{\text{Profit after tax}}{\text{Number of shares issued}}$$

Illustrative calculation:

$$\text{Earnings per share (EPS)} = \frac{\text{PAT}}{\text{Number of shares issued}} = \frac{£119.3 \text{ million}}{550.4 \text{ million}} = 21.7p$$

(*Note*   The number of shares issued is always disclosed in the published financial statements.)

The investor is really buying profits which will be earned in the *future*, and the financial analysis will only indicate *past* profit performance. The analysis should, therefore, compare the performance over time and with similar companies so that, as far as possible, the prospects for the future can be assessed. The stock markets call this assessment the price/earnings multiple (P/E ratio), which indicates the level of future growth expected in the profits of the company. The market price for any share is found by multiplying the present earnings per share figure by the P/E ratio, although the relationship is most commonly depicted as shown below.

$$\text{Price/earnings multiple} = \frac{\text{Market price per share}}{\text{Earnings per share}}$$

Illustrative calculation:

$$\text{P/E ratio} = \frac{\text{Market price}}{\text{EPS}} = \frac{246p}{21.7p} = 11.3$$

For instance, if a fast-growing high technology company is floated (sold) on the stock market, the previous profits record may not be representative of its future prospects. This may be due to the high investment in research and development and marketing which has been expensed in the profit and loss account. Consequently the market price per share may include a high P/E ratio to offset the low earnings per share. Comparatively a well-established company with mature products and low growth potential will command a substantially lower P/E ratio. Its share price may be as high because it should be generating a better current earnings level per share so that the two components, as with several of the other ratios, offset each other and must be considered together.

Some shareholders like to receive regular income from their investments and the level of dividends paid does therefore influence the attractiveness of the shares. The normal way to calculate dividend income is to express it as a yield on the market price of the shares, as shown below, so that it is comparable to the income received from alternative forms of investment (such as interest on a bank deposit).

$$\text{Dividend yield} = \frac{\text{Net dividends paid per share}}{\text{Market price per share}} \times 100\%$$

Illustrative calculation:

$$\text{Dividend yield} = \frac{\text{Dividends per share}}{\text{Price per share}} \times 100\% = \frac{7.2p}{246p} \times 100\% = 2.9\%$$

If the dividend yield fluctuates from year to year, the shareholder may become disenchanted. Thus many companies have a strategy of maintaining dividend levels, often in real terms (that is, after adjusting for the impact of inflation), or of trying to achieve a constant rate of growth in dividends. Other high growth companies have never paid a dividend, which may be equally acceptable as long as shareholders understand this and do not expect a dividend but prefer to gain through an increasing share price.

Summary

We have considered three main categories of ratios which help in the financial analysis of any business. These ratios can themselves be broken down into their component elements so that a greater understanding is gained of how the business got where it is.

The reason for doing the analysis is important as it will focus attention on certain areas for close attention, but an overview analysis will put the main issues into a general context.

The main areas for financial analysis are:

1 profitability – as a measure of financial performance;
2 liquidity – as a measure of financial strength;
3 financial structure – as a measure of gearing and as an aid to valuation.

These ratios can be applied to analysis using externally published financial statements where comparisons across similar companies and over time can be used. It is important that the ratios are made as comparable as possible by adjusting for differences and changes, most particularly the impact of inflation on time sequences.

Internal financial analysis can utilize much more detailed and more frequent information, which enables greater application to be made to the marketing areas of the business. This is considered in Chapter 5.

Exercises

As practical exercises in computing financial ratios the reader is recommended to analyse:

1 the set of financial statements prepared for Paul Cook in the worked example in the Appendix to Chapter 3 (pages 84–102);
2 the set of financial statements for a computer software company shown in Chapter 3.

5

Specific marketing aspects

So far we have tended to concentrate on analysing the business as one complete entity but most companies are made up of many products (that is, goods and services) sold in various markets by different sales people, via different channels of distribution in varying order quantities to customers with different requirements. If our financial analysis is to be of any help as a basis for internal planning it must match the way in which the activities are conducted and the organization is structured, and the appropriate marketing segments must be examined. The analytical techniques and financial ratios applied to internally produced financial information are largely the same for parts of the organization as those applied to the group as a whole, for which the externally published financial statements are produced. It is also important that the impact of marketing strategies in each area of the business and the relative productivity of alternative marketing activities are fully analysed to see how effective the current allocation of marketing resources is. This enables the planning process to build on the best available internal information but, to be of use in planning, any externally based analysis (such as competitor or acquisition analysis) utilizing published financial statements also requires a careful marketing focus (such as competitor and market analysis), which means coordinating all the various available sources of information, in addition to the published financial statements.

Organizational structure

As already mentioned, each company should be internally organized in relation to the particular requirements of its business and not by reference to any historic or legal entity considerations. Also any organizational structure so selected may be appropriate for the current phase of development but may be totally inappropriate for the following phase, where the critical success factors may be significantly different. A critical success factor is anything which must be successful if the organization is to meet its objectives and which will normally have an adverse impact across a large part of the organization if failure occurs in this particular area. Therefore internal organizations should change over time and the financial information system must adjust to reflect these changes or the financial analysis based on an outdated organization will be completely useless. If the organization is subdivided into smaller decision-making 'divisions' for planning purposes, it is essential that the financial analysis is done for these subdivisions of the business.

These divisions may be broken down in different ways depending on the critical factors facing the business in each area. Thus the divisions could be organized by particular common factors in their markets (for example, channels of distribution, size or type of customer, frequency of purchase) or by an underlying technology or process involved in the product (for example, one company may group all its information technology businesses together, while another might separate hardware and software into two divisions). It may be that in some areas of the business (for example, manufacturing and research, but only for some industries) there are large economies of scale to be obtained and these areas should be controlled as one unit for the group. For other areas it may genuinely be true that 'small is beautiful' and the group should be broken into many very specialized units focused on very specific products and services or customers, or both. Some large multinational groups (such as our software and systems company) have now set up more complex types of divisions which try to obtain the best structure for functional areas of the business and this can lead to organizations where meaningful financial analysis of the various segments is quite difficult, but even more valuable than usual.

One example of such complex organizational structures is the matrix idea of management control, which is illustrated in Figure 5.1, where functional or geographical or skill-defined areas of the business (for example, manufacturing, finance, marketing, etc.) control the overall resources but the markets where goods and services are sold are controlled separately. The resources (such as people, production capacity, etc.) needed for each market or segmented area of a market (mission) are allocated from the central functional areas and the market responsible manager uses them to achieve specific objectives, which may be defined as sales increases in terms of market share or volume, or may be a specific project for a particular customer. When no longer needed the resources can be returned to the functional area which can then redeploy them to another market segment as required.

(a) *Systems development company*

Resources controlled functionally (by particular skill group)	Markets/customer groups/missions Projects (controlled by responsible managers)				
	1	*2*	*3*	*4*	*etc.*
People: system designers	0		0	0	
systems analysts (by grade)	0	0		0	
Programmers (by grade)	0		0		
Hardware specialists		0		0	
Communications experts etc.	0		0		
Hardware: In-house computers		0		0	
Bureaux facilities etc.			0		

(b) *Business school/university*

Resources/ functional skill areas (that is, people)	Markets/products (that is, courses) Degree programmes	Managers of missions			
		International courses	Short courses	In-company programmes	Research
Marketing	0	0	0	0	0
Finance	0	0		0	
Accounting	0		0		0
Production	0	0			
Information systems	0		0		
Human resources	0	0		0	
Economics	0		0		0
Business strategy	0			0	0

0 = Allocation of resources to one particular market/mission.

Figure 5.1   *Examples of matrix-style management organizations*

This type of system is very common when large projects requiring many varied resources for a limited period are a normal way of doing business, so that flexibility in allocating resources is needed. A large advertising agency could use this type of organization to put teams of people together to work on specific accounts, as could a large international accountancy firm which needs teams of differing specialists to work on large investigations, or a large company needing a project team to develop and launch a new product. The most meaningful financial analysis is by reference to the market/mission side of the matrix but, because the resources are normally 'owned by' and hence accounted for in the other element, this information can be very difficult to obtain in many companies. A good understanding of what information is useful is more helpful than merely analysing what is available. This suggests a need for involvement of marketing management in the analysis process, at least in terms of specifying what information is needed, rather than leaving it to the financial managers, who may provide copious detailed analysis of the wrong part of the matrix.

Segmental analysis

Although breaking the business into divisions is helpful even this is not necessarily adequate to enable financial analysis to provide information for future planning. Marketing planning focuses on the allocation of marketing resources to achieve objectives which are normally described by reference to specific products and markets. A good system of financial analysis should indicate the current allocations of resources and their relative success. Therefore we need to analyse the performance into product and customer segments, and into appropriate subgroups such as channels of distribution, sales territories, etc.

The information needed to do this analysis for other companies will not be available from their summarized externally published financial statements unless a competitor is totally focused on one specific product or market. Certain trade and media sources (such as Media Expenditure Analysis Ltd normally referred to as MEAL, Nielsen Market Information Manual, Mintel Market Intelligence, and Target Group Index published by British Market Research Bureau) may give overall information on market size, marketing spend and market share, or this data can be collected by specific research, but it will be difficult to obtain explicit financial information on profitability for competitors' products and customers. However, the process of detailed internal analysis should enable the differences from competitors to be highlighted and a very good approximation of the relative competitive financial position can be built up by some logical deductions. This process requires very close involvement of many areas of the business so that all the relevant differences in operating costs, etc. are included, which again argues that financial analysis cannot be left to accountants. Competitor analysis, so that your company has the best possible understanding of a competitor's cost structure and relative profitability, can give a considerable advantage by indicating the most probable response to any new marketing initiative you may be considering. This can be done by analysing the published financial statements of competitors but for the reasons already given this analysis of publicly available information is unlikely to provide detailed insights into the particular segments of the business which would prove most helpful. By using the internal analysis which can be generated on your own business, and comparing how your operations differ from those of the competition it is often possible to produce a much more useful understanding of the cost structure of their business. For example, in a manufacturing industry the physical location of their factories relative to yours and the major customers will enable a comparative analysis of distribution costs to be undertaken, particularly if allowance is made for their method of physical distribution to customers (through their own or third party transport fleets, and whether intermediate regional warehousing is involved). The way in which their sales force is organized and remunerated will also help to indicate potential differences in relative sales expenses as a proportion of sales revenues, and their levels of promotional activity allocated to different product groups can also be analysed.

This analysis of the marketing areas should be in addition to an equally detailed comparison of their other major expense areas such as production, and research and development. In order to assemble the required comparative data all available sources from within and outside the company should be used including, wherever possible, common suppliers and customers. In some very competitive mature industries, where very small competitive advantages may be decisive, a very sophisticated level of competitor analysis is undertaken so as to try to predict the probable responses to any new initiative. This can take the form of very sophisticated computer models of cost structures which, whenever possible, are validated against published information.

A similarly detailed level of analysis is normally carried out when a company is considering making an acquisition (that is, buying another business), because a negotiating advantage can be gained through a better understanding of the other business. Detailed segmental analysis requires breaking down the sales revenues and operating costs and hence profits so that those achieved in each segment are identified. This may be quite easy for sales revenues and direct costs for the segment but may be complicated for others, and the degree of complication differs depending on the type of segmentation. Many costs, such as raw materials and packaging, can be specifically identified with individual products or product groups (these can be described as 'product costs') and thus separating out *product* profitability may be fairly easy but some of these product costs (such as advertising) can be difficult to attribute to specific customers or to different channels of distribution or even to product subgroups. There may be considerable differences in the total costs of apparently similar products sold to, say, home and export markets, or to consumer and industrial markets, or through retail and wholesale channels, due to differences in packaging and distribution costs. The marketing expenses will probably contribute significantly to these differences. It can be very difficult to split the cost of a television advertising campaign for a recently launched beer or lager product between the different channels of distribution which may include pubs, restaurants, off-licences and supermarkets, or between different product sizes which may be bulk barrels, bottles, and cans in varying configurations. Too much attempted sophistication in the financial analysis which tries to apportion these shared costs to specific channels or product subgroups can introduce spuriously accurate information which can be very counterproductive. The company may use this information to make decisions regarding the future resources allocated to particular product subgroups but these decisions may be based on a false analysis, which is not sufficiently precise and accurate to support the decisions made. The purpose of financial analysis is to aid planning and therefore the detail of the analysis should be controlled by the potential decisions which can be made. These will often hinge around expanding sales through new marketing initiatives such as developing new customers or channels, launching new products or closing existing brands – the alternatives and the appropriate decision-making techniques are considered in Part Three and more examples given in Part Five, but the basis for analysis is illustrated below.

Product/customer profitability

What is important is for the analysis to highlight the key differences among the various segments and how these affect the RONA (return on net assets) and the way in which the RONA is achieved. We are looking at another matrix analysis where the profits and assets involved can be split in many different ways, the two most common being products and customers. Some of the problems of such a matrix analysis are indicated in Figure 5.2.

In many companies the financial analysis is primarily organized to provide one side of the matrix, for example, product profitability, but the other forms of analysis (such as customer or channel profitability) are not properly considered. If product profitability is to be analysed, the costs incurred in generating the product sales revenues must be identified. As stated some of these costs will be directly attributable (that is, are incurred as a direct consequence of the particular product, and not as a general cost relating to several products) to the product and there will be no difficulty in accounting for these elements of product costs. Many costs are not directly incurred in producing any single product line and therefore cannot be easily allocated for the purposes of product profitability analysis. Among its many classifications, accounting terminology describes costs as either 'direct' or 'indirect', so that direct costs plus indirect costs equal the total (or full) cost, and any cost which cannot be totally allocated as being incurred in respect of one product (or any other cost object) is said to be indirect to that product (or cost object). (Costs can

Customers by name or grouping (for example, channel of distribution)	Profitability by products						Total customer profitability
	1	2	3	4	5	6	
(1) (2) (3) (4) (5)			X				Y
Total product profitability			Z				*Total profitability for business**

X =   The product profitability of product 3 as analysed to customer 1.
Y =   The total profitability of customer 1 as shown by all the products sold to that customer.
Z =   The total profitability of product 3, as a total for the profitability of all the customers buying that product.

   *The total profitability for the business is given by the total profitability of all the products which, on this method of analysis, equals the total profitability of all the customers.

Assumptions

1   For the matrix to balance all sales revenues and expenses must be allocated to both a product and a customer.
2   This requires one side of the matrix to be used as a start point for the process and the direct revenues and costs for that cost object are allocated first, with the other costs apportioned on a suitable basis. Thus total profitability by product is often established by the financial analysts as a first step.
3   This total product profitability is then split, on some method, to the customer side of the matrix, so as to balance the matrix.

Figure 5.2   *Profitability matrix*

be classified as direct or indirect by reference to any type of cost object. 'All costs' incurred by a company are direct as far as the company as a whole is concerned, but more costs become indirect as the cost objects of the company become smaller. A cost object can be defined as any segment of the business for which financial analysis is required, including products, cost centres and market segments. A cost centre is any segment of the business which incurs costs but does not, by itself, generate sales revenues which can offset the costs incurred.) If a cost is indirect at the product level but part of the cost is clearly incurred by the product, some system of apportionment can be used to share out the total cost across all the relevant products. A system of apportionment can be defined as the allotment to two or more cost objects of proportions of indirect costs on the basis of the relative estimated benefit received. A simple example is where the rent of a factory is apportioned to the products produced in it by reference to the floor area occupied by each product, as shown in Figure 5.3.

Products	1	2	3	4	5	Total
Square footage occupied by each product	30 000	50 000	10 000	20 000	40 000	150 000
Total rent expense						£600 000
Proportion to each product	20%	33⅓%	6⅔%	13⅓%	26⅔%	100%
Apportioned expense	£120 000	£200 000	£40 000	£80 000	£160 000	£600 000

1. *Assumption*   Factory space can be split accurately among the products, and no areas are classified as common. If there are common areas, a two stage (or more) apportionment process may be required.

Note   In many large sophisticated companies the apportionment process may have several stages where, for example, the factory rent is apportioned to the operational departments occupying the factory and the total costs of these departments are eventually apportioned to the products.

Figure 5.3   *Apportionment of factory rent to products produced in factory*

In our example of a recently launched beer or lager product there will be some costs which can be seen as directly incurred by the new product (for example, the advertising) and some which will even be direct to individual product sizes (for example, specific packaging). If the company already brews other products, a lot of the costs (for example, depreciation of machinery, labour costs and other indirect production costs) will probably be shared with the existing product range. A system of cost apportionment will need to be used to arrive at the individual product's share of these (so that the full costs of the new production can be ascertained) many of which would be direct costs if the profits of the brewing division were being considered. This financial analysis can be dangerous if not used with great care, because these *shared* costs do not represent what the company would need to spend to produce the new product on its own. New product decisions and product deletion decisions require very careful analysis using the additional techniques explained in Part Three. We can analyse the sales revenues, costs and net assets employed to decide what the profitability of the new brand appears to be but, if we are interested in a particular packaging presentation (for example, four-pack cans) sold through a specific channel of distribution (for example, supermarkets), the analysis becomes even more complicated. As we get more detailed in our cost objects less and less costs are directly attributable, and more and more reliance is placed on apportionments of costs, as is shown in Figure 5.4.

As stated above all costs are direct at some level of cost object (that is, all costs are ultimately direct to the company as a whole), but more costs

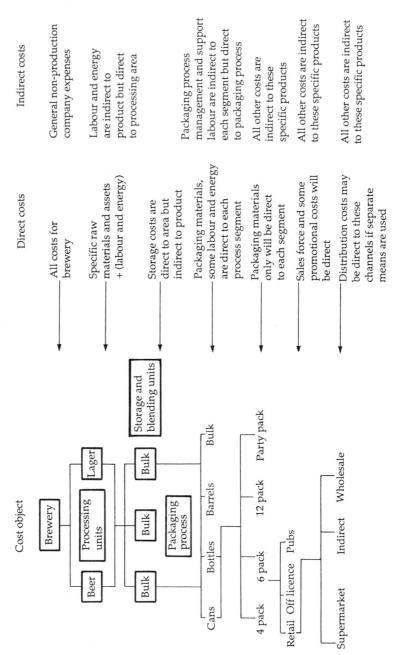

Figure 5.4   *Hierarchy of direct and indirect costs for brewery production*

become indirect as the cost objects selected become more specific within segments of the business (for example, a specific product sold to a specific customer by a specific salesperson). As the bases of apportionment (that is, the ways in which the indirect costs are spread across the cost objects) also become more complex, and sometimes more arbitrary, it is often tempting to abandon the process, and concentrate on direct costs only. This can be dangerous because the indirect costs have presumably been incurred for the benefit of all the more specific cost objects on which they have an impact. If indirect costs are ignored in the financial analysis, the relative effectiveness or profitability of any specific cost object can be completely misrepresented and incorrect decisions may be taken regarding the future allocation of resources.

One area where this impact is clearly visible is the valuation of stocks and work in progress, particularly for published financial statements. We stated in Chapter 3 that stocks and work-in-progress have to be valued at cost, but that cost has to include all the relevant costs incurred in bringing the stock to its present condition and location. A proportion of these 'costs incurred' are likely to be indirect costs and can only be attributed to the stock items by a process of apportionment. For example, if a finished product stock item is stored in a regional warehouse or in a Burton Group shop, a proportion of the distribution and storage costs should be included in the cost of that stock item. Also for the computer software company illustrated in Chapter 3 the cost of contract work-in-progress should include the cost of computer development resources used on the project, and this cost will include an apportionment of the depreciation and running costs of the computer. This system of costing is known as 'absorption costing' or 'full costing' to reflect the absorbing effect of cost apportionment to all cost objects, in this case the stock and work in progress items. Thus we can represent the full costing system by the equation:

$$DC + IC = FC$$

where DC is direct costs, IC is indirect costs and FC is full costs.

The accounting process is exactly the same as for any apportionment as the aim is to include, in the stock valuation, the appropriate proportion of the indirect costs incurred in producing the particular stock item. It must be remembered that the process of apportionment introduces a substantial degree of approximation into the full costs arrived at, and these should not be regarded as precise or accurate in any absolute sense.

Marketing productivity analysis
Another area where the inclusion of indirect costs is important is in the analysis of the productivity of marketing expenditure because if only

direct costs are dealt with distorted results can be achieved. (The analysis of the productivity of marketing expenditure relates the outputs generated by any marketing activity to the inputs required for that activity and normally uses the ratio of outputs : inputs to measure how productive the activity was compared to any alternative courses of action.) A good example would be in the area of total field sales force expenses, where the sales force is organized around customer outlets in geographical territories but where the principal analytical interest is in products and national customers. If costs are being considered in the context of either specific products or particular multisite national customers (for example, multiple supermarket chains), very little, if any, of the field sales force cost base would be considered direct because each salesperson will sell a variety of products to a mix of customers. Unless a system of apportionment is used this potentially significant element of the marketing mix would be ignored in the analysis, and judgements made regarding the productivity of any marketing activity which *was* direct to either *a* product or *a* customer could be extremely misleading. The productivity of this sales force activity might be compared to that of a product promotional campaign, or a discount offered to specific customers based on the value of their total purchases in a particular period.

The productivity of each marketing activity would be measured by comparing the increased profit resulting from the extra sales generated by each activity (the output) with the cost incurred by each activity (the input). Thus the product promotional campaign costs which can be assessed quite accurately for the product concerned, are compared to the increased sales of the product, which can also be established (some of the problems encountered in measuring increased sales levels due to marketing activities are considered in Parts Three and Five), and which enable the incremental (that is, increase in) profit to be calculated. The marketing productivity ratio (outputs divided by inputs) for this type of product-focused activity can often be calculated relatively easily and quite accurately because the majority of the costs incurred are direct, and so no significant problems of apportionment are encountered. In the case of a purchase value related discount offered to specific customer , a similar productivity analysis can be carried out by evaluating the output of the marketing activity (that is the increased profits generated by the higher sales of product to each customer) and comparing the value of this output to the cost of the input (that is, the cost of the discount granted to the customer). Again the problems of apportionment are not dramatic, although the profit increase depends upon the profit of the *products* sold to the customer, and hence requires a matrix analysis already mentioned and which is considered in more detail later in the chapter. (This example has been kept fairly simple by ignoring some of the problems encountered in obtaining the necessary information but these issues are considered in Part Three.)

However, assessing the productivity of the sales force by reference to either specific products or specific customers is not such an easy proposition because the appropriate level of input cost can only be measured by some system of apportionment, which introduces approximations and inaccuracies. Thus this productivity analysis may need to be done for the salesforce as a whole, encompassing all products and customers, which restricts its usefulness and makes it difficult to avoid the results being affected by other marketing activities taking place at the same time (this interaction of different marketing activities is a constant problem of marketing productivity analysis.)

Equally disturbing is the potential conflict which could be caused if the sales force costs *were* allocated to any customers where they were direct (for example, some small locally based customers serviced by one equally locally based salesperson), but no indirect costs were apportioned to the larger multisite customers. If only these customers had to bear any sales force costs, their relative profit contribution performance is likely to be very low and decisions may be taken to divert the sales resources to other customers (probably across a range of customers so that the cost became indirect!) due to this poor relative performance. Again misleading information is being provided on the real productivity of marketing activities. It is therefore important that sensible and consistent systems of apportionment and cost absorption are used and understood by companies, while remembering the nature (that is, indirectness) of the costs which are being apportioned as this is also important for decision-making, as is explained in Part Three.

Any system of apportionment inevitably relies on managerial judgement although some costs are easier to apportion than others. Factory space rental costs can be apportioned on the basis of the area occupied as was illustrated in Figure 5.3, and the common brewing costs in Figure 5.4 may be spread on the relative gallonage of each product produced as this is how most of these costs are incurred. Apportioning marketing costs tends to be one of the most difficult tasks and many companies use the proportions of sales revenues in the absence of any other basis. This can create problems for future planning as is discussed in detail later in this chapter, and also in Chapter 8, because the relationship is being analysed in exact reverse to the true causal links. Marketing expenditure influences sales revenues and to use sales revenues to determine the level of marketing expenditures is likely to be self-defeating, as can be shown diagramatically:

Sales ——×——▷ Costs
Costs ————————▷ Sales √

As the cost objects become more detailed it may be sensible to focus on the relative differences between the groupings rather than to try for absolute measures of profitability. In most cases a relative ranking will indicate any areas of the segment which warrant more detailed and specific analysis. If we are comparing the profitability of individual customers or customer groupings the key determinants may be the product mix which each customer buys, if the products have different profit margins, and the marketing support which each customer receives, including the service level and credit period granted, etc. For this analysis we do not want to start with the result of a previously produced detailed cost apportionment exercise on *product* profitability which has produced 'precise net profit levels' per *product*. Such an apportionment will have included some costs which can in reality be directly attributed to specific customers (for example, distribution costs, special discount rates on turnover levels) but which were indirect to any individual product. Therefore we may need to start from a higher level of product profitability measurement and may start from the gross margin for the product which only deducts specific direct costs from the actual selling price of the product and then deduct direct customer expenses. It is quite possible to break down (specifically) for any particular segmental analysis the cost headings deducted in arriving at the 'net profit' in the same way as we analysed the 'net asset turnover ratio' in Chapter 4. This process is illustrated in Figure 5.5. and this shows both how complex the analysis can be and how different the emphasis is between customer profitability analysis and that done for products.

Indeed net assets involved must not be ignored in segment profitability analysis as it would be wrong to assume that the fixed asset and working capital requirements are the same for all parts of the business. The specific levels of assets employed should be identified and allocated to each segment under consideration, but in most cases direct allocation will not be possible as many fixed assets will be used for more than one product. Raw material stocks may also be common across products and although finished goods stocks are specific to a product line, they are usually not directly attributable to customers (slightly different products may be produced for different channels of distribution and so be specific for these segments). Debtors are often the reverse of stocks, in that debtor levels can be specifically related to the individual customers who make up the total but it may be impossible to directly allocate debtors to separate products if customers buy a range of products. This is illustrated for a manufacturing business in Figure 5.6 which also shows some of the

Monthly customer profitability analysis: customer X (from multiple retailer grouping)

	£000	£000
Sales revenue in period		250
Cost of goods sold (as per gross margin analysis of specific products sold)		130
Gross margin		120
less Direct customer expenses:	*£000*	
Distribution costs (as per delivery analysis)	10.0	
Retrospective rebate allowance (as agreed for this customer)	2.5	
Specific promotions in period for multiple retailers (£100 per store)	5.0	
Specific key account salesman	5.0	
Credit cost on outstanding balance (on days credit given)	2.5	25
Gross margin after direct customer costs		95
less Indirect customer expenses		
Apportioned field sales force costs (based on sales force calls made)	10.0	
Sales management apportionment (based on sales force expenses)	2.0	
Product advertising expense (based on products sold to customer)	12.5	
General advertising and promotional expense*	7.5	
		32
Customer contribution to general indirect expenses		63
less indirect expenses (proportion of sales revenue)		50
Net customer profitability		13

*proportion of sales revenue

Notes
1 In many companies the apportionments made on sales revenues are excluded and a customer contribution concept is used.
2 We have assumed no specific stocks are held for this customer.

Figure 5.5

ways in which assets and costs are apportioned in the course of these exercises.

This indicates that as with profit levels it is necessary to do each category of segmental financial analysis on an individual basis, that is, by starting from scratch, rather than trying to take the product profitability analysis, or vice versa, and then superimposing it on to a customer profitability analysis for which some of its assumptions and apportionments may be completely illogical. This can be illustrated by reference to the marketing information system used by a major international bank in

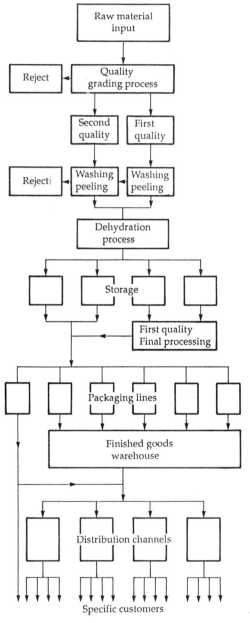

Raw material input	Common input for all potatoes
Quality grading process → Reject	Grading plant apportioned to all products based on tonnage throughputs
Second quality / First quality	Processing plant segmented to different grades of product – not yet specific to individual end products
Washing peeling / Washing peeling → Reject	Regrading and rejection possible during processing, leading to complication of using tonnage throughputs
Dehydration process	Single process but quality grades separated by batch control, assets again apportioned on throughputs
Storage	Multisegmented storage depending upon final product characteristics – apportioned on tonnage and time
First quality Final processing	Top quality product receives final processing – plant directly allocated to this product group
Packaging lines	Packaging plant is limited by pack size and form of packaging, not by quality of product. Apportion by number of packs processed not weight of product
Finished goods warehouse	Warehouse cost incurred by volume of cases and number of pallets (storage units) moved in and out of warehouse, plus by time of stay in warehouse
Distribution channels	Distribution efficiency is limited by volume of delivery not weights because product is very light and so costs recovered on cases delivered
Specific customers	Specific customers have specific debtor balances outstanding and costs allocated directly to customers, and apportioned to products based on sales mix. Same basis for customer specific marketing expenditure, some expenditure is direct to products but indirect to customers

Figure 5.6   *Simplified diagrammatic analysis of asset apportionment to products for manufacturing process (dehydrated potato plant)*

which, similarly to the problem mentioned in Figure 5.2, the analysis was originally produced by the products sold by the bank (for example, specific loan products, foreign exchange trading services, cash management, etc.) so that all direct product costs were allocated and indirect costs (including sales and marketing expenses) were apportioned to products so as to arrive at the net profit for each product. It became increasingly clear to the senior managers of the bank that they required financial analysis not so much by product but by customer because, with modern technology and increasing competition, the life cycle of any particular banking product is becoming progressively shorter, but customer relationships may continue with a succession of new products. Unfortunately they decided to take what appeared to be an easily implemented solution – complete the matrix by analysing customer profitability according to the products sold to each customer and utilizing the already analysed product profitability.

This product profitability analysis included the apportionment of many costs, not least sales and marketing expenses, which were direct at the customer level, or specific to customer groups and where more appropriate apportionment bases could have been used. As a result of this falsely based analysis, the managers reallocated resources away from certain customer groupings which appeared to be unprofitable, but which were, in fact, not only significantly profitable but also high growth opportunities.

Had the customer profitability analysis been done from scratch these facts would have become apparent – as they did when the correct analysis was subsequently done!

Market share/market growth

The principal reason for breaking down the overall financial analysis into separate marketing-focused segments is to make the information more relevant for forward planning. It has already been argued that marketing strategies should be significantly influenced by the position of the product in its life cycle and different products within any company will be at different stages of development at any point in time. Therefore segmental analysis allows the company to plan its marketing strategy for each product and each market, because one product can also be at different stages of development in different markets at any particular time. The stage of the product life cycle can be identified by an analysis over time of the rate of growth in the market and the changes in this rate of growth, but this analysis is unfortunately historic and the result is only likely to illustrate where the product *was* at a particular point in time. The company is interested in knowing where the product *is* on the product life cycle and therefore what rate of growth can be expected in the *future*. Unfortunately this *ex ante* forecasting of the position on the product life cycle is much more difficult and less accurate than the less useful but more easily obtained *ex post* analysis of where the product was. This analysis also presupposes that the information is available on the size of the market. For some well-researched markets, such as cars, televisions and other consumer durables, this information is widely available and for others (such as food products, pet foods and washing powders) the research has been built up by the main companies in the market over many years. For many more (such as consultancy services and financial services), particularly relatively new products and services, it is difficult to get an accurate view of the total existing market and even more difficult to project from this to the total potential market. In some cases it may be possible to extrapolate market size from the company's notional market share, but this can cause severe problems if the base assumption is wrong. One major food company spent a considerable amount of development marketing to build market share for a new convenience catering product based on its assumption that it had achieved an initial 6 per cent market share after launch. The increased marketing spend was not too successful in creating sales and it was subsequently discovered that the initial share was a massive 60 per cent, because the total market was only *one-tenth* of the assumed level when the marketing expenditure was justified. A better financial analysis might have stopped the company trying to expand its share from its already dominant position and saved it a lot of wasted marketing effort and cost.

The marketing strategy will, as stated above, be greatly influenced by the stage of the product on the life cycle and its consequent position in the Boston matrix as indicated in Chapter 2. A company consequently needs to know the rate of growth of the market and its market share within that market so that the appropriate strategy can be implemented. This analysis of market share over time and the relative profitability achieved is a key element in the financial analysis of marketing activities and is an integral part of the PIMS (profit impact of market strategies) studies. For any participating company PIMS will identify companies in other comparable industries (that is, at similar stages of development) with similar market shares in their own markets. Comparing the financial returns on capital employed and the different marketing strategies employed by these companies over time can be very helpful in analysing internal financial performance and planning appropriate marketing strategies for the future.

Another way of using segmental analysis is to identify particular relationships between marketing activities and sales revenues or costs and to analyse the trend in these marketing ratios. One particularly common ratio in consumer goods companies is to express advertising expenditure as a percentage of sales revenue (very commonly referred to as the A : S ratio).

The normal way of using the A : S ratio is to set a maximum level of advertising expenditure for any product or product group relative to the sales revenue achieved by the product. This would normally be referenced to the budgeting period of the business, e.g. the forthcoming financial year.

Therefore for a highly branded growth product in a competitive market an advertising allowance of 7 per cent of sales revenue might be given. This means that:

Budgeted sales revenue £10 million   Advertising budget £700 000
(at 7% of sales revenue)

But if during the year the actual sales were below budget and so were the reforecast sales revenue for the year:

Reforecast sales revenue £8 million   Advertising expenditure £560 000
(at 7% of sales revenue)

Unfortunately rigid adherence to this A : S ratio could mean cutting expenditure at the wrong time or increasing it unnecessarily. If sales were well ahead of budget in the early part of the year, and were forecast to stay ahead:

Reforecast sales revenue £14 million New advertising spend £980 000
(at 7% of sales revenue)

Many companies use the comparison over time of their A : S ratio and their relative market share as a way of planning the necessary level of advertising expenditure to achieve their target market share in the future. There are a number of dangers and assumptions in this use of marketing ratios but, if used with care, it can provide some planning guidelines.

Trying to correlate advertising activity and market share over time assumes that competitors do not vary their relative level of marketing activity during this period. If our company's share of voice declines during the period, the market share may also decline even though the advertising spend has increased (although not by as much as competitors). Using the A : S ratio helps to monitor this but if the product is in the growth phase of the life cycle sales may be increasing although market share is declining (if the market is growing at 40 per cent per year and our sales are only growing at 20 per cent per year our market share is decreasing rapidly). It is also assumed that no other part of the marketing mix changes in importance relative to advertising during the period. If our pricing levels change in real terms and relative to competition this may dramatically affect the apparent impact of any advertising activity. We have already examined the accounting problems caused by the lag effects between marketing expenditure and the resultant sales activity, and this can create severe problems in using marketing ratios as an analytical tool. Increasing advertising in this accounting period *may* generate increased sales and improved market share in a subsequent accounting period, which will confuse the A : S ratios in both periods. The company may attempt to allow for the lag in response by the way in which the A : S ratio is implemented, but this added sophistication may only add to the confusion in the decision-making process. Also what reaction should a company make to a decrease in sales levels? In a company rigidly using a target ratio of A : S the response would be to cut advertising. This may be disastrous if the sales decline was caused by increased competitive activity and the market as a whole is still growing. As with any of our other analytical techniques the major benefit lies in the skilled application by managers who understand the marketplace and do not blindly apply historic ratios to a changing environment.

Many other marketing ratios, such as sales force expenses or promotion expenses as a percentage of sales revenue, can be calculated both internally over time and for competitors where the information is available, or for similar companies (using PIMs for example). In all cases it is vital that the markets are properly segmented for significant differences and that the interactions of different elements of the marketing mix are allowed for, as well as taking into account the timing gaps between the expense and the benefit. A privately owned specialist distribution company (specializing in limited shelf-life products, such as cakes) used ratio analysis to monitor its distribution expenses as a proportion of sales, and was quite happy as the proportion was declining and the sales levels were growing very rapidly, as shown in Table 5.1.

Unfortunately it ignored the fact that its business was changing because the sales growth was generated by a new segment (large retail chains) whereas its historic business had been in selling to small corner shops. Also new imported products were being sold at higher absolute prices, further increasing sales revenues, but at considerably lower gross profit margins because of fierce competition. The company was adding less value to the business chain of supplying the product to the end consumer in its new business segment because the large retailers had their own distribution systems and much greater bargaining power – thus forcing down still further the distribution company's margin. Also this distribution company now had to finance more stock (imported product creating a longer supply chain) and much higher debtors (the large retailers using their power to minimize their investment in working

Table 5.1   *Cake distribution company: summarized profit and loss accounts £000's*

	Last year	Current year expected results	Next year's budget
Sales revenue	3 500	8 000	15 000
Bought-in goods for resale	2 520	6 250	12 000
Margin	980 (28%)	1 750 (22%)	3 000 (20%)
Distribution expenses	300 (8.6%)	625 (7.8%)	1 020 (6.8%)
Sales and marketing expenses	200 (5.7%)	350 (4.4%)	450 (3.0%)
Other expenses	320 (9.1%)	475 (5.9%)	530 (3.5%)
Total expense	820 (23.4%)	1 450 (18.1%)	2 000 (13.3%)
Profit before tax	160	300	1 000
less Taxation	56	105	350
Profit after tax	104	195	650

capital by taking a long time to pay) and so its capital employed increased as shown in Table 5.2 on much greater sales levels just as its operating profit levels were put under great pressure. This business went into liquidation when cost overruns coincided with stock shelf-life problems, even though a supposedly key marketing ratio (distribution expenses : sales) was going the right way – assuming that everything else stays the same in a dynamic marketing environment is somewhat unrealistic!

Table 5.2   *Cake distribution company: summarized balance sheets £000's*

	Last year	Current year expected results	Next year's budget
Fixed assets	325	375	550
Current assets			
Stocks	155	400	800
Debtors	175	750	1700
Sundry	90	110	250
Cash	55	–	–
Total	475	1260	2750
less Current liabilities			
Trade creditors	324	725	1250
Hire purchase loans	250	290	420
Taxation	56	105	350
Bank overdraft	–	180	345
Total	630	1300	2365
Net current assets	(155)	(40)	385
Net assets	170	335	935
Shareholders' funds	170	335	935

Breaking the business down into its appropriate marketing segments and calculating financial performance ratios for each segment can clearly be very useful as a basis for planning. However, there is a tendency to compare these performance ratios across the segments (for example, products, markets and combinations thereof) and to make judgements from this analysis. This is only valid if the segments are at the same stage of development and if similar levels of performance should be expected across these various divisions. It may be possible for a marketing division in a service industry with no heavy investment in fixed assets to show a return on capital employed of 50 per cent, whereas another division of the same group in a heavy engineering industry may do well to show a return of 20 per cent on the same accounting basis, as shown in Figure 5.7. If the group wishes to assess the relative performances of the two divisions it must separate the economic measures from the relative financial performance against expectations (that is, financial results compared to plans or budgets as discussed in detail in Part Three). The potential return from any additional investment as shown by the financial analysis of existing returns on investment clearly indicates that the group should channel most of its funds towards the marketing led service division if these high returns can be maintained. The economic performance has been better and this was probably expected (this is shown in Table 5.3). If it was expected it would have been reflected in the financial plans of each division, as shown, and the managers of each division should be judged on their performance against these plans, not against the direct comparisons of divisional performance. This separates economic from managerial performance, as introduced at the end of Chapter 1, and unless this is done every good manager will want to work in the highly profitable businesses of the company, whereas their managerial skill and judgement may produce better results when utilized in the lower performing areas of the business. This problem of comparisons can also highlight another issue for companies using financial analysis. Ratios place absolute numbers into context and are very useful ways of comparing results, but they can sometimes divert attention too far away from the absolute values (after all, the manufacturing division made a profit of £10 million). Some companies place almost total emphasis on managing the ratios, rather than managing the business (for example, rigid adherence to the A : S ratio), and this can lead to decisions, such as reducing advertising in the rapid growth period of sales for a product, which make the ratio look right but in the long term detrimentally affect the business. Remember that an infinite return on capital employed can be achieved by making a £1 profit on zero net assets, and a policy of cost minimization means spending £0. These extreme examples show how managing ratios may not build a large or a long-term business. The ratios will automatically change over time as the business matures (for example, fixed assets which are included net of depreciation and hence reduce in net book value as they get older) and so the *rate* of improvement in performance may be more important, and whether the business can afford to reinvest to maintain its position or to grow (that is, cash flow).

Comparison of divisional performance: extracts of annual results

	Marketing division £000s	*Heavy engineering manufacturing division* £000s
Sales revenue	50 000	100 000
less Total expenses	47 500	90 000
Divisional profit	2500	10 000
	Extracts of balance sheets	
Fixed assets	1000	35 000
Net current assets	4000	15 000
Net assets	5000	50 000
Profitability (ROCE) (that is, profit ÷ net assets)	50%	20%
Analysis of ROCE, that is, profit margin	5%	10%
× Net asset turnover ratio	× 10	× 2

Figure 5.7

Table 5.3   *Comparisons to budgets (£000s)*

	Marketing division		*Manufacturing division*	
	Actual	*Budget*	*Actual*	*Budget*
Divisional profit	2500	3000	10 000	9000
Net assets	5000	4500	50 000	52 000
ROCE	50%	66.7%	20%	17.3%

Financial analysis is also, by definition, historical and if it is to be of any value, it must be of relevance to forward planning. Therefore it is vital, not just to analyse where the business is, but how it got there and this information may then provide a sound basis for future marketing plans, for example, by raising questions.

PART THREE

PLANNING

6
———

Setting objectives and selecting strategies

Introduction

Financial analysis has been shown to be an essential basis for planning, as without any information to go on it is pointless to expend a great deal of time, effort and funds on financial planning. Analysing the past is largely based on known financial data (even though the preparation of financial statements requires the use of managerial judgements) whereas planning for the future means trying to achieve desired ends based on extrapolations, estimates and forecasts which are subject to significant errors and changes outside the control of any company. Therefore, even when the financial analysis has been comprehensive and rigorous, the only certain statement about a financial plan is that 'it will be wrong'.

Given this certainty of being wrong, why do we bother to plan? There are two fundamental reasons:

1 financial planning enables a company to evaluate the financial outcome of any strategy and to ensure that all the necessary resources are available to implement the plan;
2 having a plan provides a reference base against which the actual financial outcome can be compared, and modifications to either the strategy or to the objectives of the plan (or to both) can be made and the revised planned outcomes evaluated.

This use of plans to monitor progress and to control the business is considered in Part Four, but in this part we are concerned with developing a sensible and relevant plan for our business, using the financial analysis we have carried out.

Planning can be broken down into two main stages:

1 deciding what to do; and

2   deciding how to do it.

In other words a business must set itself objectives and then select appropriate strategies which will achieve those objectives. The basis of setting realistic objectives is provided by the in-depth financial analysis which has identified the current allocation of resources and the comparative success achieved to date. Financial analysis is an important element in the process of setting corporate objectives, but some aspects of the business cannot easily be converted into financial parameters; hence financial analysis can overemphasize certain parts of the business, unless a balance is achieved by the use of managerial judgement. The objectives included in a financial plan must take into account this historic analysis including any constraints which have been identified, so that all objectives are practical and possible. A business plan is not 'a wish list' but must be a fully developed set of actions for the company. Therefore planning is principally about making decisions including resolving the problems of resource allocations and generating answers to the questions raised by the SWOT analysis, which was considered in Chapter 2.

Most large companies now set their corporate objectives in two stages so that the first part can be kept almost permanently as the general 'goals' or 'mission' of the business. The other part can then be more quantified and explicit as to how these goals can be achieved in view of the current external factors and internal capabilities, which have been identified by the previously carried out analysis. The planning process, which includes financial planning, then develops strategies which are specific action plans designed to meet the corporate objectives and detailed implementation of these strategies is often further analysed into tactics. A financial control system which regularly monitors and feeds back the results of these actions is needed, so that any modifications required can be made as quickly as possible. Our overall business model can therefore be redrawn as shown in Figure 6.1.

Mission statement (or goals)

'Goals' are the statement both of what the business is (and therefore what it is not) and what it wants to be, and should encapsulate the primary mission of the company in a way which every employee and person dealing with the company can understand.

The mission statement must, therefore, indicate the industrial focus and the positioning within those industries of the company, but does not need to contain quantified financial objectives as these will change over time. Many corporate missions (for example, BP, Burton Group, British Aerospace) include words like 'leading', 'best', 'pre-eminent', 'largest',

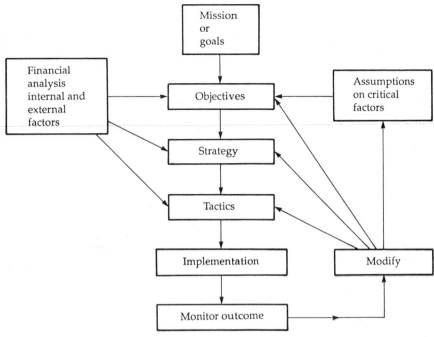

Figure 6.1 *Business model*

etc. without being clear as to how these relative measures are to be assessed. Having the biggest sales revenue seems a meaningless goal for any company unless this absolute size gives a competitive cost advantage or dominant market share which enables better financial returns to be achieved by satisfying customers' needs more profitably than competitors. This necessary marketing focus in mission statements is now more common than previously and some companies have even adopted the maxim that profit follows, rather than leads, the successful satisfaction of market requirements. For these companies long-term profitability remains an integral part of their corporate mission but profit comes *from the business* being successful and this can only be achieved by selling products or services in the marketplace and thus creating satisfied customers.

The corporate mission cannot be totally expressed in financial terms and there should be statements incorporated regarding 'corporate values' and 'business principles' which are fundamental to the way the company will conduct its operations. These values normally cover attitudes towards customers, quality of goods and services provided, and employees, as well as corporate attitudes to profits. Many leading companies (such as Ford and Citicorp) now spend considerable time and effort on refining these statements as the first stage of their planning process, and may alter the sequence of the issues if they wish to focus more attention on one particular area for the next planning period. If these statements are to be helpful in drafting the more specific corporate objectives, they must avoid being vague approbations of widely held acceptable ideals such as motherhood, the family and patriotism, and set meaningful guidelines which can be used to identify gaps between where the mission statement wants the company to be and where the financial analysis says it is, such as that shown below for Citicorp.

Example: Mission Statement
Extract from Citicorp's 1987 Published Financial Statement
'Citicorp: A Global Financial Services Company
We are: Unique in our commitment to serve all customers, including consumers, and other institutions, with a full range of financial services in virtually all marketplaces of the world.
Unique in human, managerial, and financial resources drawn from the global marketplace.
Unique also in the balance and distribution of our activities worldwide.
We recognize the need to balance short versus long-term values and are guided by shareholder and customer interest in these decisions.'
Note 1   The statement continues with more specific statements regarding separate business areas and includes clear long term financial objectives:-
'Our financial objective is to build shareholder value through'
. . . etc.
Note 2   This mission statement was published at the end of the year in which Citicorp made an additional bad debt provision of $3000 million.

Corporate objectives

Having set out 'goals' for the organization the next stage of planning is to define more specifically the corporate objectives, which if achieved will satisfy the goals. These objectives are set in the context of the actual environment in which the business is operating and therefore internal and external contraints must be taken into account as indicated by the historical business analysis. The financial part of the overall analysis can only show up existing factors and suggest, by projecting trends, what will happen in the future. For planning purposes many assumptions based on the historical analysis will have to be made regarding the external environment (for example, which opportunities and threats will occur and when) and it is vitally important that the plan recognizes as early as possible any emerging new issues, such as the introduction of new products by competitors, which can affect the business significantly. Constraints on internal resources, for example shortages of skilled labour, and major external pressures, such as overcapacity in the industry, may make it impossible for the company to set realistic objectives which fully achieve the goals of the business in the short term. The selection of specific marketing strategies may enable the business to overcome the critical constraints and achieve the goals in a medium-term period, but this may detrimentally affect the published financial performance of the company in the short term. There is a potentially serious conflict between planning for the long term and for the short term. The published financial statements concentrate on the financial performance on an annual basis, and the return on investment ratio is similarly restricted. Longer-term measures of performance are needed to evaluate the success or failure of strategic decisions, and these techniques are considered in Chapter 7.

For example, it may be part of the mission statement to be market leader in specified markets and, at present, this may not be the case for one particular area. The company could decide to increase significantly its marketing activity in that market to build its share over a two- to three-year period and thus achieve the desired market leadership. The increased marketing expense will depress profitability in the short term, and the forecast higher return in the future relies on the *assumptions* which have been made (for example, regarding future market size and competitive reaction to this increased marketing activity) proving correct. Long-term planning is not therefore simply a series of annual plans joined together, as the longer-term objectives (such as growth in market share) need to be considered and integrated with the short-term performance criteria (such as profit levels in the next year). For most companies planning is a compromise because there is an expectation and demand for a certain performance in the short term (that is, the next financial year) and a need for investment and development to achieve the longer-term objectives of the business. Even if the mission of the company included a specific financial goal which was expressed as 'maximize long-term profits' the planning process is still one of compromise. Maximizing long-term profits is not achieved by maximizing profits each year as is clear if the product life cycle (considered in Chapter 2) is considered. While any product is in the growth phase the company should be investing in market development expenditure to ensure that the growth realizes its full potential. The benefit of this expenditure is felt during the maturity or 'cash cow' period when the *larger* market generates greater profits for the company. However, if we wanted to maximize profits each year, we could increase profits in the short term by reducing marketing activity on market development and only spending on increasing market penetration. This might cause the product to become a 'cash cow' too soon and so decrease the overall profits which would be achieved by a sound long-term strategy.

Many businesses have adopted an integrated approach to planning, as illustrated in Figure 6.2, to try to overcome the worst examples of this type of problem (many companies still suffer from short-term decisions being taken without proper consideration for the longer-term implications). This integrated approach involves developing a long-range plan (normally five to seven years) with an aim of attaining the corporate goals at the end of the period. Included within this plan is a short-term operational plan (one year), which balances the need for rapid achievements and the developments necessary for the longer-term strategy. This linking of the corporate plan (long-term) to the budget (one year time frame) is vitally important as it is incompatible to adopt a particular long-term strategy and then implement short-term tactics which work in the opposite direction.

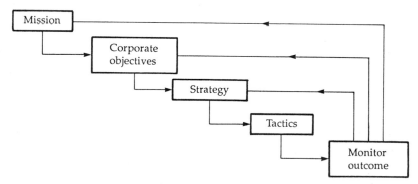

Figure 6.2   *Integrated view of planning (as a continuous process)*

Objectives, therefore, need to separate the targets of increasing short-term profits and long-term growth, while remembering that any required funding for this growth may need to be raised by generating profits and hence increasing cash flows. Indeed business objectives may need to differentiate between generating profit and cash, because some marketing strategies which increase profitability will require more cash to be invested in the business to finance higher stocks and debtors or to purchase more fixed assets. During the growth stage of any product's life cycle, a company may invest significant funds in productive capacity by purchasing new fixed assets. Although profits may be increasing, even after charging the higher depreciation expense, the net cash flow of the particular product may be significantly negative during this period, due to this expenditure on long-term fixed assets.

This indicates that the market positioning of the company should also be specified in the corporate objectives as an increased profit target could be achieved by improving the profit margin at existing sales levels. Alternatively the same objective could be met by increasing market share and hence sales volumes, even at the expense of a small decline in profit margins. Corporate objectives should identify the most desirable overall strategy which fits into the goals of the business, and thus defines the marketing strategy for the business.

Corporate objectives and strategies can be seen, in Figure 6.3, as hierarchical with each set of objectives leading to the development of strategies and each strategy requiring objectives if it is to be capable of sensible implementation. Thus the overall corporate objective will be broken down into strategies, and hence functional objectives, for each major area of the business. The process should not be regarded as exclusively 'top down' (that is, that the mission determines the corporate objectives, which in turn dictate the corporate strategies, etc.) as a degree of iteration is required in the planning system if it is to be practically useful. As indicated in Figure 6.3, the implementation of the marketing tactics and programmes may affect the marketing strategies and objectives due to their relative success. Similar upward impacts are indicated in Figure 6.3 from other points in the process. It may be that for specific areas, objectives and strategies require modification even before implementation if constraints lower down the hierarchy indicate that the objectives are inconsistent with available resources or the external environment. An example of this is where the marketing objective requires a substantial increase in market share, and the marketing strategy selected is a high level of promotional expenditure. If previous promotional efforts have indicated that the particular product has inadequate distribution to achieve significant share growth, this information should lead to a modification of the marketing strategy as it may be more sensible to try to improve the distribution of the product before increasing promotional effort. The marketing objectives and strategy are clearly critical as these will significantly influence the other functional areas of the business, not least by affecting the resources required.

This immediately suggests that these marketing objectives must be market and product focused, as shown in Figure 6.3, because very different objectives can be set for different products and markets, and even for specific market segments. The planning process should be broken down into similar segments as were relevant for the segmental analysis which was considered in Chapter 5, and specific marketing objectives should be identified for each significant business segment.

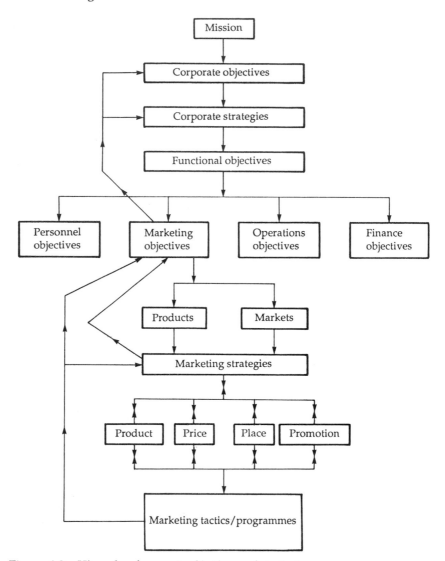

Figure 6.3　*Hierarchy of corporate objectives and strategies*

Therefore specific marketing objectives, such as increasing market penetration, should be regarded as a subgroup of the corporate objectives or as a strategy for achieving the overall corporate objectives. The profit implications of the possible marketing strategies to achieve these marketing objectives are initially important as profit levels will normally be a significant part of the corporate objectives. The planning process must have a way of comparing and ranking the probable outcomes of the many alternative ways in which any particular marketing objective can be achieved, so that the most appropriate strategy can be selected.

Selecting strategies

Strategies are alternative courses of action which can be implemented to try to achieve the corporate, or marketing, objectives. Therefore having decided on its corporate objectives, the company must select the strategy which it feels is most appropriate to its objectives, available resources, and external environment. The historical analysis, both internal and external, will have provided some information on the relative success of particular strategies when tried in the past. It is important that the analysis is sufficiently detailed, so that the planners can identify any changes, particularly in the external environment, between the time of any previous implementation and now. As it is most unlikely that any particular marketing strategy has been implemented before in exactly the same environment, there is an unavoidable level of assumption about the outcome. The aim of our in-depth financial analysis is not only to reduce the level of unknowns as far as possible but also to allow managers to concentrate their efforts on those areas where using their judgement will have the most significant impact. It will have highlighted any areas where the business may be constrained or where resources are not being effectively utilized. A major part of the planning exercise is to reallocate resources so that they are better used within the business and to acquire any additional resources which can be financially justified.

There are financial decision making techniques which are extremely helpful in this area as they force companies to quantify the benefits obtained by using resources in any particular way. In almost all companies there is a shortage of some resources within the business – it may be market opportunities, funds, production capacity, skilled managers, sales people, etc. – and if this limiting resource is not being utilized as effectively as possible, the performance of the business is less than it could be. A logical comparison is to consider what alternative financial benefit is given up by using any particular business resource in the specific way it is used at present. The simplest benefit would be to not spend the funds on the particular resource if that was a viable alternative, and the benefit would be the cost-saving. Even if the cost was already committed there might be a more profitable way of utilizing that resource. If there is an opportunity which gives a better financial return then the business can be made better off by reallocating the resources. For example: suppose a field salesperson is already fully utilized calling on a range of customers when a new potential customer wishes to place an order. If the profit potential of the new customer exceeds that of the *worst* existing comparable customer being called on, reallocating the existing sales resource can make the business more profitable. Alternatively if good sales opportunities are being lost because of lack of sales people it may be profitable to increase the resources available even though this increases the total sales costs provided that the additional contribution earned is greater than the additional cost incurred. (Planning is about reallocating resources and removing existing constraints so as to secure greater benefits.)

A general term for describing this comparison is the 'opportunity cost', which is the benefit which would be obtained from the foregone alternative, that is, the thing that could not be done because of the lack of resources (the next best available foregone opportunity). It is difficult to evaluate because the benefit has, by definition, been foregone. However, this problem of benefit being in the future applies to all financial decision-making. So the opportunity cost of taking on our new customer is the lost profit we would give up (forego) from the worst customer we can no longer supply. Also the opportunity cost of not increasing the sales force is the profit we would make from the lost (foregone) sales opportunities.

These simple examples highlight the need for the financial analysis to provide segmented marketing information relevant to the planning decisions which the business faces – in this case customer profitability analysis is essential to the decision. Any financial business decision is made under conditions of uncertainty, but appropriate financial analysis provides a good basis for the judgements which must be exercised, as these opportunity cost issues illustrate.

We use this idea of opportunity cost in many examples later in the book, but it is also important to note that the financial information relevant to any decision relates to *future* costs and benefits. The historical analysis must be used as a guide to what these future costs and benefits are likely to be, but any past costs are irrelevant to the future decision. A new product launch may make this clearer: a company has spent £200 000 on launching a new very specialized software product (which cost £500 000 to develop) into its industrial market, through exhibitions, leafleting and trade magazine advertising. The sales force is obtaining very few leads and getting even fewer conversions into orders, because the product is apparently regarded as too expensive for the benefits it provides to the customer. It is completely illogical to maintain the very high unit price (as was done by this company) on the justification of having to recover the high development and launch marketing costs. Those funds have already been spent and must be ignored for future decisions – in accounting terms they are called 'sunk' costs. The only sensible decision is to set the price at the level which will generate the maximum profit through the remainder of its product life cycle; this profit can then be regarded as a contribution towards the previously spent costs, which could help future decisions regarding potential development of similar products.

Financial decisions are based on future costs and benefits. Costs already spent are irrelevant to the decision which will affect the future not the past.

Analysis obviously helps planning decisions but, unfortunately, decisions have to be based on judgements and assumptions about the future. This makes it so vital that decisions are made by the managers with the best knowledge of the particular area, and that accountants provide these managers with the financial information needed, rather than the accountants taking the decisions based solely on their own view of their available financial information, which only forms part of the total information needed for any decision. Financial information forms an important part of decision support in most businesses, but it is only a part and it only *supports* decisions.

Within the marketing area this is particularly true as forecasting the future external environment, which is so critical to most decisions, requires detailed knowledge and even the best historical analysis needs expert interpretation as to its relevance to any particular decision. It is also important to focus the decisions, and hence the planning process, on the appropriate areas and this requires segmented planning. As stated previously, marketing is, among other things, about products and markets and therefore at their simplest potential marketing strategies are very restricted. If an overall corporate objective is to grow or to become more profitable, the marketing strategy should analyse what, where and by how much, that is, what products and which markets. A company could grow by selling more of its existing goods or services to its existing customers, or it might find new customers to buy these products. Alternatively it could develop or acquire new products to sell to its existing customers. Each of these strategies tries to build on an existing strength of the business (for example, market share, product or brand franchise, customer loyalty or channel access) and the SWOT analysis should therefore indicate which option is most appropriate. There is a fourth alternative which is to grow by selling completely new products to completely new customers, which is obviously very high risk and often cannot really be called a marketing strategy for the *existing* business. These four options, when viewed as the continuous series which they really are, cover the only ways of expanding a business and their very simple, logical analysis has become established as the Ansoff matrix, after its originator (Figure 6.4). The four boxes show a description of the marketing strategy which is appropriate for the combination of products and markets, for example, new markets for existing products require a strategy of market development.

A company may choose different marketing strategies for different segments of its business and the stage of the product life cycle may influence the selection process considerably. It is also possible to pursue more than one strategy at the same time in the same segment but the planning process must be very careful to avoid confusion, as the marketing mix tactics may be very different for each specific strategy. The financial implications of these alternatives may be dramatically different for any particular company and this may influence the choice of strategy significantly. For example, for a supermarket retailer the cost of extending its product range (for example, selling electrical goods and clothing as well as groceries) in existing stores to existing customers may be lower than the cost of breaking into new markets (for example, geographically) which would mean opening new stores and attracting new customers in a fiercely competitive market. For a high technology company, such as a computer manufacturer or software company, it may be considered less risky to try to break into new markets with an existing product so as to expand sales or prolong the product life cycle, rather than to try to develop complementary products to sell to existing customers given the potentially very high development costs. The decisions taken will depend to a large degree on the strengths and weaknesses identified in the business analysis. It does not appear to make a lot of sense for the supermarket retailer to start making computers, or vice versa, which could give both of them new products in new markets.

The Ansoff matrix is a useful way of identifying appropriate strategies for any given set of corporate objectives and it is normally used with 'gap analysis', which is illustrated in Figure 6.5. The start point for most plans is to use the historic financial analysis to extrapolate what should happen given the forecast environment if no changes are made by the company. If this outcome achieves the corporate objectives no changes are needed, but most companies would assume that the objectives are set too low or are inconsistent with the assumptions for the external environment (for example, market growth rate forecasts), and the objectives would be changed. Therefore the extrapolation normally highlights the 'gap' shown in Figure 6.5 between probable outcome and desired result, and it is this gap which the changes in marketing strategy are designed to fill. Basically the gap can be filled in the four ways shown by the Ansoff matrix and specific strategies and plans should be produced to achieve each of the elements selected.

As the diversification strategy is normally considered very risky, the company may prefer to modify its objectives so as to eliminate this element of the total gap. However, in some industries, it may signify that

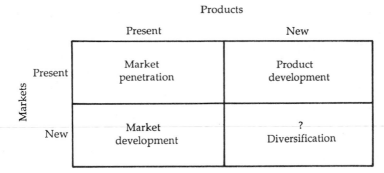

Figure 6.4   *Ansoff matrix*

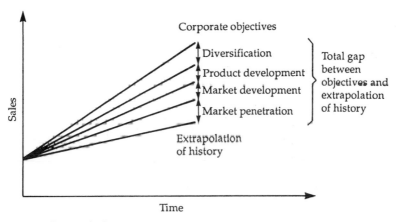

Figure 6.5   *Gap analysis*

acquisition is needed to fill the gap left by expanding the company's existing products and markets. This has been true of some financial services companies (for example, insurance broking), where the planning process identified constraints in desired growth levels and a solution has been to acquire *people* (for example, marine insurance experts) who bring technical expertise (that is, specific service products) and a new client base (that is, markets) to the company. Hence the risk of diversification is considerably lessened, and the costs are not as high as acquiring a complete company, particularly if the new services can be sold to existing customers and the new customers may be interested in existing services. An additional risk is raised which is that these people can and do leave again, or a competitor could take your key people which would create a bigger 'planning gap'; this risk is, of course, always present in any business where people are the critical 'asset'.

Summary

Planning consists of deciding what to do and how to do it, and involves reallocating resources and removing constraints. Planning is, therefore, decision-based.

It forces the business to set itself objectives which define what it is trying to do and then to establish strategies and tactics to achieve these objectives. Financial analysis is fundamental to ensuring that the objectives are practical and attainable and that the most appropriate strategy is adopted. This requires the business to choose among alternatives and the best way to do this is to evaluate the *opportunity cost* of the alternatives.

Financial decision-making only involves *future costs and benefits*, and any 'sunk' costs can be ignored, which makes the decision more dependent on managerial judgement regarding these future costs and benefits.

Most businesses face a conflict between short-term benefits and long-term objectives of the business, and the planning process must take account of this. Many companies try to resolve this by integrating the short-term planning process (the budget) within the long-range corporate plan so that the two share the same overall objectives.

We now examine these aspects of planning in detail in Chapters 7 and 8, before considering the financing requirements of the future plans in Chapter 9.

7
—

Long-term planning

Introduction

Once the business has agreed its mission statement, the long-term planning process must set out how the mission is to be fulfilled. In the long term it is possible for a company to plan to change existing allocations of resources and to remove current constraints, such as lack of access to distribution channels, on the business even if such changes will take time to achieve. This is the most fundamental difference between long-term (strategic) planning and short-term (tactical) budgeting. In a plan for the next 12 months it will be impossible to make fundamental changes to many aspects of marketing strategy as the time needed to effect changes (the lead time) is greater than the 12-month planning period. If the corporate objective for growth can only be attained by launching new products, the level of this growth will be constrained by the time-scale of product developments and this may preclude any significant new product launches in the next 12 months. For longer-term plans, the company could increase the resources dedicated to product development so that these time-scales may be reduced, or it could examine the potential for buying in new products from other companies, etc. as ways of removing the constraint to growth.

Therefore if the planning horizon is long enough almost any change in the business strategy can be accommodated, but for very long time-scales our ability to forecast the external environment is almost non-existent. Consequently long-term business planning must be broken down into those specific periods in the future when current decisions will have a significant impact, and the longer term where a broad general view of the business and its environment can be taken. Unfortunately the time-scale required for more detailed financial planning varies widely between industries due to the delay in seeing the results of current major investment decisions. A decision to build a new electricity power station depends on the market demand for electricity many years into the future. What type of power station to build hinges on the forecasts of alternative fuel prices and the available types of technology over the same period. If these forecasts prove to be significantly wrong once the investment has been *committed*, there is very little that can be done to change the cost structure that results. This requires the industry to put great emphasis on the financial analysis before making such a critical decision, and to test the sensitivity of the decision to alternative assumptions (that is, how does a change in one assumption change the financial justification of the investment). Using sensitivity analysis highlights those assumptions which are critical to the financial evaluation, and therefore where the greatest analytical emphasis should be placed. Different elements in the financial evaluation will be subject to varying levels of potential error in their estimation and sensitivity analysis uses these varying estimates in recomputing the financial evaluation. These recalculations show which elements have the greatest impact on the viability of the project and thus indicate where any analytical efforts can be most profitably invested, i.e. areas which serve to reduce the range of the possible estimates for these critical areas. The cost of fuel in a power station will be the greatest single expense which changes with the level of output (the costs which change with the level of output are described as variable costs) and fuel forms approximately 80 per cent of the total variable costs. Therefore a 10 per cent error in forecasting the cost per unit of fuel will alter the total variable costs by 8 per cent (10 per cent × 80 per cent of the costs represented by fuel). Direct labour costs in the power station (which represent only 5 per cent of the variable costs) would need a forecast error of 160 per cent to have the same impact on the total variable costs as the 10 per cent error on fuel prices, due to the dominant impact of fuel on the sensitivity of the project. In some cases it may be possible to reduce the dependence on one critical assumption, such as the type of fuel used in the power station, and although this may increase costs and so reduce the financial return, the reduction in risk may make this worthwhile, for example, building power stations which can use more than one type of fuel.

Committed versus discretionary costs

For decision analysis, costs can be classified into various types and this example illustrates the difference between costs which are discretionary and those which are committed. A committed cost is one where the company, by taking a previous decision, has already irrevocably 'committed to spend' the funds, whether the payment has physically been made or not. If the funds have not been committed the company can exercise its *discretion* through the current decision to spend or not. Thus before deciding whether to build a new power station, the electricity supply company has discretion over this cost, but once the decision is taken *all* the expenditure can be regarded as committed even though the physical construction, and the consequent payments, will be spread over several years. As decisions are based on *future* costs and benefits the most relevant costs are discretionary; however, because some committed costs may not be spent for some considerable time it may also be possible to *avoid* these costs, albeit by paying a cancellation penalty. If the cost can be avoided then it is relevant to the decision as this will affect the future level of expenditure. The demand for electricity may not grow as forecast and it may become clear that our new power station is not going to be needed until several years after it will be finished. It may be cost-effective to slow down the construction programme (that is, spend the funds later) or stop it altogether, even though this may involve penalty payments to the contractors. The net costs that can be saved are those that we avoid paying, less any penalty costs incurred, and these are classified as 'avoidable costs': these are relevant to financial decisions as they are the costs which need not be paid as the result of any decision. Therefore they represent a real saving to the business.

These costs that can be avoided, if one course of action is chosen rather than another, are obviously relevant to financial decisions and this cost classification can incorporate both discretionary (which is defined in the note below) and some elements of committed, also defined in the note below, although most committed costs cannot be avoided.

[*Note* A discretionary cost is not predetermined by any previous commitment and the optimum level cannot be calculated by any specific relationship between inputs (as measured by costs) and outputs (as measured by sales revenues). Thus management can genuinely exercise *discretion* over the level of expenditure: examples of discretionary costs are advertising, research and development, and training.

Committed costs are costs which will be incurred in the future as a result of a decision in the past, even though the actual expenditure may not yet have taken place. Control over these committed costs can only be exercised at the time of commitment, as the costs can only subsequently be affected by the taking of another major decision to alter or cancel the commitment which may incur additional costs.

An example of a committed cost is the rent of office space when a lease has been signed for (say) five years for that office space. Even though the rent cost may be payable annually over the five years, the whole amount has been committed, and the cost can only be changed by another decision (such as to terminate the lease or an attempt to sublet the space) which may incur specific costs, for example, cancellation charges.]

Fixed versus variable costs

This aspect of there being less constraints on long-term planning raises several other important issues regarding financial decisions. In the short term, for most companies a period of one year is used, most costs are committed and a lot of cost levels are fixed or static whatever happens to the level of activity. Physical distribution costs, for example, are likely to be fairly constant in the short term even if the size of each order reduces as long as the same number of deliveries has to be made to the same customers. In the longer term, for example more than one year, different methods of delivery could be adopted so that, if order sizes stayed lower than before, the distribution costs are reduced. As time-scales increase, less and less costs can be regarded as fixed because the business can vary the cost level to suit the forecast activity level. The distinction between *fixed* and *variable* costs is very important to financial decisions because if a cost is fixed and will not change as a result of the decision it can be ignored. The rent on a five-year lease for office space can be ignored if the decision being considered does not mean that the space required changes beyond that currently leased and does not have impacts beyond the five-year lease period. If a cost varies with time or activity, etc., the impact of the decision on the cost level must be considered. However, as stated, in long-term planning few costs are likely to be fixed because the company can change its strategy, and consequently its cost levels, to adjust to changing environments. Therefore fixed and variable costs, defined in the note below, are discussed in more detail in the next chapter on short-term planning where the distinction is vitally important, and where the difference is illustrated graphically.

(Note   In the relevant range, total fixed costs remain constant whereas total variable costs alter proportionately to the movement up or down the range. The relevant range can be determined in terms of sales value, sales volume, time or some other variable and may be limited in one or both directions: for example, rent is often fixed by time and floor area but the range constraint is normally only an upper limit. If more space or time is required, more rent will be payable; if less is required the same fixed rent is payable.)

Profit versus cash

The balance between the long-term objectives and short-term performance expectations has already been mentioned but major strategic decisions, such as our power station investment or the launch of a new product, have impacts across several accounting periods and thus can dramatically complicate the interpretation of published financial results.

The decisions must be evaluated by reference to all the relevant costs and benefits, and not simply those included in any arbitrary accounting period. Good financial analysis techniques and sensible accounting conventions can minimize some of the confusing impact on financial statements, but the use of managerial judgements in preparing financial statements is a cause for concern. In the case of building our power station we will have to decide what its economic life will be once it comes into use so that annual depreciation can be charged in each year's profit and loss account under the matching concept of accounting. This choice of depreciation basis, which is important for projecting profits for the periods in which the asset will be used, for something that will not even be finished for at least ten years is no more than an educated guess, and it would be worrying if such an accounting judgement affected the decision whether to go ahead.

We also have to make decisions regarding how much of the *costs* go into the fixed assets on the balance sheet to be depreciated and how much are expensed immediately as being of no future value which means that they cannot be treated as assets. This judgement will affect the timing of profit in the financial statements, but will not affect the cash spent by the business nor the benefit received from the expenditure, and should not therefore have any impact on the decision. Fortunately we can base our financial decisions on the cash flows which result from the decision (that is, future cash flows) rather than relying on the annual forecast profit and loss accounts. These forecast cash flows are not subject to the same management judgements regarding the timing of the revenue or expense and are in that sense more absolute. It should be remembered that over the full lifetime of any decision all these timing differences between cash flows and the profit and loss accounts will net themselves out, and so the same result should be obtained by either evaluation.

Time value of money

In long-term planning, as opposed to short-term planning, there is one important difference which can be reflected much more easily by using cash flows than profit forecasts. We have already considered, in Chapters 1, 2 and 4, how the passage of time affects the value of money, and any long-term decision which includes spending funds now and receiving benefit in future years cannot be properly evaluated without taking into consideration this impact of the decreasing value of money with time. It is possible to take this time value of money into account when dealing with cash flows because cash is included at the time of physical movement (that is, receipt or payment), whereas sales revenues and expenses are matched against the activities of the business. Comparing cash flows at different points in time cannot be done directly as £1000 now is worth more than £1000 to be received in five years' time, because the £1000 now could be placed on deposit for five years and earn interest which would increase its value in five years' time. Thus we need a technique which allows for the timing as well as the value of the cash flows to be taken into account.

Financial decision-making criteria

Before considering these long-term decision techniques in detail it is useful to draw together our financial decision-making criteria. We have already seen that decisions are based on future financial costs and benefits, but we now know that these decisions should also be based on cash flows rather than the more judgemental profit figures.

Therefore financial decisions are based on *future cash flows* and if these are properly evaluated, sound decisions will follow. If we are considering any particular decision many of the costs of the business will not change as a consequence of the decision (for example, the fixed costs will, by definition, remain fixed, as long as the decision does not move the level of activity outside the relevant range of the fixed cost). It is quite logical to base our decisions on a complete review of the cash flows for the business before the decision and compare this with another full cash flow forecast of the outcome after the change, but fortunately this lengthy and tedious process can be avoided. Those costs which are unaffected by the decision will be included in *both* the full cash flow forecasts for the company and hence will make no impact on the decision. This will be completely judged by the changes anticipated as a result of the alternatives being compared. The decision could be reached much more quickly and simply by concentrating on the differences between the alternatives. This is illustrated by the example shown below.

Example: Decision Criterion – Differential Future Cash Flows
This is an example of changes in pricing level for one product in one market where it is not performing well. Product X is currently selling 40 000 units a year in the United Kingdom at a price of £3 per unit. The variable cost per unit is £2 and the fixed costs for product X are £25 000 but these figures are included in the group totals shown in column 1 below.

In order to stimulate sales levels of product X, a price reduction to £2.50 is being considered which is hoped will stimulate an increase in volume to 70 000 units. This increase in volume will not affect the variable cost per unit or the total fixed costs. These adjusted figures are included in the group totals shown in column 2 below.

The adverse change in net cash flows indicates that the price reduction is not worthwhile but this is not highlighted by the scale of the other numbers included. If only the cash flows which change as a result of the decision are included, as shown in column 3 below, the result is shown more clearly and without having to consider great masses of irrelevant information.

	Column 1 £000	Column 2 £000	Column 3 £
	(Original group figures)	(Adjusted group figures after price reduction)	(Differential figures resulting from price reduction)
Cash inflow from sales revenues	40 000	40 055	55 000
less cash outflow			
Variable costs	(23 000)	(23 060)	(60 000)
Fixed costs	(12 500)	(12 500)	–
Net cash inflows	4500	4495	(5000)

This modifies our decision criteria again: financial decisions can be based on *differential future cash flows*. It is very important to ensure that all the changes resulting from any decision are included, but this difficulty would be there if the complete cash flows for each option were being compared, and simply reinforces the importance of including the expertise of the operational manager in the financial decision process. Suppose we are facing the decision in our above example on whether to change our pricing level *for one* product in *one* market where it is not performing well. We could undertake a full cash flow forecast for the whole group at the present price levels and then do the exercise again after deciding on our new suggested price for this one product, but most of the numbers would be the same as this decision is unlikely to affect other parts of the group. Even if the analysis was restricted to the product in question, it may be that the other markets would be unaffected by our proposed change and therefore all their values would be the same for both comparisons. It is adding unnecessary work to the financial decision process if we put lots of information on both sides of the evaluation when it can make no difference to the outcome. We can concentrate on the particular product and the particular market provided we are sure that there will be no other effects on sales. When we examine the specific area in more detail we can also see that some costs of this particular product and market are not affected by our pricing decision. Changing the price level will change sales volumes and thus both components (price and volume) of sales revenue will alter, and as sales volumes vary so will all those costs which are directly variable with volume. Some costs will be incurred on a period basis rather than being variable with volume and these costs (for example, rent, rates and other indirect costs) are not likely to be affected unless the volume change is so great that it moves them outside their relevant range in which they are a fixed cost.

The consequence of this is that we can ignore all the common costs which do not change as a direct result of the decision which is being considered, and concentrate on an in-depth analysis of those that are affected.

Therefore to summarize, in financial decisions, the only important considerations are the *future cash flows* resulting from the decision. If *all* future cash flows (both *in* and *out*) are considered, the most beneficial financial alternative can be selected.

However, as all common items (in other words, those occurring both with and without the decision) can be ignored, evaluation can be concentrated on *differential future cash flows*.

Decision-making example

Let us consider an example of a decision made using this technique. Our company has very recently bought a motor car for the sales and marketing director, who does around 64 000 km (40 000 miles) per year. The car cost £21 000 and because of the high mileage it was expected that the car would be sold after three years for £6000. Very soon after buying the car, an innovative company brought out a new fuel economy device which dramatically improves fuel consumption and halves petrol usage. This is forecast to produce a saving of £2000 per year for our new car and this new device is priced at £4500.

As a result of this new device and other breakthroughs in engine maintenance, a rival car manufacturer very quickly announces a new model with a similar specification to our director's car. It deliberately prices its car below the existing model at £18 000 and the annual operating savings (including the benefit of the fuel economy device which is fitted as standard to the new model) are forecast to be £4000 per year. This new model is also expected to have a three-year life and a final trade-in value of £6000. We are naturally interested in this new model and these potential savings, so the sales and marketing director calls into the dealer and enquires about the trade-in value on our nearly new, spotless executive car which cost £21 000. The dealer is very polite but apologetic, and points out that our car is now outdated technology;

therefore he is being very generous by offering us a trade-in against the fabulous new car of £10 000.

We have, therefore, lost £11 000 in a very short time on our existing car, and some companies would argue that they could not afford to make such a loss by trading in the car. They would be completely wrong in their logic. We have made the loss whether we trade the car in or not – trading the car in merely *realizes* the loss, it does not make it. (This is like arguing that, as a shareholder, you are *not* worse off if your shares go down in price *unless* you sell your shares. The value of your shareholding has reduced and hence you are worse off, whether you choose to realize the loss or not.)

In decision-making terms the original cost of our car is irrelevant to this decision as it is an historic (or sunk) cost and should not affect our future choice as to keeping the car, buying the new device to add to the car, or trading in the car to buy the new model. We can combine our two key techniques of comparing the alternative benefits and costs of the opportunities we face and using the relevant differential cash flows for each alternative, as shown in Figure 7.1.

Differential cash flow example: keep car or buy new model

Differential cash flows: buy the new model and trade-in the existing car*

Cash outflows: purchase of new model	(£18 000)
less Trade-in of existing model	£10 000
Cash outflow	(£8000)
Cash inflows: annual savings in operating costs of new model (£4000 per annum) for three years	£12 000
Net cash inflow	£4000

Keep existing car and fit fuel device

Cash outflow: purchase of fuel device	(£4500)
Cash inflow: annual savings in operating costs, at £2000 per annum, for three years	£6000
Net cash inflow	£1500

*Benefit of trading-in is £4000 which is greater than the opportunity cost (fitting fuel device) benefit of £1500, and hence best option is to trade-in our existing car and buy the new model.

Figure 7.1

One alternative is to keep the car and do nothing, while another is to keep the car and fit the fuel economy device. (For this example we ignore the time value of money and add this complication in later in the chapter.) Looking at the differences here is quite simple; we spend £4500 now to buy the device and we save £2000 each year for the three years we intend to keep the car. The total cash inflow is £6000 against an expenditure of £4500 and so we are better off buying the new device than keeping the car and doing nothing (net gain £1500).

Our other alternative is to buy the new model and trade-in the existing car and we need to compare this to see if it is even more financially attractive. Our 'opportunity cost' logic tells us that we must compare this with the *next best* available opportunity that we give up, and this has just been shown to be buying the fuel economy device which made us £1500 better off (in this case, less badly off) than doing nothing. If we compare buying the new car to doing nothing, we need a net benefit of more than £1500 to justify the decision.

Again looking at the future cash flow differences is quite easy, as is shown in Table 7.1. If we buy the new model we have to pay out £18 000 but we immediately receive the trade-in value for our existing car of £10 000 and so the net payment is only £8000. We are only interested in future cash flows and so the sale proceeds of our current car are a cash inflow, despite the sale making an accounting loss of £11 000. Against this cost of £8000 we can offset our annual operating savings of £4000 achieved by owning the new more efficient car. With an expected life of three years, our savings total £12 000 for a net financial benefit of £4000. Thus buying the new car is more attractive than keeping the existing car even if we add the fuel efficiency device.

Several important points should be noted from this simple example. In concentrating on future cash flows we do not include depreciation expenses as these are not a movement of cash but simply an accounting expense. Instead we include the actual cash outflows to buy the fixed assets where they are *future* costs. We do not include past expenditures, so the original cost of the car is irrelevant and our decision would have been the same if the historic cost had been £121 000. We are able to make the evaluation without knowing all the other costs to do with the business and even without needing to know the absolute costs of running the cars. As long as the *changes* in cash flows can be forecast sensible financial decisions can be made.

If the accounting statements, namely the profit and loss account, balance sheet and funds flow statement considered in Part Two of the book have any relevance to financial decision-making, they should, if analysed properly, lead us to the same decision. Fortunately they do but the analysis is much longer and consequently it is more likely that errors will be made. This example is evaluated using forecast financial statements as an appendix to this chapter.

It should be remembered that the cash savings are to be received annually over three years whereas the cash expenditures take place now. As money has a time value it is important that the more valuable expenditure today is compared against equivalent financial inflows and not with lower value future cash. This can be done by converting all cash flows to their equivalent 'present value' and this long-term decision analysis technique, known as 'discounting', is now considered as one of several alternative methods of evaluating major business decisions.

Techniques for major financial decisions

We have already established that financial decisions should be based on differential future cash flows and that major long-term decisions will have costs and benefits that run over several years. It is also important to remember that business decisions cannot be viewed in isolation, but must be compared against the alternative choices available to the company, that is the opportunity cost concept must be used. For short-term, minor decisions the opportunity cost comparison may involve selecting the lowest cost way of achieving any particular objective, but for longer-term major decisions it is more likely to involve the comparison of very different strategies with potentially very different outcomes. In most successful growing companies there is not sufficient finance available to implement all the new ideas that are generated by the business divisions. Therefore there is competition for the available funds and the decision-making criteria have to compare the potential returns from each investment and produce some means of ranking the alternatives.

This financial evaluation ranking can act as a means of selecting suitable projects and prioritizing various alternatives and is consequently often referred to as a *capital rationing* process, because only projects or proposals satisfying specified criteria will be carried out by the company. For any diverse business, this can create quite severe complications due to the variety of potential investments available to it which need to be compared. These could include for one specific group: building new power stations, developing new forms of turbines for industrial use, improving electrical products (televisions, refrigerators, etc.) for the consumer market, developing new telecommunications hardware and software, launching major new radar products for military use, a potential entry into the microcomputer market with a new product idea, possible major investments in new geographical areas, etc. The evaluation process needs, therefore, to be able to compare potential investments which differ as to:

1   size of investment (monetary value);
2   nature of investment (expenditure on tangible assets, research and development, marketing);

3   life of the project;
4   time-scale of investment and returns (some projects will not generate any returns for several years, for example, our power station);
5   certainty of returns (that is, the degree of risk associated with the project and the sources of risk, for example, technological versus financial).

There are three main decision techniques used by businesses for this purpose but for any complex long-term project no one measure can give a comprehensive review of all the different aspects of the project in terms of return and time-scales and hence be considered completely satisfactory. Thus many companies use a combination of these techniques and also use a comparison of accounting rate of returns (that is, the return on investment) among the alternatives to make the final decision. The techniques we are considering in this book are:

1   payback;
2   net present value (NPV);
3   internal rate of return (IRR);
4   accounting rate of return.

We will discuss each in detail, and use the same relatively simple three examples with each technique to illustrate the differences between them.

Payback

This is the simplest of the techniques as it literally calculates how long it will take to recover all the cash invested in the project. Thus it compares total cash outflows (which normally are greatest at the start of the project when the investment is made, although the operating costs continue through the life of the projects) to the cumulative forecast cash inflows from the project, and the payback period is the length of time taken for the projected cumulative cash inflow to equal the outflows. As the business is at financial risk prior to the recovery of the initial investment, the shorter the forecast payback period the better the project under this criterion. This technique does not take into account any returns which may be received after the project has broken even (that is, cumulative return equals cash invested). As companies need to receive back more than they have invested to make any project financially worthwhile, calculating only the payback period is insufficient for major investment decisions. It is vital to remember that this technique uses cash flows and hence ignores the timing of profits.

Some specific examples may make this problem clearer.

Project A

Project A consists of a potential investment in several new freehold premises for the existing retail division of our large group. The properties will cost £10 million and we will need to invest another £4 million to buy additional stocks for resale. Based on our existing retail outlets we are forecasting a constant net cash inflow level (we are ignoring taxation) of £3 million per year, which we expect to make from the first year of opening the new shops. We have decided to evaluate this project over ten years and at the end of the project we are assuming that we will sell the freehold properties and also get our initial investment back from selling the stock.

Even though we are assuming that we will sell the stock and get our cash back at the end of the project, we need to include the cash invested in working capital as a result of any new project. The cash is tied up in the project in the same way as if it was invested in fixed assets, and all the physical movements of cash need to be used in the evaluation. As discussed in Part Two of the book the fact that any particular item of stock is only held for a short period is irrelevant because, as long as we are running the new shops, we will need to have an additional £4 million invested in working capital. If there is a forecast which indicates a growing requirement for working capital over the life of the project, the *additional* investments should be included at the time they will take place. The total recovered by the liquidation of the working capital (which for some specific stocks, such as fashion products, may be zero) will be shown as a cash inflow at the end of the project.

One immediate problem of this type of project is how to assess the value of the property at the end of the ten-year period, and this requires considerable management judgement. It may also be one of the critical assumptions for the project and so we would do quite a lot of sensitivity analysis to see how different values at the end of the project (normally referred to as residual values) would affect the financial viability and this is considered in detail later in the chapter. For this example we are assuming that the company just receives back the investment cost of £10 million at the end of the ten years, and project A is summarized below:

Invest   £10 million freehold property
        £ 4 million additional stocks
        ——————
        £14 million

Annual cash inflows	£ 3 million for 10 years
Recovery at end	£10 million freehold property
	£ 4 million stocks sold
	£14 million

The payback calculation is quite simple; the cash outflow of £14 million takes place at the start of the project (the start point is conventionally known as year 0) and we then receive a cash inflow at the rate of £3 million per year. Therefore it takes four and two-thirds years to get back our £14 million, and this is the payback period.

We ignore, for this payback calculation, the additional cash which will be generated over the remaining five and one-third years of the project, and the fact that we will also receive back the £14 million at the end of ten years. We also do not take into account the decreasing monetary value of our constant cash-flow stream because of having to wait for over four years to get the last amount needed to complete the payback period.

Project B

Project B is quite different and requires an investment of £10 million in plant and machinery to make an existing product more efficiently by automating the process, and hence reducing the labour cost significantly. The new automated process requires an additional investment in specialized working capital of £4 million and we are making a conservative assumption that we only get back half of our investment (£2 million) in working capital at the end of the project. For project B the economic life will be controlled by the life of the existing product and the existing plant used to make it, and in this case the future life expectancy is only five years. It is most unlikely that the new plant and machinery will have any residual value at the end of this period. Project B, which is summarized below, will increase our cash inflows by more than project A, namely £5 million per year against £3 million, but only for the five-year life.

Invest	£10 million plant and machinery
	£ 4 million working capital
	£14 million
Annual profits	£ 3 million for five years
add back depreciation	£ 2 million for five years
Annual cash inflow	£ 5 million for five years
Recovery at end	£ 2 million working capital

These cash inflows can be reconciled to the accounting profit shown by the project which are £3 million per year, but these profits will be calculated after charging the depreciation necessary to write-off the investment (£10 million) in plant and machinery over the five-year life. Using our standard method of depreciating the cost evenly over the life of the asset discussed in detail in Part Two, this means that a depreciation expense of £2 million is included in the annual profit and loss account.

We have already established that depreciation does not affect the cash flow of the business and therefore the cash generated by the project is not just the £3 million profit but is £5 million (£3 million profit + £2 million depreciation expense.)

The payback period calculation is again straightforward. We have invested £14 million at year 0, but this time we generate £5 million per year of cash inflow from the project. The payback is therefore achieved after 2.8 years, which is considerably quicker than the 4.67 years calculated for project A. Using payback period as our decision criterion would therefore argue for project B to be undertaken rather than project A, but project A will generate cash inflows for longer and also will enable a larger cash inflow to be recovered at the end of the project.

Project C
We do have another possible investment, project C, which also requires £14 million of expenditure, but this involves launching a new service into a market segment where the company is not yet represented. Heavy launch marketing costs will be incurred and it will take time to gain market share and make the new service profitable. To simplify the calculations we are assuming all the investment in fixed assets and working capital is spent at the beginning of the project, whereas some of it would be phased in relation to sales growth and the opening of new branches, etc. as required (particularly any investment in debtors).

The expenditure is £10 million on fixed assets, including office equipment and telecommunications support and £4 million for net working capital, and the assumed life of the project is ten years. At the end of the project, the fixed assets will have nil residual value but the investment in net working capital will be recovered in full. However, the slower sales growth and the high marketing support mean that the project will make an accounting loss for the first two years, then break-even in year three, before becoming significantly profitable at £10 million per year for the last seven years. As for project B, we need to adjust the accounting profit figures to cash flows by adding back the annual depreciation expense; the fixed assets have a cost of £10 million and an economic life of ten years, therefore the annual depreciation expense is £1 million, under straight-line depreciation rules, and project C is summarized below.

£ millions	Year 0	Year 1	Year 2	Year 3	Years 4–9	Year 10
Invest in fixed assets	(10)	–	–	–	–	–
Invest in working capital	(4)	–	–	–	–	–

£ millions	Year	Year	Year	Year	Years	Year
Recovery of working capital	–	–	–	–	–	4
Annual profits	–	(3)	(2)	–	10	10
add back depreciation	–	1	1	1	1	1
Annual cash flow	(14)	(2)	(1)	1	11	15

The payback period calculation is slightly more complicated in this example because the overall cash invested actually increases in years one and two, because of the losses made by the project. Therefore whereas at year 0 the investment is £14 million it has increased to £17 million (£14 million + £2 million + £1 million) by the end of year two, and it is only in year three that our investment starts to be recouped and then only by £1 million. In years four and five we forecast receiving £11 million each year, and so by half way through year five we have received more than our initial investment back from the project (£17 million − £1 million − £11 million = £5 million outstanding at the beginning of year five). The precise payback period is 4.45 years which is very slightly better than project A but not as good as project B. Project C will generate very substantial cash inflows for a further 5.55 years after recovering this initial investment.

By comparing these projects, as is done in Table 7.1, it is possible to highlight the main criticisms of the payback period: it does not take account of cash received after payback has been achieved; the method gives equal weighting to cash flows received in year five and in year one; and, if only payback criteria are used to make major capital project investments, short-term investments are likely to be undertaken. This method does illustrate the period over which the business has to fund any project and hence indicates the period of major financial risk, and these points are shown in Figure 7.2.

Table 7.1   *Payback period comparisons*

Project	A	B	C
Investment	£14 million	£14 million	£14 million
Life of project	10 years	5 years	10 years
Annual cash flow	£3 million	£5 million	*variable* £(3) million – £11 million
Recovery at end	£14 million	£2 million	£4 million
Payback period	4.67 years	2.80 years	4.45 years

Criterion	The shorter the payback period the better.
Advantages	(1) It is very simple to calculate
	(2) Gives some weighting to timing of cash flow as earlier cash inflows will decrease payback period.
	(3) Measures financial exposure period of company.
Disadvantages	(1) Takes no account of size of cashflows after initial investment recovered.
	(2) Does not adequately reflect timing importance of cash flows.
	(3) If used as sole evaluation method, makes short-term investments more attractive.

Figure 7.2   *Summary of payback period*

Time value of money

To make any cash flow comparisons more relevant as financial decision-making techniques it is necessary to reflect the real value of the cash flows in each period. This requires cash flows taking place at different points in time to be made directly comparable. It is not possible to add up cash receivable both this year and in ten years time and get a meaningful answer; in the same way as it is meaningless to add up amounts in sterling, dollars, and deutschmarks. If we convert these different currencies to *any one* currency, the amounts become directly comparable and adding them up is quite practical and straightforward. The same principle can be applied to money values at different points in time, we need a conversion process to bring them to the same basis, that is, a time related rate of exchange.

We do have, on a personal basis, this equivalent rate of exchange which enables us to decide now whether to save, spend, or borrow to increase our current spending ability. Effectively we are comparing the value of £1 today with an amount to be received (if we are saving) or to be repaid (if we are borrowing) at a point in the future. If we were to project forward into the future our current £1 we could arrive at an equivalent value to compare with the cash flows forecast to occur at that future time. This we achieve by applying compound interest to today's money.

Another simplified example may be helpful: suppose we are considering buying a personal computer for £1000. We could buy the machine now or we could defer the purchase until next year and invest the £1000 for 12 months. If the current rate of interest is 10 per cent per year, we would earn £100 interest income and in 12 months' time we would have £1100 to buy a computer. We can now compare this £1100 value with the expected price of personal computers in 12 months' time, and if we believe that computer prices will rise less than 10 per cent in this period, we can be financially better off by deferring the purchase. (We have ignored the benefit which might be achieved by having the use of the computer during this 12-month period and which represents the opportunity cost of deferring the purchase.)

We have effectively converted today's money (£1000) into an equivalent value (£1100) for one year in the future by using a rate of interest. This logic can be applied to all the cash flows in our three examples; to make the different years comparable we would have to project the cash flows forward to the same time, and the most obvious point is the end of the project. Thus in project A, we would apply compound interest to the £14 million investment for ten years and compound interest to the annual cash inflows for different periods ranging from nine years to nil, so as to bring all these amounts to their equivalent year ten values. Compound interest means that we apply an annual interest rate to the cash flow for each year, and we earn interest on previously earned interest as well. For example, the £14 million invested in year 0 will earn interest of £1.4 million at an interest rate of 10 per cent in year one. Thus at the end of year one we would have £15.4 million and the interest for year two is calculated on this balance of £15.4 million, which effectively 'compounds' interest on previously earned interest. The calculations showing the compound interest projections for project A are shown in Table 7.2 and can be seen to consist of multiplying the previous year's figure by 1.10 to compound forward one year. Therefore to compound forward ten years, we multiply the year 0 figure by $(1.10)^{10}$ or 2.59 – this gives 14 million × 2.59 or a £36.3 million investment in year ten values.

The cash inflows at the end of the project (sale of the buildings and recovery of the working capital) do not require any adjustments as they are already in year ten values. This technique is used by a few companies and is known as 'compounding to horizon', but it makes it difficult to compare projects. In our cases projects A and C have ten-year lives and are thus comparable, but project B has only a five-year life and its projected forward cash flows would thus not be on the same basis as our other projects. Another problem is that values projected forward ten years or so are not very meaningful to most people, whereas we do have an idea of relative values *today*.

A better way of making the cash flows comparable therefore is to bring all the cash flows back to 'today's values' rather than to project cash flows forward. The technique uses the same logic but in reverse: the objective is to find an equivalent 'present value' for any future cash flow. Instead of applying compounded interest we apply a *negative interest rate* to reduce the future value to its value now. This negative interest rate (or *discount*

Table 7.2 *Compound interest illustration*

Project A	Year 0	Year 1	Year 2	Year 3	(using 10% interest rate) £ millions Year 4	Year 5	Year 6	Year 7	Year 8	Year 9	Year 10
Initial investment	(14)	(15.4)	(16.9)	(18.6)	(20.5)	(22.5)	(24.8)	(27.3)	(30.0)	(33.0)	(36.3)
Cash inflows											
Year 1		3	3.3	3.6	4.0	4.4	4.8	5.3	5.8	6.4	7.2
Year 2			3	3.3	3.6	4.0	4.4	4.8	5.3	5.8	6.4
Year 3				3	3.3	3.6	4.0	4.4	4.8	5.3	5.8
Year 4					3	3.3	3.6	4.0	4.4	4.8	5.3
Year 5						3	3.3	3.6	4.0	4.4	4.8
Year 6							3	3.3	3.6	4.0	4.4
Year 7								3	3.3	3.6	4.0
Year 8									3	3.3	3.6
Year 9										3	3.3
Year 10											3
Sale of property and working capital recovery											14
Net cash flow in year 10 values (also known as *the terminal value*)											25.4

Conclusion Project is a good investment at an interest rate of 10%.

rate, as it is called) is therefore the annual cost associated with having to wait to receive the cash.

In project A we are expecting to receive £3 million each year for ten years, and it is clear that the £3 million received this year is more valuable than the £3 million received in year ten. To decide how much more valuable we must make the figures directly comparable and we can do this by applying our negative interest rate idea. We wish to know how much cash invested today at our chosen discount rate (say 10 per cent) will give us £3 million in one year's time, and so on.

If we were compounding forward the calculation would be easy:

for example, £1000 today × 1.10 ➤ £1,100 in one year
(at 10 per cent interest rate)

The calculation is just as easy in reverse, but instead of multiplying the 'present value' we divide the 'future' value;

for example, £1000 in one year ➤ $\dfrac{£1000}{1.10}$ today or £909.09p

This tells us that at a 10 per cent discount rate the *present value* of £1000 to be received or paid in year one is £909.09p. This can be easily verified by doing the forward calculation to find how much £909.09p invested at 10 per cent interest rate would be worth in one year's time. It would earn interest of £90.909p which makes the total worth £999.999p, that is £1000 (allowing for rounding).

If we apply this technique to our £3 million annual cash inflows then at our 10 per cent discount rate the year one cash flow has a present value of:

£3 million at the end of year one ➤ $\dfrac{£3 \text{ million}}{1.10}$ today or £2 727 272.72p

You may have noticed that we are treating the £3 million as arriving at the end of the year when, in reality, it would be earned progressively over the year. This simplifying assumption of taking cash inflows at a point in time is quite common, but can be removed by using an adjusted discount rate for cash flows received over the year.)

We have cash flows each year for ten years and so we need more than a one-year adjustment. This can be achieved by bringing cash flows back one year at a time, so that £3 million receivable at the end of year two could be regarded as having an equivalent value of £2 727 272.72p at the end of year one (this is using the same calculations as for year one back to today). We want to know the equivalent value now, and we can establish this by doing the calculation again, that is,

£3 million at the end of year two ➤ $\dfrac{£3 \text{ million}}{1.10}$ at the end of year one

Therefore $\dfrac{£3 \text{ million}}{1.10} \times \dfrac{1}{1.10}$ today ➤ *present value of £2 479 338.8*

Clearly we do not need to do the intermediate calculation and the formula can be generalized as:

£X at the end of year two ➤ *present value of* $\dfrac{£X}{1.10^2}$

or if we allow *t* to represent the year and *r* to represent the rate of discount we get:

£X at end of year *t* ➤ *present value of* $\dfrac{£X}{(1 + r)^t}$

Therefore to calculate the present value of any future cash flow we need to know the projected value of the cash flow (£X) and the year when it will occur (time *t*) and we need to decide on a rate of discount to be used (*r*). Of these the forecast cash flows of the specific project will be used to estimate the cash flows and their timing, as shown by our examples, and the company will establish the desired rate of discount to be applied to these future cash flows.

Setting the discount rate

At the personal financial level it may be adequate to use our opportunity cost of funds, which may in some circumstances be our effective interest rate, as the discount factor to compare alternatives. This effective interest rate will be different depending on whether the individual is a net saver (for example, deposit holder at a bank), or a net borrower (for example, from a bank). Even if deposits and borrowings were at the same bank the effective interest rate would be different in each case because banks make their profit by lending at a higher interest rate than they pay to people depositing cash with them. Businesses can also either have net savings or be borrowers, but their situation is often more complex as they have many different sources of funds, and their choice of discount rate consequently needs careful analysis. We need to remember the reason for doing these financial evaluations and for using this sophisticated technique which allows for the different time values of money.

The company is trying to choose among alternative ways of investing its available funds, and to compare all these alternatives on a similar basis. Therefore the discount rate should logically be related to the return expected on these available funds and this will not necessarily be the rate of interest currently being charged for borrowed cash. As we have already seen in Part Two the capital employed in any business is composed of owners' funds (shareholders' funds) and borrowed funds (debt) and the overall return being achieved by the business effectively represents a weighted average of the interest rate and the return on shareholders' funds. We have also established that it is only sensible for a company to borrow funds when, by doing so, the return on share- holders' funds is increased and this only happens when the return on shareholders' funds exceeds the prevailing rate of interest. Therefore most businesses will demand a return on new investments considerably in excess of prevailing interst rates, and thus higher discount rates will be applied to forecast cash flows.

The discount rate should include the time value of money as well as the risk associated with the overall business, because a higher risk demands a higher financial return, but it is important that the company is consistent in the way it deals with inflation. The time value of money is made up of the real cost associated with having to defer present consumption and the risk that the investment may not work so that the future forecast inflow does not materialize, together with the declining purchasing power of money caused by inflation. Therefore if inflation is forecast for our future planning period, it would seem logical that it must be included in our discount rate to bring the future cash flows back to *today's real values*. This is true only if the future inflation has been included in the forecast cash flows which are being discounted, other- wise we are taking out something which we had not included in the first place. If inflation exists, the absolute levels of sales revenues and costs will increase over time and thus, if we are able to maintain our relative profit margins, so will absolute profits, and cash flows will increase in absolute terms as well. Many forecasts are done in today's money terms and so cash flows are not increased in money values to reflect the impact of inflation. This is true of our three examples where we have projected cash inflows and outflows in today's money terms and not at future inflation inclusive levels. If this is so, the discount rate used must reflect only the *real* return demanded by the business, whereas if the forecast cash flows include inflation so must the discount factor.

If this matched basis is not followed the business will make some very silly investment decisions based on false evidence, as shown below, but provided either matched system is applied the evaluation will be sensibly consistent. Below is illustrated the possible ways of forecasting cash flows, namely with or without inflation being included, and the similar possibilities for discount rates.

		Discount rate	
		Real	Inflation inclusive
Forecast cash flows	Real	√	X
	Inflation inclusive	X	√

If a company includes inflation in its forecast project cash flows but excludes inflation from the discount rate used to bring those future cash flows back to their present values, it is likely to find it very easy apparently to justify proposed projects. As net cash inflows tend to be received later than investments are made in the project, the project will benefit from inflows which are probably increased faster than they are being discounted; if inflation levels are high this will certainly be true. These justifications are completely invalid because the cash flows and discount rates are inconsistently matched.

A simple numerical example may make this clearer: Assume that inflation is forecast to be 6 per cent for the period of the project and the company demands a risk-related return from this type of project of 10 per cent in real terms. If the company builds inflation into its forecast cash flows it should use an inflation inclusive discount rate of 16 per cent, whereas if the forecast cash flows are prepared net of the impact of inflation only, the real discount rate of 10 per cent should be applied.

Similarly useless results will be obtained if inflation is excluded from the project cash flows but is included in the discount rate applied to the cash flows. In this case the company would find it very difficult to justify any new investments as it is effectively applying a very high 'real' discount rate to the 'real' cash flows of the project, and they are again inconsistently matched.

Logically matching either real cash flows to a real discount rate or inflation inclusive cash flows to a discount rate including a consistent forecast of inflation will give a similar and accurate picture of the financial return from the project after taking into account the time value of money. This may appear that, by using real cash flows and real discount rates, we can ignore future rates of inflation which would greatly simplify project evaluation but unfortunately this is not true. If a company wishes to use real cash flows, it must adjust the present-day cash flows for the net impact of inflation so that they can accurately be described as 'real' cash flows. For example, if rents are fixed in cash terms for five years under a lease the real rent cost is decreasing due to inflation; and if wage costs have been rising at 2–3 per cent per year in real terms and this is expected to continue, this real change in costs must be included in the annual real cash projections. If present-day cash flows are used unadjusted the company is assuming that revenues and costs are uniformly unaffected by inflation, which is very rarely true.

As the company is trying to relate the returns on future investment back to the expectations of its shareholders, and its published financial statements include the impacts of inflation, it is probably easier to use both inflation inclusive cash flow forecasts and an inflation linked discount rate.

Many companies use a discount rate which is set by reference to the return being achieved by the overall business at present, their argument being that by setting the discount rate at their present achievement level and thus requiring new investments to beat this rate, these investments should enhance the future financial performance of the business. In this way the capital project evaluation process can automatically ration the allocation of capital to new projects, but as is shown below the comparison between present and future performance is not completely straightforward.

Discounting: introduction

By using discount rates to calculate present values we can make future cash flows directly equivalent and these can then be compared to produce a project evaluation process which does fully allow for the time value of money. One way of using discounting is to calculate the discounted payback period which uses the present values of the cash flows to compute the period taken to recover the initial investment. The company has to select a discount rate (often called the 'criterion' or 'hurdle' rate) which is applied to all the cash flow projections, and thus removes one of the principal objections to the use of simple or crude payback calculations. This technique still has the major objection of not taking into account any cash flows received after the initial investment is recovered and is thus less useful than full discounting techniques, such as net present value (NPV) and internal rate of return (IRR), which are considered later in the chapter. However discounted payback will be used as an easy introduction to the use of discount factors and it is used by many large companies as part of their investment decision process.

If this technique is applied to our three projects at a discount rate of 10 per cent, we can see how the evaluations change. To do this we need to generate the discount factors to apply to each year's cash flows and this is very simple. (Discount factors are the numbers used to multiply future cash flows so as to reduce them to their present values.) As already illustrated we apply a negative interest rate to each year of deferral and so by dividing any year's factor by 1.10 we get the following year's factor (if we were using a 20 per cent discount rate, we would divide by 1.20 each year, and so on). The relevant factors are shown in Table 7.3 below:

Table 7.3   *Discount rate of 10%*

Year	Discount factor	Comments on calculation
0	1.000	Year 0 has no need of discounting
1	0.9091	$\dfrac{1}{1.10} \rightarrow$ present value
2	0.8264	$\dfrac{1}{1.10^2}$ or $\dfrac{0.9091}{1.10} \rightarrow$ present value
3	0.7513	$\dfrac{1}{1.10^3}$ or $\dfrac{0.8264}{1.10}$ or $\dfrac{0.9091}{1.10^2} \rightarrow$ present value
4	0.6830	$\dfrac{1}{1.10^4}$ or $\dfrac{0.7513}{1.10}$ or $\dfrac{0.8264}{1.10^2}$ or $\dfrac{0.9091}{1.10^3} \rightarrow$ present value
5	0.6209	$\dfrac{1}{1.10^5}$ (Similar basis to above)
6	0.5645	$\dfrac{1}{1.10^6}$
7	0.5131	$\dfrac{1}{1.10^7}$
8	0.4665	$\dfrac{1}{1.10^8}$
9	0.4241	$\dfrac{1}{1.10^9}$
10	0.3855	$\dfrac{1}{1.10^{10}}$

Although this is very easy to work out on a pocket calculator, most companies use preprinted sets of tables (see Appendix 1, page 425), and which give all the factors for each year and each possible discount rate. The tables are very easy to use: to find the discount factor for any year and any discount rate, you simply go to the intersection of the appropriate year row and rate column. For example, using Appendix 1 (page 425) the discount factor for year seven at a discount rate of 25 per cent is found in the seventh row of the 25 per cent rate column and can be seen to be 0.210. Readers should familiarize themselves with the use of the tables by looking up random combinations of years and discount rates before continuing. Also, it is good practice to look up all the discount factors given in the text so as to check that you know on what the calculations are based.

Table 7.4 restates the cash flows of our three projects and shows their timings which now need to be adjusted by calculating the present values of the future cash flows. Calculating the discounted payback period for project A is straightforward. The present value of our investment is £14 million as the money is spent now and we recover £3 million each year, but the present value of each £3 million is declining. The present values are shown in column 3 of Table 7.5 and can be seen to be declining; for example, year one's present value is £2.727 million whereas by year five the present value has decreased to £1.863 million. The cumulative present value of the cash flows is shown in column 4 and this reduces from the initial investment (cash outflow) of £14 million as the present values of each year's cash inflows are added to the total. The initial investment has been recovered, after allowing for the time value of money, when the cumulative present value is equal to zero. If it is negative at the end of one year and positive at the end of the next, the discounted payback period can be estimated by pro-rating the cash flows received in the final year to see when the cumulative present value became zero.

Table 7.4　*Cash flow summaries of projects A, B and C*

Project	A	B	C
Investment Year 0	£14 million	£14 million	£14 million
Cash inflows year 1	£3 million	£5 million	£(2 million)
Cash inflows year 2	£3 million	£5 million	£(1 million)
Cash inflows year 3	£3 million	£5 million	£1 million
Cash inflows year 4	£3 million	£5 million	£11 million
Cash inflows year 5	£3 million	£7 million	£11 million
Cash inflows year 6	£3 million	–	£11 million
Cash inflows year 7	£3 million	–	£11 million
Cash inflows year 8	£3 million	–	£11 million
Cash inflows year 9	£3 million	–	£11 million
Cash inflows year 10	£17 million	–	£15 million

For project A, Table 7.5 shows the cumulative present value to be £(0.934 million) at the end of year six, but to be £0.605 million at the end of year seven. The present value of the cash flows received in year seven is shown as £1.539 million and £0.934 million of this was needed to repay the original investment. Assuming, as we normally do for this purpose, that the cash flows are evenly spread through the year, we can estimate that it took £0.934 million of year seven for the initial investment to be

Table 7.5   *Project A: discounted payback*

Year	(1) Gross cash flow	(2) Discount factor	(3) Present value	(4) Cumulative present value
0	£(14 m)	1	£(14 m)	£(14 m)
1	£3 m	0.9091	£2.727 m	£(11.273) m
2	£3 m	0.8264	£2.479 m	£(8.794) m
3	£3 m	0.7513	£2.254 m	£(6.540) m
4	£3 m	0.6830	£2.049 m	£(4.491) m
5	£3 m	0.6209	£1.863 m	£(2.628) m
6	£3 m	0.5645	£1.694 m	£(0.934) m
7	£3 m	0.5131	£1.539 m	£0.605 m
	£7 m		£0.605 m	

Column (3) = column (1) × column (2).
Column (4) is last year's balance plus this year's present value.
Discounted payback period = 6.60 years.

repaid. Therefore the discounted payback period for project A is six years + 1.539 years or 6.6 years.

The detailed computation illustrated in Table 7.5 shows that the discounted payback period is 6.6 years compared to the original non-discounted calculation of 4.67 years. The present value of the cash inflows in year seven can be seen to be only half that of the same inflow received now and at far higher rates of discount the drop in value is even more dramatic (for example, at 20 per cent discount rate, cash flows four years hence are worth less than half their face value when expressed in today's equivalent present values).

The same calculations are shown in Tables 7.6 and 7.7 for each of the other projects and readers should do these calculations and check their answers with those given. The resultant discounted payback periods are: project B: 3.46 years, and project C: 5.25 years.

Table 7.6   *Project B: discounted payback*

Year	Gross cash flow	Discount factor	Present value	Cumulative present value
0	£(14 m)	1	£(14 m)	£(14 m)
1	£5 m	0.9091	£4.545 m	£(9.455) m
2	£5 m	0.8264	£4.132 m	£(5.323) m
3	£5 m	0.7513	£3.756 m	£(1.567) m
4	£5 m	0.6830	£3.415 m	£1.848 m
	£6 m		£1.848 m	

Discounted payback period = 3.46 years.

Table 7.7   *Project C: discounted payback*

Year	Gross cash flow	Discount factor	Present value	Cumulative present value
0	£(14 m)	1	£(14 m)	£(14 m)
1	(£2 m)	0.9091	£(1.818) m	£(15.818) m
2	(£1 m)	0.8264	£(0.826) m	£(16.644) m
3	£1 m	0.7513	£0.751 m	£(15.893) m
4	£11 m	0.6830	£7.513 m	£(8.380) m
5	£11 m	0.6209	£6.830 m	£(1.550) m
6	£11 m	0.5645	£6.209 m	£4.659 m
	£17 m		£4.659 m	

Discounted payback period = 5.25 years.

These discounted payback calculations give the same rankings (that is, B, C, A) as our original classifications, but project C has moved considerably nearer to project B and project A is now a poor third, as can be seen in the comparison below.

Project	A	B	C
Simple payback	4.67 years	2.8 years	4.45 years
Discounted payback	6.6 years	3.46 years	5.25 years

However, as already mentioned the technique still suffers from the major criticism that it does not include the impact of cash flows after the investment has been recovered. The discounting technique makes it very easy to include this and most companies now use discounting methods which include all the cash flows from the project as their main capital project decision criteria.

Discounting methods

Net present value (NPV)

These methods of evaluation simply use all the cash flows from the project and adjust them to their present values by applying the appropriate discount factors. Each cash flow item therefore becomes directly comparable and the net position for the project can be calculated. There are two similar methods used to evaluate projects, net present value (NPV) and internal rate of return (IRR), and both are considered in this section. The net present value method requires the company to determine a discount rate which it will apply to the cash flows of projects so as to compare present values of those cash flows. If the present value of the cash inflows exceeds the present value of the cash outflows having applied the company's selected discount rate, the project is showing a positive cash flow return for the business. The higher the positive value of this net present value the better, but if the net present value is negative the project does not achieve the target return set by the discount rate applied by the company.

Before applying this technique to our examples we can simplify the calculation quite considerably. When working out the discounted pay-back periods we multiplied *equal* annual cash flows by different annual discount factors and then added up the answers. If we had added up the discount factors first we would have got the same answer, only by doing fewer calculations. Again companies have these cumulative discount factors, which are calculated by adding together the appropriate discount factors for the years of constant cash flow, preprinted in tables (Appendix 2, page 426), and these make the calculations even faster. These cumulative discount factors can only be used with constant annual cash flows and, since an annuity is the name for such a constant annual flow, these factors are often called annuity factors. Redoing the calculation for project A and using the annuity factor for years one to seven at a 10 per cent discount rate from Appendix 2 gives the following simpler layout:

Year	Cash flow	Discount factor	Present value	Cumulative present value
0	£(14 million)	1	£(14 million)	£(14 million)
1–7	£3 million	4.868	£14.605 million	£0.605 million

We can now calculate the net present value for each of the projects, using our existing 10 per cent discount rate and the simplifying annuity factors where the cash flows are constant from year to year, and these calculations are shown in Table 7.8. As can be seen from this table the use of annuity factors can dramatically reduce the number of calculations needed when the annual cash flows are constant as in projects A and B. Even in project C the cash flows from years four to ten are constant at £11 million (if we ignore the recovery of working capital in year ten and do that calculation separately), and we can still use annuity factors but with some adjustments. We want an annuity factor for years four to ten and not as in previous examples, years one to ten. We can achieve this by using the annuity factor for years one to ten (which at 10 per cent is 6.145), and deducting from this the annuity factor for years one to three (which at 10 per cent is 2.487), which leaves us with the annuity factor for years four to ten as being 3.658. This calculation works because annuity

Table 7.8 *Net present values of projects A, B and C (at discount rate of 10%)*

Year	Discount factor (including annuity factors)	Project A Cash flow (million)	Project A Present value (million)	Project B Cash flow (million)	Project B Present value (million)	Project C Cash flow (million)	Project C Present value (million)
0	1	£(14)	£(14)	£(14)	£(14)	£(14)	£(14)
1	0.909	–		–		£(2)	£(1.818)
2	0.826	–		–		£(1)	£(0.826)
3	0.751	–		–		£1	£0.751
1–5	3.791	–		£5	£18.955	–	–
5	0.621	–		£2	£1.242	–	–
1–10	6.145	£3	£18.435	–			
4–10	3.658	–		–		£11	£40.238
10	0.386	£14	£5.404	–		£4	£1.544
Net present value			£9.839	–	£6.197	–	£25.889

factors are calculated by adding together the discount factors for the years involved, and therefore shorter periods of annuity cash flow can be computed by deducting one annuity factor from another.

Comparing the results of this evaluation shows that project C is now significantly the leader as its higher cash flows from years four to ten give it a significantly greater net present value (NPV) than the other projects. Also project A is to be preferred to project B as reclaiming the original investment in year ten more than outweighs the higher cash flow generated by project B but for a shorter period.

Under this technique all the cash flows are included and hence influence the result but obviously the timing of the cash flow has a dramatic impact on its significance. One problem raised against this method of evaluation is that it can be difficult to make decisions based on the absolute size of the NPV. This is not so in our example as all our projects require an initial investment of £14 million, but if we had a project D with a NPV of £50 million and a project E with a NPV of £15 million, we might at first sight want to do D but not E.

If we also knew that project D required an investment of £100 million whereas project E required only £5 million the situation is likely to be reversed, as the relative return on E is much greater than that on D. We need some relative measure of NPV to help us rank projects with different initial investment requirements. The most sensible way to do this is to calculate the profitability index, shown below for each project which compares the present value of future cash inflows to the initial investment required, by looking at the return per £ of investment.

$$\text{Profitability index} = \frac{\text{Present value of future cash flows}}{\text{Initial investment}}$$

We can now compare the relative returns of our initial five projects, including a further two additional possibilities (projects F and G), as shown in Table 7.9.

Table 7.9   *Comparison of seven projects*

Project	A	B	C	D	E	F	G
Initial investment	£(14 m)	£(14 m)	£(14 m)	£(100 m)	£(5 m)	£(50 m)	£(17 m)
Net present value	£9.8 m	£6.2 m	£25.9 m	£50 m	£15 m	£30 m	£10 m
Present value of future cash flows	£23.8 m	£20.2 m	£39.9 m	£150 m	£20 m	£80 m	£27 m
Profitability index	1.7	1.44	2.85	1.5	4	1.6	1.59

If we have unlimited funds available for long-term investment at a cost of 10 per cent we would want to do all the projects as they all show a positive return at 10 per cent which would involve a total investment of £214 million; but most companies have finite resources. Therefore there may be a need for an opportunity cost assessment of which projects will most enhance the future financial performance of the business. If, in our company, the maximum available for investment is £100 million this year we could spend all of it on project D, which would generate a NPV of £50 million. This is the highest individual NPV of any project but it does not have the highest profitability index by any means. If we consider how else we could invest £100 million we can, in fact, do considerably better by selecting those projects with the highest profitability indices as shown in Table 7.10.

Table 7.10   *Ranking of five projects using profitability index (PI)*

Project	Profitability index	Investment		Net present value
E	4	5 m		15 m
C	2.85	14 m		25.9 m
A	1.7	14 m		9.8 m
F	1.6	50 m		30 m
G	1.59	17 m		10 m
		Total	100 m	Total 90.7 m

By selecting the best available projects we can generate a NPV total of £90.7 million from our available £100 million investment rather than the £50 million generated by project D. Thus using profitability indices can be very valuable to any company as it focuses investment resources on those projects which produce the maximum return per £ of cash invested and is particularly useful where capital rationing has to take place. Merely selecting the project with the highest NPV may not give the best answer.

Internal rate of return (IRR)

There is another, increasingly popular, way of trying to compute some relative measure of return for alternative projects but this uses a very different basis of calculation from the profitability index. Instead of selecting one rate of discount and applying it to each project's cash flows, this technique sets out to find what rate of discount will make the present value of the inflows equal to the present value of the outflows. An alternative way of defining this *internal rate of return* (also described as the time-adjusted rate of return) is that rate of discount which generates a NPV of zero. Rather than arriving at an answer which is an absolute value (NPV) we arrive instead at a percentage discount rate and the criterion becomes: the higher the percentage the better the project.

The actual calculation requires a number of calculations using different rates of discount in order to find the internal rate of return for the project. Computer software can now do the necessary computations very quickly whereas previously this could be time-consuming for large complex projects. This accounts for the growing popularity of the technique. The logic is again straightforward; we try a rate of discount and calculate the NPV – if it is positive we try a higher rate, if it is negative we try a lower rate. By a process of iteration (that is, trying different rates and calculating NPVs for each rate tried), we get closer and closer to the internal rate of return (IRR) for the project. The basis of discounted cash flow is therefore fundamental to this technique and there are few technical and financial differences in the way it operates, but it can show different results.

If we wanted to do the calculation for project A we might try a discount rate of 25 per cent as we already know the IRR is above 10 per cent, since the project's NPV is positive when a discount rate of 10 per cent was used. The calculation for a discount rate of 25 per cent for project A is given in Table 7.11.

This calculation tells us that the IRR is between 10 per cent and 25 per cent because the NPV at 25 per cent is negative. We can approximately calculate the answer by linear interpolation, which pro-rates the change in NPV between the two discount rates used (the lower one giving a positive NPV, and the higher one giving a negative NPV) to find out

Table 7.11 *Discounted cash flow: project A at 25%*

Year	Gross cash flow	Discount factor	Present value
0	£(14 m)	1	£(14 m)
1–10	£3 m	3.571	£10.713 m
10	£14 m	0.107	£1.498 m
		Net present value	£(1.789) m

where the NPV is zero – the calculation uses the same basis as that for calculating exactly when, during the year, the discounted payback occurred. For our example of project A, the calculation is as follows:

If NPV $= +£9.8$ million at 10%
and NPV $= -£1.789$ million at 25%

$$\text{NPV} = 0 \text{ at } 10\% + \frac{9.8}{9.8+1.789} \times 15\% \text{ or } 22.68\%$$

where the change in NPV is from £9.8 million to −£1.789 million or a movement of £(9.8 + 1.789) million for an increase in discount rate of 15 per cent. Assuming that the decrease in NPV is evenly spread over the range (of 15 per cent), which is not quite true mathematically, the NPV will be zero at the rate given above.

Another alternative method of determining the internal rate of return approximately is to graph the relationship between NPV and discount rate. If we assume a straight-line relationship, which is the same as was assumed for the linear interpolation method above, we can plot the line from the two points which have been established for the discount rates of 10 per cent and 25 per cent, as is shown below.

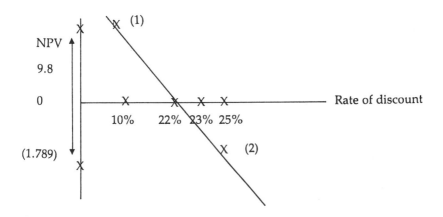

Point (1) is given by the NPV of £9.8 million at 10 per cent discount rate and point (2) is given by the NPV of −£1.789 million at 25 per cent discount rate. Joining the two points shows that the line cuts the axis (which is a NPV of zero) at a discount rate of just over 22 per cent but below 23 per cent.

Therefore the IRR for project A is around 22 per cent and this can easily be confirmed by doing the computation in detail at a discount rate of 22 per cent, as is shown in Table 7.12.

Table 7.12   *Discounted cash flow: project A at 22%*

Year	Cash flow	Discount factor	Present value
0	£(14 m)	1	£(14 m)
1–10	£3 m	3.923	£11.77 m
10	£14 m	0.137	£1.92 m
		Net present value	£(0.31) m

This more accurate calculation shows that the IRR for project A is, in fact, slightly below 22 per cent, because at 22 per cent discount rate the NPV is negative. (The linear interpolation technique will only give approximate results, because it assumes a straight-line movement in NPV over the range of discount rates, and the relationship would in fact generate a curve, not a straight line.)

Table 7.13   *Project B: Internal rate of return calculation (discounted cash flow at 25%)*

Year	Cash flow	Discount factors at 25%	Present value
0	£(14 m)	1	£(14 m)
1–5	£5 m	2.689	£13.445 m
5	£2 m	0.328	£0.656 m
		Net present value	£0.101 m

Table 7.14   *Project C: Internal rate of return calculation (discounted cash flow at 28%)*

Year	Cash flow	Discount factors at 28%	Present value
0	£(14 m)	1	£(14 m)
1	£(2 m)	0.781	£(1.562) m
2	£(1 m)	0.610	£(0.610) m
3	£1 m	£0.477	£0.477 m
4–10	£11 m	1.401	£15.411 m
10	£4 m	0.085	£0.34 m
		Net present value	£0.056 m

If we do the same calculations for projects B and C we get IRRs of 25 per cent and 28 per cent respectively from Tables 7.13 and 7.14. We now have several differing criteria for comparing our three projects (Table 7.15).

These produce different rankings for the projects, as shown in Table 7.16, which reflect the weightings given to various aspects by the alternative techniques. Project B is preferred on the payback criteria because of its high short-term cash returns, but its shorter economic life makes it the least desirable under the NPV evaluation at 10 per cent

Table 7.15   *Project comparisons*

Project	A	B	C
Payback	4.67 years	2.8 years	4.45 years
Discounted payback	6.6 years	3.46 years	5.25 years
Net present value @ 10%	£9.8 million	£6.2 million	£25.9 million
Profitability index	1.7	1.44	2.85
Internal rate of return (IRR)	22%	25%	28%

Table 7.16   *Rankings of projects*

Projects	A	B	C
Payback	3	1	2
Discounted payback	3	1	2
Net present value @ 10%	2	3	1
Profitability index	2	3	1
Internal rate of return (IRR)	3	2	1

discount rate. Project C becomes much more attractive due to its high cash generation potential once the higher market share has been developed, and it has the best IRR as well.

Interestingly, project B has a higher IRR (25 per cent) than project A, although the position was reversed for NPVs at 10 per cent discount rate. This is caused by the higher discount factor which is applied to all the cash flows, and this dramatically reduces the present value of the investment recovery for project A, making this a much less important part of the project cash inflows (present value of the year ten inflows in project A falls from £5.404 million at 10 per cent discount rate to only £1.92 million at 22 per cent discount rate).

Higher rates of discount affect later cash flows very significantly and can therefore alter the relative attractiveness of different projects. This reduced impact of far ahead cash flows can be regarded as one of the great practical strengths of the discounted cash flow technique because it balances the lack of forecasting accuracy by reducing the real value of the future cash flows. Most companies can forecast most accurately (or, as some people would say, less inaccurately) in the short term and the level of certainty declines as the time period increases; fortunately, by applying the appropriate discount factor, the impact on the overall project declines as well. The problems caused to long-term projects by calculating IRRs have led many companies to use NPV and profitability indices as their prime decision criteria.

Allowing for risk

In order to do this, the company has to select a criterion or hurdle discount rate to be applied to all projects, but the *risks* associated with the different projects will not be uniform. If valid comparisons are to be made some allowance for different risk levels must be included in the evaluation. For example, project A could be said to be a relatively low risk project because the company is already in that market and if the particular shops are not successful the capital investment can be recovered by selling the freehold premises. Project C involves investing in a new market and places at risk not £14 million but a maximum of £17 million if the development expenditure is included, with no guarantee of success and little prospect for significant recovery of cash spent if the launch does not work. Therefore the risks associated with this project are greater, and a higher level of return will be required to compensate. How much more return is demanded will depend on the willingness of the particular company to accept risks, and differences between companies regarding risk aversion explain many of the different investment strategies employed within the same industry.

If a company is willing to accept a greater degree of risk than its competitors for the same level of return then it will be willing to invest in projects that the competition will reject, and different investment strategies will be seen in the same industry. This argument is based on the assumption that companies are able to calculate the degree of risk inherent in a particular project and set an appropriate target level of return (in the form of a higher or lower criterion rate of discount or required IRR) commensurate with that measured level of risk.

In textbooks on financial decision-making writers often distinguish between uncertainty and risk, although the division can become somewhat semantic and we will not allow it to interfere with our analysis.

Uncertainty is created because we cannot be certain what will happen in the future (in other words, we lack complete foresight) and, because all financial decisions involve estimates of future results, all decisions are made in conditions of greater or lesser uncertainty. Risk is distinguished from uncertainty only because we can, in the case of risk, identify the potential outcomes and measure the probability (degree of likelihood) of each of these potential outcomes taking place. Both terms imply the possibility of losses being incurred or smaller profits made than the anticipated or forecast profits, but risk also implies that a degree of action is required by managers to analyse the potential outcomes and to manage the risks, as well as managing the project. (No-one can manage uncertainty because, by definition, we do not know what may happen.)

One method of risk management requires the identification of the stages in the decision process and the evaluation of the potential outcomes at each stage. If possible, mathematical probabilities (odds of occurrence) should be attached to each potential outcome but, more importantly, the potential for management action to alter events at each decision point should be assessed. It is almost certain that any project will not turn out exactly as forecast, and the ability of managers to respond by taking appropriate decisions during the project to minimize the damage or even restore the project to its initial targeted result will be very important indicators of the risks of the project, as will the potential for the project to outperform the original forecast. This can be most clearly demonstrated by preparing a decision tree analysis for the project, which breaks the project down into the sequential decisions which have to be taken and shows what alternatives are possible at each decision point. The decision tree then follows each of these alternatives and shows what further decisions follow from each initial branch (hence the description 'decision tree'). Unfortunately, decision trees for complex projects can themselves become incredibly complex because of the multitude of decision points and the range of alternatives which can occur at each point. For very major projects computerized decision trees are often developed, and these are continuously updated as actual decisions are taken and future forecasts become reality, so that the vast range of original possibilities is gradually reduced as the project develops.

The principle involved can be illustrated by producing very simplified decision trees for our three projects (A, B and C) to see what can affect their financial returns and how this analysis can be used to assess the risk of each project. If we restate the NPV calculations for each project from Table 7.8 as is done in Table 7.17 we can start to highlight the potentially critical influences on the overall success or failure of each project, and to discover the degree of control which the business has over these events – the greater the degree of control the lower the risk.

Table 7.17 *Restated net present value calculations for projects A, B and C (at 10% discount rate)*

	Project A				Project B				Project C		
Year	Cash flow	Discount factors	Present value	Year	Cash flow	Discount factors	Present value	Year	Cash flow	Discount factors	Present value
0	(14 m)	1	(14 m)	0	(14 m)	1	(14 m)	0	(14 m)	1	(14 m)
1–10	3 m	6.145	18.435 m	1–5	5 m	3.791	18.955 m	1	(2 m)	0.909	(1.818 m)
10	14 m	0.386	5.404 m	5	2 m	0.621	1.242 m	2	(1 m)	0.826	(0.826 m)
								3	1 m	0.751	0.751 m
								4–10	11 m	3.658	40.238 m
								10	4 m	0.386	1.544 m
	Net present value		9.839 m		Net present value		6.197 m		Net present value		25.889 m

The decision tree for project A is shown in Figure 7.3, and this shows that the investment can be broken up into the costs associated with each individual shop, and hence approval of the project does not necessarily place at risk all £14 million as the purchase of each shop can be considered as a separate investment decision. It also shows that if trading for any shop is more successful than was predicted we can take advantage of this extra potential to earn profit (the American saying is 'play the upside') by expanding the shop, or opening still more branches. Possibly even more important to our risk assessment is the action which can be taken if trading is below expectations (that is, profits are less than £3 million per year). For this project, the decision tree shows that we can either continue trading and receive a lower return on the project, or we can cease trading and sell the shop and stock to recover our investment of £14 million earlier than originally forecast. If the cash is received earlier than year ten it will have a higher present value and a consequently greater impact on the overall financial evaluation of the project. This ability for managers to take direct action both if the project is overperforming or underperforming can be argued to reduce the risk of this project significantly.

Another risk assessment technique, which can be used alongside decision tree analysis, is sensitivity analysis and this was briefly mentioned earlier in the chapter. We can apply sensitivity analysis to the forecast cash flows for project A as shown in Table 7.17 and see what changes will have the greatest impact on the project's outcome if the cash flow is not as forecast. The company should be able to forecast the cost of the shops and the required investment in working capital very accurately as they are already in the business and the cash outflows are planned to take place immediately. The projected £3 million cash inflows are more likely to turn out differently and Table 7.18 shows the impact on the NPV if the cash inflows are actually 10 per cent above or below the forecast level.

The adjusted NPVs of £11.682 million, if inflows are 10 per cent higher, and £7.995 million, if inflows are 10 per cent lower, are respectively an increase and decrease of 18.7 per cent on the base NPV of £9.839 million. Thus the project is affected much more than (that is, is very sensitive to) the relative change in the cash inflows and this is due to the great weighting applied to the value of the cash inflows through the annuity process (the annuity factor used being 6.145). If the residual value of the freehold shops is to make the same impact on the NPV it needs, as shown in Table 7.19, to be adjusted to £18.775 million minus the £4 million recovery of working capital, i.e. £14.775 million. This represents a 47.75 per cent increase over its forecast level of £10 million compared to the 10 per cent change in cash inflows. The greater relative change is caused by

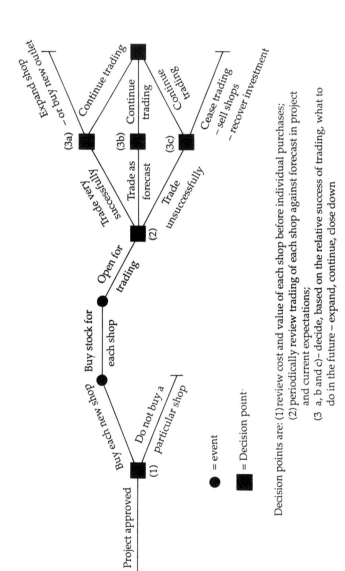

Figure 7.3   *Decision tree for Project A*

Decision points are: (1) review cost and value of each shop before individual purchases;
(2) periodically review trading of each shop against forecast in project and current expectations;
(3 a, b and c) – decide, based on the relative success of trading, what to do in the future – expand, continue, close down

Table 7.18 *Project A: sensitivity analysis (a)*

Year	Discount factors	Base cash flow	Inflows 10% up	Present value	Inflows 10% down	Present value
0	1	(14 m)	(14 m)	(14 m)	(14 m)	(14 m)
1–10	6.145	3 m	3.3 m	20.278	2.7 m	16.591
10	0.386	14 m	14 m	5.404	14 m	5.404
	Net present value	9.839 m	Net present value	11.682	Net present value	7.995

the low weighting (a discount factor of 0.386) given to this cash inflow received ten years hence, and shows how much more sensitive the project is to forecast errors in cash inflows from trading. If this very sensitive element in the forecast cash flows is uncontrollable by the company the project risk is increased, and the risk is even more increased if managers cannot respond to adverse movements in the most sensitive items. Fortunately for the company in project A we can take action to recoup our initial investment by selling the shops and stock if the very important cash flows from trading are not satisfactory and this reduces the risk of the project.

Table 7.19 *Project A: sensitivity analysis (b)*

Year	Discount factors	Adjusted inflows + 10%	Present value	Adjusted residual value	Present value
0	1	(14 m)	(14 m)	(14 m)	(14 m)
1–10	6.145	3.3 m	20.278	3 m	18.435 m
10	0.386	14 m	5.404	18.775 m	7.247 m
		Net present value	11.682	Net present value	11.682

The same analysis for projects B and C is set out below with a briefer narrative for reasons of space but readers are advised to work through the examples and ensure they follow the conclusions drawn. The simplified decision tree for project B is shown in Figure 7.4 and highlights the lack of control which can be exercised over this project, once started, due to its dependence on the continued role of the product concerned (the project is for an efficiency improvement in the manufacture of a particular product).

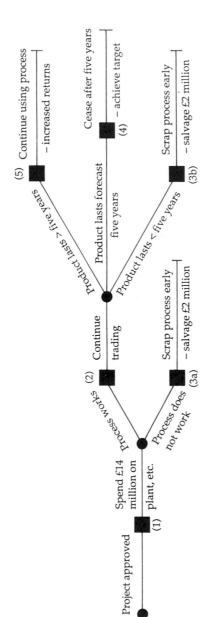

Figure 7.4   *Decision tree for Project B*

This lack of control increases the risk of the project and highlights the importance of the life of the product concerned, which is independent of this project. The sensitivity analysis also shows the importance of the time period for which the project lasts in terms of the impact on the NPV. This is highlighted in Table 7.20 which shows that a project life of four years reduces the NPV to £3.211 million – a massive reduction of 48.18 per cent from its original value of £6.197 million. This is because the impact of year five cash flows is very significant, being subject to a discount factor of 0.621. The level of project cash inflows which is needed to create the same relative change in NPV is shown by Table 7.21 to be £4.213 million per year, but £2 million of this cash flow is produced by the non-cash movement depreciation expense which is added back to profits to calculate cash flow from operations.

Table 7.20 *Project B – sensitivity analysis (a) option 1 (shorten life to four years)*

Year	Discount factors	Base cash flows	Year	Discount factors	Cash flows	Present value
0	1	(14 m)	0	1	(14 m)	(14 m)
1–5	3.791	5 m	1–4	3.1670	5 m	15.85
5	0.621	2 m	4	0.683	2 m	1.366
	Net present value	6.197 m			Net present value	3.211 m

Table 7.21 *Project B: sensitivity analysis (b)*

Year	Discount factors	Adjusted cash	Present value flows	Maximum residual value effect	Present value
0	1	(14 m)	(14 m)	(14 m)	(14 m)
1–5	3.791	4.213 m	15,972	5 m	18.955
5	0.621	2 m	1.242 m	0	0
	Adjusted net present value (equal to four-year life calculation)		3.214 m	Net present value	4.955 m

Thus profits from the project have to reduce from £3 million to £2.13 million, which is a change of 29 per cent, if the same impact is to be felt as would be caused by the loss of one year's life of the project (a 20 per cent reduction). Table 7.21 also shows that even if no recovery of working capital was achieved, the NPV would not decrease as far as £3.211 million, being £4.955 million with £0 recovery at the end of the project.

As the project gives no effective control over its life due to the dependence on the particular product which it is supporting and given the importance of this project life to the NPV, project B should be regarded as a high risk project.

Project C requires a more complex decision tree but we can simplify it, as is done for Figure 7.5, by assuming that each year similar decisions and actions occur regarding the relative sales success achieved.

In project C, the company can take subsequent actions through increasing or decreasing marketing activities to try to achieve the sales revenues and thus long-term cash inflows which were used to justify the project. If additional market research carried out soon after the launch of the service indicated that this would be a further waste of money, the service could be scrapped and the investment in working capital (£4 million) recovered earlier, as well as saving the investments in marketing which were forecast for years one and two. This ability to have some control over the long-term success of the launch reduces the risk of the project, and this can be seen to be even more critical once the sensitivity analysis has been carried out.

Table 7.22 shows the impact on the NPV if the project does not achieve the high level of profits until year five instead of year four which was used in the project justification. The impact of a one-year deferral is a reduction in NPV to £19.059 million from £25.889 million (a reduction of 26.4 per cent). This indicates that the company could consider spending considerable resources on increased marketing activity to ensure that the projects did achieve high profits in year four if early sales revenues indicated that this success might be delayed. (If these early sales revenues suggested that the forecast profit levels would never be reached and that the long-term prospects for the service were not attractive, the company could cancel all future marketing plans and abort the project, as suggested by the decision tree.)

Table 7.22 also shows the changes in cash inflows required to have the same impact as a one-year profit deferral, which is a reduction to £9.13 million for years four to ten from £11 million. £1 million of this cash inflow is the depreciation expense add-back which is common to both alternatives. Therefore the change in profit levels is from £10 million down to £8.13 million, which is an 18.7 per cent reduction and causes a reduction in NPV of 26.4 per cent – this is caused by the high weighting given to the cash inflows as was shown for project A. In project C's case the company can try to stimulate these profits by increased marketing support as it is a new service which is being launched.

As this project is so sensitive to both the size of cash inflows and their relative timing, the company might consider a test market launch for the new service, so as to minimize the investment put at risk. A national

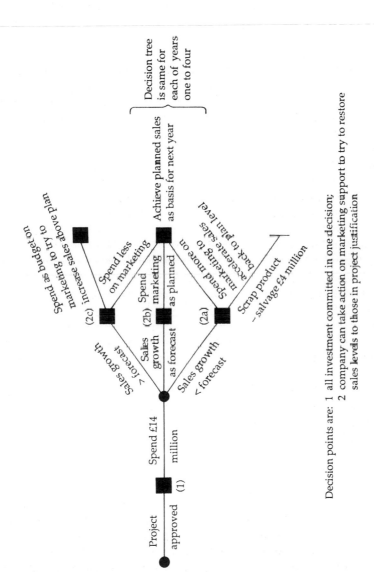

Figure 7.5 *Decision tree for Project C*

Decision points are: 1 all investment committed in one decision;
2 company can take action on marketing support to try to restore
sales levels to those in project justification

Table 7.22   *Sensitivity analysis for project C: (a) Impact of deferring high profit from year four to year five; (b) adjusting the cash inflows for years four to ten to have same impact*

Year	Discount factor	Base cash flows	Present value	Adjusted (a) cash flows	Present value	Adjusted (b) cash flows	Present value
0	1	(14 m)	(14 m)	(14 m)	(14 m)	(14 m)	(14 m)
1	0.909	(2 m)	(1.818 m)	(2 m)	(1.818 m)	(2 m)	(1.818 m)
2	0.826	(1 m)	(0.826 m)	(1 m)	(0.826 m)	(1 m)	(0.826 m)
3	0.751	1 m	0.751 m	1 m	0.751 m	1 m	0.751 m
4	0.683	11 m	7.513 m	1 m	0.683 m	9.13 m	33.408 m
5–10	2.975	11 m	32.725 m	11 m	32.725 m	9.13 m	
10	0.386	4 m	1.544 m	4 m	1.544 m	4 m	1.544 m
		Net present value	25.889 m	Net present value	19.059 m	Net present value (set equal to (a))	19.059 m

rollout could follow from encouraging early sales achievements in the test market, when a greater level of certainty had been established around the critically sensitive factors. In some markets this is not practical for product reasons or because of competitive reaction (giving away knowledge of the service before launching it nationally) but the company can still concentrate its analysis on how much influence it can have by marketing activities on the demand for the service once it has been launched and the £14 million investment committed. The fact that some control can be exercised may make the company view project C as less risky than project B, where no subsequent control was possible over the critically sensitive components.

Some of the examples in Part Five of the book will consider risk in other situations. They will use decision trees or sensitivity analysis as part of the analytical process, but as has been illustrated, risk analysis is an important part of project evaluation and requires the exercise of managerial judgement however sophisticated the analysis which is made.

Accounting return on investment (accounting rate of return or ARR)

In addition to the various methods of evaluating projects using cash flows, there is one remaining technique which compares the accounting return (that is, profit) generated by the project with the investment made in the project. The main argument produced in favour of this technique is that it is most similar to the criterion used to judge the success of the existing business (that is, return on capital employed, ROCE), and thus helps overall comparability. While true, it reintroduces the previous complications discussed in Part Two regarding the timing of profits and the judgements required to establish the level of accounting, as opposed to cash, investment in the project. It also requires, for long-term projects, that some method of averaging be used to calculate an annual return as the accounting return may vary in each year of the life of the project. There are considerable problems of using averages as the basis for making decisions, when what we require are the changes which will occur in the future, but we need to use an average profit figure and some similar measure for the investment as well, in order to make the computation manageable for any long-term project. The only alternative would be to calculate an accounting rate of return for each year of the project using some measure of net book value of assets for each year as the measure of investment. In order to generate a return for the project as a whole this would still require some process of aggregating and averaging the annual ARRs.

Most companies take a simplistic view of this calculation and use the average annual profits over the life of the project and compare this to the initial investment in the project, including any relevant investment in working capital. Some companies use an average calculation for the investment, which reflects that the fixed assets are depreciated over the life of the project. Using a simple average calculation does not weight the profits depending on their timing and so a profit in year ten is treated as being equal in value to a profit in year one. Also because the calculation produces only an average, this particular return on investment may not be achieved in any specific accounting period.

$$\text{Accounting return on investment} = \frac{\text{Average annual profits}}{\text{Initial investment}} \times 100\%$$

If we calculate the accounting return on investment for our three projects and then calculate the actual return achieved in each year this may become clearer, and this is shown in Table 7.23 for the average and Table 7.24 for each year.

Table 7.23 *Accounting return on investment*

Project	A	B	C
Average profits	$\frac{£30\text{ m}}{10} = £3\text{ m}$	$\frac{£15\text{ m}}{5} = £3\text{ m}$	$\frac{£65\text{ m}}{10} = £6.5\text{ m}$
Initial investment	£14 m	£14 m	£14 m
Return on investment	21.43%	21.43%	46.43%

Table 7.24   *Annual accounting return on investment*

Project	Year									
	1	2	3	4	5	6	7	8	9	10
Project A based on:	21.4%	21.4%	21.4%	21.4%	21.4%	21.4%	21.4%	21.4%	21.4%	21.4%
Profits	£3 m	£3 m	£3 m	£3 m	£3 m	£3 m	£3 m	£3 m	£3 m	£3 m
Net book value of assets	£14 m	£14 m	£14 m	£14 m	£14 m	£14 m	£14 m	£14 m	£14 m	£14 m
Project B based on:	25%	30%	37.5%	50%	75%					
Profits	£3 m	£3 m	£3 m	£3 m	£3 m					
Net book value of assets	£12 m	£10 m	£8 m	£6 m	£4 m					
adjustment to fixed assets due to depreciation of	(2 m)	(2 m)	(2 m)	(2 m)	(2 m)					
Project C based on:	N/A	N/A	0	100%	111%	125%	143%	167%	200%	250%
Profits	£(3 m)	£(2 m)	0	£10 m	£10 m	£10 m	£10 m	£10 m	£10 m	£10 m
net book value of assets	£13 m	£12 m	£11 m	£10 m	£9 m	£8 m	£7 m	£6 m	£5 m	£4 m
adjustment to fixed assets due to depreciation of	(1 m)	(1 m)	(1 m)	(1 m)	(1 m)	(1 m)	(1 m)	(1 m)	(1 m)	(1 m)

Project A is the only project with a consistent level of accounting return in each year and this is only because we are assuming that the company would not depreciate the freehold land and buildings which are recovered in full at the end of the project. This would mean that, for this project, a profit of £3 million would result in cash flows of £3 million as have been used in the previous calculations. Project B, which shows the same return as project A when calculated on the initial investment, shows increasing accounting returns each year as the fixed assets reduce in book value through depreciation. Project C shows a meteoric rise in annual return once it reaches profitability, which is caused by the declining book value of the fixed assets rather than continually increasing profits, as these are constant at £10 million per year for years four to ten.

If we compare the average accounting returns to the discounted cash flow calculations which produced the IRR, we can see from Table 7.25 that there is no general relationship between the two criteria. Project A is unusual because it has constant profits which equal the cash flows as mentioned above, and the initial investment is exactly recovered at the end of the project, but for other projects there is no definable relationship.

Therefore accounting return on investment is another method of comparing alternative projects, which provides another insight into the potential impact on the business. It is widely used as a supporting calculation to the more sophisticated discounting techniques, and this example does highlight one of the accounting problems mentioned in Chapter 5. Project C incurs substantial marketing expenditure in its early years in order to develop a market share which generates the high profits in the later years of the project. In the accounting return on investment calculation this expenditure is written off and produces an accounting loss for the first two years and break-even in year three. The presentation would be significantly altered if the expenditure were treated as another asset (an *intangible marketing asset*) and shown on the balance sheet alongside the more tangible fixed assets, which have very little value if the launch marketing activity is a failure. The strength of the cash flow-based techniques is that they do not differentiate between different types of expenditure and all cash outflows are treated identically which makes the evaluation more meaningful and less judgemental.

Summary

Long-term planning is not restricted by existing business constraints and decisions can be taken to reallocate or increase resources if necessary so as to attain the corporate objectives and hence achieve the mission of the business.

Planning is about making decisions, and business decisions depend on evaluating alternatives. Financial decisions can be made by relying on those items which will change as a result of the decision and therefore fixed and committed costs can be ignored for decision-making purposes. Indeed decisions can be based on differential future cash flows which simplify the evaluation process considerably.

However, money has a time value and if we are to make sensible decisions we need to incorporate the real value of future cash flows into our evaluation criteria. We can achieve this by applying discount rates to all future cash flows so that we bring them back to their equivalent present value, which makes all the project cash flows directly comparable. The most common way of doing this is to select a discount rate for the company and to apply this to all the cash flows of the project. A positive net present value indicates that the financial return from the investment is acceptable, but the opportunity costs evaluation against other potential investments must still be done. This requires comparison

Table 7.25 *Comparison of internal rate of return (IRR) and accounting return on investment*

Project	A	B	C
Internal rate of return	22%	25%	28%
Accounting return on investment	21.4%	21.4%	46.43%

of what benefits could be achieved by investing in a different mix of projects and where there are constraints on the total amount of capital which can be invested, this comparison is very important. In such a situation of capital rationing, the profitability index can be used to compare relative investment returns between projects; this is done by dividing the present value of the net inflows by the value of the initial investment.

Several major investment evaluation techniques are used by companies:

1   payback period;
2   discounted payback period;
3   Discounted cash flow
    (a) net present value (NPV)
    (b) internal rate of return (IRR);
4   Accounting return on investment (ARR).

These provide different views of any project and no single criterion can be regarded as giving the answer, so many companies use a combination of techniques and adjust the results to allow for the relative risk of the investment being examined.

Appendix

New car example using financial statements comparison

Resumé

Our sales and marketing director's car cost £21 000 and is assumed to have a £6000 residual value at the end of three years. A fuel efficiency device becomes available for £4500 with projected savings of £2000 per year.

A rival manufacturer launches a new car model, including the fuel efficiency device, for £18 000 with additional benefits yielding a total of £4000 per year in savings.

Assumption: The operating expenses of the existing car total £6000 per annum.

Method

All three options are compared from their presentation in the financial statements:

Keep car and do nothing

Profit and loss account

	Year 1	Year 2	Year 3	Total
	£	£	£	£
Operating expenses	(6000)	(6000)	(6000)	(18 000)
Depreciation expense	(5000)	(5000)	(5000)	(15 000)
	(11 000)	(11 000)	(11 000)	(33 000)

Balance sheet (end of year)

	Year 1	Year 2	Year 3
	£	£	£
Fixed assets at cost	21 000	21 000	21 000
less Accumulated depreciation	5000	10 000	15 000
Net book value	16 000	11 000	6000

(Assuming car sold at beginning of year 4)

Cash flows

	Year 1	Year 2	Year 3	Year 4	Total
Fixed assets purchased	(21 000)	–	–	–	(21 000)
Fixed asset sale proceeds	–	–	–	6000	6000
Operating expenses	(6000)	(6000)	(6000)	–	(18 000)
Total	(27 000)	(6000)	(6000)	6000	(33 000)

Note: Depreciation expense is calculated as follows:

$$\frac{£(21\ 000 - 6000)}{3} \text{ per annum} = £5000 \text{ per annum, that is reduction in value}$$

from £21 000 to £6000 spread over the three years

Keep car and add fuel device

Profit and loss account

	Year 1 £	Year 2 £	Year 3 £	Total £
Depreciation expense – car	(5000)	(5000)	(5000)	(15 000)
fuel device	(1500)	(1500)	(1500)	(4500)
	(6500)	(6500)	(6500)	(19 500)
New operating expenses	(4000)	(4000)	(4000)	(12 000)
Total	(10 500)	(10 500)	(10 500)	(31 500)

Balance sheet (end of year)

	Year 1 £	Year 2 £	Year 3 £
Fixed assets at cost	25 500	25 500	25 500
less Accumulated depreciation	6500	13 000	19 500
Net book value	19 000	12 500	6000

(Assuming car sold at beginning of year 4)

Cash flows

	Year 1	Year 2	Year 3	Year 4	Total
Fixed assets acquired	(25 500)	–	–	–	(25 500)
Fixed assets sale proceeds	–	–	–	6000	6000
Operating costs	(4000)	(4000)	(4000)	–	(12 000)
	(29 500)	(4000)	(4000)	6000	(31 500)

Comparing options 1 and 2 shows that the impact over three years is £33 000 of expense if we do nothing and £31 500 of expense if we buy the new fuel device. This improvement of £1500 is equal to the answer achieved by the total cash flows shown and was also arrived at by the differential cash flow method in the body of the chapter. It is also useful to note that over the whole period the cash movements equal the profit and loss account impact, but they are significantly different in each year.

Sell the car and buy new

Profit and loss account

	Year 1 £	Year 2 £	Year 3 £	Total £
Loss on sale of car				
(Cost £21 000 – proceeds £10 000)	(11 000)			(11 000)
Depreciation expense on new car				
$\frac{(18\ 000-6000)}{3}$	(4000)	(4000)	(4000)	(12 000)
Reduced operating expenses	(2000)	(2000)	(2000)	(6000)
	(17 000)	(6000)	(6000)	(29 000)

Balance sheet

	Year 1 £	Year 2 £	Year 3 £
Fixed asset at cost	18 000	18 000	18 000
less accumulated depreciation	4000	8000	12 000
Net book value	14 000	10 000	6000

(Assumed sold year 4)

Cash flows

	Year 1	Year 2	Year 3	Year 4	Total
Fixed assets acquired					
(£21 000 + £18 000)	(39 000)				(39 000)
Fixed assets sale					
proceeds	10 000	–	–	6000	16 000
Operating expenses	(2000)	(2000)	(2000)	–	(6000)
	(31 000)	(2000)	(2000)	6000	(29 000)

Net expenses at £29 000 again show the same imrovement of £4000 against the do-nothing alternative as given by the differential cash flows method in the body of the chapter and the cash flow movement equals the total profit impact over the life of the car. However timing differences are even more significant with the accounting loss all being shown in year one and some companies may argue that this detrimental impact in the profit and loss statement makes the decision to sell and buy the new car untenable. They would argue that by retaining the car they can spread the loss over three years through the annual depreciation expense. This logic is flawed because the application of the prudence accounting concept requires companies to recognize losses as soon as possible and the value to the business of the existing car has decreased with the launch of the new, more efficient car. Therefore a more sensible accounting presentation would be to recognize this loss in value in year one whether the car is sold or not; this could be done by charging an exceptional level of depreciation in the profit and loss statement. Unfortunately this treatment is not usually followed and the car, if retained, would be depreciated in the previous way, effectively disregarding the reduction in its value to the company.

Conclusion

The use of financial statements does generate the same answers as the differential cash flow method used in the chapter, but it does require the inclusion of more information and can complicate the timing of costs and benefits.

8

Budgets and forecasts

Introduction

In Chapter 7 we considered techniques for financial planning on a long-term basis, but we also established in Chapter 6 that planning is effectively a continuous and integrated process. No business can sensibly make long-term plans without any consideration of their impact on the immediate future, and equally a company which concentrated exclusively on short-term objectives would be unlikely to achieve its long-term goals. The logical process is to establish a long-term corporate plan and then to develop, in a coordinated way, a short-term detailed operational plan.

The long-term corporate plan may allow for the alteration of many existing constraints and resource allocations within the business, because the period of the plan allows these adjustments to be made. In the shorter time frame of the operational plan some changes are possible but major strategic issues, such as new product launches and moves into new markets, will often be constrained by actions already set in motion in previous periods; therefore many more costs of the business are committed and fixed in nature.

This difference between short-term and long-term planning is very important as it dictates where most managerial effort should be allocated. There is little point in allocating effort to an area which cannot be changed within the relevant time-frame of the plan, and so short-term planning concentrates on those areas that can be changed and where managerial judgement is important. It should be remembered that planning is not a 'wish list' for the business but a detailed series of actions which aim to achieve the corporate objectives. The short-term plan should therefore contain the most specific actions and is of critical importance to the success of the longer-term corporate plan, and is also an integrated part of the longer-term plans of the economy, as shown in Figure 8.1. As the flowchart illustrates, the short-term plan (or budget) is the way in which the long-term strategy of the company is implemented, and the objectives of the short term must be carefully integrated with the overall corporate objectives.

We need to set action-based budgets within the overall plan and these must be broken down into the relevant business segments, which fit the products and markets of the company. Thus the budget (normally the one year operating plan) should be put in the context of the overall marketing plan and the objectives and strategies for each element of the budget must be consistent with those of the overall plan. A budget can be defined as a statement, agreed by responsible managers, of policies and actions to be implemented in the forthcoming budgetary period to try to achieve the corporate objectives. The budget should include the forecast financial outcomes of the proposed actions in the form of a set of projected financial statements, and it requires a set of assumptions regarding the external environment for the budget period.

Although the annual budget focuses on a much nearer time period than the long range plan, it is still subject to the same problem which afflicts all forward forecasts: *it will be wrong!* However, the same reasons also apply for preparing short-term financial plans:

1   providing a basis for accepting the financial implications of the future proposed actions; and
2   providing a reference base for comparing the actual achievements against as the year unfolds.

These reasons can be even more forcefully applied to the budgeting process because of the relatively short planning period and hence short gap between plans being made, actions being implemented and results being observed. This again highlights that budgets should be action oriented and decision based, in the same way as long range plans should be. The monitoring and feedback process is also vitally important because if the original assumptions prove to be incorrect, the plan must be adjusted to take account of the actual circumstances in which the business is operating (Figure 8.1). This is also true if the outcome of current actions is not as originally envisaged, and different future actions are required as a consequence.

A budget, therefore, is not a static document which must be rigidly adhered to at all times, but it is very difficult to use something which is always changing as a reference base. This is akin to trying to hit a constantly moving target but, in a dynamic business environment, short-term actions should be based on the best, most up-to-date information available, and not on estimates made at the time of the last annual budgeting exercise. Most companies reconcile these inconsistencies by preparing an annual budget which is then not changed after completion,

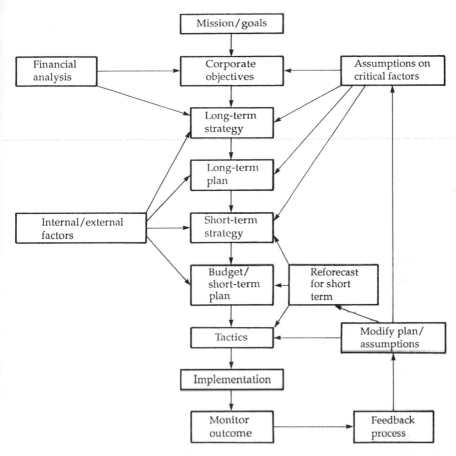

Figure 8.1 *Updated planning model*

and using regularly updated *forecasts* to take account of changing circumstances. This adds another dimension to our planning cycle; not only do we need to monitor the actual outcome of our actions against the budgeted results, but we must use these actual results to prepare updated forecasts for the remaining budget period, and this additional stage is also shown in Figure 8.1. Analysis, planning and monitoring really do become one continuous integrated process if we implement such a system. The distinction between a budget and a forecast is clarified below.

A *budget* is an agreed quantified plan of actions and policies to be implemented in a specified time period so as to try to achieve the corporate objectives. The budget is agreed against a set of assumptions regarding the external environment, and the overall long term plan of the business.

A *flexed budget* takes account of actual changes from budget which occur in sales volumes and incorporates the planned impact of those changes into the budget; in other words, it shows how the budget would have been prepared if the sales volumes were correctly predicted.

A *forecast* is the latest prediction of the results of the business using the most up-to-date information available on the internal and external environment. Thus it does not have to be an agreed plan, and may not be aiming to achieve the same set of corporate objectives as set in the budget (if circumstances have changed).

Monitoring also becomes more complex as we now have to compare the budget to the actual results for the latest period and also understand why the updated forecast predicts a different result from that estimated in the original budget. Ideally the subsequent actual results should be compared to the latest forecast for the period as well as, if not in place of, the original budget. A further way of incorporating the inevitable changes between the budget and the actual outcomes without losing control of the business or making the original budget completely irrelevant is by using a 'flexible budget'. A flexible budget takes account of actual sales *volumes* differing from the original budget and 'flexes' all the variable costs in line with their expected amounts at the actual sales volumes achieved. Thus if sales volumes exceed the budget expectations, variable cost allowances would be increased by the same proportion in the flexible budget to reflect what would have been forecast if the sales volume budget had been accurate. These problems of control are considered in more detail in Part Four. Before considering the budgeting process in detail it may be helpful to summarize the benefits of a good budgeting system as the 3 Cs:

Coordination, which ensures that the individual plans of the parts of the business are consistent and are targeted at the overall corporate objectives.

Communication, whereby each interrelated part of the business is made aware of the plans and proposed actions of the other parts and, often even more importantly, of the overall corporate objective. This process of communication and involvement can have a major positive impact on motivation of the management of the business.

Control; as already stated, budgets help as a reference base against which actual achievements can be measured and decisions taken as the year unfolds. The subdivisions of the budget can also be used to judge the performance of the various operating areas of the business and, to some degree, the managers responsible for those areas.

The budgeting process

When we are preparing a long-term plan, it is logical to start from the corporate objectives and devise strategies to achieve those objectives, even though there may be short-term constraints on implementing some of these strategies. In preparing a one year budget these constraints are much more significant and may dictate the way in which the budget is prepared, due to the time-lag involved in removing the constraint.

If our business has an objective of being market leader in its main market within five years but at present is only in third place we need to understand what constraints are stopping us achieving our objective. Our business analysis, as described in Part Two, if properly carried out, should have provided most of these answers but it may take a considerable period of time to redress the position by reallocating resources or increasing the resources available. The constraint could be lack of access to critical channels of distribution or a shortage of direct sales resources. Each of these may be capable of being tackled in the budget period by increasing resources (for example, hiring more sales people) in the appropriate area but the financial benefit of such a decision may not be felt through higher sales until after the end of this budget period whereas the increased expense will be felt immediately. If management is concentrating too heavily on short-term financial results (for example, the profit forecast in next year's budget), this development type of expenditure may not be spent as it clearly reduces profit in the short term. A good budgeting system should, therefore, distinguish between maintenance type expenditure and development activities which may have longer-term benefits for the business.

This emphasizes the essential need for a balance between the short-term and long-term objectives so that managers are discouraged from meeting their own objectives at the expense of the overall success of the business (this is described as achieving 'goal congruence' and is examined in more detail in Part Four). The problems of accounting for marketing, due to writing-off significant expenditures in accounting periods prior to those when the benefits will be received, can exacerbate conflicts between different timings of objectives. Budgets should be decision-based and so can partially offset this accounting problem by using the appropriate decision-making techniques, thus relying on forecast cash flows and ensuring that all the future benefits are included in the evaluation rather than simply those falling within the next annual accounting period.

Another way of redressing the balance is to analyse the budget into 'task' related segments so that specific 'development' activities are identified and cannot be hidden by being included under large total expenditure headings, which are very vague and broad. For instance the marketing budget could be separately analysed into expenditure designed to maintain existing sales levels and expenditure on whichever elements of the Ansoff matrix (Figure 6.4, pages 170–1) were to be used to expand sales, assuming this is a budget objective. Such a split avoids the business automatically reallocating expenditure in order to achieve a short-term profit target (or not spending some of the development marketing budget) at the expense of being able to achieve the longer-term growth target.

A third method is to make the budget objectives sufficiently comprehensive that any undue imbalance in emphasis will lead to non-achievement of at least some financial or quantified targets. This could be done by having profit as only one of the objectives and adding sales growth, or level of market share at the end of the budget period as a further objective. Alternatively if a specific key constraint affecting the longer-term objectives can be identified, the additional targets can be made even more specific and, in our previous illustration on page 231, these could be opening identified new channels of distribution or expanding the size of the direct sales force by a specified number of people prior to the end of the budget period.

The budgeting process can help to achieve this essential balance, but any budget must also be internally consistent across the whole company and so the budgeting process can be regarded as circular; this circular process is illustrated in Figures 8.2 and 8.3. Each area of the business must be able to provide the resources required to achieve its part of the budget and the output from this area will then place demands on and provide inputs to other areas of the business. An example of a plan for a new product launch for a fmcg company with a long-term growth objective but a continuous requirement for annual profit improvements, may make this clearer. Market research identifies an opportunity for a new product aimed at a specific segment of the market and so the specification for the product is passed to the research and development department. They must allocate resources to developing a product with satisfactory performance characteristics and at a cost which enables the target price level to be achieved. Once developed (and preferably as part of the development process) the manufacturing department must be involved in deciding how the product should be produced and this may involve acquiring or developing new equipment. The purchasing department may need to be involved in this phase but certainly will be involved in sourcing any new raw materials and packaging required for the new product. It is possible that more labour may need to be hired to produce the new product, but even if existing labour is to be reallocated there may be a requirement for training before production can commence, and thus the personnel department will need to be involved. Once these plans are drawn up and any inconsistencies are resolved the potential launch date can be agreed. Sales and marketing department now have to plan the launch activities which may require accessing new channels of distribution and filling the channel pipeline prior to launching the product to the end consumer.

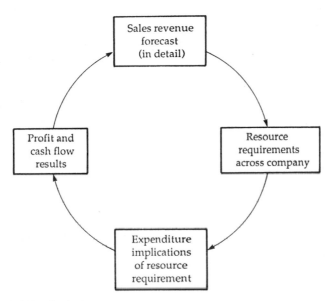

Figure 8.2   *Circular budgeting process*

Each area of the business has an input to this operational planning process and unless all these inputs are coordinated the new product launch could rapidly degenerate into a fiasco, such as is created by launching a product before any stock is available for sale.

A major role of the budget is to ensure that the internal resources are adequately matched and that the plans of each area are mutually compatible with each other and the overall corporate plan. Due to its essential circular nature it is not critical in which area the planning process starts, but since in a budget period many resource constraints cannot be removed the logical starting point is at a key immoveable constraining factor. For many companies this will be sales revenues (that is, sales levels at current selling prices) but for some (for example, mining

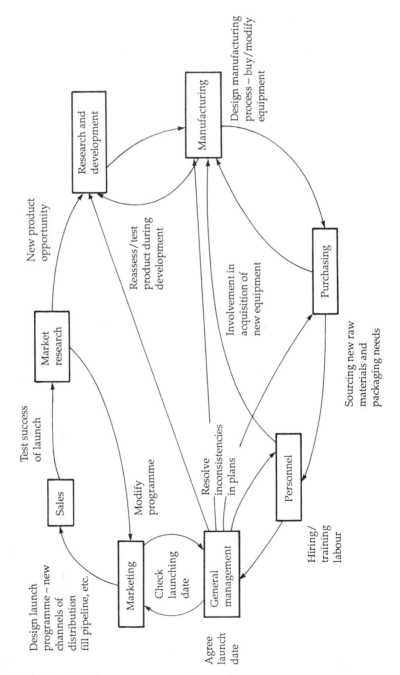

Figure 8.3   *Circular budget process – new product launch plan*

industries) it may be production capacity (for example, the maximum tonnage which can be extracted from a mine in a year) or some other factor. The critical issue is that the company is consistent about stopping the planning process at the same point that it starts the budgeting cycle. It is very tempting, if the initial result of a budgeting cycle is unacceptable in terms of profit outcome, to increase planned selling prices slightly so that the forecast profit goes up and not to go round the business cycle again and include the impact of the price increase on sales volumes, etc! – thus ignoring any impact caused by the elasticity of demand for the product; this normally suggests that at higher selling prices, sales volumes will be lower.

Once the long-term objectives for the business have been broken down into relevant objectives for the budget period, this circular budgeting process can get under way. If we start with the sales budget as being a prime constraint we can follow some of the stages to see how the integrated process works. Marketing managers will have a detailed analysis of the existing markets, forecasts for price movements, competitive activity, etc., and can produce their view of the optimum combination of selling prices for the budget period ahead. These prices, together with the proposed level of marketing activity, will dictate the levels of sales (that is, volumes of goods or services) which will be made. This sales volume forecast is the principal item of interest to the production or service providing department (the output department), as this will dictate its own planning and determine its resource requirements. Any potential resourcing constraints must be removed (for example, by new machinery, working overtime or additional shifts) so that the desired output level is attainable, or the sales plan will require modification to fit what is achievable. The consequent output plan is the input to purchasing and personnel for resourcing the necessary inputs as required by the output department in terms of machinery, raw materials, packaging, energy and skilled labour, etc. It is important to note that the necessary lead times for these resources will differ for each area and a time sequenced action plan is as important as a financial budget to ensure that resources are available when required (for example, labour must be hired in time to be trained so that output can be started and stocks, if needed, built up prior to the new product launch).

If, at any stage, the budget becomes inconsistent it is vital that this inconsistency is removed, even if this means going back to the beginning by reforecasting sales and then reiterating the entire process. This need for consistency and the use of money as the only common language among the business functions have been the main reasons for the degree of control exercised by financial managers over the budget process. This involvement should be as a *coordinator* to ensure this consistency and *not as the imposer* of the financial budget because of their accounting expertise.

Budgets should not be *imposed* on managers but should be *agreed* with the operational managers, because if there is no acceptance of the targets there will be no commitment to achieving them. In that situation the budget becomes 'somebody else's problem' and no-one is actually taking responsibility for 'making it happen'. If this occurs, all the time and effort that is put into the analysis and planning processes is wasted, and there is little point in implementing a sophisticated monitoring and control system because this type of budget cannot be used as a basis for future decisions.

What is required is a budget analysed into its controllable elements so that specific but coordinated objectives can be agreed for each area. These objectives should include financial and non-financial objectives and it is important that the financial aspects of the budget are integrated with the tasks and activities of each separate area and are not simply a total money value representing expenditure levels or sales revenues to be achieved. In order to do this it is necessary to break down the overall costs and revenues into the specific relationships that can be derived and used to predict the levels of costs which will need to be incurred in the future. Such a cost relationship can be defined as an 'engineered' cost if it is possible to calculate the level of output expected from a given level of input or when the forecast volume of sales is known and the level of time from labour required, for example, can be worked out.

Standard costing

A standard cost is the level of cost which *should* be incurred for any given level of activity, normally as determined by some measurable *input–output* relationship, under specified conditions. A standard cost can be established per unit of activity where appropriate, whereas budgeted costs are normally established for the budgeted level of activity.

If the input–output relationship is predictable as it often is in an engineering or manufacturing area of the business, it is possible to build up an 'expected' or 'standard' level of cost for any given level of activity. The specified task can literally be any repetitive task where the resources needed can be predicted with reasonable accuracy and the cost of those resources identified. Therefore standard costing need not be restricted to the production environment as it is in most companies and can be used with reference to sales operations for setting standards for the calls expected from a field sales force and establishing a standard cost per call. In the clerical and distribution areas of the business, many operations are repetitive and standard costs can be established for these functions. A good example is in the sales order processing area where the time taken to input a line on an order form can be established and by establishing the average lines of data per order, a standard time allowance (and hence standard cost) for inputting an order, including all the customer product and delivery information needed, can be calculated. This standard cost can be used to set the level of resources needed by the department, and to monitor the actual costs incurred against the level which should, according to the standard cost relationships, have been used to process the actual volume of orders. Standard costs can also be used in the distribution area of the business where the order-picking function is largely repetitive and in the goods receiving and storage functions the same analysis can be carried out.

This idea of standard costing can be very useful in budgeting as it greatly assists in setting a reference base to compare actual outcomes against. Companies differ in the level at which they set 'standards' because it is possible to set standards which establish a very tight target to aim at or to set standards which are what you actually hope to achieve. In a production environment, where the use of standard costing is most common, companies define standards at three alternative levels:

1 'ideal' standards, which mean that a machine is running at its rated capacity, etc. These standards are only achieved under exceptional circumstances and then for very short periods of time, and normal performance will always fall short of this 'ideal';
2 'expected' standards, which are genuinely the best estimate of what is 'expected' to happen over the budget period. If things go according to plan, the business expects to beat the standard as often as it fails to achieve it and over the year the gains and losses should balance out;
3 'target' standards, which tend to be based on previous performance but with an allowance built in for improved future productivity. This assumes a learning process over time which makes the operation more efficient, and this gain in efficiency is included in the forecast standard cost.

None of these methods is right or wrong, but it is important that the company and the appropriate managers understand how the standards are set because this will influence the reaction to actual achievements against them. The normal control process is to calculate what costs should have been incurred according to the standard allowances and to compare these against the actual costs experienced. This accounting calculation is known as 'variance analysis' and, for obvious reasons, if the actual cost incurred was lower than the standard the variance is described as 'favourable' and if actual cost exceeds the standard allowance the variance becomes 'unfavourable'. It is important for the reader to understand that the accounting term 'variance' simply means the *difference* between the standard and actual costs, and is not used in the same way as the variance calculated in statistics. If the standards used are set at the 'ideal' level, the company must expect to incur regular unfavourable (also known as 'adverse') variances. If 'expected' standards have been established, both favourable and unfavourable variances would be recorded during the year, and the company would 'expect' the overall net variance to be zero.

Standards are most commonly set at some sort of 'target' level and because a good performance is simply to achieve a target, it is most likely that some level of adverse variances will be recorded during the year when the actual costs are compared to standards.

Some budgeting systems which use standard costing also include a budgeted (that is, expected) level of variance to allow for the non-achievement of 'ideal' or 'target' standards.

Standard costs are, in fact, always composed of two elements as shown below and if properly utilized standards can, as mentioned, be of great value in many areas of the business as well as production and engineering, including marketing.

Standard cost	= Standard physical units	× Standard price per unit
for example, Standard labour cost per customer enquiry	= Standard time per enquiry	× Standard clerical costs per hour

A standard cost is a cost level expected to be incurred in carrying out some task and consists of some physical units consumed in some way multiplied by a price per unit to generate the financial costs. The input–output relationship is in most cases determined by the physical aspects of the standard and not by the price; for example, we can derive a physical standard for the amount of steel in a motor car body which will be constant over a period of time and does not change merely because the *price* of steel changes at a point in time. If we can assign physical input–output relationships to non-production activities, we can apply the logic of standards as a planning and control technique.

One obvious area of application is within clerical operations where it is often practical to establish 'standard' timings for inputting data to systems, as illustrated for the sales order processing area. Even for apparently non-routine tasks in the clerical area such as answering customer enquiries the use of statistical techniques and the high volume of transactions may make it possible to derive very meaningful measures of physical inputs required for any forecast level of enquiries. Although the time taken to deal with any specific enquiry may range from a few seconds to over one hour, it is possible to analyse all the enquiries from customers over a specified period and to group them into various categories. Each category can be examined to establish an expected time (often the average) for the customer service clerk to satisfy one enquirer in this category and this can be set as the standard time allowance. By using the expected mix of the various types of enquiry (that is, the categories), the standard time allowances for the forecast (or standard) workload for the department can be calculated.

As before, this standard or expected workload can be used to establish the required resources for the department and to monitor how the efficiency and/or the workload is changing over time. If one category of enquiry is 'customers who are complaining' the change in that level of workload is of great interest to the marketing department as it indicates a change in the level of customer satisfaction, and regular monitoring and feedback is essential. In order to ensure this happens and that these customer complaints are properly handled, a more sophisticated customer enquiry system can be established which tries to segment the enquiry into the various categories, on its first receipt by the company. Each category can then be handled by different groups of staff, with consequently more specialized training, and standard time allowances can be more accurately assessed for each repetitive process. It is normally true that the more a repetitive process is broken down into its specific task components the more accurately the standard cost can be established.

This logic can, as mentioned, be extended into the area of deciding on the budgeted size of the field sales force provided that the objectives of such a field sales force are properly established. If a major aim is to make calls on existing customers and to take orders, we can produce a series of physical relationships which reflect: (a) the number of customers to be called on, (b) the desirable call frequency based on the likelihood of obtaining an order (that is, each customer is given a call frequency grading); (c) and the number of calls which a salesperson can make per day based on an assumed level of utilization in the field. These relationships can generate the required size of the field sales force and this can be taken as a 'standard' if the objectives are to be met.

It is important to understand that the 'standard' enables us to measure the level of efficiency of the operation and not its effectiveness, and the difference between the two is important as shown below.

Efficiency measures the units of output relative to the units of input.
Effectiveness measures how well the objectives have been achieved.

Therefore: efficiency is a measure of technical success/failure in the input–output relationship, whereas effectiveness reflects whether the right outputs were achieved to meet the objectives set, irrespective of the technical efficiency regarding level of inputs.

Thus using input–output relationships to decide on the required size of a field sales force monitors whether the sales force actually achieves the 'standards' of performance set for it, in this case by meeting the objective of calling on existing customers at a predetermined frequency. The sales force may overachieve by making more calls than the standard (that is, be more efficient), but this could reduce the effectiveness of meeting the business objectives as less long-term sales may result from this style of pressurized sales operation. Effectiveness can only be judged by how appropriate the specified objectives are. The company should also remember that these 'physical relationships' are themselves subject to change and errors in forecasting, and so the discovery of large adverse variances may indicate that the 'standard' is no longer relevant rather than performance has been inefficient. Trying to measure effectiveness of performance is very difficult and this is why key non-financial objectives should be included as part of the budgeting process.

For most industries, it is relatively straightforward to establish a normal cost for employing a field salesperson which can, with all the other associated costs (such as a car, travelling, accommodation and subsistence, entertaining, and samples), build up to a total employment cost per person. The company has relatively little choice or discretion in paying at least this market rate because if it pays materially below this level it will lose all its good sales people and be unable to recruit good replacements from the market. (It may choose to pay above the going rate so that it has a greater choice of applicants, and hopefully it can justify this extra cost by obtaining a more effective sales force in return – the supporting analytical evidence would be a comparatively higher level of contribution per sales person which more than outweighs the additional employment costs.)

When we are examining the overall budget for such a field sales force it is interesting to consider the options open to the sales director. At first sight it might appear that a sales director has total discretion (that is, freedom of choice) over how to spend a budget of, say, £1 million. This £1 million expenditure has to cover salaries, commission, car expenses, travel, accommodation and subsistence, entertaining, etc. for the field sales force and in reality the level of discretion is very limited. If the total all-inclusive cost of one salesperson is £40 000 per year the sales director can employ 25 people and this can be regarded as his discretionary choice. In this case we are effectively establishing a standard cost of one salesperson at £40 000 per year. In our example the sales director may also have non-financial objectives relating to calling on customers and generating orders. If we apply the relationship model for possible calls per sales person we can also develop the number of sales people required to achieve these non-financial objectives. Again we have established a standard, but this time it is a physical standard not a financial standard. Unless our physical evaluation establishes a need for the same level of 25 sales people, our sales director has an incompatible set of budgetary objectives.

This is very common and is most frequently caused by the financial budgetary objectives not being derived from the physical activities which have to be performed by the budget holders in order to achieve their objectives. Instead the financial objectives are often the result of a separate financial planning exercise done 'for the budget' and not as an integral part of the operational planning of the business. The budget must be an integrated planning process and must have both financial and non-financial objectives for each budget holder which are compatible with each other and with the other elements of the budget. One very good way of linking in the non-financial objectives is to use the physical relationships which form an essential part of the standard costing concept. This use of standards for planning also helps dramatically when the company faces decisions which require the comparison of alternative courses of action. Decisions depend on an evaluation of what changes as a result of the decision and this will hinge upon the discretion (degree of choice) which can be exercised by the budget-holder. In other words what costs can be changed and what costs are determined by the engineering relationship discussed?

In the case of our sales director, what decision should be made if sales force costs increase unexpectedly by 10 per cent, so that unless something is done the total expenditure will be £1.1 million against a budget of £1 million? The various reactions of this kind of problem would be hilarious if they were not so seriously damaging to the future success of the business. We have already established that reducing the salesperson's basic salary is likely to lead to a loss of the good members of the sales force and so most companies try to avoid altering this element of the cost. Some employers achieve much the same result by altering the incentive schemes so as to reduce total earnings! Other companies attack some of the other costs incurred by the sales force, such as car expenses. Savings can be made in this area by giving sales people smaller, cheaper cars and by reducing the mileage rate paid per mile travelled. The smaller cheaper car, assuming that the current car had been established as suitable for the task, is likely to affect the efficiency of the sales force and may mean that less calls per day will be made, as well as being detrimental to employee morale and encouraging some good, employable sales people to leave. Reducing total mileage allowances reimbursed by the company, which is another cost-saving idea used by companies, again affects the ability of the salesforce to call on customers, unless they are willing to pay some of the mileage expenses themselves. Calling on customers is why they are employed! A similar result is achieved by reducing accommodation and subsistence allowances. One company reduced allowable mileage levels and restricted accommodation to one night away per week which meant that some of their sales people could not stay in a hotel, nor did their new mileage allowances allow them to drive home for the night; and, of course, their new, smaller, cheaper car was not really suitable for sleeping in! The resultant loss in good sales personnel and decline in sales revenues for that company illustrate the dangers in misusing the budgeting process and not properly understanding the interrelationships between costs.

If we examine the more logical planning options available to the company when the cost level has increased by 10 per cent there are relatively few alternatives. Each sales person on average now costs £44 000 per year and not £40 000; this may mean that it is no longer worthwhile calling on a certain category of customer, or calling as frequently, and so less calls could be made which would reduce the number of sales people required. This increase in cost could also make it more attractive to service some of the existing customers by a different method, for example, telephone selling based on a glossy brochure mailed direct to the customer; again this might result in fewer sales people being required. The company therefore has a degree of discretion over the number of sales people it employs if it can achieve its non-financial objectives in a different way, whereas, if the original budget was realistic, it has little discretion over the cost of each sales person which is determined by an engineering relationship (that is, a cost built up of the component elements). What is required is a full opportunity cost evaluation of how else the non-financial objectives could be achieved now that the base cost of using a field sales force has changed – again the planning and control process is decision based and should focus on what practical alternatives are available to the business.

Another example of the potential use of standard cost relationships in the marketing area is with regard to setting advertising budgets. As mentioned in Chapter 1 it may not be sensible to try to control advertising expenditure solely by rigid adherence to an absolute financial limit when the effectiveness of any expenditure may be fundamentally affected by the physical scale of the activity in terms of 'opportunities to see'. If a particular advertising campaign has been designed around a certain number of opportunities to see but advertising media costs have suddenly increased, the normal reaction of many companies is to limit total expenditure to the amount in the budget. If the price per showing has gone up, this inevitably requires the opportunities to see to be reduced and these may be reduced below what is felt to be the 'critical mass' level at which any beneficial effect will be achieved. The key decision once again is what aspects of the expenditure do the business really have discretion over and where are engineered (input–output) relationships more important?

In neither of these examples is the business objective simply to spend the budget allowance, and specific non-financial objectives are required for each area if sensible plans are to be drawn up. Even more importantly the budget should be analysed into segments which help make decisions when, as in these cases, external factors change and budget assumptions are found to be wrong. Clearly the budget needs modification when this happens and a reforecast should be carried out, rather than rigidly adhering to the previously established budgeted levels of expenditure. The use of standard costs and the underlying engineering (input–output) relationships can be very helpful in focusing attention on how the costs will change as a result of particular decisions and where the business really can exercise its discretion. These decisions should use the concept of opportunity costs to compare alternatives, but it is important that the real benefits of the alternatives are compared in terms of their contribution to the business objectives. In other words, decisions should be based on effectiveness criteria and not merely on ways of doing the *wrong* thing more efficiently. Sensible budgets therefore depend on a good understanding of the relationships between costs and revenues within the budget period and we can now consider these in detail.

Cost–volume–profit analysis

In Chapter 7 we analysed costs into those that change with the level of activity (variable costs) and those that remain at a constant level for a given period of time and range of changes in activity (fixed costs). For long-range planning most costs will change over the period of the plan but when we are considering budgets with a much shorter time-scale many more costs will be fixed.

As previously stated a fixed cost remains unchanged for a specified relevant range which may be defined in terms of time, output, space or some other variable, whereas a variable cost will vary proportionately with a change in the level of activity. It is therefore possible to classify all the expenses of a business as either fixed or variable costs and this can be very helpful as a planning and decision-making technique.

Some business costs do not, at first sight, fall readily into either the fixed or variable category as they partially increase with activity but not in direct proportion to the change in activity because part of the cost is fixed.

Many utility costs such as telephone, electricity and gas fall into this classification being a combination of a fixed rental or standing charge per period and a price per unit consumed. It is possible to separately classify these costs into a third category, mixed costs (also called either 'semi-fixed' costs or 'semi-variable' costs), as shown in Figure 8.4, but this simply confuses all our decision-making criteria and is unnecessary. Each of these costs can be split into its fixed components and its variable components and these components can be treated accordingly.

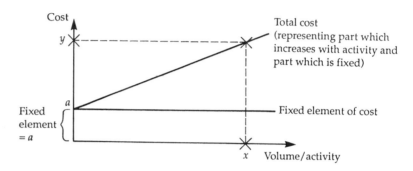

The cost (*y*) is given by the sum of the fixed element (*a*) and the variable element (*bx*), where *b* is the variable cost per unit and *x* is the measure of volume activity. Therefore the graph can be depicted by $y = a + bx$

Figure 8.4 *Mixed costs (semi-fixed or semi-variable costs)*

This complete cost analysis into fixed and variable costs can be used to represent graphically, as in Figure 8.5, the profit position of a business for any particular set of circumstances within the short-term time-scale. The total costs of the company are split into fixed and variable costs and we can restate our normal profit equation as follows:

Profit = Revenue – expenses
     = Revenue – (fixed costs + variable costs)

The most common way of representing this 'cost–volume–profit' relationship is to highlight how profit is earned by the business and particularly at what level of activity the business starts to make a profit. Where profit is exactly zero, the business is said to be 'breaking-even', and it is very useful to know the 'break-even point' for any company. Sales revenue is calculated from the sales volume multiplied by the selling price per unit and variable costs are similarly calculated by multiplying the same volume by the variable cost per unit (as variable costs, by definition, vary proportionately with activity or volume). Fixed

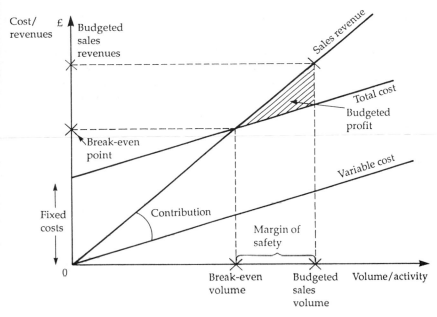

Figure 8.5   *Break-even chart*

costs are also, by definition, fixed provided that the graph is only drawn
for a particular relevant range and within a given time period.

   This break-even chart in Figure 8.5 is only valid for the particular set of
assumptions on which it is based and therefore, if any cost relationships
change, the chart must be redrawn. The following important points
should be noted and checked against Figure 8.5.

1 Sales revenue and variable costs are drawn as straight lines because of
   the assumption that only one selling price and a constant variable cost
   per unit are applicable to the whole range of the chart. For large
   changes in volume, the selling price will need to be changed and the
   chart would have to be redrawn. This restricts the range of activity
   which can be covered by one chart. The straight line used for sales
   revenue also assumes one sales mix for the products covered by the
   chart and if the mix of sales change the slope of the line will need to be
   redrawn. In the same way, not going outside the relevant range for
   the fixed costs restricts the range covered by the chart.
2 As fixed costs are treated as a constant, the total cost line given by
   fixed costs plus variable costs can be drawn parallel to the variable
   cost line.
3 The break-even point is where neither profit nor loss is made and is

thus at the point where the total cost line crosses the total sales revenue line.

4   If budgeted, forecast or actual sales levels are also plotted on the chart their relationship to the break-even point can be examined. In Figure 8.5 our budgeted sales revenues are above the level needed to break-even and so we are budgeting for the profit. The level of the profit is shown by the shaded area of the chart, and there is a 'margin of safety' available to the business which is the degree to which the sales levels can fall before the business fails to make a profit. This margin of safety can be expressed as a percentage of break-even sales volumes by using the formula:

$$\frac{(\text{budgeted sales} - \text{sales at break-even})}{\text{sales at break-even}} \times 100\%$$

It is now quite common for the break-even position to be expressed as a percentage of the total capacity of the business (that is the maximum volume or activity which can be supplied by the company) as this can indicate the scale of the risk that the business will be trading at a loss. A high percentage of total capacity represented by break-even indicates a high risk that sales volumes may be below this level and the company would, in the short term, be unable to reduce its costs to avoid making a loss. It also indicates that there are limited opportunities for the company to make large profits even when sales volumes are above break-even if the break-even volume is close to capacity.

5   The angle between the sales revenue line and the variable cost line indicates the contribution rate of business. This shows the rate at which the business covers its fixed costs by sales activity and then contributes to profit (hence the description).

$$\text{Contribution} = \text{Sales revenue} - \text{Variable costs}$$

[which can be expressed in per unit terms as:

Contribution per unit = Sales revenue per unit − Variable costs per unit]
but   Profit = Sales revenue − Variable costs − Fixed costs
Therefore Profit = Contribution − Fixed costs
thus   Contribution: 1 covers fixed costs
2 makes profits

This concept of contribution (sometimes described as contribution margin or economic profit) as the difference between the sales revenue and the variable costs is one of the most useful concepts in financial decision-making. As the volumes applied to sales and variable costs are the same we can use the *contribution per unit* as the difference between the

unit sales price and the variable cost per unit. This enables us to derive a
very useful relationship for the break-even volume, shown below.

Profit   = Revenue − Expenses
and Revenue   = Selling price per unit × Volume
and Expenses = Fixed costs + Variable cost per unit × Volume
but Break-even is where Profit = 0
     Therefore Revenue = Expenses
     Therefore Selling price per unit × Volume = Fixed costs +
     (Variable cost per unit × Volume)
     Therefore Volume (selling price − variable cost per unit) = Fixed
     costs

     Therefore Break-even volume = $\dfrac{\text{Fixed costs}}{\text{Contribution per unit}}$

This shows that the break-even point is dictated by the level of fixed
costs incurred by the business and the rate at which these fixed costs are
covered by making a contribution on each unit of sales. It is also possible
to graph the relationship between sales volumes and profits directly,
simply by combining the relationships shown on the break-even chart
into one line, as shown in Figure 8.6.

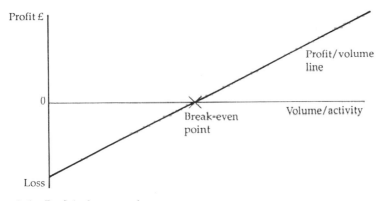

Figure 8.6   *Profit/volume graph*

So far we have considered charts which show how to measure break-
even but the main interest of companies is in making profit, and the
relationship of contribution − fixed costs = profit (see above) is critical to
this evaluation. The profit/volume graph in Figure 8.6 is devised directly
from this equation and illustrates how contribution covers fixed costs
until break-even and then contributes to profit above this level of activity.

While these charts are restricted to a given set of assumptions, they can
be quite flexible in their applications, because they can display the impact

of many potential changes in the business and in its environment. Any specific demands for profit can be incorporated, either as a fixed target profit (when it is treated as if it were an additional fixed cost) or as a fixed percentage of sales (when it is treated in an analogous way to an additional variable cost) and these are illustrated in Figures 8.7 and 8.8. Also, the impact of any known or possible changes in fixed costs, selling prices or variable costs can be assessed by redrawing the chart, using the new values in place of the old.

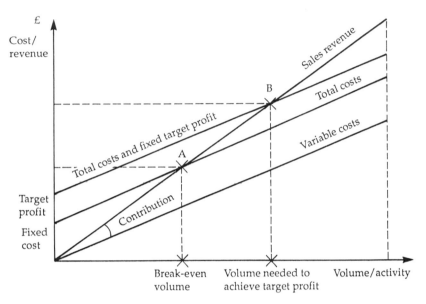

1 The fixed target profit can be added as a fixed element to the fixed costs and therefore generates another line parallel to the variable cost line, being total costs and target profit.
2 Where this line crosses the sales revenue line the company achieves its fixed target profit (that is, at point B on the chart)

Figure 8.7   *Fixed target profit incorporated in chart*

Potentially the greatest value is to compare the relative cost structures of different strategies and businesses, and the consequent risks associated with each. A business with a high level of fixed costs and low variable costs per unit needs to achieve a high contribution per unit or a very high volume if those fixed costs are to be recovered and a reasonable profit achieved. If a high contribution per unit can be achieved, once the fixed costs are covered, that is the break-even point is passed, the business will make profits at a rapid rate – after the break-even point profits are earned at the contribution rate. However, it is equally true for

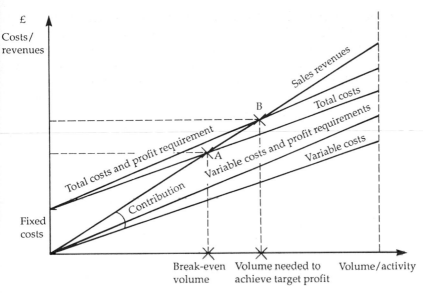

1 The target profit which is expressed as a percentage of sales revenue can be added to the variable cost line increasing the gradient and producing a new line – variable cost plus profit requirement.
2 This produces a net excess profit contribution towards fixed costs and where the new total cost and profit requirement line crosses the sales revenue line, the company achieves its objectives

Figure 8.8   *Target profit as a fixed percentage of sales revenue included in chart*

this business that substantial losses will be earned if the level of activity falls below the break-even level as the high fixed expenses will still be incurred. This situation is illustrated in Figure 8.9, which shows how a small movement in level of activity can make a dramatic difference to the profits of the business.

If a different strategy was possible which incurred much lower fixed costs but earned a lower level of contribution per unit as a consequence (as shown in Figure 8.10) the risk profile of the business could be altered significantly. The potential losses could be minimized because costs would decrease with decreasing sales, but the profit potential from increased activity is also greatly reduced.

It may seem unlikely that any business could operate in the same industry with such different cost structures but one obvious cause could be the level of vertical integration. If a business manufactures all its own products it may incur very high fixed costs of equipment, labour and other indirect expenses and the variable costs may be limited to raw materials at one end of the process and some of the marketing and distribution expenses at the other end and these, even in total, could be

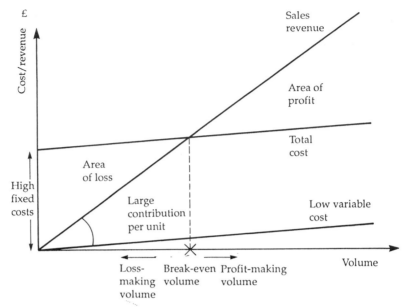

Figure 8.9   *High fixed cost/high contribution*

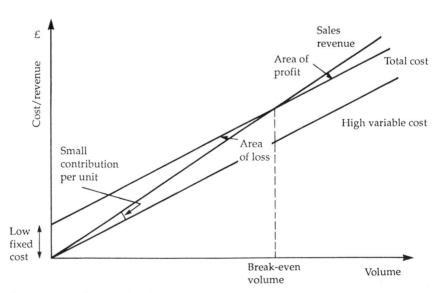

Figure 8.10   *Low fixed cost/low contribution*

quite small relatively. Alternatively the business could buy in the finished products and act as a marketing and distribution specialist, where a much greater proportion of its costs (that is the bought-in product costs) are variable and its contribution per unit will be correspondingly smaller. Its fixed costs will be dramatically lower also as it has transferred most of those costs back to its suppliers, and therefore its risk of making large losses is reduced; together with its opportunity of making as large profits as its vertically integrated competitor when sales demand is high.

Different marketing strategies can have an equally dramatic impact on the cost structures of parts of the business. If a company selects a high direct advertising expenditure strategy or direct sales campaign to create demand for its products or services it will be incurring a *fixed* cost because the expenditure incurred is independent of the consequent sales achieved. An alternative, possibly lower risk, strategy is to try to stimulate demand by some promotional activities which directly link the expenditure to the sales created, for example, money-off offers or collectable campaigns. This type of promotional activity is much more of a *variable* cost and hence reduces the contribution per unit earned on each sale, but it does not force the company to incur the cost unless sales are being achieved. Clearly these activities will often serve different marketing objectives and will therefore be complementary parts of one strategy, but the relative weighting given to each area of expenditure can vary significantly between companies in the same industry.

Similar logic can be applied in the service sector where a large consultancy operation could employ a lot of permanent staff who would represent a very high fixed cost. As a consequence it would have almost no variable cost to deduct from its fee income and so its profit or loss level would be completely controlled by the level of staff utilization (that is, the proportion of staff time which is chargeable to clients) and profits would fluctuate dramatically as these utilization rates changed. If it decided not to employ these people on a permanent basis but to hire in self-employed consultants as needed, it could dramatically reduce its fixed cost base, but would now incur a high variable cost to match against its fee income which reduces the contribution rate. Several more illustrations of these types of alternatives are examined in Part Five, but the selection of cost structure is clearly a very important issue for a business.

If we consider individual industries the impact of the relative proportions of fixed and variable costs becomes even clearer and helps to explain many specific marketing strategies. An airline has almost entirely fixed costs for its scheduled flights and the extra cost incurred for carrying another passenger is very, very small. Therefore any sales revenue generated from an additional traveller is almost totally contribution. Thus airlines are very keen to fill all the seats on a plane, and it could be argued that it should sell any remaining seats at any price above its variable costs. We do have to remember the opportunity cost argument which insists that we consider whether greater alternative benefits could be obtained by selling the seats at higher prices.

Airlines can select a range of different marketing strategies based on their cost structure of predominantly fixed costs. One option is to have a high selling price (for example, only first class fares) and accept a lower level of utilization due to the lower volume of sales. The other extreme is to have a very low price level and consequently fill every seat on every flight, so that full capacity utilization is achieved. The best strategy, assuming a profit-motivated company, is the one that generates the highest contribution to help pay for the fixed costs. This is likely to be achieved by segmenting the market as far as possible, and charging the maximum fare achievable in each segment. Given that the overall service which is being delivered to each customer is the same, that is, air transportation from point A to point B, the degree of differentiation that has been achieved is quite staggering and is reflected in the vast array of prices that are charged (for example, first class, club, economy, Apex, package rate, standby). Each of these alternatives must cover its direct variable costs (for example, specific marketing expenses) and make an adequate contribution to fixed costs. However, the contribution from each segment is not the same and therefore it is more profitable to sell a club or business fare ticket than to fill that seat with a lower fare-paying passenger. It is still better to sell a standby ticket for the seat than to forego any sales revenue at all, and this is one of the key problems for the airline. What is required is both flexibility in seating on the aeroplane, which can be achieved by extending or compressing the club section as required or seating business class passengers in first class if necessary, and a marketing strategy which guarantees some revenue for a seat but does not pass up the opportunity of higher revenue if this becomes available at the last moment. This aspect can be partially achieved by having a very sophisticated information system which projects the final sales mix for each flight based on the actual booking position at any point in time, and which enables prices to be altered if desirable. Also a sales format (standby fares) which allows the company to defer the low fare-paying passenger onto a later flight, if higher contribution generating passengers wish to travel, is an additional way of ensuring the maximum contribution per flight.

This example illustrates several important points regarding the use of cost structures in decision-making. A ticket on a particular airline flight is an ideal example of a perishable product in that once the flight has taken off the opportunity to generate any sales revenue from the ticket has been lost forever – in the same way as a hotel room for any night has no value once the night is passed. This increases the need for flexibility in pricing so as to generate some *contribution* before the opportunity is gone forever. The degree of flexibility will be conditioned by the cost structure of the particular business and where the vast majority of the costs are fixed the greatest flexibility is possible. If we fill the aeroplane at very low prices we may maximize our contribution level but fail to cover our fixed costs. If sales revenues do not more than equal total costs over a reasonable time period, we may be unable to pay for our level of new high fixed cash costs as they arise in the future and then we will go out of business. This reflects the difference between the short term and the long term, and between committed or sunk costs and discretionary costs.

In the short term we have the fixed costs associated with our scheduled flight programme and maximizing the contribution from any flight even though this only seems to minimize our total accounting losses may be our best alternative. This is because some of the fixed costs of operating the flight are sunk (for example, the purchase costs of the aeroplanes which generates the depreciation expense) and the remainder are committed for some time period (for example, salaries for employees and fuel for each scheduled flight which we are contracted to fly). In the longer term we have much more discretion because we can redeploy our staff and aeroplanes (or decide not to replace them) to profitable routes. Unless each route can be seen to be generating sales revenues in excess of its total costs in the longer term we may decide to cease that particular operation. Therefore contribution pricing (which sets prices so as to maximize contribution levels and ignores fixed costs) may be the best solution in the short term but in the long term all costs must be recovered, and in the very long term no costs are fixed and hence all costs vary with activity. It is also important that the longer-term implications of short-term pricing strategies are carefully considered, as creating a market expectation of a particular price level which does not fully cover total costs can be very dangerous, even if it is done for apparently very sound short-term financial reasons. The company will need to increase its prices to cover its total costs at some point in the future, but if its customers have become used to the lower level of contribution pricing they may be unwilling to pay the higher prices being demanded by the company. If sales volumes decline substantially, the company may still be unable to recover its total costs.

Marginal costs

There is another term for describing the direct variable costs associated with any decision and this is 'marginal cost'. The *marginal cost* of a product is strictly defined as the cost of producing one more unit but in accounting it is extended to cover the cost of producing the incremental volume under consideration for any specific decision. Normally the marginal cost will equal the directly variable costs but if the decision moves the activity level outside the particular relevant range the fixed costs may alter as well, and marginal cost is then equal to the differential cost considered in Chapter 7. We will continue to use the term differential cost but readers will find marginal cost used in other reading material and should be aware of its definition.

Fixed costs remain fixed for a specified relevant range and time span and often when they change they immediately become fixed again for another relevant range (for example, rent, which increases when a new building is occupied but becomes fixed again for the new rental period on the total buildings now occupied). Therefore, many fixed costs can be graphed as a step function or a series of plateaux, depending on the size of the relevant ranges for the timing of movements from one plateau to the next, as illustrated in Figure 8.11.

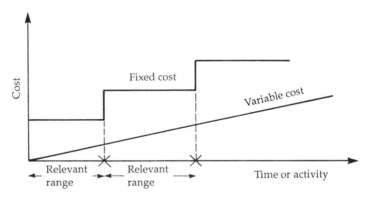

Figure 8.11   *Plateaux of fixed costs*

If the fixed costs increase in sizeable steps it becomes important to know if a particular decision means that a fixed cost will move outside its relevant range and will thus increase. For example, a decision to hire several more office employees would not necessarily increase occupancy costs (the cost of occupying space, that is, rent, rates, lighting and heating, etc.) unless there was no spare space available and a new building had to be rented. If no spare space was available the differential cost of hiring a few people might be very high if the only way to acquire additional space was to rent another building or an additional floor in a new office block. If this new fixed cost was taken on, there might well be a lot of spare office space now made available which would mean that more people could be hired at no additional rent cost. Thus differential costs are not uniform, and are specific to the particular decision being considered.

Differential versus average costs

In this sense differential costs can be contrasted with the average costs incurred which are much more uniform and are the normal costs obtainable from published financial statements. Average costs are simply the total costs divided by the relevant volume measure. For example, the average cost per mile of running a company car could be calculated by finding the total annual costs and dividing by the number of miles travelled per year. Suppose a particular car costs £500 per year to tax and insure, £700 for maintenance (which is planned by time and not mileage) and the depreciation expense is £1200 per year: it also costs 10 pence per mile in petrol and oil, which will, of course, vary with the mileage. If the current mileage is 12 000 per year, the average cost is 30p per mile (see below).

$$\text{Average cost per mile} = \frac{\text{Fixed cost}}{\text{Mileage}} + \text{variable cost per mile}$$

$$\frac{£2400}{12\ 000} + 10p = 30p \text{ per mile}$$

The financial director considers that this average cost is too high and, looking for ways to reduce it, hits upon the idea of increasing the mileage travelled by each car. If this could be doubled, the average cost would reduce to 20p per mile:

$$(\frac{£2400}{24\ 000} + 10p = 20p \text{ per mile}).$$

Clearly this decision has really incurred a differential cost increase of 12 000 miles (19 300 km) at 10p per mile, that is, £1200, provided that the fixed costs really do remain fixed given the increased level of activity. If extra maintenance costs had to be incurred, the differential costs would be even higher for the extra 12 000 miles (19 300) km).

This concentration of differential costs on the changes which result from decisions makes it ideal as a decision technique and it is much more relevant than the more readily available average cost. (Because this type of costing technique concentrates on the differences in costs resulting from a decision and does not differentiate between fixed and variable costing, it is most logically described as 'differential costing' and that is why we are using the description throughout the book.) Differential costing can also usefully be contrasted with another widely used costing method, absorption costing.

Differential costing versus absorption costing

In Chapters 3 and 5 we discussed the valuation of stocks and work in progress and considered how stock is valued at cost in financial statements. The question must then be asked as to what level of cost should be applied to value this stock, and for financial statements absorption costing has typically been used in preference to the differential costing technique. *Absorption costing* takes all the costs incurred (including fixed and variable) and spreads these full costs across the output of the business, so that each element bears a proportion of the total cost. Thus all stock and work in progress values will include a proportion of relevant indirect costs, whereas the differential cost of the stock would only include the direct costs incurred. As with previous examples the particular accounting technique used cannot alter the total profit made from any specific project but it can change the period in which the profits are reported, and this can have a significant impact on the perceived performance of the business. An example may clarify the difference.

Example

Peter White runs a small specialist electronics business and has developed a new attachment for microcomputers which enables the most sophisticated computer games to be played on the cheaper machines. He realizes that the product life cycle will be very short (less than one year) because his invention will be copied and incorporated by the major manufacturers. He decides to manufacture and sell through distributors, giving high volume discounts to stimulate high volume sales. Peter's financial year end is in six months' time, in the middle of this product's life expectancy and he is preparing his budgets to show the impact of this new product on his financial position in each year.

The relevant information has been established as follows:

	Year 1	Year 2	Total
Forecast sales: Volumes	12 000	16 000	28 000
Sales values @ £30 per unit	£360 000	£480 000	£840 000
Forecast Production: Volumes	20 000	8000	28 000
Direct variable cost of manufacture @ £15 per unit	£300 000	£120 000	£420 000
Other expenses including development, marketing, indirect manufacturing, etc.	£200 000	£40 000	£240 000

Overall the plan looks substantially profitable as it should generate a profit of £180 000 (sales revenues of £840 000 less direct variable costs of £420 000 and less other expenses of £240 000), but Peter wants to know when this profit will be shown in his accounts. In view of the short-term nature of the project he is regarding all the indirect expenses as being fixed in nature because he has committed himself to these levels of expenditure whatever the success or failure of sales volumes.

If we apply the logic of differential costing, we would only bring into consideration the costs which are directly incurred as a result of a particular decision. Therefore we have made a decision in that we plan to produce 20 000 units and sell only 12 000 units in year one, and the costs directly incurred as a result of producing the 8000 units for stock are the variable costs of production only, that is, £15 per unit. Thus we would value our stock at £15 per unit under differential costing rules, and this would give us the profit and loss accounts for the two years which are shown in Table 8.1.

Table 8.1 *Profit and loss accounts for each year (using differential costing)*

	Year 1	Year 1	Year 2	Year 2	Total
Sales (at £30)		12 000 £360 000		16 000 £480 000	£840 000
Opening stock	–		£120 000		
Direct production costs	£300 000		£120 000		
Subtotal	£300 000		£240 000		
less Closing stock	£120 000	180 000	–	240 000	420 000
Contribution		£180 000		£240 000	£420 000
less Indirect expenses		£200 000		£40 000	£240 000
Net profit/(loss)		£(20 000)		£200 000	£180 000

By writing off all the indirect expenses incurred in year one a small loss would be reported, whereas in year two a very sizeable profit will be shown as a consequence of the very low indirect expenses in that period. However, for published financial statements at least some of these expenses would be included in the stock valuation and therefore carried forward to year two. If we suppose for simplicity that all of them could be included in the stock valuation (the non-manufacturing expenses, and particularly any marketing expenditure would normally be excluded) and we apply absorption costing to the stock valuation we can change the presentation of profits quite substantially. The indirect costs per unit produced in year one can be seen to be £10 which is given by total indirect costs of £200 000 divided by the production volume in year one of 20 000 units.

Therefore the stock value becomes:

Variable cost per unit	£15
+ Indirect cost per unit	£10
Total absorption cost	£25

The impact of using this absorption costing based stock valuation is shown in Figure 8.12. The total profit has not been affected but year one now shows a healthy forecast profit of £60 000 rather than the previous loss of £20 000. This increase is reflected in the increased stock value (£200 000 compared to £120 000) which has the effect of decreasing the year two results when this higher valued stock is sold. As previously mentioned there is an essential degree of managerial judgement in valuing stock and this is particularly true in the area of indirect costs recovery but using the very simple and decision-relevant differential costing basis produces an answer which is considered unacceptably prudent for published financial statements.

Profit and loss accounts for each year (using absorption costing)

	Year 1		*Year 1*			*Year 2*	*Total*
Sales (at £30)		12 000 £360 000			16 000	£480 000	£840 000
Opening stock –	–			£200 000			
Production costs (including indirect expenses)	£500 000		£160 000				
	£500 000		£360 000				
less Closing stock	£200 000		–				
Total expenses		£300 000				£360 000	£660 000
Net profit		£60 000				£120 000	£180 000

Figure 8.12

Cost apportionment

Absorption costing has a much wider impact than just being the basis for stock valuations because it is also the basis for spreading indirect costs to products, markets, customers, channels, etc. In Chapter 5 of the book we separated direct costs from indirect costs and stated that indirect costs can and should (for certain purposes) be apportioned or spread to cost objects when necessary. Direct costs are incurred because of specific cost objects and can therefore be directly allocated to them in total. Indirect costs are, be definition, shared by more than one cost object and therefore need an *absorption costing basis* to spread the costs across the relevant cost objects. Differential costing only includes those costs *directly* incurred as a result of the particular decision, and thus does not include any indirect costs and therefore has no need of apportionment. In many cases the basis of apportionment is obvious, as it is the main determinant of the size of the indirect cost; for example, rent will normally be shared out on the basis of the area occupied. For some indirect costs there does not seem to be any sensible method of apportionment, such as corporate advertising and public relations expenditure, and some companies will use an arbitrary method such as sales revenue whereas other companies will not spread these costs and leave them at the centre of the company as a general indirect expense.

It is important that companies understand the dangers inherent in apportioning all costs to any cost objects, as well as those caused by leaving these costs at the centre in this central cost 'bucket'. If all costs are apportioned the danger is that managers may forget that these costs are not necessarily all direct or variable, and make decisions based on the information supplied including the apportioned costs. A simplified example from a very large multinational may make this clearer. The group consists of three operating divisions and a head office, which provides a very wide range of general support services, such as computing, legal and professional, accounting and treasury, public relations and senior corporate management. The divisions generate all the sales revenue and head office costs are apportioned out to the divisions on the basis of sales turnover (in the absence of a better method of apportionment) in an attempt to assess the profitability of each division. As part of the budgeting process one of the head office finance team was studying the summarized budgets shown.

Division	A £	B £	C £	Total £
Sales revenue	30 m	20 m	10 m	60 m
Variable costs	20 m	15 m	5 m	40 m
Contribution	10 m	5 m	5 m	20 m
Divisional fixed costs	7 m	4 m	2 m	13 m
Divisional profit before head office costs	3 m	1 m	3 m	7 m
Group head office costs				6 m
Group net profit				£1 m

At first sight, the position seemed quite satisfactory because each division was forecasting a profit before head office costs and the group overall was projecting a profit of £1 million, but the finance manager decided to look at the budgets after the apportioned head office costs as these would be used by head office managers to examine the divisional results in more detail. This exercise gave the results shown in Figure 8.13, using the group's system of apportioning head office costs on the basis of sales revenue.

Restated: budgeted profit and loss accounts

	A £	B £	C £	Total £
Sales revenue	30 m	20 m	10 m	60 m
Divisional profit before head office costs	3 m	1 m	3 m	7 m
Shared head office costs	3 m	2 m	1 m	6 m
(the apportionment is based on £1 m per £10 m of sales revenue)				
Net profit	£0	£(1 m)	£2 m	£1 m

Figure 8.13

This showed a very different picture and suggested that division C was highly profitable whereas division B was making a loss for the group! 'Surely the group would be better off by closing B down and stopping the loss!' thought the finance manager, who therefore looked at the analysis which would result without division B, and this is shown in Figure 8.14.

Restated profit and loss accounts after closing division B

	A £	B £	C £	Total £
Sales revenue	30 m	X [*closed*]	10 m	40 m
Divisional profit	3 m	0	3 m	6 m
Original apportionment of head office costs	3 m	2 m	1 m	6 m
Reallocate B's share of head office based on sales revenue	1.5 m	(2 m)	0.5 m	0
Net profit	£(1.5 m)	0	1.5 m	£0 m

Figure 8.14

This was not going the way it should, the group was now only at break-even overall and division C was less profitable, but division A was making a bigger loss than division B was before it was closed down. Therefore perhaps it should also be closed down. If this was done the analysis became much simpler as there was now only one *profitable* division left as shown in Figure 8.15. According to the results shown in this table the whole group was now a disaster and it should be closed down completely!

Restated profit and loss account after closing divisions A and B

	A £	B £	C £	Total £
Sales revenue	X	X	30 m	30 m
	[closed]			
Divisional profit	0	0	3 m	3 m
Apportioned head office costs	4.5 m		1.5 m	6 m
Reallocate A's share of head office	(4.5 m)	–	4.5 m	0
Group net profit	0	0	£(3 m)	£(3 m)

Figure 8.15

Prior to the apportionment exercise the group was projecting a profit of £1 million but if apparent profit improvement decisions were based on the apportioned information it would be projecting a substantial loss which is clearly nonsense. These decisions ignored the basic rules which we have established for financial decisions: financial decisions are based on things which *really* change as a result of the decision.

In this potentially disastrous series of decisions we have included costs which only appear to change as a result of our decisions, for example, the divisional allocation of head office expenses. These are still included at a total of £6 million after we have closed down divisions A and B, which means that they are not affected by our decision and should be excluded from the evaluation because they are not differential costs. The more logical decision process would be to compare what we give up and what we gain from the decision, in other words to base the decision on the differential costs only.

The first decision was whether to close division B because it appeared to be making a loss, but if we closed the division we would lose the divisional profit contribution of £1 million. Therefore unless we can save more than £1 million out of our head office expenditure as a consequence of closing B, we will be worse off as a result of such a decision. Here 'saving' means exactly that – not spending the cash in future – rather than simply reapportioning the costs to another part of the group. Hence decisions are still based on differential costs, and this type of exercise requires that we can identify the 'avoidable' costs which will result from any change. (Avoidable costs being those that can literally be avoided as a consequence of the decision and which are also known as, not surprisingly, severable costs. These were discussed in Chapter 7.)

Therefore, we need to be careful how we use apportioned costs, but if we do not spread indirect costs to those areas of the business which benefit from the expenditure we may experience different but also serious problems. If a business segment has use of central facilities but is not required to 'pay' for them (through a cost apportionment system) there is a high possibility that it will not utilize them in the same economic way that it would if it was charged for the full costs incurred. Thus 'free' central or indirect facilities can be used uneconomically and the total costs of the business can increase as a result. What is required is a sensible system of pricing for the indirect resource so that managers can make sensible judgements as to whether 'to buy' the facilities or not. This internal system of pricing (known as 'transfer pricing') needs to be applied sensibly or it can create great internal dissension and demotivation.

An example from a different large group may highlight some of the reasons for concern, and others are discussed in Chapter 10. Earlier in this section on cost apportionment we said that rent was normally an easy expense to apportion on the basis of the area occupied, but it can in certain circumstances still create complications. Our large services group occupied a seven-storey building right in the centre of London which served as its head office but also had space for some of the operating divisions as well. Most of these operating divisions had some employees based around London but they tended to be in cheaper areas of the city, and hence occupancy costs were lower. The group used a system of charging out central services, including rent, to those divisions using the services so as to avoid some of the problems of arbitrary cost apportionment (this was a recent change caused by some severe decision-making issues resulting from generally spreading all head office costs). Thus the rent for the unoccupied parts of the head office building were charged to those divisions occupying the space and initially divisions X, Y and Z occupied one floor each. The total occupancy costs for the building were budgeted at £1.4 million for the forthcoming year, and on a simple apportionment across the seven floors a charge of £200 000 was to be made to each division.

The general manager of division X was under competitive pressure in the marketplace for that division's products and consequently was very keen to make savings wherever possible. She therefore suggested that her division should move out of head office and rent cheaper accommodation on the outskirts of London at a total cost of £100 000 – a saving against budget of £100 000. This seemed sensible but nobody else wanted to take up the now vacated floor in the head office building, so the budgeting system recalculated the occupancy cost per floor by dividing the total cost of £1.4 million by the six floors now occupied. Therefore division Y and Z were now to be charged £233 333 each for occupying their space and division X's apparent saving was getting bigger by the minute!

Not surprisingly division Y now decided to move out and was able to rent space quite close by for £180 000 per year, and thus show a saving of £53 333 against the new projected costs. Before division Z could follow suit, head office were able to find an outside tenant for the two floors now vacant, as a result of the other divisions moving out, at a rental per floor of £75 000 per year. They therefore recalculated the budgeted charge to division Z as shown below at £250 000:

Total cost of occupancy for seven floors	£1.4m
less Rent received for two floors	150k
Net cost to group for five floors	£1.25m
Therefore New cost per floor	=£250 000

If we consider the actual impact on the group of this sequence of events which is shown by the differential costs, we will see how much costs have increased. In cash flow terms divisions X and Y are now paying out a total of £280 000 in rent which is extra cash leaving the group, whereas head office is only receiving £150 000 in extra cash from the outside tenant. Costs have increased in cash terms by £130 000, although the divisional accounts of both X and Y will show an improvement against the budgeted levels based on apportioned costs. Had the business looked at the opportunity costs available, it should have been able to agree a rent with divisions X and Y which reflected the cash cost of these divisions renting alternative space, or the potential rent achievable from an outside party. This group has very recently moved its head office completely out of London on the justification that the occupancy costs had become too high!

Contribution analysis

We have seen how spreading indirect expenses can cause problems when trying to make decisions, and how a concentration on differential costs can help companies to focus on the relevant decision costs. If fixed costs are fixed, the differential costs are equal to the directly variable costs and therefore if a decision affects the level of sales the decision requires the use of contribution analysis, shown below.

Contribution per unit =Sales revenue per unit −Variable cost per unit

Contribution analysis enables us to ignore costs which do not change or are common (that is, will be incurred) both before and after implementing the decision, and therefore provides a very direct solution to a wide range of marketing problems. However, it must be remembered that costs only remain fixed in the short term and thus contribution analysis is particularly relevant to short time scale decisions. A series of examples can illustrate how contribution analysis works.

Example 1

A company proposes to increase its advertising expenditure by £100 000 on a product which sells for £5 per unit and which has a variable cost per unit of £3. How many more units must be sold to justify the expenditure? Ignoring complicating issues such as the time value of money and the risk associated with the additional activity, it is quite straightforward to use a variation of our break-even calculation.

The product has a contribution of £2 per unit (that is, £5−£3) and we need to recover £100 000 to break-even. Therefore we must plan to sell at least 50 000 additional units to justify the extra advertising expenditure.

Example 2

We can apply a similar approach to decisions that affect price levels and hence alter the contribution rate achieved. Our retailer, George Taylor, buys some of his goods from a wholesaler who makes a small contribution of 5 per cent on his sales (that is, he sells for £1 something which he has bought for 95p). The wholesaler wishes to give George a discount to encourage him to buy more goods from him, and therefore is considering reducing his effective prices to George by 2½ per cent in the form of a retrospective rebate, which hardly seems a massive change in price level. He wishes to know how much additional business he must generate to break-even on this idea. At present George is spending £50 000 per year on goods from this wholesaler and so the contribution earned is as follows:

$$\text{Contribution at present} = £50\ 000 \times 5\% = \underline{£2500}$$

If the wholesaler reduces his prices by 2½ per cent he will not automatically reduce his variable costs per unit, and so this reduction will come out of his contribution. This will reduce his contribution to half its previous level; strictly the contribution earned will be given by selling for 97½p what he has still bought for 95p. In order to earn the same overall contribution of £2500 he therefore needs to *double* the sales made to George:

Sales of £100 000 × contribution of 2½% = £2500 total contribution

The requirement for such a dramatic increase in sales is caused by the low level of contribution. The percentage price decrease is irrelevant to the calculation. What is important is that the wholesaler is giving away half of his existing contribution.

Example 3
If we compare this situation to a jewellery retailer making a 50 per cent contribution (that is, selling goods for double what he bought them for) the difference becomes quite clear. If the jewellery retailer reduces his effective selling prices by 2½ per cent through a free giveaway offer he needs to increase sales by just over 5 per cent to break-even as shown below.

If sales now are £2000 per week
Contribution @ 50% is £1000 per week
After price decrease of 2.5% contribution is reduced to 47.5%
If retailer wishes to maintain contribution at previous £1000 per week
Equation is now:
New Sales @ 47.5% = £1000.
Therefore   Sales will have to increase to £2105.26p. This is a sales increase of:

$$\frac{£105.26}{£2000} \times 100\% = 5.26\%$$

Due to a higher contribution rate, the jeweller is giving away proportionately less of his total contribution and can, in fact, afford to reduce effective prices by 25 per cent before sales have to double to break-even. The critical relationship is between the contribution which is lost and the contribution which is retained, and the sales increase required can be generated into the formula given below.

$$\frac{\text{Sales change required}}{\text{to break-even}} = \frac{\text{Contribution change}}{\text{contribution retained}} \times 100\%$$

If we apply this formula (the mathematics of which is set out in an appendix to this chapter) to the cases of the wholesaler and jeweller (examples 2 and 3) we get the sales increases shown below which support our previous calculations.

$$\text{Wholesaler: Sales increase required to break even} = \frac{\text{Effective price change} \times 100\%}{\text{Contribution after price change}}$$

$$\text{Sales increase required} = \frac{2\frac{1}{2}\%}{2\frac{1}{2}\%} \times 100\%$$

$$= 100\%$$

$$\text{Jeweller: Sales increase required} = \frac{\text{Price change}}{\text{contribution after price change}} \times 100\%$$

$$= \frac{2\frac{1}{2}\%}{47\frac{1}{2}\%} \times 100\%$$

$$= 5.26\%$$

George Taylor could obviously use this logic on his own business where he is at present making 25 per cent contribution on some products which are not selling well. If he reduces the price by 5 per cent to break-even he will need to expand his sales volumes by:

$$\frac{5\%}{(25-5\%)} \times 100\% \text{ or } 25\%$$

Before the change he is selling £500 worth per week of these goods, which is making £125 contribution to his business. New sales of £625 per week at a lower contribution rate of 20 per cent would also generate £125 contribution to the business.

This technique is clearly relevant to any type of business and focuses attention on changes in levels of contribution rather than changes in prices. It can be used to assess the level of decline in sales which could be tolerated on a price increase before the company becomes worse off. If our wholesaler considered putting prices up $2\frac{1}{2}$ per cent rather than down the expectation would be for sales to decline but a drop of less than $33\frac{1}{3}$ per cent would leave the business better off. This can be shown by using the formula in a similar way for price increases:

$$\text{Sales decrease which can occur and still break-even} = \frac{\text{Contribution gain}}{\text{New contribution}} \times 100\%$$

$$= \frac{2\frac{1}{2}\%}{5\% + 2\frac{1}{2}\%} \times 100\%$$

$$= 33\frac{1}{3}\%$$

The expected volume change will obviously depend on the assumed price elasticity of demand in the particular market, but the technique can very quickly calculate the level of change needed for any proposal. This required or acceptable change can be assessed for reasonableness, or compared against separately developed forecasts.

Contribution per unit of limiting factor

We can apply this contribution analysis procedure to identify the optimum allocation of resources within a business or a segment of the business, which can be extremely useful when we face resource constraints. As mentioned earlier in the chapter, immoveable resource constraints are particularly common in budgeting time scales which are also when the separation of fixed and variable costs is most appropriate. For longer-term planning most costs can change with activity, and thus contribution rates are not constant and many constraints on resources can be removed by specific management actions.

In many businesses a range of goods or services are sold which share common resources, not least being the sales and marketing resources, and to maximize the performance of the business it is important to use these resources in the optimal way.

Let us consider the position of a division of a fmcg company which has three products but is currently trading at a loss after all the divisional and group apportionments have been made. The division is trading in a very competitive and mature market, but one where differentiation is possible and marketing initiatives can prove successful.

The monthly budget is set out below, and includes the apportioned costs to the products from the division and from the group to the division.

Product	A	B	C	TOTAL
Current volume in cases	30 000	30 000	40 000	100 000
Selling price per case	£5	£5	£6	
Variable cost per case	£3	£2	£4	
Contribution per case	£2	£3	£2	
Therefore total contribution	£60 000	£90 000	£80 000	£230 000
Direct fixed costs	£30 000	£10 000	£20 000	£60 000
Divisional fixed costs (apportioned to products on basis of revenue)	£45 000	£45 000	£60 000	£150 000
Divisional profit	£(15 000)	£35 000	£0	£20 000
Apportioned group costs				£50 000
Net (loss) per month				£(30 000)

For the purposes of our analysis we can ignore the direct fixed costs and the apportioned costs except to the extent that our decisions may result in changes to them, and we can concentrate on the contribution levels of the various products. If we can improve the product mix achieved by the division we may be able to improve the profitability quite significantly. This can be done by reallocating resources to the products with the higher contributions relative to any constraints, or by using up any unutilized resources to produce a positive net contribution. At first sight it would appear logical to try to expand sales of product B, even at the expense of products A and C, because it has a higher rate of contribution per unit. In a competitive market it may be necessary to reduce the selling price to expand sales and this would reduce the contribution level, but it would still be worthwhile until the contribution rate reached that of one of the other two products. This is where the planning process, the analytical work and the managerial judgement of the operating managers all come together to forecast the impact on sales of changes in the marketing strategy. The benefit of using the contribution rate is that it immediately helps to concentrate management attention on the critical areas of the business, rather than being confused by a mass of financial information.

In this particular example there is an added complication of a specific production constraint which cannot be removed in the short term. These three products are all produced on a particular machine which is already running 24 hours per day, seven days per week and therefore total production cannot be expanded. However, the products do not all take the same amount of machine time to produce, and the relative times are given below.

	A	B	C	Total
Machine-hours per '000 cases (1)	4	8	8	
Total cases per month (as per budget) (2)	30 000	30 000	40 000	100 000
Total hours per month $\dfrac{(1)\times(2)}{1000}$	120	240	320	680

(680 hours equals full effective utilization of the machinery each month)

This new constraint stops us from expanding sales of any product, unless we free production capacity by producing less of another product, but the different production rates give us a new picture of the relative product contributions. To maximize the overall contribution we need to use our limiting resource to our best advantage, and this requires an evaluation of contributions per machine hour, as shown below.

	A	B	C
Contribution per case (1)	£2	£3	£2
Therefore contribution per 1000 cases (2) [(1)×1000]	£2000	£3000	£2000
Machine-hours per '000 cases (see above) (3)	4	8	8
Therefore contribution per machine-hour (4) [(2) ÷ (3)]	£500	£375	£250

Product A now displays a clear advantage over the other products due to its more efficient use of the limiting factor, machine time, because (as shown above) it generates a contribution per machine hour of £500 whereas C only produces £250 contribution per machine hour and even B trails with £375. Therefore it is logical to divert resources away from product C, with the lowest contribution rate, to increase output of product A. This will enable us to expand the total volume of product produced above 100 000 units per month, as one extra hour used producing A increases output by 125 cases, and hence enhance the overall divisional performance. In increasing sales of product A we will probably have to reduce its selling price and so lower its contribution but we can continue to divert resources until product A's contribution reaches that of product B.

In this example if we wish to increase sales of product A by 66.7 per cent we need to reduce its selling price to £4.50 and this reduces its contribution per case to £1.50. Even more importantly it reduces the contribution per machine hour to £375, as shown below, and this is equal to that produced by product B.

Product	A	B	C	
Adjusted selling price per case	£4.5	£5	£7	
Variable cost per case	£3	£2	£4	
Contribution per case (1)	£1.5	£3	£3	
Adjusted contribution per machine-hour	£375	£375	£375	Total
Adjusted volumes in cases (2)	50 000	30 000	30 000	110 000
Total contribution (1)×(2)	£75 000	£90 000	£90 000	£255 000
Total machine hours used	200	240	240	680

This means that it is illogical to try to increase sales of product A any further by even greater reductions in price because its contribution rate per machine-hour would then be lower than product B, which would then become the division's most financially attractive product.

In order to increase output of product A, we have had to divert resources away from product C, but because of its relatively inefficient production rate the loss in production is less than the increase in A. As the volume of product C available for sale is reducing, it may be possible to increase the selling price on that remaining, and in this example the selling price of product C is increased to £7. As shown above this increases the contribution per case and also raises the contribution per machine-hour to £375, thus equalling products A and B. As all three products are now producing the same contribution per machine-hour (that is, per unit of limiting factor) there is no financial advantage to be gained from reallocating resources, and this can be described as an optimal solution to the allocation of resources problem. In the real situation of this company there were over 250 products involved, not three as in our simplified example, and one of the major practical problems in using this technique is the sheer number of computations involved. Fortunately there is a mathematical technique which can be set up on a computer and which will solve the problem of vast numbers of products and even of several constraints (that is, limiting factors which affect different products in different ways). The technique is known as 'linear programming' and will find the optimal solution provided all the necessary information is made available in the form of mathematical equations. Linear programming is widely used for resource allocation problems, but the input to the required equations normally involves the exercise of a great deal of managerial judgement, particularly if the problem relates to the marketing area and sales forecasts at different selling prices.

In our simplified example (above, page 269) we can see that the total contribution achieved by reallocating our production resources is £255 000 which is an improvement of £25 000 over the original total contribution of £230 000 (see monthly budget, page 267). This improvement is not enough completely to remove the budgeted loss per month of £30 000, after the direct fixed costs and apportioned costs have been charged; but, as stated at the beginning of the example, these are not differential costs for the decision under consideration and can be ignored. It is better to make a small loss (£5000) than to make a bigger loss (£30 000), and therefore our decision has improved the financial performance, and the analytical process has been worthwhile.

The key to this process is identifying the limiting factor (key constraint) for each segment of the business and then selecting the appropriate strategy to optimize the contribution per unit of this limiting factor. If this is achieved the total contribution for the segment will be maximized, but the limiting factor may change over time, and for different parts of the business. Therefore this evaluation of contributions should be done for customer groupings and channels of distribution as well as for products. Understanding the different profit contributions generated from these segments is the start to reallocating resources to maximize the overall return, and linear programming can be a great aid to the analysis.

Analysing the budget

For this segmented contribution analysis to be practical the budget must be broken down into the controllable elements of the business (that is, the elements over which managers can exercise genuine control through decisions and not arbitrary or legally defined subdivisions of the total organization). Thus sales and variable costs will be split by products and markets to fit the way the company is organized, but it must also be possible to group products or customers together in different ways if this will help decisions on the allocation of resources. Products may be principally analysed into the market groupings where they are sold (for example, consumer, industrial, etc.) but the key limiting factor may be a particular aspect of production or distribution and this form of analysis may be more relevant to a resource allocation decision. A matrix type structure can be used which allows the budget to be reanalysed and modern computer systems can cope with such issues very readily provided the information is input correctly in the first place, that is, by coding the inputs so that they can be sorted into the desired groupings for subsequent analysis.

It is also important that the budget objectives are broken down in a compatible form to the contribution analysis, and this includes non-financial objectives which may be 'task' related. To do this properly at the operational level the overall objectives and strategies must be analysed down to the specific tactical level, where contribution analysis and differential costs can be used. These techniques are ideal for comparing alternatives and this is clearly a major part of the planning process, and particularly so for budgets where specific alternative action plans can be evaluated. The relative risks of these alternatives must be taken into account and this may be indicated by the different cost structures of various alternatives (higher fixed costs indicate increased risk) and the critical success factors for any plan should be identified. A critical success factor will be highlighted by doing a sensitivity analysis on the major variable elements (as illustrated in Chapter 7) in the budget and seeing where small changes in the variable elements make a significant impact on the outcome of the budget. Obviously managerial attention should concentrate on these critically important areas and every attempt should be made to ensure that the budget levels are attained. However, many areas of the business are subject to non-controllable influences and therefore the critical costs may be increased or the sales levels reduced relative to the assumptions in the budget; as stated at the beginning of the chapter, the budget is bound to be wrong.

The techniques introduced in this chapter can be used to prepare alternative strategies and tactics to deal with the most obvious changes tothe budget. These contingency plans can dramatically speed up both a company's ability to react to changes in the environment and the ability to recognize that the budgetary assumptions are incorrect. The company cannot afford to continue to follow a budget which has been overtaken by current events, and regularly updated forecasts should be used to incorporate the appropriate contingency plans with amended financial results.

Zero base budgeting

After a budgeting system has been in operation for some time there is a natural tendency for next year's budget to be justified by reference to the actual levels being achieved at present. Indeed this is part of our financial analysis process discussed in Part Two, but the proper analysis process takes full account of all the changes which should affect the future activities of the company. However, even using such an analytical base some companies find that the historical comparisons and particularly the existing level of constraints on resources can inhibit really innovative changes being incorporated in budgets. This can develop into a severe handicap for the business because the budget should be the first year of the long-range plan. Therefore if changes are not started in the budget period, and the status quo is allowed to continue, it is difficult for the business to make the progress necessary to achieve the longer-term objectives which allow it to attain its corporate mission.

One way of breaking out of this cyclical planning problem is to go back to basics and to develop the budget from an assumption of no existing resources (that is, a zero base). This means that all resources have to be justified and the particular way chosen of achieving the specified objectives has to be compared with the alternatives (using opportunity cost logic). Therefore in the sales area, the existence of a field sales force would be ignored and the optimum way of achieving the sales objectives in that particular market for the particular goods or services should be developed. This might not include any field sales force, or a different-sized team, and the business then has to plan how to implement this new strategy.

The obvious problem of this zero-base budgeting process is the massive amount of managerial time needed to carry out the exercise. Consequently some companies do the full process every five years, but in that year the business can almost grind to a halt. Thus an alternative way is to look in depth at one area of the business each year on a rolling basis, so that each sector does a zero base budget every five years or so.

Summary

The budget is an integral part of the financial planning process and suffers from the same problems (being wrong) and has the same benefits of providing a financial justification for the planned actions and a reference base to control the business against.

The benefits of a good budgeting system can also be summarized as the three Cs: coordination, communication and control.

The fact that the budget will be wrong requires that regularly updated forecasts are prepared, so that short-term plans are based on the best information available.

Budgets should be decision-oriented and therefore utilize a number of financial decision techniques which are particularly relevant to short-term decisions. These include differential costing (also known as marginal costing) and contribution analysis, which are evolved from the cost–volume–profit relationship which analyses all costs into fixed and variable.

By accepting fixed costs as fixed in the short term, financial decisions can focus on the relationship between sales values and variable costs which is described as contribution. These techniques are used in decisions, but are not applicable when preparing published financial statements and so these differences must again be remembered.

The shorter time-scale of annual budgets means that the essential ingredient for long-term financial decisions, namely the time value of money, is of less significance and other techniques become predominant.

—

Appendix: price changes – changes in contribution

(Change in sales volume to compensate for any change in contribution.)

Contribution before a price change can be given by $C_1 \times V_1$ where $C_1 =$ original contribution per unit and $V_1 =$ original volume.

If the price is reduced by Y% (so that Y is negative for a price increase) the new contribution can be given by $C_2 \times V_2$ where $C_2 =$ new contribution per unit and $V_2 =$ new volume.

The assumptions are:

1   variable cost per unit is constant;
2   fixed costs are fixed.

Break-even is achieved when the two contributions are equal.

That is $C_1 \times V_1 = C_2 \times V_2$

But $C_2 = C_1 - Y$ and therefore $C_1 = C_2 + Y$.

Therefore $V_1 (C_2 + Y) = C_2 \times V_2$

This can be rearranged to show $V_1 \times Y = C_2(V_2 - V_1)$

or $\dfrac{V_2 - V_1}{V_1} = \dfrac{Y}{C_2}$

Where $V_2 - V_1 =$ volume change and so $\dfrac{V_2 - V_1}{V_1} =$ proportionate change in volume

and   Y change in contribution

and $C_2 =$ new contribution $=$ (original contribution $-$ change in contribution).

Therefore   the relationship can be stated as:

$$\text{Proportionate change in volume needed} = \frac{\text{Change in contribution}}{\text{Contribution retained}}$$

9

Financing the plan

Introduction

Throughout the book we have emphasized the importance of cash flow
to all businesses, not least because running out of cash can spell total
disaster. It is vitally important, therefore, that any business plan includes
an adequate evaluation of the financing required to achieve the plan's
objectives and that proper consideration is given to the ability of the
company to generate this finance. An inability to raise the necessary
finance could be a major constraint on the implementation of the plan.
Again the different time scales of long-range plans and budgets can be
significant in terms of the company's ability to remove any such
financing constraints. In the longer term the business may be able to raise
additional funds to pay for planned investments, whereas in the budget
period the existing levels of available finance may be a restriction on the
implementation of any rapid growth plans.

The analysis section in Part Two considered, in general terms, the
available sources of finance for any company and these are relevant to
financial planning. It is also important that the plan takes account of the
existing financial structure of the business, as the relative strength of the
existing financial structure can significantly affect the future ability to
raise any required additional finance. Financial structure can be defined
as the relative weighting of the existing sources of finance used by the
business (that is, the ratio of debt to shareholders' funds or the financial
gearing) and the degree of matching, in terms of timing, between the
sources of funds and the uses to which these funds have been applied. If
the financial analysis shows a business is in a weak financial position (for
example, with excessive debt outstanding) one of the key objectives in
the short term may be to restore the financial structure to a healthier
position, and this objective may well conflict with some of the marketing
planning objectives regarding expanding market share or developing
new products and markets. As has already been mentioned, planning is

normally a compromise between conflicting objectives, but the cash flow requirements of the business are of such paramount importance that it is ridiculous for the company to adopt a plan which is inconsistent with its ability to generate the required funding. The result is normally a disastrous failure to achieve any of the objectives of the plan, as strategies have to be modified half-way through their implementation with the build-up of cash flow pressures.

At the other extreme a company with a very strong current financial position which adopts a very conservative plan that does not build on this existing financial strength may find its shareholders unhappy with the returns generated from its strategies. There may be considerable pressure to impose more aggressive objectives or there could be moves by other companies to acquire such a business. It is a very dangerous premise to believe that if your company is financially strong you cannot be taken over. Some companies (such as Hanson plc) make acquisitions because they believe they can achieve a better return from the acquired business than is currently being achieved by the current management with their existing strategy, and this can apply not just to companies in a weak financial position. A business which has been successful and so has a very sound balance sheet structure but is now 'fat and happy' with limited plans for future success can often appear as a very attractive takeover target.

Thus the planning process must start with a good understanding of the existing financial position of the business which is provided by the financial analysis, and the corporate objectives must appropriately try to restore or build on this existing base. However we have also seen in Chapters 4 and 5 that these measures of financial strength need to be applied in the specific contexts of the business, its strategy and its environment. The absolute levels of the financial status ratios, such as financial gearing and the liquidity ratio, for example, are of far less importance than their trend in the past and their forecast levels which will be generated in the future by any proposed plan.

The calculation of these forecast levels requires the preparation of a full cash flow projection for the period of the plan, as shown in the appendix to Chapter 3. This also allows any gaps between the cash flows generated from the planned levels of activity and the cash investments demanded by the planned strategies to be identified. As we need cash at specific points in time, the timing of cash flows is of paramount importance and so assumptions must be made for the leads and lags associated with all the payments and receipts related to the trading and financing activities. We have already seen in Chapter 7 how important cash flows are to the various types of decisions which are a fundamental part of the planning process, and the use of forecast cash flows is consequently an integral and essential element of financial planning. However, using the correct decision evaluation techniques is not a substitute for preparing full cash flow projections. Even if the long-term investment decisions are properly evaluated using discounted cash flow techniques and only those generating positive net present values are implemented, this does not necessarily remove the need for additional financing during the period of the plan.

These new investment decisions will be made after adjusting all the relevant cash flows to their equivalent present values so that they are truly comparable, but for business financing evaluations we need to consider the actual timings of the absolute cash outflows and inflows. Investments made today use up available current financing until they start to generate their own cash inflows and if the total funding needed cannot be raised by the business, some potentially beneficial projects may have to be deferred or cancelled. Therefore we need to add another element to our long-term investment decision criteria that were established in Chapter 7 – 'affordability'. Many companies now consider their investment projects on a portfolio basis, which looks at the total cash flows required or generated each year and ensures that the overall portfolio of live projects *can be afforded* by the business.

A 'portfolio' is a term which is normally used to describe a range of investments of different types and which, consequently, have different roles. By investing in a well-balanced 'portfolio' of shares in the stock market, an investor can reduce, but not eliminate, the investment risk relative to investing all their available capital in one share. A company can apply the same 'portfolio' argument to its investments in projects and ensure that they have an acceptable return for the remaining overall risk. The company can decide that it wishes to carry out all or most of the potentially profitable projects but this can only be done if adequate funding can be found and this could necessitate increasing the amount of finance available.

The business can increase the total funding in the three basic ways considered in Part Two: it can ask its shareholders to invest more cash in the company or it can reinvest some or all of the profits made by the business (instead of paying them out to the shareholders in the form of a dividend) or it can borrow more cash from an external source. Whether it decides to do any of these, and which source of funds it chooses to utilize will depend on the potential return from the plan and the risks associated with the investments under consideration. It is sensible for any business to match the appropriate sources of funds to the required uses to which the cash will be put in terms of both time-scale and risk. Later in the chapter specific sources of finance will be described and matched against appropriate uses of funds (for example, acquisition of assets).

Operational gearing

The required time-scale is indicated both by the nature of the investment and by the cash flow forecasts, and the risk factor can be assessed by carrying out a sensitivity analysis on these cash flows, as was done in Chapter 7. In Chapter 8 we examined the impact of different cost structures and saw how a business with high fixed costs is likely to have great volatility in its profitability from small changes in the level of trading activity. This is also true for cash flows if the high fixed costs result in cash outflows from the business irrespective of the level of trading activity. Any business with such high fixed costs will be seen as high risk and the ratio of fixed cost to total costs can be regarded as the *operational gearing* of the company. Thus in the same way as high financial gearing (debt to total capital employed) is seen to increase the business risk, high operational gearing also increases risk and requires a higher potential return to compensate.

However, the impact on the suitable sources of funding is even more important because businesses with high 'operational gearing' should ideally select financing strategies with low 'financial gearing'. If the planned level of activity is not achieved but the high fixed costs still have to be paid, the forecast cash flows will be severely affected. If this cash flow is heavily dependent on borrowed funds which also require cash outflows to pay interest and repay principal, the company could rapidly run into a cash flow crisis, at a time of adverse trading conditions (indicated by the lack of achievement of its planned level of activity) which could make it impossible to raise any additional finance. It would be more sensible to ensure that the additional finance required by all the contingency plans prepared, which should reflect those potentially lower levels of activity, is guaranteed to be available to the company, and that as many cash outflows as possible can be restructured when necessary (dividends to shareholders can be suspended and are therefore discretionary, but interest and principal payments on debt are committed and cannot be withheld).

Sensitivity analysis

Sensitivity analyses of the planned cash flows are clearly very important whatever the cost structure of the business but they should not be restricted only to the amounts of the cash flows. All cash flow forecasts are based on assumptions regarding the *timing* of the cash flows and if these assumptions are wrong, the financing of the business can be dramatically altered. Thus the impact of changing these assumptions should be checked to ensure that the company can survive a delay in receiving certain cash flow items, etc. Some companies have a policy of including payments on their due date but only including receipts after an appropriate delay caused by having to chase their customers. Their logic is that if this cash flow forecast can be financed, the business has some operational flexibility to cope with the inevitable changes that will occur during the actual period covered by the plan. This can be illustrated by reference back to the cash flow forecasts prepared for Paul Cook in the appendix to Chapter 3 (pages 88 and 100).

In the cash flow forecast for his first six months' trading Paul assumed that he would generate some sales revenues (£20 000) in month one and increasing sales thereafter, but that he would have to wait 30 days to receive the cash from his customers. The timing of this cash inflow is as important as the size, as a delay in payment by the customers would have significant cash flow implications for the new business. If, in reality, the customers took 60 days to pay for the sales made, all of the cash inflows from sales revenues would be put back one month later and the impact is shown in Figure 9.1.

Paul Cook: adjusted cash flow forecast first six months

Months	1 £	2 £	3 £	4 £	5 £	6 £	Total £
Cash in							
Capital + loan	50 000	–	–	–	–	–	50 000
Sales income	–	–	20 000	30 000	40 000	45 000	135 000
Total (1)	50 000	–	20 000	30 000	40 000	45 000	185 000
Cash out							
Total (2)	8500	27 800	38 400	51 400	57 800	59 400	243 300
Movements in months (1)–(2)	41 500	(27 800)	(18 400)	(21 400)	(17 800)	(14 400)	–
Balance brought forward	–	41 500	13 700	(4700)	(26 100)	(43 900)	–
Balance carried forward	41 500	13 700	(4700)	(26 100)	(43 900)	(58 300)	(58 300)

Figure 9.1

The delay in receiving cash means that the business moves into a cumulative deficit in month three and has an additional financing need of £58 300 at the end of month six (compared to an original position of having positive cash until month six and needing only £8300 extra cash funding). The extra cash required can be easily reconciled as it is the £50 000 of sales revenue originally forecast to be received in month six but now delayed until month seven. If we were to also adjust the second six months' cash flow forecast the same difference of £50 000 would be seen with the cash funding gap required at the end of the period increased to £62 600 – again a significant increase from the previous level of £12 600. It is important to remember that the profit and loss accounts for the periods (except due to increased interest costs on the higher financing requirement) would not change, as we have not changed our assumptions regarding the timing of sales transactions, only the timing of the cash flows resulting from those transactions. The impact would be reconciled on the face of the balance sheet which would have a larger overdraft (or similar source of financing) as a liability which would be balanced by much higher outstanding debtors, reflecting the 60 days sales not yet paid for. The adjusted balance sheet at the end of the first 12 months trading is shown in Figure 9.2, together with a restatement of the original figures so as to highlight the changes.

Paul Cook: balance sheet as at the end of first 12 months

	Original figures £	£	Adjusted figures £	£
Fixed assets				
Current assets				
Stock	60 000		60 000	
Debtors	50 000		100 000	
Prepayments	1200		1200	
Total current assets		111 200		161 200
less Current liabilities				
Trade creditors	45 000		45 000	
Unpaid expenses	300		300	
Bank overdraft	12 600		62 600	
Total current liabilities		57 900		107 900
Net current assets		53 300		53 300
Net assets		53 300		53 300
Owner's capital		23 300		23 300
Loan account		30 000		30 000
Capital employed		53 300		53 300

Figure 9.2

The impact of a delay in the receipt of the cash from sales revenues is so great that Paul Cook should set up contingency plans to finance the increased cash requirements before starting his business. This could be done via an overdraft or by factoring the outstanding debtors (which is explained later in the chapter) or by injecting more long-term capital himself, if possible. The source of the funds should be matched against the use as far as practical. The timing need of the cash will depend on whether Paul believes the risk of slower payment is only present as he starts his business; as it may be difficult to insist on payment according to his stated terms of business in the early months of trading. If he feels that once his business is established he will be able to reduce outstanding debtor days to the target level of 30 days, the increased financing need could be satisfied by a short-term source such as an overdraft. If this plan is unrealistic and debtor days are more likely to stay at 60 days, the increased financing requirement is much longer term and debtor factoring or an increased capital injection would be more appropriate.

Paul should also examine the sensitivity of his cash flow forecast to changes in other items and prepare contingency plans to reduce the risk of business failure due to running out of cash in the early months of trading.

The type of strategy being implemented in the plan can have a major impact on this sensitivity evaluation. When the business is continuing in its existing markets with existing proven products, the timing and absolute size of the cash flows may be forecast with some level of accuracy based on past experience after allowing for any forecast changes in the external environment. However, if the marketing plan includes launching new products, going into new markets, or even dramatically changing the marketing strategy in existing markets the cash flow implications are much more uncertain. The added risk involved can be handled as described in Chapter 7 by using decision trees to identify the level of control exercisable by the business. Remember that the higher the risk, the greater the return required.

This increased range of potential outcomes clearly increases the risk and should suggest that more secure, low-risk financing should be used for such projects. The example of Peter White's new computer add-on product outlined in Chapter 8 illustrates this point. Peter had developed a new attachment for microcomputers which would have a very short life cycle and which he had decided to sell through distributors. He had no previous experience of either dealing with distributors or of products which were only expected to last for less than one year. Therefore this project was quite risky from the marketing perspective but the financial return looked very good (£180 000 profit) and as no investment was needed in new capital equipment the financing risk was initially perceived as low. If we consider the real potential financial commitment a different picture is revealed. In order to develop and launch the product Peter has to commit to spending fixed costs of £200 000 this financial year and £40 000 in the next financial year. He also needs to build stocks quickly and so plans to manufacture 20 000 units within six months which will commit all the costs of production before he has any real information on how sales of the product are going. At a variable cost per unit of £15, this is committing another £300 000 of cash, bringing the total cash which is at risk if the product does not get off the ground to

£540 000. For a small electronics business this is quite a substantial absolute sum of money and a very large amount to have at risk on one new project. Even if the product does sell well, Peter may have to wait for some time to receive payments from his new distributors, who will be reluctant to pay out until they have been paid by *their* customers. This could require Peter to finance, albeit on a short-term basis, the cost of manufacturing the other 8000 units forecast for the second six months period at a cost of another £120 000.

Peter White: financing requirement: cash outflows

Research and development and launch costs	£240 000
Variable manufacturing costs	
Initial 20 000 units @ £15	£300 000
Second phase 8000 units	£120 000
Maximum cash outflow	£660 000

Figure 9.3

If he is unable to fund this very heavy investment (maximum £660 000 as shown in Figure 9.3) in a secure manner he may find that his business gets into financial difficulties, even though the product is very successful eventually (he should make an accounting profit of £180 000 from the product). There are, unfortunately, many examples of businesses collapsing because of trying to increase their scale of activity without adequate financing being made available – this has already been described as 'being undercapitalized' or 'overtrading'. There are even more examples of businesses failing because they put the entire business at risk over *one* supposedly low risk project, which goes badly wrong and absorbs a vast amount of cash. It is useful in these cases to work out the break-even volume as a proportion of forecast sales, as this gives a measure of the sensitivity which can be tolerated without such overwhelmingly disastrous consequences. This break-even calculation could include a maximum loss which can be accepted by the business. For Peter this should be looked at in two ways. In accounting terms he has fixed costs of £240 000 and a forecast selling price of £30 per unit compared to a variable cost of £15 per unit which leaves a contribution per unit of £15, and a break-even volume of 16 000 units or 57.1 per cent of total forecast sales as shown in Figure 9.4.

This may be considered quite acceptable, but the other way to evaluate the project is in terms of committed cash outflows. In cash flow terms Peter has committed more than the fixed costs because he also has to manufacture stock in advance of sales. Therefore the maximum cash which could be at risk before any success for the product is assured is

Peter White: Break-even calculation

$$\text{The break-even volume} = \frac{\text{Fixed costs}}{\text{Contribution per unit}}$$

$$= \frac{£240\,000}{£15}$$

$$= 16\,000 \text{ units}$$

As a proportion of forecast sales this represents $\dfrac{16\,000}{28\,000} \times 100\% = 57.1\%$

$\therefore$ the margin of safety

$$= 100\% - 57.1$$

$$= 42.9\%$$

Figure 9.4

£540 000. This cash will be recovered at the unit selling price of £30 because the variable costs are already included and so 18 000 units must be sold before all the cash committed is recovered. In this case, because of the high profit margin, there is little difference between the two calculations but the use of cash commitments as a financing break-even indicator (or payback) can be very useful as part of the plan's funding evaluation.

The maximum cash outflow from a project is, therefore, another measure of risk which can be included in the capital investment evaluation process and several companies do calculate this. Where the absolute value is significant for the business as a whole, as it is in Peter White's case, it is vital that a suitable source of finance is identified which avoids putting the whole business at risk if the single project fails or is simply slower than planned in producing the projected cash inflows. This essential matching of sources and uses of funds, both in terms of timing and risk, requires the identification of appropriate sources of finance for each potential category of investment highlighted in the business plan. These will now be considered in terms of relative time scales, that is, long-term, medium-term and short-term, even though inevitably the distinctions become a little blurred in practice.

Appropriate sources of finance

Long term

Shareholders' funds, which were defined and discussed in Chapter 3 and are also known as 'equity', represent the major source of long-term finance for most companies, and the level of owners' investment in the business will also affect the amount of debt that can be obtained (via the debt to equity or gearing ratio). For a successful business it is often possible to produce the additional financing requirements of its business plans out of the internally generated funds from existing operations (that is, profit plus depreciation), perhaps by restricting the level of dividends paid, but large new projects or aggressive growth targets may require additional funding. These internally generated funds are the largest source of finance for most companies.

If additional funding is required, it can be obtained from the existing owners of the company if they are willing to put in more cash. Normally this would be done by 'a rights issue' whereby each existing shareholder is given 'the right' to buy *new* shares in the company in proportion to the existing number of shares owned (for example, a '1 for 5' rights issue means that for every five shares owned, a shareholder can buy another one). To encourage shareholders to buy these shares which increase the total shares in existence, the company normally sells them at a slight discount to the current market price for the existing shares, but to guarantee that it receives the required amount of cash (it cannot after all *force* shareholders to buy any more shares) it will also arrange to have the issue 'underwritten'. This is a form of insurance policy because the underwriters (large City institutions) guarantee to buy any shares not taken up by the shareholders in exchange for a fixed fee, which is paid whether they have to buy all the shares or none of them. A rights issue is clearly quite an expensive process because it requires communicating directly with each shareholder and paying quite substantial fees to professional advisers. Therefore most companies only use this method for raising very sizeable amounts when the costs incurred form a smaller proportion of the capital raised.

In some cases the existing shareholders are not seen as a good potential source for the additional cash needed but new share capital can still be obtained by selling shares to outsiders. The practical result is the same in that the company receives cash in exchange for issuing new shares, but this introduces new owners into the business and consequently may change the balance of power within the company, by diluting the proportionate shareholdings of the existing owners. This does not happen if the additional financing is raised by a 'rights issue' which is taken up (that is, all the shares offered are bought) by the existing shareholders. In fact the most common way in which this occurs (in other words, introducing new owners into the business) is when one company acquires another, but does not want to use cash to pay for it; it does the acquisition by issuing new shares in itself and the shareholders in the acquired business swap their shares for different ones. Therefore in this case the company never actually receives cash in exchange for the shares which it issues, as it immediately swaps these new shares for ownership of shares in the company being acquired. The examples below show how this works.

Example 1: Acquisition using shares

Company A wishes to acquire all the shares in company B but does not have sufficient cash to pay for them. As an alternative it could offer the shareholders in company B an exchange where it issues new shares in itself and swaps these new shares for the shares existing in B.

Company A (the acquiror) currently has 10 million shares in issue with a market value of £5 each, giving a total company value (referred to as the 'market capitalization') of £50 million.

Company B (the acquiree) has 2 million shares in issue also with a market value of £5 each, giving it a market capitalization of £10 million. In order to buy these shares, company A has to offer the shareholders of B an equivalent value of £5 (we will ignore the extra price which may be payable to secure control of B), which is represented by one extra share in A.

Thus: before acquisition the total shares in A were	10 million
Number of new shares issued in exchange for the shares of B	2 million
Total shares in A after acquisition	12 million

The number of shares in company A has increased from 10 million to 12 million, and A now owns all the shares in company B and has not used up any cash in achieving this. As a result of issuing these extra shares, company A has increased its market capitalization to £60 million (assuming the share price stays at £5 after the deal).

Example 2: Acquisition using different value shares

Company A – which now has 12 million shares at £5 each – wishes to acquire company C which has 10 million shares issued with a market value of £1 each (that is, a market capitalization of £10 million). As each of A's shares is worth much more than each of C's shares, A can offer a share exchange which equates the market values and not the number of shares.

Again ignoring any premium price which may be required, A could offer the shareholders of company C an exchange of: one new share in A for every five shares owned in C. In total this would require A to issue another 2 million shares (£10 million acquisition value divided by share price of £5) and this would give the following position:

Company A shares issued prior to acquisition of C	12 million
issued to acquire shares in C	2 million
Total shares in issue	14 million

Again company A now owns all the shares in the acquired company but has not used any cash in achieving this. The ownership of A's shares has changed again because new shares have been issued to the previous shareholders in B and C, and they now own a proportion of the enlarged company A.

The relative number of shares exchanged depends on their relative market prices, but the end result is that the acquiring company has bought another business and not used up any substantial amounts of cash – it will have had to pay fees and may have offered a cash alternative to the previous shareholders, both of which will use up some of the available cash resources. Any company's ability to do this type of acquisition deal depends on the attractiveness of its shares to outsiders, and this explains why so much effort goes into the external corporate communications process of which the published financial statements form a major part; this is sometimes now described as 'investor relations', which is a specialized area of public relations.

Increasing the share capital of the company is a permanent change and therefore would not be appropriate as a source of finance for short or medium-term applications. However, if the long-term plans of the business indicate that these funds can continue to be reinvested ('rolled-over') in new expansion projects, it may be the best way to raise the cash even for an apparent medium-term need, particularly if the first identified need, that is, the project, is seen as a *high-risk* investment so that a *low-risk source* of finance (from the company's perspective), such as shareholders' funds, is recommended.

As an alternative source of long-term funds, the business can seek to increase the level of external borrowings on a long-term basis, with the exact term of the loan being decided as appropriate for the assets being acquired. The availability of this type of finance will be subject to the projected cash flows and the particular type of assets which are being financed, and there will be the overall constraint of maintaining an acceptable level of debt to equity from the lender's perspective. The attractiveness to the company of borrowing depends on the rate of interest charged compared to the return which is forecast from the investment (as previously illustrated in Chapter 4, it is nonsensical to borrow at 20 per cent and invest the money in a project which returns 15 per cent), but it may also be affected by any operational constraints (for example, loan covenants which are specific conditions imposed on the business in a loan agreement which restrict such things as additional borrowings and levels of dividends which can be paid) imposed on the business by the lender.

Long-term debt and shareholders' funds (whether by retaining cash in the business or issuing new shares) are appropriate sources of finance for long-term uses of cash within the business. One major area of long-term uses of cash is the investment required by the company in the fixed assets which will be used in the business. This immediately indicates that the financial structure of each company must be specifically tailored to its own requirements as the relative investment in each area of the company will differ depending on the business carried on by the company and the specific strategy employed by the company in its particular business. In order to illustrate this we will consider the various headings on the assets side of a normal balance sheet (see below) and the appropriate sources of finance for each heading; this treatment will also indicate the problems of trying to group sources into the headings; long, medium and short term.

Fixed assets
Land and buildings
Plant and machinery
Motor vehicles
Computers and office equipment
Current assets
Stocks, including raw materials, work-in-progress and finished goods
Trade debtors
Prepayments
Cash at bank and in hand

Land and buildings
If a company needs to occupy substantial land and buildings in the course of its business (a retailer, for example), the first decision is whether it wishes to invest large amounts of capital in these assets. It may be possible for the company to rent the necessary properties so that it pays for the occupancy as it uses the facilities, thus dramatically reducing the investment made in the asset. The problem with short-term rental contracts is that they do not match the time-scale of the use of the asset (long-term) but this can be overcome by taking out a long-term lease on the properties required.

A lease is a rental contract for a specified period of time (for example, for 999 years) and so the company does not acquire ownership of the property but does secure guaranteed use as long as the lease payments are kept up to date. The terms of leases can vary dramatically and the company using the property (described as the lessee) may have to spend some cash in buying the lease (often described as the lease premium or 'key money') or in fitting out the property. This expenditure will be classified as a fixed asset on the balance sheet and depreciated (the term 'amortization' is often used instead of depreciation but the impact is identical) over the period of the lease. As any cash spent on such leases will be tied up for some, or many, years the company may use shareholders' funds or long-term debt as the source of finance; whereas the periodic lease payments (which may be made monthly, quarterly, half-yearly or annually) will normally be financed out of operating cash inflows as required.

The problem of leasing property is that no outright ownership is obtained and the company therefore foregoes any potential gain from the increase in the value of the property; this is retained by the person owning the property and leasing it out (known as the lessor). This gain in value has been very substantial in most areas of property in the postwar period and many companies have changed their strategies to owning their land and buildings, rather than merely having the use of them. In many cases this investment in land and buildings may be much larger than the financing required for any other part of the business (for example, large retailers such as the Burton Group, Marks and Spencer and Sainsburys) and the investment is also very long term. It may be that the company chooses to use shareholders' funds to finance the majority of this use of funds (as Marks and Spencer do) or it could raise long-term debt.

Freehold land and buildings (that is where full ownership is held) are very attractive to any potential lender of cash to the company as it can provide very good 'specific security' for the outstanding debt. This means that if the debt is not repaid when due or the interest payments are not made on time the lender can take over the land and buildings and sell them to recover the balance outstanding. Hence the risk on the loan is reduced because eventual repayment is more likely as the land and buildings may well increase in value rather than decrease as most fixed assets do. The lender may require that a mortgage is taken over the land and buildings, which publicly registers their interest in the property and stops the borrower from selling these assets without first repaying the principal on the loan and any outstanding interest and charges. In this way the property is providing the specific security for the debt rather than the lender having to rely on the other general assets of the borrower. If the lender regards the property as being the main element of security, the loan will be restricted to the value at which the property could be sold by the lender if necessary, and this may differ significantly from the amount being paid by the borrower to buy the property. (On a personal basis, this explains why a building society or bank is prepared to lend a higher proportion of the purchase price of a standard house on an estate, where the resale value can be easily and accurately estimated, than for the purchase of a converted seventeenth-century windmill or a light-house on a deserted clifftop.)

These decisions regarding financing land and building assets appear to be very long term and yet the circumstances of a company can change quite quickly. Suppose a retailer decides to buy its shops and to use a mix of shareholders' funds and long-term debt to finance these acquisitions. In a few years' time it may wish to increase the rate of expansion but finds that it cannot increase the level of shareholders' funds quickly enough to finance the investment required. One option is to change its strategy from buying property to leasing it, so that the investment required is reduced. However, it can go one stage further if necessary and sell some of the properties which it currently owns, even though they may still be required for the business. It can retain the use of the properties by agreeing to lease them, and thus a 'sale and leaseback' arrangement can be used to provide additional financing for other projects within the business.

Other fixed assets

If we now turn to the other fixed assets of a company we can consider them as a group even though the time-scale of their asset lives will differ considerably, from possibly two to three years for computers and cars to over 25 years for some plant and machinery. The financing options relevant to land and buildings are also applicable in some cases to other fixed assets, but different sorts of debt products tend to be used, as the resale value of the particular fixed assets may make a mortgage seem unattractive to the lender, that is, if the resale value declines rapidly over the early period of use of the asset as with a computer.

A very common way of financing major investments in plant and machinery is through some kind of instalment credit deal, where the financing company provides the cash to buy the asset and the loan is repaid over time – this is the same logic as used for a mortgage. Instalment credit ranges from a straightforward term loan where a bank, for example, lends the company the cash required and the company buys the plant and machinery directly from the supplier and repays the loan over the agreed period, which could be from three to 25 years, and pays interest on the balance outstanding. The lender may not rely specifically on the residual resale value of the asset being purchased for the repayment of the loan, but may take general security over all or most of the assets of the company (this can be publicly registered as a 'floating charge' on the assets of the company and warns any other potential lenders of the interest which already exists in the assets of the business. It also gains the lender priority should the company get into financial difficulties).

A more asset specific form of instalment credit is a credit sale where the purchaser buys the asset and owns the asset immediately but pays for it over a period of time (linked to the useful economic life of the specific asset). The interest cost is often included in the periodic payments rather than being charged separately as with a term loan and this type of financing is often provided by the suppliers of the fixed assets – either directly or by them introducing a financial institution. It can be more expensive than a term loan because the lender often relies only on the cash flow of the business to pay for the fixed assets, and no other security is taken. Some of the risk can be reduced by requiring a proportion of the cost to be paid immediately (as an initial deposit) but the ownership of the asset has passed to the purchaser, and so the lender cannot retake possession of the asset to sell it and recover the outstanding balance.

In order to overcome this problem a form of financing known as hire purchase was introduced, whereby the purchaser does not become the owner of the fixed asset until all the payments have been made. Therefore, during the credit period the financing company 'hires' the asset to the purchaser who makes an additional nominal payment on top of the 'hire' charges in order to acquire legal ownership of the asset. In most practical aspects hire purchase and credit sales are very similar, but legally under hire purchase the seller is still the owner until final payment is received and hence can repossess the asset if the purchaser defaults during the payment period.

A third variation is a lease of the asset for the whole of its economic life, which is known as a financial lease, where the asset can be used but is never owned by the company. Ownership is retained by the lessor (the financing company) and the lease charges have to take account of the interest costs on the outstanding balance and the depreciation of the fixed asset since this is being suffered by the owner and has to be recovered from the user. Effectively this kind of lease can be viewed as giving ownership of the asset to the user. This is how it is now treated in published financial statements because all assets acquired under financial leases should be included as fixed assets on the balance sheet, even though they are not 'owned' by the company, and the leasing obligation should be shown as a liability on the balance sheet. This presentation should also be followed for hire purchase contracts during the 'hiring' period, and so the company will depreciate all these assets as if they were owned. Table 9.1 contrasts these three types of specific fixed asset financing, and they are also applied to car fleets later in the chapter (page 298).

Table 9.1   *Fixed asset financing*

	Credit sales	Hire purchase	'Financial' leasing
Ownership of fixed asset during financing period	Purchaser	Financing company (hirer)	Financing company (lessor)
Obligations of purchaser	Pay full price and interest costs	Pay hire charges equivalent to full price and interest costs *plus* nominal transfer of ownership	Pay lease charges which include interest and depreciation elements
Payments after financing period	*None*	*None*	Pay low but continuing lease payments – ownership always stays with lessor
Balance sheet presentations	Show fixed asset and outstanding debt balance	Show fixed asset and outstanding principal due to hirer	Show fixed asset at equivalent cost of purchase and equivalent balance of cost unpaid (that is, same as other two)

Current assets
It may seem strange to include current assets in the long-term financing category, but a large proportion of current assets may require financing on a permanent or long-term basis even though the individual items are turned over rapidly. Thus current assets need to be split into the short-term seasonal portion, which is considered separately, and the base level of constant usage. This segmentation of financing need can be represented diagrammatically as in Figure 9.5.

Stocks
Most manufacturing companies invest cash in raw materials, work-in-progress and finished goods and although these individual items change rapidly, the financing is required on a permanent basis as long as the company continues trading at the same level of activity. Even service companies may tie up resources in finished goods (for example, wholesalers and retailers) or in stocks of consumables and these may require financing.

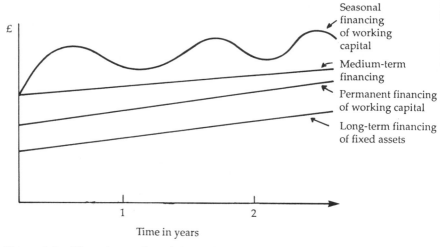

Figure 9.5   *Financing needs and timescales*

The most obvious source of financing for stocks is trade credit because most companies buy on credit (that is, they do not pay for their purchases immediately) and so not all of the stocks held will have tied up the company's cash. In many industries, trade credit may be the most important source of financing for stocks, but it is a mistake for companies to regard it as a source of 'free' financing and hence extend their payment period as far as possible. Their suppliers, who are consequently having to wait longer for payment, will themselves have to finance their businesses to a greater extent and, in the long term, they will need to recover the increased cost of this financing from their customers, namely our example companies. Where the operating cycle of the company (the number of days taken to turn raw materials into finished goods and sell the goods) is longer than the available trade credit, the company has to find additional means of financing its stocks. If a specific source of financing can be generated this will avoid using the shareholders' funds or any general lines of credit available to the company and financing stocks has been a problem for many companies for hundreds of years. Not surprisingly such a specific financing product has been developed and is still widely used today. Many industries (particularly commodity processing industries such as the pulp and paper industry) buy their raw materials using 'bills of exchange' which enable the supplier to be paid without using cash from the purchaser. A bill of exchange is a 'written promise to pay a specified amount of money at a specified future date to the named person or to the bearer of the bill at the expiry date' and can be likened to a postdated cheque, as shown below.

Example of a BILL OF EXCHANGE

1 September 1988

TO: ABC Purchasers Ltd
Three months after date, pay to our order the sum of £100 000, value received.

Signed
XYZ Suppliers

Note   The bill of exchange differs from a postdated cheque or promissory note (illustrated on page 294) in that it is actually written by the person to be paid, and is a demand for payment at a specified future date. Because the bill is written by the creditor, it has to be accepted (signed) by the debtor before it can be traded.

The supplier can wait for the specified period of the bill and then receive payment, or they can sell the bill immediately because it is a negotiable instrument (hence the inclusion of 'bearer') and receive the discounted payment – reflecting the time value of the period until payment will be made by the purchaser. Bills of exchange are normally made for periods of 90, 120 or 180 days, and are actively traded in bill discount markets. Anyone purchasing a bill of exchange runs a risk that the company which is receiving the period of credit will not honour the payment when due and they would require a bigger discount off the face value of the bill if the company was not well known with a good credit rating. This would restrict the availability of this source of financing to very large companies, but the banks recognized that they were large well known companies with good credit ratings who could also assess the credit risk of their customers. Therefore if they added their name to a client's bill of exchange as a guarantor of payment (known as 'accepting the bill') the bill would be capable of being discounted against the bank's credit standing and not that of their smaller unknown customer. Thus most bills of exchange are drawn under 'bill acceptance facilities' granted to customers by banks, and discounted in the market by suppliers at very good effective rates of interest (a bank-accepted bill of exchange is described as a 'first-class bill' or 'prime bill'). The banks charge an acceptance fee for adding their name to the bill (normally between $\frac{1}{2}$ per cent and 1 per cent of the face value of the bill) and regard the amount of bills outstanding as part of the borrowing of the company – after all the payment date and amount are known as so the cash flow forecasting impact can be assessed with great accuracy.

Remember we are considering a long-term financing requirement for stocks and yet we are using a bill of exchange with a duration of less than

180 days normally. If the company rolls-over the bills of exchange (that is, replaces the bills with new ones as they mature), using the overall acceptance facility granted by its bankers, the financing can also be made long term. This type of facility is satisfactory for those companies who need the additional backing of a bank acceptance, but for larger companies the bill-discounting market can be accessed directly at a reduced cost due to the saving in the bank acceptance fee. This would normally be done by issuing promissory notes (see below) which are now described as 'commercial paper'. The commercial paper market is very large in the United States and is rapidly developing in Great Britain, as it allows very large creditworthy companies to access cost-effective financial markets directly. The rate of interest charged for bill discounting or commercial paper is a very competitive reflection of general current short-term interest rates.

Example of a PROMISSORY NOTE (simplest type of bill)

1 September 1988

We hereby promise to pay the sum of £100 000 to XYZ Suppliers Ltd, or bearer, on 1 December 1988, value received.

Signed

ABC Purchasers Ltd

Payable at:
Main Bankers Ltd
High Street
London

Using a bill of exchange facility also gives the company flexibility in financing because, although the facility gives access to long-term funds by rolling-over bills, the company does not have to use the facility if it does not need the additional financing for the following period. If a long-term loan had been used, the cash could not be returned to the lender during a short-term cash surplus period. The costs of financing would be commensurately increased due to the normal gap between the cost of borrowing and the interest income which can be earned on cash deposits.

Debtors

The other major component of current assets which often requires long-term financing is the outstanding balance of debtors, representing those customers who have not yet paid for their purchases. Again each specific debtor may be a very short-term item but will normally be replaced by a new debtor, so that the need for the financing of debtors while the business continues with its present strategy and at its current scale of activity, will be permanent.

Wherever practical a specific source of financing should be identified so that more general long-term sources are not unnecessarily utilized and with debtors this is particularly possible. With almost all other assets the specific security value is dependent on the continued successful trading of the business (the exception being freehold land and buildings), but once a sale has been made, the customer is legally bound to pay the company for the goods or services supplied. Therefore any financial institution lending against the security of outstanding debtors is lending not against the credit rating of the trading company but against the credit rating of its customers; as the risk of non-payment is primarily caused by the customers being unable to pay, rather than being unwilling. For any company which has a broad range of customers with good credit ratings, it is consequently possible to raise the financing required for outstanding debtors against the specific balances due from these customers.

This can be done in a variety of ways but the most common is some form of invoice discounting, where finance is advanced against specific invoices, or factoring. Factoring consists of selling the outstanding debtor balances so that the selling company receives cash very quickly after the sale is made and does not need to wait for the customers to pay. The financing company, which buys the debtors, charges an interest cost which reflects the time value of the delay which they suffer between paying out cash and receiving the balance due from the customer. Normally the factoring company (the finance house which is buying the debtors) will pay between 65 per cent and 80 per cent of the sales invoice value at the end of the month when the sale is made, and the remaining balance will be paid (less interest costs and administrative charges) when the cash has been received from the customer.

Many different forms of factoring service are possible ranging from a full sales ledger service (where the factor will send out monthly statements and chase customers to collect outstanding and overdue cash) to confidential factoring (where the customer is completely unaware that a factor is involved and that their outstanding balance has been sold to a third party). In non-recourse factoring the finance company will even assume the risk of non-payment by the customer (the occurrence of bad debts), but will charge for any additional services provided or risks undertaken, so that the cost of factoring varies with the type of service provided. The normal level of interest charges are at a similar rate to those charged for an overdraft facility, where security is given through a floating charge on the debtors of the company.

Medium term

It is difficult to select specific sources of finance which are appropriate for medium term needs but several of those already mentioned are most frequently used for financing needs in the two to five year category which is regarded as the medium term.

Term loans are a very good example of such a product and a five year term loan is ideally suited to finance the acquisition of a fixed asset, with an economic life slightly longer than five years, but which will generate increased net annual cash flows which will repay the loan and cover the interest costs on the outstanding balance. Such self-liquidating financing is ideal in the medium term as it does not involve the company taking on long-term commitments which go beyond the period for which the financing is needed, and which may restrict the flexibility of the company in the future. Most term loans have restrictive covenants included as mentioned earlier and often long-term loans have penalty clauses if the company wishes to repay the loan earlier than specified in the loan agreement.

Another specific form of medium-term financing is a financial lease where the asset involved (such as a computer) will have almost no residual value within five years. The lease charges have to take account of the entire cost of the asset, as well as including the interest payments on the outstanding balance; and the result is only very minor differences from a term loan agreement over the same period to enable the company to buy the asset.

Short term

As shown in Figure 9.5 the outstanding balance on medium-term finance should decrease over time, until new assets are required using new medium-term financing. Short-term financing needs should fluctuate over much shorter time-scales, and very often reflect seasonal peaks and troughs in the business activity levels. The cash flows of many seasonal businesses (for example, the holiday industry, toy manufacturers, and even tissue producers) are very highly concentrated in short periods of the year. This would inevitably lead to cash deficits and cash surpluses during the year if a constant level of financing was used throughout the year. In order to avoid this, the seasonal company should use flexible sources of finance which allow it to adjust the level of cash used to that required by the business.

In some cases it may be possible to do this by adjusting the utilization of certain financing facilities already discussed (for example, bills of exchange and factoring), but the most immediately effective way of achieving this required flexibility is by using an overdraft. An overdraft is a borrowing facility which is *immediately* repayable on the demand of the lender, and should therefore only be used as a short-term financing method – surprisingly many large and otherwise sophisticated companies use overdrafts as long-term or almost permanent components of the core sources of finance for their businesses. In order to balance the ability of the lender to demand repayment, the borrower only has to pay interest on the actual cash borrowed (this is literally computed on a daily basis) and short-term excess cash can be used to reduce the outstanding overdraft balance and hence reduce the interest charged immediately. No company should risk incurring seasonal peaks in financing demand without being sure that the required cash would be available, and this can be achieved with an overdraft by agreeing an overdraft facility (normally for the forthcoming year) with the lender. Even though an adequate overdraft facility has been agreed, there remains a financing risk as, by its nature, the overdraft facility can be withdrawn, without notice, by the lender. The borrowing company can remove this risk by paying a fee (a facility or commitment fee) to the lender to ensure that the facility will be kept available for the required period. The lenders will correspondingly try to reduce their risk by putting conditions and restrictions on the methods of doing business by the borrower, and probably insist on compliance with certain measures of financial strength during the facility period.

Any form of borrowed funds will put some constraints on the business because interest payments and principal repayments will have to be made at specified times, but, as illustrated, nowadays the range of available ways in which lending is packaged provides a great deal of potential flexibility to match the specific needs of individual companies. Thus companies can now tailor their borrowings to fit the projected levels, timing and *currencies* of the cash flows in their financial plans even if this includes the need for a capital repayment holiday for one or two years (that is, making no repayments of principal for the first one or two years of the loan) to take account of a particular project with a long period before positive cash flows are generated, such as a major new product development and launch. The rate of interest charged may be increased in accordance with the lender's perception of the risk associated with the loan, but this will be reduced if there is the prospect of high realizable values from any assets which could be sold if the business venture fails. Therefore if the lender can take specific security which helps to guarantee the repayment of the loan the rate of interest charged will be reduced.

For very large companies, most borrowing is done on a global basis against the overall strength of the business rather than against specified assets or for individual projects, but the type of assets involved in the business will still affect the level of debt to equity ratio that is considered acceptable by lenders. Thus it is now not unusual for a large multi-national to raise many millions of pounds in the form of a completely unsecured long-term loan stock or marketable debenture (which means that the debenture or loan stock can be bought and sold like any share in the company; financial markets allow investors to trade in these securities just as they do in shares) with a period to repayment which can exceed 25 years (the loan can even be set up so that all the principal is repaid at the end, just as with an endowment mortgage) and so debt financing can almost equal equity in degree of permanence. (Some banks such as National Westminster have, like governments, issued unsecured loan stock which will never be repaid, that is, it is irredeemable, and the company only has to pay the interest as it falls due.)

The variety and complexity of these forms of lending has been partially caused by the demands of borrowers but more significantly by the aggressive marketing strategies of lending institutions which are attempting to segment the market by offering differentiated products. Thus any company which is seeking external financing should evaluate the available alternatives in terms of costs (which may include arrangement fees, early repayment penalties, etc. as well as interest charges) and compare these total costs with any constraints which will be imposed on the business as a result of each source of financing before making a final decision – after all, we should expect to apply our opportunity cost logic to financing decisions as well as to all our other financial decisions.

If we compare the specific available alternatives for one further particular decision with specific relevance to the marketing area, the wide range of options may become clearer. Many large companies regularly carry out reviews of the best way to finance the fleet of cars used by their sales-forces. One option is to buy the cars, pay for all the maintenance as it is incurred and then sell the cars after two, three or in some cases even four years. This ties up a considerable amount of capital particularly if the fleet of cars is large relative to the other assets of the business and this money could well be needed elsewhere in the business. Thus the most attractive alternatives utilize financing which is specifically related to the cost of the cars, and where the interest cost on the financing may be included in the total costs, including any other operational charges, levied by the financing institution. The simplest of these is to lease the cars, whereby a finance company (not surprisingly the two largest in the world are owned by the two largest motor car manufacturers) purchases the fleet of cars on behalf of the company and charges a periodic rental (lease) for their use based on the forecast depreciation as well as the interest cost. Ownership of the cars stays with the finance company, but any additional charges caused by them incurring a loss (that is, additional depreciation) on the eventual sale of the vehicle at the end of the lease period are normally charged back to the company using the cars. Maintenance costs are normally paid directly by the user under most leasing contracts but a further alternative includes maintenance costs as well in the periodic charge. This option is normally known as contract hire and some firms give a guaranteed cost which means that the hirer (that is, the company providing the financing) takes the profit or bears the loss on the eventual sale of the vehicles. Yet another option is to purchase the car fleet using hire-purchase as the source of finance. Which of all these options proves the most attractive is affected by the effective rates of interest charged but this is also complicated by the impact of taxation. There is, as one would expect, no clearcut winner on all occasions and as one company switches from buying to leasing another may decide, based on their evaluation, to do the opposite; with the alternative uses for the capital involved (that is, the opportunity cost of capital) making a significant difference to the decision.

One area of the business plan which can have a dramatic impact on the financing requirements and the availability of alternative sources of funding is any substantial investment in developing intangible marketing assets. It is often difficult to borrow cash specifically to fund marketing expenditures, due to the intangible nature of any asset created and the relative subjectivity required to produce any assessment of their realizable value (remember that these intangible marketing assets are not normally included on balance sheets in published financial statements). Therefore marketing expenditures utilize part of the overall level of funding available to the business, and if any borrowing is to be used the amount available will be subject to the overall gearing level considered acceptable for the company. This may act as a constraint on the ability of the company to finance aggressive marketing strategies which could restrict the growth objectives which are achievable within the planning time-scales.

Summary

In order to make any plan capable of implementation it is essential that the necessary amount of funding can be made available at the right time and in the appropriate form.

This appropriate form means that the sources of finance are matched to the uses for which they are required in terms of time-scale (that is, duration) and complementary degree of risk. The level of business risk is increased if the company has a high proportion of fixed costs (high operational gearing) and suitably low-risk financing should be used.

Equity is the lowest risk funding available because repayment is unnecessary and dividends can be a discretionary payment if absolutely necessary, whereas any form of debt increases the funding risk. Debt can now be raised in many different forms and the appropriate form should take account of the potential sensitivity of the projected cash flows in both absolute size and timing. This is to ensure that the entire business is not placed at an unacceptable level of financial risk due to the non-performance of one project.

Unfortunately some marketing expenditure even if creating a marketing asset tends to be looked on unfavourably by lenders due to its intangible nature, which means that it has to be financed out of the generally available funds of the business and not from specifically raised financing which can be used for other types of assets, such as plant and machinery or salesforce cars.

PART FOUR

CONTROL

10

Designing control systems

Introduction

In Part Three we noted that the only certain thing about financial planning, no matter how thoroughly it is done, is that it will be wrong in that the actual results will differ from those planned. Some of the assumptions regarding the external environment on which it is based will prove to be inaccurate but the most common area for differences is in the expectations of the results of the plans, some of which will turn out to have been unrealistic. If we reconsider the main justifications for all the effort that is needed to carry out these first two stages, namely financial analysis and planning, it becomes clear that producing a plan which then proves to be wrong gets no less than half the potential benefits of a full system of financial involvement.

The planning stage does, of itself, enable us to be aware of and thus accept the financial implications of our plans, to reallocate resources where necessary so as to increase their productivity, and to increase total available resources where appropriate. This planning stage should also ensure that adequate financing is available to meet the needs of the plan and, by using sensitivity analysis and contingency planning (that is planning for unexpected events by preparing alternative action plans) we can provide alternative plans of action for differing circumstances.

If we do not monitor the actual outcome of the various actions included in the plan we will not know when such alternative strategies should be put into operation, and we also need to be sure that they are still appropriate, given the actual circumstances at the time. The monitoring process should also be seen as a way of updating our financial analysis as this should not be regarded as a one-off exercise which can then be ignored. We have already indicated in Chapters 6, 7 and 8 that the planning process should be continuous with updated forecasts being used to supplement the more formalized budgeting and long-range planning procedures. Thus the whole process of financial involvement is circular and continuous, as shown in Figure 10.1, with analysis forming the basis of planning and these plans being monitored to provide up-to-date inputs to the analysis function of where the business now is.

This circular process highlights a fundamental aspect of financial control, which is that financial control should be viewed as a learning process. Monitoring and analysing, so as to explain the actual results achieved by implementing the financial plans of the company can provide the feedback from which better plans can be prepared next time; so the linkage provided by financial control systems between the past and the future is very important. It also indicates that the emphasis in financial control systems should be placed on those areas of the business where additional knowledge, gained through this learning process, can be of the greatest value in the future. In other words, monitoring and explaining in great detail non-recurring events can be a relatively unproductive use of resources from a learning point of view.

However, planning is fundamentally about making decisions and therefore merely monitoring the outcome of our plans is inadequate. The business should set up control systems, which are decision aids and enable changes to be made to the planned strategies when necessary to achieve the most effective results possible. This immediately highlights another fundamental principle of designing financial control systems – there is no point in having a control measure if it cannot lead to some form of action, when this is shown to be necessary. Control can, in this context, be defined as a process of assisting in managing the business by comparing actual performance against planned (for example, the budget) and taking remedial action where necessary. Control can, by definition, only be exercised over the present and the future, as no one can change the past, only explain it. This explanation of the past can, if used as a learning process, aid the control of the future and thus form part of the financial control system. Managers who can anticipate future events can be said to have greater control over their business, and this ability to anticipate correctly can be enhanced by the learning process provided by explaining the past. This idea of control can create a potential conflict which must be resolved through the design of the control system because in the planning stage we specify *activities* which we wish to be carried out, but the control process can only be implemented by *people*.

The logical way to resolve the conflict is to link the activities in the plan to appropriate areas of the business and to specific managers who are then made 'accountable' for the outcome of these activities, ideally by linking this accountability into their job specifications. This process is known as 'accountability planning' and requires the overall plan to be analysed into specific tasks which can be allocated to the operational areas of the business, hence the need for a hierarchical system of

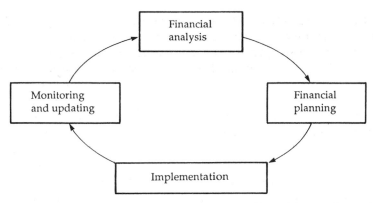

Figure 10.1 *Circular process of financial planning (financial control as a learning process)*

objectives and strategies (as shown in Figure 6.3 on page 166) leading to detailed tactics which can be implemented. If this linkage is established it is possible to design the control system around the idea of 'responsibility accounting', where the financial reporting system provides information, which compares actual performance to that indicated in the plan, to those responsible for specified sections of the plan. These 'responsible and accountable' people must have the ability to make any decisions which are needed to bring actual performance into line with planned, or even to modify the strategy or objectives where necessary. Without such decision-making power they are placed in the impossible position of having 'responsibility without authority' and the link between the planned activities and the controlling managers has not been properly established. If a marketing manager is held responsible for the profitabi- lity of a particular range of products sold through a particular channel of distribution, but has no authority over the direct costs of providing the products or over the costs of distribution through that channel, the marketing manager can be described as having 'responsibility without authority'. A different measure should be used to judge the managerial performance of the particular manager and this problem is discussed at length later in the chapter.

Ensuring that the financial control system really can function as a decision aid is of crucial importance and requires that the right *information* is provided to the right *people* at the right *time*; we can now examine each element which Chapter 11 will then consider in more detail.

The right information

Managers require information which can be used to control their areas of the business and not unprocessed raw data which can simply overwhelm them (not least with pieces of paper) and not help them to concentrate on those key elements where their decisions can significantly affect the success of the business. Marketing managers need information, for example, on how sales of their products are going, but sending them a copy of each individual sales invoice (which is the raw data for the analytical information required) would not be very helpful, whereas a segmented report of periodic sales analysed by customer groups and geographical or distribution channels and shown relative to the budget would be of great value. In this context, therefore, information can be defined as inputs which assist managers in decision-making and controlling the business, including explanations of past history. This information will result from the selective processing (including summarizing, comparing to other sets of data as appropriate, etc.) of the detailed raw data which is generated as part of the accounting recording system or the planning process.

The information supplied to managers should be relevant to the decisions which *they* can take and this raises two critical issues.

1   We are now well aware that financial decisions are based on future cash flows, but cost accounting information systems inevitably report on past events, and so we have a problem in providing managers with future-oriented information required for decision-making. A well-designed financial control system will use the latest actual information (that is based on events which have just happened) to predict the likely impact in the future, which helps the decision-maker. For example, if the product costs for last month have increased significantly it is important for the product manager to have information which distinguishes between a one-off production problem which is unlikely to recur and a permanent increase in the price of a major raw material. The decisions which should be taken are very different in each case and unless suitably analysed information is provided, decisions will unnecessarily be based on assumptions or guesses, not facts. Also up-to-date information can provide the best inputs for the revised forecast for the remaining budget period, which may indicate the need for changes in strategy or tactics, if the original objectives are to be achieved.

2   We must not overload managers with information, and this particularly includes providing a mass of information where no decisions are required, but where the manager may waste a lot of time coming to this 'no action needed' conclusion. If most of the plan is on target and the strategies are being successfully implemented, we should concentrate on any specific sections of the business where problems or

opportunities can be identified, as we do not wish to make changes unnecessarily.

This can be done by providing detailed financial information only on those areas which are not in line with the plan, that is, *on an exception basis*. Summary information can be supplied to managers on the areas which are achieving planned objectives to confirm this position and the more detailed exception reports will show where most management time should be spent. Also if the format of these exception reports shows the causes of the variances (differences) from plan, the manager is able further to concentrate on those areas where decisions can change the current position. This is illustrated in Figures 10.2 and 10.3 which show two different ways of presenting the same financial results to a particular marketing manager, who is in charge of a group of consumer products.

Figure 10.2 contains a mass of figures which does not help the marketing manager to identify any problems and to take effective corrective action. Many of the detailed figures cannot, in fact, be affected by the marketing manager as they represent shared costs or costs controlled in other areas of the business. Even the information relating to variable costs is not particularly helpful as it looks at consumer products in total and shows sales revenues and contributions above budget in both the period and year to date.

In Figure 10.3 (which is only an extract, and therefore does not show all the analytical information) the non-controllable information is effectively ignored by summarizing the overall figures. The fall in percentage contribution indicates that although sales revenues are above budget, the contribution rate is below budget and this requires further investigation. Part 2 of the report shows the specifically controllable costs for the marketing manager and again indicates the relative percentages of sales revenue as a guide to performance. This is not done for the non-variable portion as this should not be affected by small changes in sales revenue (the report analysing these is not included for reasons of space). The exception report, illustrated as part 3 of Figure 10.3, highlights the problems of one product which, despite maintaining higher proportionate marketing support is not achieving budgeted sales levels. This is hiding the overperformance of the rest of the business, and also may mean that proper action on this product would not be taken if this type of product analysis is not carried out.

The right people

Even using a very well-designed exception reporting system the business will be unable to take corrective action if the appropriate information is

Marketing manager report: monthly financial report on consumer products

Actual	Budget	Variance	£000s	Actual	Budget	Variance
Year to date					*Month 4*	
21 400	20 000	1400	Sales revenue	5210	4960	250
			less Direct variable costs			
6435	6000	(435)	Raw materials	1579	1434	(145)
1528	1400	(128)	Packaging materials	360	340	(20)
2042	2000	(42)	Labour	525	523	(2)
837	600	(237)	Energy	140	150	10
842	800	(42)	Indirect variable manufacturing	230	222	(8)
910	800	(110)	Variable distribution	240	205	(35)
1506	1400	(106)	Variable marketing	380	350	(30)
14 100	13 000	(1100)	Total variable costs	3454	3224	(230)
7300	7000	300	Contribution	1756	1736	20
920	800	(120)	*less* Other sales and marketing	260	200	(60)
1124	1050	(74)	Other manufacturing	275	261	(14)
960	1000	40	Finance and administration	230	250	20
750	800	50	Commercial and supply	180	200	20
			less Share of:			
800	800	–	Research and development	200	200	–
1000	1000	–	Divisional management	250	250	–
880	880	–	Head office costs	220	220	–
6434	6330	(104)	Total other costs	1615	1581	(34)
£866	£670	£196	Profit before interest and taxation	£141	£155	(£14)

Figure 10.2

supplied to managers who cannot do anything with the information because the required action is beyond their levels of authority, or relates to areas of the business where they have no direct authority. This would indicate that the linkage between the activities required to be controlled by particular managers to achieve the objectives of the plan and the accounting information system (that is, the historical part of the financial control system) for those responsible managers has not been properly established. It may be sensible to provide information to other managers in the company as it will help them to understand how the overall business is doing and which parts are doing well or badly against plan,

Specifically tailored report for marketing manager: monthly financial report on consumer products

£000s

Summarized overall results

(1)

	Year to date				Month		
	Actual	*Budget*	*Variance*		*Actual*	*Budget*	*Variance*
Sales revenue	21 400	20 000	1400		5210	4960	250
Total variable costs	14 100	13 000	(1100)		3454	3224	(230)
Contribution	7300 (34.1%)	7000 (35%)	300		1756 (33.7%)	1736 (35%)	20
Other costs	6434	6330	(104)		1615	1581	(34)
PBIT	866	670	196		141	155	(14)

(2) *Controllable costs*

	Year to date				Month		
Variable costs:	*Actual*	*Budget*	*Variance*		*Actual*	*Budget*	*Variance*
Distribution	910 (4.2%)	800 (4.0%)	(110)		240 (4.6%)	205 (4.1%)	(35)
Marketing	1506 (7%)	1400 (7.0%)	(106)		280 (5.4%)	250 (5.0%)	(30)
Non-variable costs:							
Sales and marketing	920	800	(120)		260	200	(60)

(3) *Exception reports [budget variances >10%]* (*Sample only)

Comments (a) The period and year to date contribution rates are below budget largely due to sales mix factors (detailed schedules – attachments 6, 7 and 8) of which large-size cans of branded tomatoes (product 21C) are the largest contributor:

Product 21C	Year to date				Month		
	Actual	*Budget*	*Variance*		*Actual*	*Budget*	*Variance*
Sales revenue	840	1600	(760)		180	400	(220)
Contribution	350 (41.6%)	640 (40%)	(290)		62 (34.4%)	160 (40%)	(88)

(b) Other products are uniformly above budget at approximately budgeted rates of contribution. Product 21C has a higher than average variable marketing cost allowance (10% of sales revenue against an average of 7%) and the budgeted expenditure levels have almost been maintained to try to stimulate demand for the product. Thus expenditure levels have been:

	Year to date		Period	
	Actual	*Budget*	*Actual*	*Budget*
Variable marketing on product 21C	120	160	30	40

This largely explains why variable marketing is above the budgeted rate in the period

Figure 10.3

but this 'nice to know' information cannot replace the 'need to know' information for the relevant decision-makers.

The financial control system should therefore take account of the decision-making organizational structure of the business, and the information supplied should be in sufficient detail for the types of decision taken at each level. At the lowest operational level managers will probably want detailed information on each category of expense which they control compared with the budgeted level, whereas at senior management level in a large organization summarized information only on the performance of operating divisions may be requested, with details being supplied on an exception basis. It is very important that a sensible balance is achieved, both at these extremes and at each managerial level in between, as many companies have control systems which generate too much detail at the high levels and too little at lower levels with the result that the information is of hardly any value in making decisions. Figures 10.4 and 10.5 illustrate respectively the ways in which some of our marketing manager's information might be presented to the area sales managers responsible for implementing specific promotional activity and an overall report made to the main board of directors at group level.

Area sales manager's monthly financial report: area 8 – consumer products (extract only)

Year to date			*£s*	*Month 4*		
Actual	*Budget*	*Variance*		*Actual*	*Budget*	*Variance*
			Variable marketing expenses			
			In-store promotions			
21 300	16 500	(4800)	Product 16A	5350	4000	(1350)
35 600	26 500	(9100)	Product 19	8150	6400	(1750)
15 400	18 000	2600	Product 21C	4100	4500	400

Figure 10.4

The plan should have been developed by reference to the interrelationships of activities and categories of expenditure, and the control system should be designed around these relationships. Thus the distinction between discretionary expenditures and engineered expenditures is important, as discussed in Chapters 6 and 8, because if an input–output relationship, such as in the manufacturing area, exists this will have an impact on the degree of control which can be exercised by the manager. Responsibility should normally rest with the manager who can exercise discretion over whether, and how, expenditure should be committed, as this is the level at which the plan and the strategy can be changed by

**Group board – monthly financial report consumer product group
– division 26**

Overall results			£000s		
Actual	*Variance*		*Actual*	*Variance*	*Comments*
21 400	1400	Sales revenue	5210	250	One product 21C is significantly below budget, others are above
7300	300	Contribution	1756	20	Lower sales of 21C are major reason for low increase
866	196	*Profit before interest and tax*	141	(14)	Sales and marketing costs are £60 k above budgets due to increased sales force headcount

Figure 10.5

management decisions. This can require that more detailed information may be needed at specific levels in the organization to support decisions because particular discretion can be exercised in this area, and this may cut across the formal organizational hierarchy. The financial control system has to provide the information to the 'right people' and not to the most senior people simply because of their place in the organization. This can often cause organizational problems for companies particularly within the marketing area, because relatively young product managers, possibly with very little 'people management' responsibility, will have discretion over many marketing aspects of their product group. They will consequently need information on the performance of these products to support their decisions on pricing, promotions, packaging design changes, distribution methods, etc. which will have far-reaching implications across the business and directly affect managers who, in the organization structure, are far more senior, as can be seen from the organizational chart shown in Figure 10.6. If the company restricts access to the necessary information for these product managers it will inevitably find that the quality of their decisions will be considerably lower and their performance consequently will be much less effective. However, it is possible to find many businesses where responsible, but junior, marketing managers (such as product managers) are unable to see product profitability information or customer contribution analyses for which they are supposedly responsible simply because of their level in the organizational hierarchy.

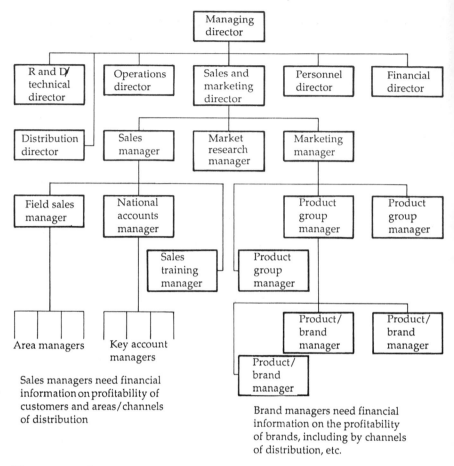

Figure 10.6 *Organizational chart (1)*

The right time

Once a company has decided what information should be provided to which managers, it must still resolve two major questions regarding the timing of supplying this information. The first question concerns the speed of supply and the second relates to the frequency of supply, and the general overall answer to both questions is very simple. The information must be supplied *as quickly and as often* as is demanded by the types of decision for which it will be used, but this general statement clearly needs some clarification.

There is always a cost associated with providing information and as was established at the beginning of the book we must make sure that the benefit obtained from the information exceeds the cost of providing it (by doing a cost benefit analysis). It may be difficult to evaluate the precise benefit obtained from providing information but a common way is to consider the potential costs which could be suffered by the business in the specific circumstances or as a result of particular events which can be avoided by providing the information. By assessing the likelihood of these circumstances or events (that is, their profitability), an expected value can be calculated for the information which can be compared to the cost of providing it. It is also normally true that requiring information to be supplied faster increases its cost because more sophisticated systems and resources have to be committed to its preparation, and this extra cost must also be justified. Part of this extra cost can be offset by allowing for a slightly lower level of accuracy in the information which is needed quickly. A level of approximation which supplies a good overall picture of performance may enable the business to make timely alterations to its strategy which otherwise might not be possible if it had to wait for more accurate but less timely reports. Many managers prefer to be 'approxima- tely right' rather than 'precisely wrong', in that they would rather get some information when it is useful than get a very detailed explanation with full reconciliations when it is too late to do anything with it.

The same logic can be applied to the frequency of supplying financial information to decision-makers in that the frequency must be linked to the time-scale of the decisions being made. Most of the regular decisions can be supplied by equally regular financial reports generated by the control system on a suitable schedule, but many major business decisions are taken on an ad hoc basis triggered by force of circumstances (such as the unexpected launch of a new competitive product by a rival company) and these will normally require specially produced inputs. It is important that the financial control system can cope with such irregular requirements and that the information can be presented in the appropri- ate format to suit the particular decision under consideration, which requires a high level of flexibility to be built into the design of the system. For example if a food manufacturing company gets the opportunity to tender for a very large contract to supply various products to all the national health hospitals for the next three years, it would be ridiculous to rely on the standard product costs prepared for the budget, which might have been put together nine months ago and which are not due for updating for another three months. It could be almost as bad if the entire accounts department had to be taken off its normal work for several weeks to do the ad hoc exercise necessary to produce sensible base information for the tender pricing decision, as the rest of the business would be effectively without sound financial information during this period.

Impact of computers

In Chapter 11 we consider these aspects in more detail with examples of the issues involved, but modern technology can help tremendously in the area of financial control. One of the problems of attempting to supply 'the right information to the right people at the right time' is that these 'individualized' requirements can lead to a plethora of financial reports which have to be produced on differing timetables. Even if the massive clerical workload could be coped with, there was historically a more fundamental problem caused by lack of consistency across the various reports because they were prepared from different base documents, with differing degrees of approximation, at different times, by different people, with differing levels of financial aptitude and enthusiasm for financial control procedures. Consequently considerable management time was spent trying to reconcile the alternative results given in the various reports and this often caused a high degree of distrust as to the accuracy of any output from the accounting department. For example, it was not unknown for the various sales and profit analyses used by marketing managers to add up to different total sales revenues and profit figures than were given by the overall profit and loss account due to the different ways in which sales by customers, products and channels were extracted and the different bases used in apportioning certain costs. Not surprisingly this could cause a degree of confusion in marketing management meetings. In many companies this resulted in the various operating areas setting up their own internal, informal financial control systems, in order to obtain financial information which was relevant to *them*, and which they believed in sufficiently to use as the basis for decisions, for which they, not the accounting department, were held responsible. The duplication and consequent waste of resources are clear, but the diversion of skilled management resources away from their areas of expertise was, in many cases, even more expensive.

Fortunately the general level of support provided by accounting departments has improved substantially, but the great breakthrough for financial control systems has been provided by technology. The dramatic increase in processing power, and equally dramatic decline in cost, of modern computer systems has given even relatively small businesses the potential to develop quite sophisticated financial planning and control systems. The great ability of these systems to process large volumes of data at great speed means that all managers can have, theoretically at least, the specific financial information which is needed to control their section of the business without having to sift through reams of paper to find the key pieces of information which they require. In many companies the previous problem has been superseded by a lack of ability of user managers either properly to specify the information they require or to understand and use the tailored information correctly.

Many of the financial decision-making techniques that we have considered rely in most businesses on the extraction and processing of substantial volumes of financial data (for example, internal rate of return (IRR) calculations, break-even charts and contribution analysis), and these calculations have been speeded up dramatically by computerization. However the greatest improvement is the ability of the computer systems to allow changes to be made in the assumptions on which the computations are based so that many alternatives (usually described as 'what-ifs') can be compared. This allows much more sensitivity analysis to be carried out at the planning stage, and contingency plans can be developed for the most probable alternatives. Thus when it is seen that the actual business situation is different from the plan's assumptions the contingency plan can very rapidly be implemented, and the consequences of the changes which are to be made can be evaluated by the information system. This can be seen by returning to our example of our marketing manager's financial reporting system and the underperformance of product 21C as was shown in Figure 10.3.

If an integrated planning and control system is in use, the opportunities are far greater because the appropriately analysed plan can be used as the base to compare the actual outcomes against as normal, but now on an automated basis. This enables the 'actual versus plan' control reports to be produced very quickly after the end of any accounting period, and the production of the exception report can also be automated. To do this the company has to specify tolerance limits or acceptable levels of deviation (that is, variances from the plan) for each relevant subdivision. For any area in which the actual to plan difference is greater than the specified level an exception report is produced. This automated processing power can take the clerical effort out of producing regular routine control reports but it does not actually carry out the financial control process.

The financial control process is carried out by the various managers throughout the business but if the financial control system provides all managers with their tailored information requirements on a totally consistent basis across the company, the decision-making process is substantially improved. If such a system is also able to cope with ad hoc decisions which require the information to be arranged in a completely different configuration over unusual time periods, without unduly disrupting and delaying the production of the regular routine reports, the company is almost certainly using a good 'database' financial control system. 'Database' has been a computer system 'buzz-word' for many years, but only recently have databases become practically operational in many companies and a very high proportion are still struggling with problems of design and implementation. The concept is very simple and immensely logical in that it requires each piece of data to be input into the computer system once and only once. This includes the financial plan inputs, and actual transactions and any updated forecast data that the company may consider relevant. By coding all this input *appropriately*, and this is the key to the successful design of the system, it is possible to access any desired combinations of data and produce either summarized or detailed reports for specified managers. Hence all the reports are consistent since they all use the same base data, and in very sophisticated environments they can be formatted by direct user request via a VDU (visual display unit) screen, which further eliminates both clerical workload and delay in preparation.

The potential impact of being able to compare the financial plan, rolling forecast and actual achievement at varying levels and in various combinations with a minimum of effort is clearly dramatic and it can free management from the problems of having to make major decisions based on inadequate information. However, there is a new danger in that managers can tend to become overtaken by 'analysis paralysis' as the new-found ability to evaluate many more possible alternatives and take account of additional factors mean that decisions are delayed, deferred or just not taken because managers are too busy 'planning'. Analysis, planning and control are still meant to help support the business, and the business is only successful if it sells products in a market at a profit and this requires decisions to be taken as to what products and which markets, which depend on where the profit comes from.

Therefore a good financial control system, whether it uses a computer database or the backs of envelopes, should focus attention on providing information to support decisions and this requires an ability to differentiate the types of information relevant to the different types of business decision.

Economic decisions versus assessment of managerial performance

In normal business decisions we are interested in selecting the option which brings the maximum benefit to the business, even if the best choice only results in the company making a smaller loss than under all the other alternatives. The selection of this maximum benefit can only be made in the knowledge of the corporate mission and the objectives and strategies which have been built into the plan so as to achieve the mission, or get as close to it as the external environment will allow. Decisions in business are made by the managers and it may be dangerous to assume that a particular manager is motivated to achieve the same objectives as have been set for the company by the most senior managers. The corporate strategy may include a quite high level of risk which is felt to be acceptable to the shareholders of the company because the potential return is commensurately even higher, but to the manager the career risk may not be perceived as being matched by any related return, and the return demanded could in any case be dramatically greater.

The normal corporate reaction to this problem is to attempt to make the manager *motivated* to achieve the corporate objectives, but this concept of 'goal congruence' is not that easy to achieve in practice. The simplistic approach is to measure the manager's performance by how well the company meets its objectives but this can have a very negative motivational influence if, for example, a sales manager wins several very large orders which the rest of the operation fails to deliver in terms of date, quality, and cost and so the business overall does not achieve its targets. Indeed no single manager, not even the chief executive, can be regarded as having complete control over the achievement of the corporate plan's objectives because the plan is subject to many assumptions about the external environment. For example, a large bank may find that its expansion plans are impossible if a rapid rise in world interest rates, triggered by a US federal budget deficit, causes a dramatic decline in borrowing levels, but the management cannot really be held responsible for the actions of the US government. This does not mean that the company can afford to ignore the external environment, and changes from assumptions made in the plan can significantly affect the economic performance of the business. The financial control system should distinguish those things for which managers can be held accountable (and this can include forecasts made of the external environment in which the company will be operating) from other things for which no accountability can be attached to the managers. The analysis of both categories can contribute to the learning process, by explaining any variances, and may enable better forecasts to be made in future. It is, therefore, important to separate issues relating to managerial performance measurement from the external environment's impact on the economic results of a company, while still trying to maintain the link in motivating the managers to try to achieve the corporate goals.

This can be achieved if managers are primarily evaluated against measures where they have a high level of control over their performance. Therefore we need to separate controllable areas of the business from those where they exercise no control. The analysed budget can be very useful, because if properly broken-down the budget will provide objectives, strategies, etc. for the various areas of the business which are consistent with those for the whole business, and these can be used for managerial performance evaluation. The problems come from the inter-action of the budget areas within the business and the impact on the relevant area of the business of the external non-controllable factors which can differ from their planned levels. If key tasks or activities within the specific budget area can be identified, then the successful completion of these tasks or management of particular activities to achieve the specified objectives can be used for managerial performance evaluation. As far as possible items should be selected which are independent of other influences, that is, our sales manager could be given the objective of winning a certain volume of *new orders* and could be judged primarily on that performance rather than on the overall business performance. The logic is that if all managers achieved their own objectives then the company overall should achieve its objectives. Hence we have obtained goal congruence if the individual objectives can be properly set. If our sales manager worked for the bank with the expansion plans and was given an objective to obtain new customers for the bank to lend to, the external environment would make this objective much more difficult than was previously intended, and a good performance might be the achievement of 10 per cent growth against a target of 35 per cent. In some areas of the business, it may be possible to vary the objective to suit the changed conditions (known as 'flexing' the budget), and this is what updated forecasts are supposed to do for all the business but it is difficult to use a continually changing forecast as a benchmark against which to measure managerial performance. For our banking sales manager it may be possible to set the growth objectives in the context of the growth of the whole market, for example, the objective is to grow 10 per cent faster than the market. Therefore if our forecast for market growth was 25 per cent, our own growth objective would be 35 per cent as shown by the target. However, if the change in business environment meant that the overall market was static, our 'flexed' objective would be a growth rate of 10 per cent, and the budget could be altered accordingly.

The most logical areas where 'flexible budgeting' is of value are where there is an input–output engineering relationship so that the managerial performance can be assessed against the changed target in a relatively objective way. The distribution area of a business is significantly affected by the sales performance of the company but cannot be held directly responsible for it. However, if a good model of distribution costing has been developed, the total cost which *should* have been incurred to deliver the actual sales can be calculated and compared to the *actual* costs incurred as indicated in Figure 10.7.

This approach can also cope with many of the external changes which cannot be directly affected by the particular area, such as increases in fuel costs, because the impact of these changes in the costs can be calculated

Distribution costs (simplified example)*

	Budget	Actual	£000s Flexed budget	Adjusted variance
Outside hauliers: delivery charges	175	250	262.5	12.5
Number of cases delivered	5000	7500		

*Under our simplified distribution model, outside hauliers are budgeted to charge 3.5p per case delivered (that is, £175 000 for 5 million cases) and so we can flex the budget for the actual volume of cases delivered. This would give a flexed budget of 7.5 million cases × 3.5p or £262 500, with which the actual cost incurred in delivering 7.5 m cases can be compared. It is not helpful to analyse the original budget and the actual, and highlight an apparent *adverse* variance of £75 000.

Figure 10.7

and these variances can be excluded from the managerial performance evaluation. Even though these costs cannot be 'controlled' by the company, its ability to forecast and anticipate changes will affect the 'degree of control' which can be exercised over the business. Thus the company may not be able to avoid increases in fuel costs, but a good financial control system, which enabled it to predict the increase, would greatly assist it in minimizing the impact. These changes will still be included in the economic performance assessment and are to be used in future forecasts as relevant base information – any such change does after all affect the financial performance of the business.

This use of specific individual objectives for managerial evaluation has the benefit of focusing management attention on those areas where managers exercise greatest personal control, which are the parts of the business where their decisions will have greatest effect. However, it can also be divisive to the management team approach to running the business and it may create an apportionment of blame approach to the financial control system rather than as a business support system. This negative use of the financial control system as a way of apportioning blame must be avoided, and the more positive use as a learning process must be emphasized by the company. In many large organizations it is possible to subdivide the total business into smaller business areas with more closely focused management teams and to use these as motivational management teams, because the smaller areas will have more closely identifiable aims and objectives which the managers can associate with as a team. This can stop individual managers becoming too introspective about their own area. The organization structure, as illustrated in Figure 10.8, can therefore be used to avoid some of the problems of managerial performance assessment but issues regarding measurement and comparability remain and are considered later in the chapter.

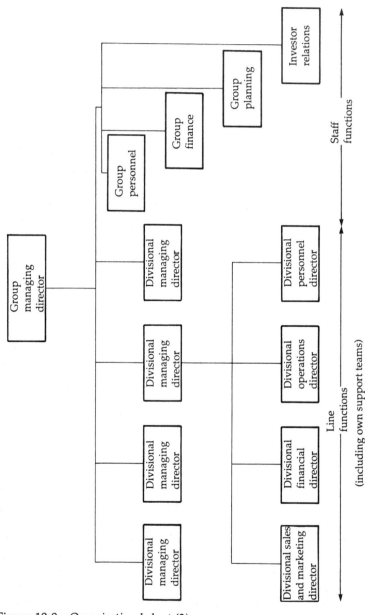

Figure 10.8   *Organizational chart (2)*

The divisions may themselves be broken down into subgroups which focus on particular markets with particular products, etc. depending upon the ability to discretely separate resources (i.e. assets and people).

We can try to use objective measurements which enable some of the lack of total independence of any business subdivision to be allowed for, but we must be careful to remember what the financial control system is comparing and evaluating.

Efficiency versus effectiveness as control measures

If we use an input–output relationship we can adjust the level of activity in the plan to reflect what should have happened under the updated situation, but we are only able by this calculation to measure the *efficiency* of the management concerned. Whether the correct level of distribution cost was incurred for the actual sales achieved can be measured by using the cost model already established. The answer to this question makes no comment on the effectiveness of the management in helping to achieve the overall corporate objectives, and assumes that the previously planned relationship is appropriate for the new situation. It is possible that one reason why sales are below budgeted levels is because our distribution service no longer compares acceptably to the competition, which may have dramatically upgraded their service levels. An excessive emphasis on efficiency measurements, particularly in cost areas, may lead to a decrease in quality if some measure of quality is not included in the managerial performance assessments.

To overcome this risk we must identify additional objectives, quite probably non-financial ones, which can also be used to measure the performance of management, but where the effectiveness of the management is being assessed rather than just their efficiency. In the example of distribution, the non-financial objectives might include a measure of delivery time from release of order to receipt by the customer, or a measure of achievement of forecast delivery dates, and comparisons where possible with the service level achieved by competitors. This inclusion of effectiveness can only be achieved if the financial control system is very closely linked to the corporate objectives and strategies. If this is done then 'critical success factors' can be identified for various areas of the business, which really do mean that if each area achieves its 'critical success factors' then the business should hit its overall targets. A critical success factor can, in this context, be defined as any action which must be successfully carried out if the overall objective of the business, or any particular part of the business, is to be achieved. If our company distributes to retailers short shelf-life products such as cakes, as in our example in Chapter 5, the critical success factor for distribution may be to minimize the delay in delivery to the retailers so that the maximum shelf-life is available during the period on sale in the shop. This will minimize the level of out-of-date returns by customers, and also increase customer satisfaction levels. The non-financial objective should, therefore, be expressed in terms of days elapsed between the stock being released to the distribution department and received by the customer, or as an overall percentage of the total shelf-life of the product which must still be available when the product is received by the customer. This latter measure should focus attention on those products which have very short product lives where even one day's extra delivery delay may be critical, rather than on those products, such as fruit cakes, where a much longer storage life is available. This objective for distribution is in addition to the promised delivery time-span for customers as to the gap between an order being placed and the delivery made.

The financial control system should emphasize the monitoring of these factors and will include, wherever possible, 'early warning indicators' of problems which may require the commencement of certain contingency planning actions, that if taken quickly enough can put the critical success factor back on target. For example, the growth objective in the budget may be dependent on the successful launch of two new products in the second half of the financial year. The control system obviously cannot monitor any actual sales until after the launch, but there are a number of critical actions which must take place well before the launch date if the corporate growth objective is to be achieved through additional sales of these two new products. Thus dates for completion of the various product development stages, and for initial production trials, etc. can be monitored; if these slip it may be possible to add in additional resources to still meet the launch date, by for example diverting engineering or production resources to this project. This shows that the control system will monitor non-financial issues as well as financial results. If the launch date has to be delayed, the sales volume for the year may be unachievable, without increasing the launch marketing support so that sales growth is faster than forecast. The impact of this additional expense would need to be evaluated against the original objectives of the plan, but it may mean a choice between hitting the sales revenue objective and making a smaller profit in the period than targeted, or not achieving the sales growth objective.

As discussed earlier, *planning* is often a compromise between competing objectives, and the *actual* position is normally the same. One of the major reasons for implementing a financial control system is to ensure that the company is able to choose which objectives it aims for rather than getting any particular actual result by default, so that our company could at least choose to achieve the sales growth objective or to achieve the profit objective but not grow as fast as planned. Clearly internal failures to meet subobjectives, such as launching the new products, may mean that the overall objectives have to be lowered and strategies changed accordingly, but the business will always have a mix of objectives and the required amendment may only need to modify one, or a few, of these objectives. The financial control system should highlight the alternatives in terms of which objectives can be compromised, but must ensure that the revised objectives and strategies are internally consistent and conform to the updated set of externally based assumptions. For example, if the external environment has deteriorated so that sales of the new product would have been lower anyway, this information will have an important impact on the choice of new strategy made by the company.

The real economic decisions facing the business require a continually updated set of assumptions on the external environment, such as the market size and rate of growth, because they are so important to many decisions. These reviews may indicate that, through no fault of the business, the original objectives are no longer attainable and, again, the control system must be capable of adjusting the objectives or strategy, or both, so that the impact of these external factors is minimized. Of course, if the change is advantageous, the control system must enable the company to take maximum advantage of the opportunity, and therefore flexibility and speed of response are of great importance. If the market is growing more rapidly than expected, it may become even more important to divert resources to bring forward the launch date and to increase the level of launch activity to take advantage of this increased sales opportunity.

Responsibility centres

The best way of ensuring flexibility and speed of response is if the control system and the plan are broken down into smaller but logically structured subdivisions of the business, the managers of which are the principal operating decision-makers in the company. Each of these divisions (or Strategic Business Units) should have their own subset of objectives and strategies which fit into the overall objectives of the business but which allow the division to operate as a relatively self-contained responsibility centre.

A responsibility centre within a business can be defined as any area of the business which has inputs and outputs, and where management responsibility can be associated with a particular individual or responsible group of managers. The responsibility centres may be broken up in two main ways:

1 functionally by type of management responsibility, such as marketing, research and development, finance and accounting, production or operations;

2   divisionally by products, market segments, customer groupings or channels of distribution.

A division of a business is therefore a responsibility centre which has some measurable form of output (normally as some sort of sales revenue), whereas in a functional organization it is often very difficult to measure outputs. However, a division may have sales revenues from 'internal' customers, that is, other parts of its own organization. Therefore a newer classification of division has been created by some large groups which must have external customers.

Strategic business units (SBUS) are divisions of the company the managers of which have control of their own resources and which make sales to external customers. SBUs are normally created to focus on a market segment or a product group.

Every division will have non-financial objectives, such as achieving quality or market share objectives, as well as financial constraints, and there are four major ways of classifying responsibility centres depending on their degree of financial independence. It must be remembered that no division can ever be completely independent financially, because this would involve it in raising its own financing from its own shareholders and it would therefore be a completely separate company. Thus no matter how operationally independent divisions may be the financial linkage back to the larger group will be maintained.

If divisions are to be given financial objectives, these must be capable of being monitored by the control system, which requires that they can be measured in a regular and meaningful way. For management control purposes, these financial objectives must be controllable which can restrict the level at which they can be set. Some managers of areas of the business cannot be regarded as generating any meaningful sales revenues, whereas other responsibility centre managers can control their revenues but do not control all the expenses which would create a profit. Still others can be considered not only to generate profit but to control the level of assets used and so they can be held accountable for that investment on a suitable basis.

This gives us the four main types of responsibility centre:

1   cost centres;
2   revenue centres;
3   contribution and profit centres;
4   investment centres.

Cost centres

When a business subgroup or responsibility centre does not generate any sales revenue or other financially measurable output, the only realistic level of financial control is by reference to the expenditure level incurred. A cost centre can be generally described as involving physical output, rather than financially measurable output, and only a modest level of managerial discretion, for example, regarding the level of expenditure which can be incurred. If a meaningful budget has been established, the actual expenditure can be compared against budget and any material overspend reported. However, this is a very tenuous system of control and requires very tight links to the non-financial objectives of the responsibility centre, so as to ensure that sensible decisions are taken in line with overall corporate objectives. Research and development into new products is often run as a cost centre due to the lack of financially measurable outputs, and the financial control can be only comparisons of actual to budgeted expense levels. The budget should be set at a level which enables research and development to develop sufficient new or improved products in a timescale to meet the needs of the marketing plan. Consequently underspending their budget (that is, producing a favourable variance) but failing to deliver the new products on time should not be regarded as good management performance. Here again we are in danger of concentrating on 'apparent efficiency' and not effectiveness. What we require is a system of 'milestones' (or key decision points at which project reviews should be undertaken) which enable the level of expenditure to be related to some practical achievements set out in the plan, and on which decisions to commit further resources can be based.

In no cost centre do we want managers to just spend the budget, we want them to spend the resources wisely so that their objectives are achieved. Marketing departments are often treated as cost centres and the problem of measuring effectiveness can be particularly difficult. If the budget is broken down into specific marketing programmes (that is, marketing activities with identified financial and non-financial objectives), then the remainder (mainly salaries and indirect expenses) can be regarded as a cost centre, which should also be a relatively fixed cost. Controlling a cost centre which has mainly fixed cost expense centres should not be a major problem as periodic variances from budget should be fairly small and any changes that need to be made should be justified and approved in advance, that is, before any additional fixed costs are incurred. The individual marketing programmes should be financially justified before the expenditure is committed, by using the appropriate techniques already discussed and the control procedure should be to evaluate the actual outcome of the activity (often referred to as a 'post-completion audit'). Any attempt to compare actual outcomes of marketing activities to the stated objectives is almost always complicated by changes in the external environment from that forecast at the time of the justification, but the use of outcomes means that this portion of the expenditure does not need to be controlled as a cost centre because measurable financial outputs result from the activity. Thus a price-reduction promotion may be justified on the forecast level of increased sales and the consequent overall improvement in contribution (using the calculation examined in Part Three), but an unexpected change in the external environment, such as a fall-off in total demand or aggressive competitive activity, can make the actual sales considerably lower than those forecast. This does not necessarily mean that the promotion was a failure financially, because the actual results *should* be compared to 'what *would* have happened without the promotion' rather than to the now outdated forecast (that is, the forecast should be 'flexed' to take account of the external changes). This is demonstrated in the example below.

Example: Price Reduction Promotion – Pre-justification and Post-justification
A confectionery product has a selling price per case (48 bars in a case) of £4 and a variable cost per case of £2.50, and the marketing manager decides to stimulate demand by reducing the price per case to £3.60 (a 10 per cent price reduction for a three month period). The current monthly sales volume is 50 000 cases per month and the forecast increase is 50 per cent (that is, another 25 000 cases per month) as the market is very price sensitive.

Pre-promotion analysis – three month period
Contribution without promotion   = 150 000 cases × £1.50
                                   = £225 000
Contribution with promotion   = 225 000 cases × (3.60−2.50)
                                   = £247 500
Therefore promotion increases total contribution by £22 500

Note   Remember it is the change in contribution which is important and applying the formula given in the appendix to Chapter 8 gives a break-even volume increase of:

$$\text{Volume increase needed} = \frac{\text{Contribution given up}}{\text{Contribution retained}} = \frac{40p}{(1.50-40p)} = 36.3\%$$

Unfortunately the three months of the promotion period saw very heavy competitive activity particularly by overseas companies trying to gain market share, and actual sales in the period were only 64 000 cases per month. Against a base of 50 000 cases this does not justify the price decrease, but the marketing manager can quite validly argue that without the promotion 50 000 cases would not have been sold in the actual external environment. It is normally difficult to establish what sales would have been, but using the appropriate budgeting model in this case it was agreed that 43 000 cases would have been sold each month without the promotion.

Post-promotion analysis – three month period
Contribution with promotion (flexed)   = 129 000 cases × £1.50
                                               = £193 500
Contribution with promotion (actual results) = 192 000 cases × £1.10
                                               = £211 200

Unless a very sophisticated market model is in use within the business, it is very difficult to carry out an objective 'what-if' analysis when the actual result is known. The best way to overcome this is to do several 'what-if' alternatives at the justification stage to test the sensitivity of the activity and to see how financially robust it is. If small changes in the external assumptions make it financially unattractive, the risk is clearly higher than for any activity which is worthwhile for a larger range of situations.

Revenue centres

Some areas of the business, most notably sales, can be regarded as controlling sales revenue levels but not controlling all the costs which go to make up a profit or loss on their activities. Hence sales departments are often financially controlled by reference to sales revenue targets, while their cost levels are controlled as a cost centre. We have already discussed in Chapter 8 how sales force costs can be much more positively controlled if the allocated resources are justified on the input–output relationship utilizing the non-financial objectives set for the sales force activity. This requires that very clear non-financial objectives are specified for their activities and actual costs are not simply compared to budgets. It is equally dangerous to rely on overall monetary revenue targets for the sales area.

We really want the sales force to make profitable sales and hence the product and customer mix is very important, and any global sales revenue targets ignore changes in the sales mix. This problem can be overcome by including segmented targets which focus attention on achieving an acceptable sales mix, but if sales *prices* vary from the budgeted levels, the original target value may be made irrelevant. Establishing volume targets can remove the most obvious impact of alterations in price levels, but changes in the external environment (for example, through changes in the price elasticity of demand for the product) which may have caused the need to change prices can also have affected the probable sales volumes. It may be practical to set the objectives in relative terms which are automatically flexed according to external changes and market share could be useful as such a measure. Market share cannot, however, really be used as an exclusive objective of the sales area as it is influenced by all the company's marketing activities, and a different marketing mix could dramatically alter the level of share achieved, irrespective of the effort of the sales force. If sensible control measures cannot be found for the particular subdivision of the business, it may be that the way in which the business is being divided is not logical, and alternative divisional structures should be considered (for example, group sales and marketing together so that market share is appropriate as a control measure).

Profit centres

Profit (P) is given by revenue (R) − costs (C), so a basic equation for a profit centre can be shown as $R - C = P$, which indicates that in order to control the level of profit both R and C must be capable of being controlled.

As a major corporate objective is related to earning a profit, most businesses prefer to break the total operation into divisions which also have profit as a major performance measure. For this to be practical divisions have to be set up which generate identifiable and measurable sales revenues and control the cost levels which are deducted to arrive at a profit. If some costs are controlled centrally and arbitrarily charged out to the divisions, the control system can focus on the contribution made by the division because non-controllable apportioned costs should be excluded from the managerial performance evaluation. (We have already established that managerial performance evaluation should not include costs which cannot be controlled by the managers concerned, as opposed to the economic evaluation of the area when all relevant costs should be included.)

The only areas of the business, which really control both sales revenues and costs, are vertical subdivisions of the business which have their own markets and products (for example, strategic business units, SBUs) and are, consequently, almost self-contained businesses. Almost all large companies (such as GEC and Hanson) break their operations down into this level of divisional structure, but many try to create even more subdivisions so that even more specific objectives can be agreed. If these divisions do not have direct external sales (that is, are not SBUs) but supply other parts of the business, it is possible to create internal sales and purchases by setting up a system of transfer prices. Thus if the

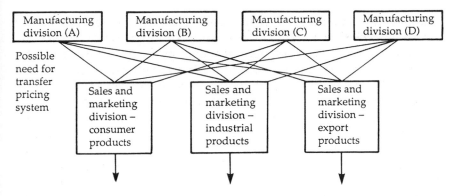

Figure 10.9   *Transfer pricing: sales between divisions of a large group*

organization is broken down into sales and marketing units which are serviced by large specialized production units, it may be practical to set prices for 'internal sales' from the production units to the sales and marketing units as shown in Figure 10.9.

Some companies go even further and set transfer prices for the provision of various internal services, such as computing, to other parts of the business. In all transfer pricing exercises it is important that the business does not confuse the idea of setting prices so as to allocate resources efficiently (which is an economic decision and hence requires the application of the opportunity cost concept) and the use of transfer prices as a means of assessing managerial performance. The latter should be assessed on controllable costs of the responsibility centre, and transfer prices *imposed* on the division by the centre, or the supplying division, cannot be regarded as controllable unless the purchaser has the right to go outside the group to obtain lower prices.

As long as transfer prices are kept at the levels set in the budgets, their impact on the divisional performance against their budget (which should form the basis of managerial evaluation) may not be very significant and these costs charged at fixed transfer prices are often effectively a fixed cost at the divisional level, as seen in Figure 10.2. The effect on economic decisions regarding the *absolute* level of performance of the business can be very important, as the apparent performance can be distorted if profit margins are being taken on internal transfers by other divisions of the group. Any decision on whether to close the division, or drop the product, etc. must be taken in the context of the impact on the *overall group* and not just the impact on the particular division. For example, a particular product may contain elements produced by several different profit centre divisions, assembled in another and distributed to the end marketing division by yet another profit centre, all of whom earn a margin on their input to the final product. Even though the end marketing division may not make a viable profit margin on its costs, the group must take all the other contributions into account when deciding on the future of the product. Such a system may cause internal problems because the managers of the end marketing division may not devote very many resources to supporting this product which only earns a low profit margin as far as they are concerned. Indeed there are many examples of marketing divisions wishing to drop products which are very profitable to the overall business, but where an incorrect transfer pricing system shows a false financial return to the division with unfortunate consequences. This can be illustrated in a multinational car manufacturer and this is examined in Part Five, on page 389. These problems are the main reason why some major car companies do not run their individual manufacturing plants on a profit centre basis.

Investment centres

Although an overall corporate objective is to earn profit, we established, right at the start of the book, that this profit needs to be put into the context of the investment required, and therefore a return on investment measure for a division of the business represents the most compatible divisional objective. In order to use the investment centre concept the division should not only be able to control the profit levels but also to decide on the level of investment which will be employed in the division. Thus an investment centre should concentrate on its level of profitability, that is, rate of profit per £ of investment, and not on the absolute level of profit. (A basic equation can therefore be developed for an investment centre as: $\dfrac{R - C}{I} \times 100\%$ = return on investment, where R is revenue, C is cost and I is investment.)

Therefore investment centres tend to be very self-contained businesses which are often run as relatively independent entities. As previously indicated, divisions are never completely independent and the main control exercised over many investment centres is by the centre of the group acting in the role of financier and providing the necessary investment funding. The group wishes to allocate its available funds to those divisions which will produce the best return and this can, to some extent, be measured by the return on investment (ROI) measurement. This is the most common method of assessing divisional performance on the investment centre basis but, as discussed in Chapter 7, ROI does have a number of measurement problems (that is, in accurately measuring both the return and the investment involved) and the level in any particular year may not be particularly representative of the long-term return which will be achieved by the division. ROI is also a backward looking (historic) accounting measure, whereas for investment decisions we require a forward-looking cash flow based measure, such as internal rate of return (IRR), as established in Chapter 7.

An alternative method, which is also used by several large businesses, is for the group to make a notional interest charge to the division for any funds used by the division. This interest charge reduces the divisional profit in proportion to the investment base of the division and results in a lower absolute level of 'residual income' (RI) or economic profit after paying the costs of capital. Some companies are now quite sophisticated in the way in which they charge different 'interest' rates for varying types of funds used by the division. Different types of assets will have very different levels of risk and the consequent type of funds which they will absorb will differ accordingly. Thus a division with significant investments in marketing assets, which are considered high risk and normally have to be financed by high cost equity, would be charged a higher 'interest rate' than a division with comparably sized investments in freehold land and buildings.

It should be remembered that the financial control system will compare all these performances against the expected levels shown in the budgets, and this relative comparison against expectations does help to alleviate some of the measurement problems which exist in the absolute ROI evaluations, as previously illustrated in Table 5.3 in Chapter 5.

However, it also highlights the need for careful coordination in the setting of objectives and the consequent control mechanism, so that decisions are made that are in the group's overall interests, and not in the specific interests of one division. We have seen, in Chapters 4 and 5, how it is possible to 'creatively manufacture' any desired level of ratio, and if divisions are judged on ROI criteria they may well try to improve the *measure* rather than the *real performance* of the business. This is shown in the example below.

Example: Use and Abuse of ROI as a Control Measure
A leading multinational group judges the performance of its many operating divisions on their return on investment (ROI) compared to budgeted levels. Also because the divisions are funded by the group the investment base used is 'total assets less trade creditors', and in summarized form the UK division's position is as follows:

Balance sheet (£m)

		Actual		*Budget*
Net fixed assets		60		62
Current assets				
stock	40		35	
debtors	60		50	
sundry	5		5	
	105		90	
less Trade creditors	30	75	25	65
Investment		£135 million		£127 million
Profit		£54 million		£57 million
ROI	=	40%		45%

The division is below budget and if the managers are paid large incentive bonuses to achieve budget, they may be strongly motivated to alter this position. A number of 'creative' possibilities exist

1   sale and leaseback of the fixed assets;
2   sale to a broker of a portion of the stocks held;
3   factoring of debtors;
4   paying the suppliers for extended credit or for holding stocks and delivering at very short notice (that is, off-balance sheet inventories).

Any of these will reduce the profit of the division but, because of the very high ROI being achieved, the consequent reduction in the investment base will improve the division's ROI – potentially above budget so that 'performance' bonuses are paid by the group.

It should be clear that these different forms of control for responsibility centres are hierarchical levels and thus any investment centre can, and probably should, be broken down into profit, revenue and/or cost centres as appropriate. This hierarchy can be illustrated by the level of managerial discretion in each level. In cost centres managers can only affect costs, whereas in revenue centres, sales revenues and some costs can be changed by management action. At the profit centre level discretion is exercised over all sales revenues and costs and in an investment centre there is also discretion over the level of investment made. The vital issue is that the financial measures are used in conjunction with the evaluation of specific non-financial objectives, rather than as a complete replacement for them. It is also important that the business does not concentrate exclusively on the performance of organizational subdivisions because success is determined by performance in the marketplace and the control system must provide relevant financial information on product and customer performance; this is discussed further in Chapter 11.

Summary

Financial control systems are designed to give the right information to the right people at the right time, and their fundamental basis is to support decision-making rather than merely explain what has happened. The explanatory process is important as it aids learning which can lead to better decision-making in the future. Therefore it should provide information, not data, which is relevant to decisions to change the plan when required and the control system needs to link the accountable, responsible managers to the planned activities.

Control systems can be made much more comprehensive due to the power of computer systems, but the basic types of decision must still be separated. Economic decisions are based on all the *real* factors affecting the business and these include those that are non-controllable by any manager at a particular level within the business. However, the managerial performance evaluations of that manager at the particular level should only use controllable items as otherwise the process is unfair and can be very demotivating. It is important to separate measures of efficiency (that is, the maximum level of output for a given level of inputs or the minimum inputs for a given required output level) from measures of how effectively the objectives of the business are being achieved, and to combine the two logically wherever possible.

Breaking the business down can greatly assist in the financial control process and the level of control will be set by the measurable and controllable financial inputs and outputs of the division. Four main types of responsibility centre can be identified: cost, revenue, profit and investment centres, but problems exist in all cases of using only financial performance measures which can all tend to become measures of efficiency not divisional effectiveness.

11

Operating control systems

Introduction

The design of financial control systems should provide 'the right information to the right people at the right time' and thus the operation of control systems should check that this is happening and that the original design is still relevant. One way of proving that all is well is to examine what is being done with the information and many companies now carry out this kind of regular review of their financial control reporting systems. After all, the cost of originally providing the information should have been justified by a cost/benefit analysis and if the benefits are no longer of sufficient value, the system should be changed.

In a dynamic, rapidly changing environment, the information requirements of the business may alter quite dramatically. This is another excellent reason for the control system to be designed for maximum flexibility so that changes in the information needs can be catered for without having to redesign the control system completely. The use of a computerized database system can be of tremendous assistance, but equally if the required data is not included in the original system specification it can prove extremely expensive to change a comprehensive integrated computerized system. As mentioned in Chapter 10, some businesses are already facing the nonsensical situation of separately producing certain essential information from a manual system, alongside relatively new sophisticated computer systems, because future information requirements were not considered when these supposedly comprehensive systems were designed. This can be caused by not properly involving in the design process the 'right people' who are obviously the managers who will use the information in their future decisions.

Sales information system example

An example regarding a sales information system may help to illustrate this idea of a database system. The ideal control system is one where all the necessary data can be collected directly from essential accounting records, which saves any duplication of effort inputting data into the system. This also means that all outputs utilize the same base data which guarantees consistency of the financial information, and so removes the need to reconcile the various reporting formats which are required in any large organization. The main inputs for a sales information system are contained on the sales invoice, which must be processed by the business in order to record the transaction and collect the cash. The invoice will show details of:

1 the invoice reference number and contact person;
2 the order reference;
3 the customer, including name, address, responsible salesperson, and reference number;
4 the products sold, including
   (a) types
   (b) quantities
   (c) prices (both gross and net of any discounts and allowances given)
5 distribution information, including delivery address, required delivery date and time;
6 the settlement terms applicable to the transaction.

By suitably coding all of these pieces of data and cross-referencing them to other information stored in the system (often referred to as 'master files') many different types of sales analysis can be extracted without any additional inputs and with minimal effort. Sales can be grouped by customers classified by size, geographical location, industrial or similar classification, sales-force territories, order size, products purchased or other distinguishing characteristics. These analyses can be very helpful in segmenting the market or identifying new potential customers which have similar characteristics to existing customers to whom the firm's products appeal. However, if all this information is not properly coded when the invoice is produced, the cross-referencing is impossible and the subsequently required analysis can only be done by specially sorting the raw data (that is, all the individual invoices), which may not be practical in terms of cost, available resources or time-scale of obtaining the output. The people who will know the types of analysis that are most likely to be of value are in the sales and marketing area and they should obviously be consulted when the system is being designed.

Unfortunately any additional work required to code the input for subsequent analytical purposes is likely to be carried out in the clerical section of the accounting area, and the people inputting the data are probably not very interested in the quality of this analytical output. This means that the coding used for information purposes should, if possible, be the same as is used for basic accounting referencing so that it must be validated before the invoice is passed. A customer accounting reference number is needed to input the invoice into the accounting system and ensure that the invoice value is included in this customer's balance owing to the company. This reference number can, for example, be composed of the data needed to analyse the customer by type, size, area, etc.; or a matrix look-up table (that is, a reference catalogue system stored in the computer) can be used to obtain the cross-referencing necessary. Not only does this force the analytical input requirements to be validated but it minimizes the additional work which has to be done by the outside agent (in this case the accounting department). A simple form of such a customer reference number could be as follows for a fmcg company: T734695.

This customer reference number should provide the company with the ability to include all invoices in the required sales analyses of customers without further input of data. The initial letter would be the first letter of the customer name, such as T for Tesco's, and this simply assists in alphabetic sorting routines and provides a visual check of the validity of the reference number for clerical staff. (It should be clear that, if a clerk is trying to input a Sainsbury's invoice which has a reference number beginning with T, there is something wrong!)

The first number identifies the type of customer so that analysis of customer groupings can be done. Customer types in this example could be: national multiples, regional multiples, wholesaler groups, smaller wholesalers, voluntary buying groups, discount stores, etc. The next number classifies this particular store (that is, the delivery outlet) by size (in square metres), as sales analysis by size of outlet is often required.

The next category of information concerns location of the particular shop or outlet; one number (4 in our example) shows the geographical region where the shop is located, and the next number shows the area within the region. These regions and areas would be the same as are used for the organization of the field sales-force, and for this type of business the regions would correspond as closely as possible to the major television regions so that differences in TV advertising weightings could be monitored.

Having identified the area, we need to be more specific for some purposes and so the next number identifies the salesperson within the area who is responsible for this customer outlet. This enables analysis to be very specific and, by holding information on a master file regarding the frequency with which the salesperson calls on this outlet (known as call frequency), an analysis of the cost of servicing relative to the contribution received from the sales revenue achieved can be made.

In most companies a check digit is added to the end to ensure that, if a clerk changes around (transposes) two of the numbers or hits the wrong input key on the VDU, the altered number will not be accepted by the computer. If this is not done the whole analysis will be invalidated by the inevitable clerical errors and the old computer adage, 'garbage in, garbage out' (GIGO) will be shown to be true. In our example the check digit makes the whole number divisible by 13.

Having established the most 'efficient' way of inputting the data to our 'effectively' designed control system, we now need to consider the optimum balance of extracting information from the system. If 'too much, too often' is the result, managers will stop reading the reports altogether or become buried in trivial detail and miss the important trends where decisions are needed. If the opposite extreme is reached so that very little information is supplied, managers tend to assume that there is more happening which they are not being told about or they make decisions based on their 'gut feel' for the business because they have 'no numbers to go on'. Control systems should supply information to assist in making decisions and the frequency will be determined by the decisions which can be taken as a result of the information supplied. Hence any request for more information can legitimately be met with another question, 'what would you do with the information if it were supplied?' If the answer is 'look at it, file it, graph it, write a report about it or sit on it', the extra cost involved cannot be justified, but if the answer is 'decide whether to change something because of the information' then the benefit may well be worth evaluating further.

Thus the logic of decision-taking can be used to redefine financial control systems as 'decision support systems' (which is how some companies describe them) and this helps considerably in establishing the frequency and level of detail needed.

Frequency of reporting

The reporting cycle should be set principally according to the frequency with which action can be taken, and an example from our expanding retailer, George Taylor, can illustrate the differences. George now has seven shops and a wholesale cash 'n' carry warehouse and so requires more financial control systems than when he started with one shop which he ran personally. At the most frequent level he needs to know that the cash taken at each location has been paid into the bank and this should be controlled on a daily basis. The system can be very simple in that it requires a balanced total of takings from the tills, less any deductions for expenses paid in cash, to be reconciled to (that is, checked-off against) the paying-in slips deposited at the local banks. These paying-in slips can be reconciled to the bank statements once or twice a week. The reasons for the high frequency are the volume of transactions and the fact that it is cash. If long gaps are left between control checks a lot of money can suddenly disappear, or the business can develop a cash flow crisis because receipts have been lower for a period and nobody has noticed!

This daily cash reconciliation of sales could be used as an excuse to produce sales analyses of product groups daily, and if the system is an integrated computer system, as George Taylor's now is, product contributions could be printed daily as well. One very large, sophisticated consumer durables manufacturer is very proud of producing a full profit and loss account by product every day – they do not actually seem to *do* anything with it, but they apparently have the technology and so they produce the reports! It is difficult to imagine anyone being able to make meaningful product decisions based on daily information, so product sales information should be geared to decision time-scales as well. Some major retailers believe very strongly that they can predict the success of new products, which are on limited test launches, by the sales levels in the *first week* at certain key stores, and their financial control system is geared to delivering this information very quickly as decisions are made equally quickly when it is received. For other products sales information is needed according to the reorder cycle, which will differ by product category, and exception reports can be triggered automatically by the control system when the stock level reaches a preset reorder level. Of course if sales of the product are going badly, this level may not be reached for an unacceptably long time and another exception report can highlight products which have sold *less* than a preset volume. Therefore slow moving lines are quickly identified and action can be taken immediately to reduce prices, cancel further orders, etc.

For completeness, full sales analyses may be produced for George on a monthly basis as back-up within the monthly management information package but the major decisions on products will have been taken as required during the period. These monthly management reports will concentrate on a review of the business performance in a more overall way, with the product analysis concentrating on relative contribution levels per square metre of shelf space, for example, so that the allocation of resources can be changed if necessary, a decision which requires comparative information across product groups.

Thus we should differentiate between information which is genuinely produced as part of a financial control system, (that is, because decisions need to be made and these decisions need to be taken in the light of the best available information including the historical analysis) and information which is explanatory in nature and is not designed to lead to specific actions. Unfortunately many businesses do not distinguish between the two and, in fact, dedicate a lot more of their effort to producing the explanatory, informative 'nice to know' than the hard, decision-supporting 'need to know'. This is partially caused by their seemingly overwhelming compulsion to produce a full set of management reports on a monthly basis, including a profit and loss account, funds flow statement and balance sheet, whether this meets the appropriate time-scale for decisions or not. For example, in a very long-term project such as building a nuclear power station we should tailor our control system to the decision time-scales relevant to the project. This may mean no regular reporting on a daily, monthly, or even quarterly basis, but full reporting at the important 'milestone' review points when the next phase of resources are due to be committed. Even worse than too frequent reports are the companies which want to maintain, in some way, the sanctity of their management accounts and so no sectional reports are produced in the intervening period, and all managers must focus their decision time-scales around the production of the monthly set of financial information (often known as 'the bible').

It can be argued that if operational managers are really in control of their areas the monthly management reports do not tell them anything they do not already know about the previous accounting period. This may, and indeed should, be true but it also completely misses the point of the financial control system. The accounting information which simply relates what happened in the previous accounting period can be no more than a detailed explanation and this should not provide new information on 'what happened' to the managers directly involved; indeed they should have been involved in developing the explanatory notes. The explanation may provide new information to other managers more distant from the day-to-day operations, and they may well use this information, in the absence of anything better, to make decisions which affect the future operations of the business, but they should get something better than just an explanation of the past. The financial control system, if it is operating properly, should be looking for the causes of the past events and using these causal relationships to predict the likely impact in the future, which provides a much more relevant input for decisions than a simple explanation of the past. In this way the financial control system really can operate as a learning process which can help to improve the performance of the business in the future.

Budgeting, standard costing and variance analysis

One of the best ways in which these causal relationships can be analysed is by using budgets and standard costing, and analysing the deviations from the budgets and standards by calculating the appropriate variances. We will work through, in detail, the variance analysis for a simplified example to illustrate how such an analysis can be of great value to decision makers.

Division X of a large multinational has three products and operates a sophisticated system of standard costing, within an overall budgeting system. For its most recent accounting period it is showing a surprising and alarming result with sales significantly above budget but with profits slightly below. The summarized results (profit and loss account for last month) are shown below.

	Budget	*Actual*	*Variance*
Sales revenue	£500 000	£600 000	£100 000
Expenses	£400 000	£520 000	£(120 000)
Profit	£100 000	£80 000	£(20 000)

As an aid to decision-making this summarized presentation is less than helpful as it indicates that division X either might be more profitable by reducing its sales levels dramatically or that it has completely lost control over its expenses. If we break down the budget into more detail as in Table 11.1, and then compare it to the total actual results, we find a quite different position. This shows that the products

Table 11.1   *Budget analysis for division X*

Product	A	B	C	Budget total	Actual total	Variance
Sales volumes	20 000	10 000	20 000	50 000	67 500	
Standard values per unit:						
Selling price per unit	£10	£20	£5			
Variable cost per unit	£5	£5	£4			
Contribution per unit	£5	£15	£1	£	£	£
Total values	£	£	£			
Sales revenue	200 k	200 k	100 k	500 k	600 k	100 k
Variable costs	100 k	50 k	80 k	230 k	360 k	(130 k)
Contribution	100 k	150 k	20 k	270 k	240 k	(30 k)
less Direct fixed costs						
(principally marketing)	30 k	40 k	0	70 k	100 k	(30 k)
	70 k	110 k	20 k	200 k	140 k	(60 k)
less Indirect fixed costs	40 k	40 k	20 k	100 k	60 k	40 k
Budgeted profit	30 k	70 k	0	100 k	80 k	(20 k)

differ substantially in their contribution per unit and indicates that sales mix, as well as volume, is likely to have a significant influence on the profitability of the division.

It is always helpful to analyse differences between budgets and actual results in stages, which each focus on what you expect to happen and what did really take place in one particular area of the business. Therefore as the volume of sales is so substantially different it is obvious that we would expect a different result to the budget, and it would help us to focus on the real changes if we immediately split the total variance into these two parts: the variance expected because of the volume change and the variance between this new expected result and the actual outcome at the new volume. We do this by 'flexing the budget' which calculates what should have happened if all the budget assumptions had been the same and the volume had been correctly forecast.

Thus in our example the flexed budget would be given by using 67 500 units instead of 50 000 units, but at the same sales mix and cost levels and the restated result is shown in Table 11.2. This highlights the real scale of the problem because the actual profit was £20 000 lower than budget and not £94 500 higher as it should be.

Table 11.2

	Original budget	Flexed budget	Variance	Comments on calculation of flexed budget
Sales volumes	50 000	67 500	17 500	
	£	£	£	
Sales revenue	500 000	675 000	175 000	Actual volume multiplied
Variable costs	230 000	310 500	(80 500)	at budgeted average sales
Contribution	270 000	364 500	94 500	and cost levels
less Direct fixed costs	70 000	70 000	–	Fixed costs are assumed to be
	200 000	294 500	94 500	fixed for this volume change
less Indirect fixed costs	100 000	100 000	–	
Profit	100 000	194 500	94 500	

A more detailed analysis of the actual position (volume comparisons by product) is shown below; individual sales levels are significantly different from those which would have been budgeted at the flexed level.

Product	A	B	C	Total
Actual sales volumes	12 500	15 000	40 000	67 500
Flexed budget volumes	27 000	13 500	27 000	67 500
Variances	(14 500)	1500	13 000	—

Although sales volumes have increased significantly, the sales mix has also changed substantially and this has affected the actual sales revenues because average selling prices per unit have not been maintained as is shown below. The budget shows £500 000 of sales revenue from 50 000 units which gives an average selling price per unit of £10. If we apply this value in flexing the budget to our actual volume of 67 500 units, the actual sales value should be £675 000 but it is only £600 000. We are therefore worse off by a total of £75 000 and some of this is due to changes in the sales mix, which we can quantify exactly by multiplying the actual individual product volumes by their standard selling prices to see what the sales revenue should have been for this actual sales mix:

	A	B	C	Total	Flexed budget
Actual volumes	12 500	15 000	40 000	67 500	67 500
Standard selling Price per unit	£10	£20	£5		
Total	£125 000	£300 000	£200 000	£625 000	£675 000

This shows that the change in sales mix should have caused a £50 000 drop in sales revenue to £625 000 but the actual sales revenue total is £600 000 and so we have lost a further £25 000 which is not caused by sales mix but by a decrease in the selling prices of one of the products, which is revealed by another piece of more detailed analysis regarding the *actual* sales values by product as shown below.

	A	B	C	Total
Actual sales revenue	£100 000	£300 000	£200 000	£600 000
Actual selling prices per unit	£8	£20	£5	
Standard selling prices per unit	£10	£20	£5	
Variance per unit	(£2)	–	–	

Note   Actual selling prices per unit are calculated by dividing the actual sales revenue per product by the actual sales volume per product.

From the above we can see that product A has reduced its selling price by £2 per unit, which has reduced sales revenue by £25 000 because of the actual volume sold of 12 500 units. We also know that the change in sales mix reduced sales revenue by £50 000, but that the increased sales volumes should have increased sales revenue by £175 000 (£675 000−£500 000).

Thus at the sales revenue level we have now split out the sales revenue variance of £100 000 into its three components, summarized below.

Volume increase of 17 500 units – at standard selling prices and budgeted sales mix would have increased sales revenue by	£175 000
Change in mix – actual mix of products at standard selling prices showed lower sales revenue than budgeted mix by	£(50 000)
Decrease in selling price – product A is not being sold at standard price per unit and this reduced sales revenue by	(25 000)
Net sales revenue variance from original budget	£100 000

Therefore by working at three different levels we can break out the overall variance into its component elements, which show what we would have expected compared to what actually happened, and *why* it happened, which is the really important point of the analysis (that is, in this case *why* sales revenue increased from a budget of £500 000 to *exactly* £600 000).

However, we are mainly concerned with the drop in profitability and so we can do a similar analysis to the one we did at the sales level, at the cost and contribution level. We would expect the average contribution rate per unit to be reduced because the sales volume increase is in product C which has the lowest budgeted contribution rate per unit at £1. Using the actual sales volumes we would expect, at the standard contribution rate, the total contribution to be as is shown below:

	A	B	C	Total	Flexed budget
Actual volumes	12 500	15 000	40 000	67 500	67 500
Standard contribution per unit	£5	£15	£1		
Total	£62 500	£225 000	£40 000	£327 500	£364 500

This shows that the actual sales volumes should have increased the contribution to £327 500 from the budget level of £270 000 but the flexed budget level was £364 500 and the actual is only £240 000.

Therefore in the analysis of the contribution totals we can see the same

breakdown as we did for sales revenues: we originally expected the
volume increase to raise the total contribution from £270 000 to £364 500
(a gain of £94 500) but the sales mix changes tell us that we should only
hope to achieve £327 500 (a loss against the flexed budget of £37 000).
However, the actual contribution at £240 000 shows a further loss of
£87 500 against the contribution level which should have been achieved if
each product earned its standard contribution per unit, and indicates that
some major problems have occurred. If we examine the detailed actual
results as set out in Table 11.3 we can see what has happened. The selling
price decrease of A has been partially offset by the decrease in the
variable cost per unit, but B has suffered a very severe increase in its
variable cost per unit which has dramatically affected the profitability of
the division.

Table 11.3 *Actual results*

	A	B	C	Actual total	Budget total	Flexed budget
Actual volumes	12 500	15 000	40 000	67 500	50 000	67 500
Actual selling price per unit	£8	£20	£5			
Actual variable cost per unit	£4	£10	£4			
Contribution per unit	£4	£10	£1			
Total values	£	£	£	£	£	£
Sales revenue	100 k	300 k	200 k	600 k	500 k	675 k
Variable costs	50 k	150 k	160 k	360 k	230 k	310.5 k
Contribution	50 k	150 k	40 k	240 k	270 k	364.5 k
Direct fixed costs	30 k	40 k	30 k	100 k	70 k	70 k
	20 k	110 k	10 k	140 k	200 k	294.5 k
Indirect fixed costs	10 k	30 k	20 k	60 k	100 k	100 k
Actual profit	10 k	80 k	(10 k)	80 k	100 k	194.5 k

We again need more detailed analysis of products A and B and if we
compare each product, as in Table 11.4, we can identify the exact
differences to be explained. In order to achieve this more detailed
analysis of A and B we have to break down the variable costs into their
component elements. For simplicity we are only going to consider two
elements, direct labour and direct raw materials, in this analysis.
Although, in practice, the detailed cost build-up of most products is
considerably more complicated, the *process* of analysis is exactly the
same. It is sensible to consider first the components of the standard

variable cost per unit of each product, as is done in Table 11.5 and then to compare each component with the actual cost incurred.

From Table 11.5 the standard cost components of each product can be built-up by multiplying the usages by the relevant costs. For example one unit of product B requires 10 units of component Y (this usage allowance takes account of expected wastage levels) which have a standard cost of 40p each, and so the raw material cost of each unit of product B is £4. The standard labour rate of £10 per hour is multiplied by the standard time required to produce one unit (0.1 hours) to give a standard direct direct variable labour cost of £1 per unit.

Table 11.5 shows that the products have different proportions of the components, direct material and direct labour, and this may give rise to different results by product in any particular set of circumstances. We could now go straight on to the analysis of the actual circumstances in the period but, for completeness, we will first set out the standard cost analysis for the original budget as per Table 11.6.

This shows that the originally budgeted total variable cost of £230 000 was composed of £120 000 of raw materials and £110 000 of direct labour, which represented 11 000 hours of direct labour worked. However, we are already aware that the actual level of activity was considerably higher than budgeted and that these costs would have been exceeded even if the company was working exactly as efficiently as planned, that is, achieving the costs and usages set out in the standards. Our analysis of the contributions expected from the original budget, the flexed budget and the actual sales mix (Table 11.2 and p. 341) showed that the total contribution would not increase from £270 000 (original budget) to £364 500 (flexed budget) but only to £327 500 (actual sales mix at standard contribution rate) even at these planned efficiency levels, due to the changes in the sales mix. We also saw (page 343) that the actual sales mix generated £50 000 lower sales revenue than if the increased volume had been in proportion to the budgeted sales mix (flexed budget sales revenue of £675 000 versus an actual mix at standard selling prices of £625 000). The loss in standard contribution between the flexed budget and the actual sales mix is £37 000 (£364 500 − £327 500) but the lost sales revenue from the changes in sales mix is £50 000. The changes in the components of standard variable costs are consequently quite interesting as is shown in Table 11.7.

The analysis in Table 11.7 shows that the total standard variable cost is reduced under the actual sales mix by £13 000 from that expected under the flexed budget assumptions. This is logical as it explains the gap between the £50 000 loss in sales revenue and a loss in contribution of £37 000, and we can summarize the position, as shown below (reconciliation of sales mix variance). The change in the actual sales mix was an

Table 11.4   *Contribution analysis by product*

Product contributions	(1) Contribution as per original budget	(2) Actual volume at standard contribution rates	(3) Actual contributions	Variance (2)–(3)
	£	£	£	
A	100 k	62.5 k	50 k	(12.5 k)
B	150 k	225 k	150 k	(75 k)
C	20 k	40 k	40 k	–
Total	270 k	327.5 k	240 k	(87.5 k)
	(Table 11.1)	(Page 343)	(Table 11.3)	

Table 11.5   *Analysis of standard cost per unit**

Product	A	B	C
Standard cost components per unit of product			
(1) Raw materials usage:			
Component X	3 units		
Component Y		10 units	
Component Z			2 units
(2) Raw material cost per unit			
Component X	£1		
Component Y		40p	
Component Z			50p
(3) Direct labour usage in hours	0.2	0.1	0.3
(4) Direct labour cost per hour	£10	£10	£10
Standard cost build-up:			
Raw material (1) × (2)	£3	£4	£1
(usage × cost)			
Direct labour (3) × (4)	£2	£1	£3
(usage × rate)			
Standard cost per unit	£5	£5	£4

*In most companies standard costs are worked out per '000 units of production, but again the principles are exactly the same, and it is easier to see the source of the number when the calculation is set out per unit. If working in '000s of units the labour usage figures would be respectively 200, 100 and 300 hours per 1000 units.

Table 11.6 *Standard cost analysis – original budget*

	A	B	C	Total
Budgeted volume	20 000	10 000	20 000	50 000
Standard raw material *usage*				
Component X (unit)	60 000			60 000
Component Y (units)		100 000		100 000
Component Z (units)			40 000	40 000
Direct labour hours usage	4000	1000	6000	11 000

Note We cannot add up these heterogeneous units to arrive at a meaningful total and this again illustrates the use of accounting as a common business language, because by translating each into a cost in £s, we can add them up.

	A	B	C	Total
Standard raw material cost	£60 000	£40 000	£20 000	£120 000
Direct labour cost	40 000	10 000	60 000	110 000
Total	£100 000	£50 000	£80 000	£230 000

increase in the lowest cost product (C) and a decrease in a higher cost product (A) which resulted in an overall saving against the cost level expected (actual sales mix costs of £297 500 against flexed budget standard costs of £310 500).

Loss of sales revenue due to change in sales mix (p. 342)	(£50 000)
Savings in standard variable cost due to change in sales mix (Table 11.6)	£13 000
Loss of contribution due to change in sales mix (p. 343)	(£37 000)

Note The impact of changes in sales mix can be calculated in either way (that is, as the component elements of sales revenue and variable costs, or by going directly to the impact on contribution) but, for completeness, we are illustrating both ways.

Equally important in Table 11.7 is the change in the relative weighting of the component costs because the increased usage of labour (an extra 1150 hours) is more than offset by the reduced raw material cost. This is caused by the switch from a high raw material content product (A) to a high labour content product (C), and illustrates why a detailed analysis is required. If the company assumed that the increased activity (that is an increase of 35 per cent in volume) would mean a uniform increase in resources across the business there could be a dramatic and potentially costly shortage of direct labour, as the requirement in the original budget (11 000 hours) has increased to 16 000 hours as per the actual sales mix (an increase of 45 per cent).

So far we have looked at the impact on cost components under the planned cost structures, but we are more concerned with the comparison of actual costs with planned costs. We already know from Table 11.3 that the actual variable costs are different from the standards, and can be compared in total, as shown below. When analysed into their components they can provide the basis for a range of marketing decisions.

Product	A	B	C	Total
Actual volume at standard cost	£62 500	£75 000	£160 000	£297 500
Actual costs	£50 000	£150 000	£160 000	£360 000
Variance	£12 500	(£75 000)	–	(£62 500)

Table 11.7

	(1) Original budget	(2) Flexed budget	(3) Actual volume at standard rates	Variance from flexed budget[b] (3)–(2)
Product A volumes	20 000	27 000[a]	12 500	(14 500)
Standard raw material cost	£60 000	£81 000	£37 500	£43 500
Standard labour cost	£40 000	£54 000	£25 000	£29 000
Total	£100 000	£135 000	£62 500	£72 500
Product B volumes	10 000	13 500[a]	15 000	1500
Standard raw material cost	£40 000	£54 000	£60 000	(£6000)
Standard labour cost	£10 000	£13 500	£15 000	(£1500)
Total	£50 000	£67 500	£75 000	(£7500)
Product C volumes	20 000	27 000[a]	40 000	13 000
Standard raw material cost	£20 000	£27 000	£40 000	(£13 000)
Standard labour cost	£60 000	£81 000	£120 000	(£39 000)
	£80 000	£108 000	£160 000	(£52 000)
All products total volumes	50 000	67 500	67 500	–
Standard raw material costs	£120 000	£162 000	£137 500	£24 500
Standard labour cost	£110 000	£148 500	£160 000	(£11 500)
	£230 000	£310 500	£297 500	£13 000

[a]The flexed budget volumes are generated by prorating the total increase in volume across the products so as to maintain the budgeted sales mix. As previously analysed the actual sales mix is significantly different with major growth in C and dramatic shortfall in A.

[b]Adverse variances, that is cost increases, are shown in brackets. A volume shortfall is normally regarded as adverse, so this is shown in brackets even though the effect in this figure is to reduce costs.

Product A has a lower variable cost because the price of the component X has reduced to 50p per unit, by using a new source of supply, and we also know that 2500 hours of direct labour and 50 000 components of X were used in producing product A in the period.

Component Y has increased in price substantially from 40p per unit to 90p, and 150 000 components of Y and 1500 labour hours were used producing product B in the period.

The increased demand for product C created labour problems and even though labour was transferred from A where demand had reduced substantially, 3000 hours of overtime were worked during the period. Overtime attracts a 50 per cent premium rate and therefore increased the total rate to £15 per hour. Including the actual overtime hours worked, 10 500 hours of direct labour were used producing C and a total of 80 000 components of Z were used. (No change took place in the price of Z.)

It is very difficult to make meaningful decisions using the analyses shown in Table 11.8 and on page 347, but if we start to carry out a logical variance analysis for each product we can produce information that explains the actual results in a way that helps the business to learn from the past, to make sound business decisions and to plan better in the future. We have already analysed the impact of sales mix and the selling price changes, so we can now compare the actual costs against the actual volume evaluated at standard costs.

Table 11.8   *Summary of actual cost analysis*

Product	A	B	C	Total
(1) Raw material price per unit	50p	90p	50p	
(2) Component usage	50 000	150 000	80 000	
(3) Raw material cost (1) × (2)	£25 000	£135 000	£40 000	£200 000
(4) Labour hours worked	2500	1500	10 500	
(5) Labour cost (4) × £10 per hour	£25 000	£15 000	£105 000	£145 000
(6) Extra cost of overtime (£15–£10) × 3000 hours	–	–	£15 000	£15 000
(7) Total labour cost (5)+(6)	£25 000	£15 000	£120 000	£160 000
Total variable cost (3)+(7)	£50 000	£150 000	£160 000	£360 000

Product A – detailed variance analysis

There are two separate impacts on the cost performance which relate respectively to the changes in the *cost* per unit, known as the price or rate variance, and the level of *usage* of the cost component, that is, how efficiently the business utilized this resource, known (not surprisingly) as the efficiency variance. Splitting out these two factors is quite straight-forward as long as it is done in a logical sequence, and we will start with the price variance. The cost per unit has reduced significantly with the change in supplier and we can quantify the impact of this by multiplying the per unit cost variance by the number of units used in the period as shown below (raw material price variance). (In practice, price variances are calculated on the units *purchased* in the period to allow for changes in stock levels and to match the timing of the cost variance to the period in which it is incurred, but we are assuming, for simplicity, no changes in stock levels throughout this example.)

Raw material price variance – Product A

Standard cost per component unit	£1
Actual cost per component unit	50p
Variance per unit (1)	50p
Number of components used (2)	50 000
Price variance (1) × (2)	£25 000

This shows that the company has reduced its costs by £25 000 due to the reduction in price from the new supplier but if we look at the usage efficiency we get a different picture. The usage of components is substantially higher than the standard allowance and may be caused by the quality of the component X supplied from the new source. This is shown below (raw material usage variance) which illustrates an increased cost of £12 500 due to inefficient material usage. We have already taken account of all the impact resulting from the change in price level and so we now work usage variances out at standard cost levels.

Raw material usage variance – Product A

1	Standard component usage per unit of A	3
2	Units of A produced	12 500
3	Standard usage allowance (1) × (2)	37 500
4	Actual usage	50 000
5	Quantity variance (3)–(4)	(12 500)
6	Standard price per component	£1
7	Usage variance (5) × (6)	(£12 500)

We can now see that the two elements of raw material variances are working against each other (see below); the £25 000 saving has been partially negated due to the overusage of raw materials leaving a net saving against planned costs of £12 500.

Standard cost allowance at actual volumes – £3 × 12 500		£37 500
Less favourable price variance		£25 000
		£12 500
Add Adverse usage variance		£12 500
Actual raw material cost		£25 000

If we compare the actual labour usage and price to the standards, as shown below, we see there are no variances and so the only area of concern is in raw materials.

	Standard	Actual	Variance
Labour rate per hour	£10	£10	–
Hours allowed/taken to produce 12 500 units	2500	2500	–

We have already seen for product A that the selling price has been reduced from £10 to £8 but the volume has still fallen sharply, which is clearly worrying. However, the cause for concern may now be more clearly seen because the price decrease may not be as great as it should be if determined by the change in raw material cost prices. These have dropped by 50 per cent but the selling price has only fallen by 20 per cent; if competition has responded differently, or if customers were expecting a greater reduction in selling price, the company's pricing policy may now be out of line with market expectations. The adverse usage variance is reducing profitability and clearly requires management attention to bring this back under control, but if the component price decrease is expected to continue, the selling price may need to be reviewed again if volume sales are to be restored. This will depend upon the price elasticity of the product and the cost relationship is examined in Table 11.9, where the usage variance is first excluded on the assumption that quality from the new supplier can be improved. (It may be that the company cannot get the previous quality level at this lower price and therefore must decide between this new supplier and the next supplier's higher price but with perhaps a consequently better quality; that is the company should do an 'opportunity cost' evaluation.)

Table 11.9 shows that even if the adverse usage variance is removed the volume must be increased to 18 182 to achieve the budgeted

Table 11.9   *Product A: per unit costs and selling prices*

	Standard		Adjusted raw material cost	Current actual costs		Adjusted raw material cost/current selling price
Raw material	£3.00		£1.50	£2.00		£1.50
Labour	£2.00		£2.00	£2.00		£2.00
Contribution	£5.00	(50%)	£3.50	(50%) £4.00	(possible)	£5.50
Selling price	£10.00	(possible)	£7.00	£8.00		£8.00

Note   Maintaining the percentage contribution rate (that is, 50% of selling price) does not guarantee the absolute value of the contribution generated by the product. Indeed to generate the same absolute contribution as forecast under the standard costs and original budget now requires a volume given by:

	Budget	Adjusted selling price (£7)	Current actual	Adjusted costs current selling price
Volume	20 000	28 571	25 000	18 182
Contribution per unit	£5.00	£3.50	£4.00	£5.50
Total contribution	£100 000	£100 000	£100 000	£100 000
Current actual volume		12 500		

contribution of £100 000 and at a lower selling price the volume required is substantially increased to 28 571. It is probable, therefore, that the budget is no longer relevant as a planning reference base and the company needs to use this current analysis as the basis for reforecasting product A.

Product B – detailed variance analysis

We can do the same analysis for product B but the results will differ as the component cost has increased substantially (Table 11.10). It is now clear how dramatically the component cost increase has affected product B and this indicates that the company must consider a sizeable selling price increase, that is, 25 per cent, so as to restore the contribution level. Whether such an increase is possible will again depend on the competitive reaction and the forecast price elasticity of the product and how sales volumes would be affected. The zero usage and efficiency variances show that the company performed exactly to its standards at the higher production levels. With product A the company experienced an adverse raw material usage variance and this indicated a need to improve its performance in this area, which may be possible but it is unlikely that the raw material cost increase for product B can be avoided in the future and this is an important aspect of variance analysis: differentiating between changes in cost levels which are temporary and permanent because the type of decision and action required for each is significantly different.

Table 11.10 *Product B: variance analysis*

	Standard		Actual	Variance
Raw material price				
(1) Component price per unit	40p		90p	50p
(2) Usage in producing 15 000 units	150 000		150 000	
(1) × (2)	£60 000		£135 000	(£75 000)
Raw material usage				
(3) Production of 15 000				
units – allowed	150 000	used	150 000	
(4) Standard cost per component				
unit	40p		40p	
(3) × (4)	£60 000		£60 000	–
Direct labour				
(5) Rate per hour	£10		£10	–
(6) Usage – allowed	1500	used	1500	
(5) × (6)	£15 000		£15 000	–
Total	£75 000		£150 000	(£75 000)

Most temporary cost changes are self-correcting or can be corrected quite quickly by management action but the more permanent changes, such as the increased raw material cost in product B, require more fundamental management decisions which may affect many other areas of the business, such as changing selling prices. Both require the properly analysed information to be delivered in a timely manner to the managers who can take the decisions required (that is, our originally stated prerequisite of a good financial control system – the right information at the right time to the right people), but the managers concerned may be different and the time-scale may also be different. In practice information regarding a substantial cost increase, as in this example, should be obtained at the earliest possible opportunity (for example, when the supplier indicates a change in price, or when the next order for supplies is placed at the higher cost, or at least when the invoice is received) rather than when the new cost has been incurred through usage and sale of the more costly product without the company being able to adjust its marketing strategy accordingly. Thus a good financial-control system must obtain updating inputs at appropriate points from within the business, and not rely exclusively on the historical recording of accounting transactions and the subsequent preparation of financial statements.

Product C – detailed variance analysis

At first sight, product C does not require any variance analysis as the actual costs (£160 000) equal the standard costs expected for the actual volume in the period (£160 000), but a more detailed analysis reveals that this apparent balanced position is misleading.

Table 11.11 shows that working overtime cost the company an extra £15 000 which, by chance, was recovered because the labour was used more efficiently to produce the substantially increased volume (40 000 units against a budget of 20 000). If this increased efficiency indicates economies of scale (for example, reducing costs as volumes increase) the company may consider trying to maintain this higher volume by changing its marketing strategy (for example, by pricing or promotional activity). However, the use of overtime should also urgently be reviewed by the company due to the impact on the product profitability, as shown below.

Table 11.11   *Product C: variance analysis*

	Standard	Actual	Variance
Raw material price			
Component price per unit	50p	50p	–
Raw material usage			
Allowance for 40 000 units	80 000	80 000	–
Direct labour rate			
£10 per hour × actual hours (10 500)	£105 000	£105 000	–
Overtime premium £5 × 3000 hours	–	£15 000	(£15 000)
Direct labour efficiency*			
(1) Allowance/used for 40 000 units	12 000	10 500	–
(2) Standard labour rate per hour	£10	£10	–
Total (1) × (2)	£120 000	£105 000	£15 000
		Net total	–

*As before, we have already taken áccount of all the rate (price) variance and so all subsequent variance analysis is done at standard cost rates

	Standard	*Overtime production*
Labour allowance per unit	0.3	0.3
Labour rate per hour	£10.00	£15.00
labour cost	£3.00	£4.50
Raw material	£1.00	£1.00
Total variable cost	£4.00	£5.50
Contribution	£1.00	£(0.50)
Selling price	£5.00	£5.00

Because of the high labour content and the low budgeted contribution the company actually makes a negative contribution (that is, a loss after directly variable costs) if product C is produced while working overtime. It is illogical to link the favourable efficiency variance to this cost of working overtime, as this is arguing that labour is more productive when working overtime at the end of the normal working week!! Unless the detailed analysis of the labour costs were worked out, these variances and their required management actions could have been missed by the company.

Table 11.12 *Overall summary of profit variances*

		£
Original budgeted profit		100 000
Increase in contribution expected from increased volume (Table 11.2)		94 500
		194 500
Loss in contribution due to adverse change in sales mix (page 347)		(37 000)
		157 500
Product A Lower selling price (page 342)	(25 000)	
Offset by lower raw material cost (page 353)	25 000	
Raw material over usage (page 353)	(12 500)	(12 500)
		145 000
Product B Adverse raw material price (Table 11.10)		(75 000)
		70 000
Product C Adverse direct labour rate (Table 11.11)	(15 000)	
Favourable direct labour efficiency (Table 11.11)	15 000	–
		70 000
Fixed costs Direct overspend (Table 11.1)	(30 000)	
Indirect Underspend (Table 11.1)	40 000	10 000
Actual profit		£80 000

It may be helpful to summarize the variances for the period to see how much more information we now have compared with the overall summarized profit and loss account shown on page 340 and this is shown in Table 11.12.

We have not analysed the fixed cost expenditure variances but this is more straightforward and normally results in an explanation of overspending or underspending: there is, by definition, no volume effect to be accounted for. (It should be noted that throughout the analysis we have dealt with direct costs and have not attempted to analyse apportioned indirect costs. Any such detailed analysis should be approached very carefully.) Therefore, we can now explain in great detail the reasons for the decrease in profit from an original budget of £100 000 to the actual level of £80 000 as well as having highlighted a number of other areas requiring management attention.

This lengthy and detailed example shows some of the complexity and many stages involved in operating a comprehensive financial control system. It would obviously be very helpful if the workload involved in the analytical process could be reduced.

Use of computers

As mentioned in Chapter 10 this is quite possible using the immense processing power of modern computers, and the detailed calculations of flexed budgets and variance analysis can very largely be automated. The computer system does not carry out the financial control process; it merely provides managers with the information needed to carry out the process which involves learning from the analysis, making decisions and updating plans.

We have only considered, in detail, the product analysis, but for many companies the customer or channel of distribution analysis may be as important or more important. Some service companies (for example, some consultancies) argue that they cannot carry out product profitability analyses as the divisions between 'products' are nebulous and continually changing, and therefore they concentrate their financial control system on customer groups or ways of accessing the market (channels). In Chapter 5 we considered customer profitability analysis, and in Chapter 10 we briefly discussed distribution cost modelling, and it should be clear that the variance analysis process can be applied equally validly to any of these types of business segmentation. In fact for these different types of analysis the changes, particularly in the external competitive environment, are likely to be more dynamic than for some product-based analyses and a more easily updated control system would be of great value.

Again computers can be of great assistance because it may be possible to develop a computer model (that is, a simulation) of the company, its competitors, its customers, or the market in which it is operating so that planned, potential or actual changes can be 'run through' the model to see what the forecast impact is. Some models are now very sophisticated and highly mathematical, and try to take account of a vast range of potential influences on the success of the company, including those over which the managers have no 'control'. In Chapter 10 we pointed out that managers who can predict changes in uncontrollable costs can have better control over their businesses. It is equally true that being able to forecast accurately the impact of these changes further enhances the level of control and, even if the change was not predicted, being able to assess very rapidly the impact of any actual change also dramatically increases the level of management control and can improve the quality of managerial decisions.

Summary

Financial control systems should be operated to provide – the right information, to the right people, at the right time.

This may require a great deal of data to be processed and, as far as possible, this data should be collected as an automatic part of the accounting process and should be input to the system only once (that is, a database should be established).

The detailed analysis should be structured to provide meaningful information to managers who can take action where appropriate, which requires that the information should be provided according to the time-scale of the decisions which can be taken, based on the information being supplied. In order for managers to learn from the analysis of the past, the information must be appropriately detailed and, where relevant, standard costs and variance analysis are an ideal way of carrying out this analysis. This is because variances can be broken down for the various cost components, for example, raw materials and labour, and for their causes, for example, price and usage.

This analysis can be very time-consuming, so computers should be used if possible, but their use can enable even more complex models of the business environment to be developed.

This use of modelling and comprehensive analysis as part of a financial control system shows how the actual results of implementing plans are used to continually update the analysis from which better plans can be developed and implemented in the future. Therefore we end, where we began, with a continuous financial involvement through the process of:

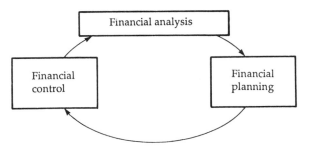

PART FIVE

APPLICATIONS AND EXAMPLES

Throughout the book we have been looking at illustrations of the various financial concepts and techniques but it may be helpful to try to place these financial tools in a more specific marketing context by looking at examples under the headings of the four Ps. In many examples it is difficult to single out any one aspect of the marketing mix as being dominant, and so several of the illustrations have impact and relevance in other marketing areas but they have been, as far as possible, classified by reference to the principal or dominant element. For reasons of space most of the examples are simplified and may consider only particular aspects of the problem; as with most marketing issues it would be possible to continue the analysis and discussion at much greater length.

After Chapters 12 to 15, respectively on one element of the marketing mix each, a final chapter on overall financial aspects of marketing has been included. This is not an attempt to try to summarize the entire book, but is merely a way of illustrating a few of the more interesting overall marketing problems with financial impacts which do not fit happily in any of the particular individual chapters on the marketing mix.

12

Product

Introduction

One of the most fundamental product decisions which any company faces is the question of how to develop and launch new products and whether the overall investment required is financially justified. As discussed in Chapter 7 and elsewhere, the financial analysis of such long-term decisions (the relevant time-scale for the decision is clearly linked to the particular product's life cycle) is complicated and necessarily based on a series of assumptions and managerial judgements. Therefore the use of sensitivity and risk analysis is important and this may include the use of decision trees and similar techniques.

However, the decision is further complicated in some cases by the option of whether to develop the new product internally or to buy in an existing product from another company – this was considered for George Taylor in Chapter 1 at the start of his business. The potential for buying in a new product will often be determined by the stage of development of the market and the products in it because, in the very early stages of the product life cycle, it may not be a practical option. In a mature established market it may appear cheaper (or less expensive) to buy another company's product, which is already established, than to try to develop and then launch a product which will have to compete with this potential acquisition and the other existing products in a fiercely competitive market. The Ansoff matrix analysis, used in Chapter 6, can be helpful as it indicates the appropriate marketing strategy for particular stages of development and the potential ways of generating growth in sales revenue. It is also important for the market to be analysed into the appropriate segments so that potential new products are targeted at the most attractive segments of the total market.

Developing a new product internally

Thus although the wines and spirits industry is not growing significantly in total in the more developed markets, such as the United States, some segments are showing quite good growth in sales volumes, for example, wines and white spirits such as vodka. Therefore when a major company in the industry, such as International Distillers and Vintners (IDV), a division of Grand Metropolitan, was looking for growth in sales revenue internationally, it would be logical to consider these growing segments rather than segments which are static or declining. At this time, the business had the choice of developing and launching a new brand itself or of acquiring an existing brand – the market generally is heavily branded, as is IDV, and marketing support levels are generally high.

The relevant financial analysis was further complicated because IDV had an existing licensing agreement under which it manufactured and sold Smirnoff Vodka in several markets around the world, for example the United Kingdom, but not in the United States. The licence had been granted by Heublein, a division of RJR Nabisco Inc, who owned the brand name and marketed the product in the United States, in exchange for a fee and a royalty on sales. (Licensing is a common way of companies gaining access to markets, where they do not have a presence, without having to invest substantial funds in creating a new business of their own – it consequently fits under 'place' in the marketing mix and is considered again in Chapter 15.) The existence of an existing interest in the Smirnoff brand, the market leader, would clearly reduce the attractiveness of launching a competitive product in the United States, not least because such a launch would probably have led to the loss of the existing licensing arrangements outside the United States but the financial analysis process may still have been carried out. The projected cash outflows should be developed based on the investment in plant and machinery required to produce the projected volumes (from a technology risk perspective this is clearly a low risk new product because the company already has the 'knowhow' to make a quality vodka product). This investment can be assessed quite accurately but the subsequent investment required to develop market share is much more difficult to assess, particularly as it depends to a large extent on competitive reaction to the launch. The cost structure of the product can also be forecast accurately but the selling price achievable and costs required to develop distribution channels are more uncertain (the existing distribution channels were dominated by Smirnoff and the number two brand, Popov, also owned by Heublein). Therefore the projected cash inflows which could be generated by the new product are very speculative and the ranges needed for the sensitivity analyses would be quite wide. Also the accounting treatment of such a major new product launch can create presentation problems for a large publicly quoted group, such as Grand Metropolitan, because all the marketing expenditures (but not the investment in tangible fixed assets) would be expensed in the profit and loss account immediately. This could depress, in the short term, the published accounting profits and earnings per share of the group which can be argued as not being critical to making a rational decision, but the product launch also requires the business to spend cash which has to be sourced from somewhere.

As discussed in Chapter 9, a company can raise additional debt funds in a multitude of ways but most of these require some form of tangible asset backing as a means of security and only part of this new product expenditure (that is, the expenditure on plant and machinery) provides this. Also any debt will incur interest costs and it may be several years before such a major new product development becomes profitable and can cover the additional interest expense incurred by the group. In the early years of launch the use of debt financing would consequently decrease the overall profit of the group by the extra interest costs taken on. We have also indicated that any expenditure with a high business risk should ideally use low risk financing, such as shareholders' funds, and a new vodka branch launch would have to be viewed as a high risk marketing activity. Therefore the more logical funding source would be either through retained earnings or directly increased shareholders' funds by selling new shares, probably through a rights issue.

As discussed in Chapter 4, a key financial performance ratio for publicly quoted companies is earnings per share (EPS) and this is shown in the published financial statements. Consequently, increasing the number of issued shares through a rights issue, so as to invest the cash proceeds in a new product which is likely to take several years to become profitable, is not very logical, as it would automatically reduce the EPS of the group in this development period. The allocation of the funds generated by existing operations would probably, in a well-diversified group such as Grand Metropolitan, also be governed by a capital rationing process using discounted cash flows and a criterion or 'hurdle' rate of discount. Therefore the decision would be made using the opportunity cost concept, discussed in Chapter 6, by comparing this project to the alternatives available to the group. The rate of discount applied to the somewhat vague and nebulous cash flow forecasts would be higher to allow for the potential risk of failure of the new brand, compared to an alternative project to invest in new hotels, for example.

Buying-in an existing product

An alternative new product strategy for the United States became available and was implemented when, in January 1987, IDV acquired Heublein from RJR Nabisco and thus gained Smirnoff in its home market as well as permanently guaranteeing the brand in the other markets which were previously under licence. The acquisition meant that profits would be earned immediately and the group could plan to develop from a strong base in the United States market, instead of having to battle to establish a new brand. Such obvious benefits are not purchased cheaply and the acquisition cost $1.2 billion, for which IDV gained net tangible assets of approximately $400 million. Thus the difference of $800 million represents the marketing assets built up by the brand franchise of Smirnoff (the distribution network, customer base, etc), none of which were included on the published balance sheet of Heublein. These marketing assets are not included on the latest published balance sheet of IDV or Grand Metropolitan either (neither, of course, are the assets of their own developed brands such as J & B Rare Scotch Whisky), because on an acquisition a UK acquiring company is allowed to write-off the goodwill (excess of the purchase price over the net book value of the balance sheet assets) against the reserves included in shareholders' funds on the balance sheet. This avoids this cost having to be reflected in the profit and loss account as the intangible assets (such as marketing franchises) are depreciated or amortized over time. Therefore the EPS for the company can be improved in the short term due to the immediate inclusion of the acquisition's profit stream in the group's published financial statements, rather than having reduced EPS while the new product moves slowly into profit.

From a cash flow point of view all of the investment outflows have been brought forward to the date of acquisition and are now known, and the cash inflows have been made more certain, thus reducing the apparent risk of the project. However, the acquisition is only worthwhile if it matches the corporate objectives which should include an objective regarding the creation of 'shareholder value', and buying something does not of itself achieve this. Shareholder value is created by acquisitions only if the product bought eventually proves to be worth more, in terms of NPV, when managed by the acquirer than the price paid for it. If the future growth of the business is critical to this value, the eventual purchase price can be calculated by reference to the future growth achieved. This is normally done by making an initial payment and agreeing a formula for the final price which includes the rate of growth or future profitability. In acquisitions where the managers acquired are going to be left to run the business this can be particularly relevant and was, for example, used by Hestair plc in their acquisitions of several entrepreneurially managed employment bureau companies in the United States in 1987. Hestair is a conglomerate type group which has some similar service businesses in the United Kingdom but no sizeable presence in the United States market, and so it was a lower risk strategy to enter the United States market by acquisition and to try to expand dynamically the business acquired; thus the final price payable was based on the future growth in profits of these businesses.

Other types of new products

Some companies have strategies under which they prefer to develop their own new products even though they may be in mature markets, such as confectionery. In this case some very semantic arguments are sometimes advanced as to what is a new product development and what is an old product development (which generally means an extension or new form of an existing product). We will not worry about the semantics of definitions because the financial evaluation process is the same, and if the company is a dominant competitor in the market, such as Mars in the confectionery market, we can argue that almost any new product is linked to existing offerings. In considering new product justifications in this environment managers will be looking for gaps in the existing range of product offerings or new movements in demand which can be satisfied by a specifically targeted new product. Thus in such a mature, highly competitive and heavily marketed industry most new products are strongly focused at specific market segments and the financial evaluation has to be carried out against this background.

In addition to taking account of the normal competitive reaction to the new product the company must also consider the impact on sales volumes of existing products in the same market, whenever the new product is positioned near to other existing offerings. (This is true of many industries and would, for example, have been a consideration in the launch of the Ford Orion, which was likely 'to steal' sales from Ford's existing Escort and Sierra products.) This can be a factor for Mars when they consider a new chocolate bar line (competing against the Mars Bar, Milky Way, etc.), and given an already high market share the lost contribution from these potential lost sales may take away the financial justification for the new bar line.

However, the attractiveness of expanding sales volumes for any business with substantial levels of fixed costs has been discussed in Chapter 8. Therefore generating new sales revenues, which increase the total contribution of the business, will, as long as the fixed costs stay fixed, improve the profitability of the company, and this forces the company to look for new product opportunities which have lower 'steal' factors from existing products (the 'steal' factor is the proportion of sales of the new product which are made at the expense of, that is in direct substitution for, sales of existing in-house products). Ideally the company wishes to utilize the existing asset base of the business to increase the total profits, thus increasing the return on assets, and this is most easily achieved by launching new products based on existing technologies. Indeed the idea of using up spare productive capacity of the existing fixed assets (as discussed in Chapter 4) is often a major attraction of new products, but the company should not restrict the definition of assets to this narrow balance sheet context.

In many major marketing-led companies the principal assets of the business are the intangible marketing assets (such as brand franchises, distribution networks, etc.) and the business should be considering the impact of new product decisions on these company assets, in exactly the same way as the increased fixed asset turnover ratio is included. Thus new products which utilize existing distribution channels and sales force organizations may be more profitable than those which require expenditure on new methods of reaching customers. However, the company must be careful when correctly using the incremental cost approach for such decisions and ensure that the opportunity cost of adding a new product is taken into account. The direct customer steal factor is one element in such an opportunity cost analysis, but it is also possible to overload both distribution channels and sales forces with additional small 'incremental products' which can lead to 'diseconomies of scale' (increasing costs with number of products) and, in fact, reduce rather than increase the overall profit of the business. For example, if the product range handled by one sales person becomes too broad, the sales person may not have complete product knowledge and will not be able to present each product properly to the customer (say the buyer for a major retailer) and therefore the sales performance is likely to be lower. Some companies have partially solved this problem by segmenting the sales force and giving specific product ranges to each segment, thus introducing a new type of divisional structure to those previously considered in Chapter 10.

For Mars the most attractive new products are likely to be those which will generate sales in segments of the market where they have their lowest share or where they do not currently have a presence. If it was possible to create new sales opportunities altogether and so expand their total sales potential, this would be even better, but this would have to be done using existing technology and people skills. It can be argued that this was achieved with the launch of Twix, which is perceived and positioned as a chocolate-coated snack product rather than a confectionery product, and may attract new customers to the company. This trend of repositioning products in the markets has been around for a long time, for example, Maltesers (another Mars brand). A more recent opportunity to segment the market and create additional 'non-stolen' sales has been taken by the development and launch of 'Fun-size' Mars products, which are sold in smaller individual sizes in larger bags of product and are seen as different products by consumers (that is, eaten on different occasions, in that a consumer is unlikely to buy, on impulse, a bag of 'Fun-size' Mars to eat as they walk down the high street) and therefore potentially increase the total market.

The financial assessment of these new products (range extensions, etc.) is clearly not easy but the techniques illustrated in the book can and should be applied to this type of decision.

Packaging – value analysis

The 'Fun-size' concept is also an illustration of how packaging can be used to create differentiated new products and to add value, and hence increase profits for a company. Packaging can be regarded, in its most basic form, as providing necessary protection for the product and therefore should be done at the minimum cost. For this aspect of the role of packaging, the argument of cost reduction may well be valid, but many companies now regard packaging in a very different role and carry out sophisticated packaging value analysis exercises. This idea is based on the argument that good packaging can add considerable value to the customer/consumer both in ease of use and in initial presentation and that the customer/consumer will be willing to pay more for this value added than it costs the company in increased packaging.

Therefore a packaging value analysis exercise would normally start from the cost minimization base of 'what do we have to do to protect the product' and then analyse each attribute of the proposed packaging formats. This tries to ensure that the pricing of the product reflects the value added by the packaging advantages and more than recovers the incremental costs incurred in the improved packaging. The packaging improvement could be minor (for example, a plastic scoop included in washing machine powder or dishwasher powder boxes) or quite major (for example, a flexible squeezable bottle for tomato ketchup) but the cost increase involved should have been evaluated, and this is a major use for the value added concept introduced in Chapter 3.

For some products it could be argued that developments in packaging have been a major contributor to the growth in market share and the packaging presentations certainly have not been justified on a cost minimization basis. Individual portions of chilled convenience foods are a good example where the total packaging cost may even outweigh the cost of the other raw materials used in the product, but a major part of the 'consumer value' created by the product is in the convenience and attractive presentation of the food. Hence the consumer is prepared to pay a high price which more than justifies the incremental cost incurred in the packaging format used.

Branding – product development as a strategy

In some markets distinctive and separate styles of packaging are seen as an integral part of the individual branding and segmentation process and the additional cost should be evaluated and justified as such. There is also a financial cost involved in any one company having a number of brands rather than one single brand in any market, not least because the company has to incur substantial marketing costs to maintain the awareness of several names and their different brand attributes (the idea of corporate brands is discussed in Chapter 16). If this segmentation strategy expanded the total size of the market it would be possible to financially justify the increased expenditure by considering the increase in contribution from the additional sales volume generated by the extra brands with the extra expenditure on developing and maintaining these extra brands in the market.

However, there are several markets where it is very difficult to argue that the vast array of brands available from one company has increased the size of the market and therefore the argument would appear to be about market share within the existing market. This makes the financial justification for many products more questionable, particularly if the market is well developed and mature, as was discussed above. It is especially debatable if the market is dominated by only two companies but where each has a range of brands in the market. The washing powder market (dominated by Proctor and Gamble and Lever Brothers, part of Unilever) is a good example, and as both companies are very sophisticated financially, there should be a good justification for the very large increase in overall marketing cost caused by the proliferation of brands in the market.

One potentially very strong argument is that a large number of brands acts as a strong barrier to entry (this was mentioned in Chapter 2) and therefore maintains the total market share of the company at its present level – thus justifying the increased marketing cost. The rationale for this argument is that although a high proportion of consumers are loyal to one product, another group will oscillate between brands and will try new products when offered. If this latter group is sizeable and the current market is shared by only two brands, any new product will be able to gain a reasonable market share from this oscillating consumer group. It will also be easier for the new entrant to gain distribution to reach the consumer and to establish a clear brand identity against only two competitors. Where there are 20 existing brands in the market, the potential for a new brand is much less and the costs of establishing a brand image and gaining distribution are likely to be greater. Thus an effective barrier to entry (branding) has been created which does not rely on production technology etc. but is based on marketing and product strategy. The mathematics of this argument are shown below, in very simplified form (with the assumption that 45 per cent of consumers switch brands and 55 per cent are loyal):

Number of existing brands	2	20
Potential shifting market	45%	45%
Share potential for new entrant on random choice by shifting market	$15\%\ \left(\dfrac{45\%}{3}\right)$	$2.1\%\ \left(\dfrac{45\%}{21}\right)$

Branded versus own label

For many manufacturing based companies with high investments in fixed assets, a critical success factor in achieving a better return on assets (ROA) is an improvement in the utilization of the fixed assets (that is, increasing the fixed asset turnover ratio). This can be achieved by increasing the sales volume without investing in more plant capacity and thus is dependent, as mentioned in Chapter 4, on there being spare capacity available. If the company's sales revenues are currently generated from branded products, it may be difficult to increase the sales volumes substantially without a material decrease in the unit selling price, and such a price movement may require a complete change in the marketing strategy for the product. Also the total contribution generated by the new sales revenues (that is, lower unit selling prices less the same variable costs per unit multiplied by the increased sales volumes) may not be greater than the existing total contribution – we can use the formula in the appendix to Chapter 8 to calculate the required volume increase for any loss in contribution.

Therefore many companies have looked for an alternative solution whereby sales volumes can be increased without affecting the existing brand marketing strategy. For many fmcg companies selling to the retail distribution channel, the recent concentration of retailer buying power created a demand for a new category of product which, at first sight, appeared to satisfy this criterion. Major multiple retailers were trying to establish and build their own brand franchises by developing own label products (that is, exclusive brands sold under their own or generic names); Marks and Spencer have, of course, had this concept for many years with their exclusive St Michael brand name. In many maturing industries, the inevitable slowing down in the market growth rate had led to excess capacity in the industry (a common problem caused by companies not planning on the basis of the product life cycle, but extrapolating future requirements for capacity from existing growth rates). When this excess capacity was coupled with the increasing dominance of major retailers the combination gave rise to fierce price negotiations on these new own label products. It was relatively easy in the short-term for companies under this severe customer pressure and with a desire to improve short-term profitability, to use direct variable costing as a basis for their pricing of own label products.

The argument was that the fixed costs had been incurred anyway and the volume obtained would be incremental; and so any contribution over the increased variable costs would be an increase in profits. If the investment base of the business did not have to increase because existing assets would be more fully utilized, the return on assets would rise due to the higher profits. The indirect costs were minimal, it could be argued, because the branded product formulation could be sold as the new product in a different packaging form and the retailer would bear the cost of marketing the product. In some cases this discounted pricing enabled retailers to make a larger contribution on own label products than on the comparable branded product and still sell them to the consumer at a considerably lower price. Not surprisingly in such cases, particularly where the product quality was exactly comparable, the own label products very rapidly took a substantial market share, and the retailers were renegotiating with manufacturers to increase the future repeat order size substantially.

Normally when customers substantially increase their order size they expect a decrease in the per unit selling price. However, because of the variable costing originally used, these manufacturers actually required an increase in selling price to cover their indirect expenses, which had to be apportioned to the own label product as the volume became a more significant proportion of their total output. Unfortunately for them, the new brand franchise and product rights were owned by the retailer, who was able, if necessary, to transfer the increasing business volume to another manufacturer with excess capacity, who was willing to tender a per unit price based on variable costing!! Some own label products are now, when all the retailer brands are added together, clear leaders in market share and the major supermarket retailers (for example, Sainsburys) have established large brand franchises for their own label products, which now form a substantial, if not majority, share of their sales revenue.

Interestingly, some major branded product manufacturers (such as Kelloggs, Heinz, Nescafé) have decided to invest significant funds in trying to defend their brand franchises by launching advertising campaigns which very explicitly state that they only manufacture branded products and do not produce own label products for any retailers. It can be argued that other manufacturers might not have been so willing to 'shoot themselves in the foot' if they had properly regarded their brands as a marketing asset, and had evaluated the financial impact on these assets of producing private label products. Instead the financial analysis seems, in some cases, to have been limited to the traditional concept of tangible assets.

Focused own-label strategy

The above argument is not meant to imply that it is impossible for a manufacturer to make a satisfactory return on investment by producing own label products. This would clearly be wrong as many companies have become very successful by concentrating on such products, and the critical success factor may be their 'concentration' on this segment. If the retailer (or any customer of any goods or services) is the party adding the major element of value to the product by giving it a clear identity (their own brand name) and by communicating the attributes of the brand to the consumer, the only strategy for the manufacturer which is likely to be successful in the long term is to be very efficient and become the lowest cost producer in the industry (as discussed in Chapter 6).

This low-cost strategy requires not only efficient production capabilities (that is, low direct variable costs) but also a low level of indirect expenses (both fixed and variable). This is often incompatible with a high profile marketing-led strategy which depends on new product development and building a strong image and presence in the market (which clearly increases the cost base of the business). Therefore there can often be a conflict in companies which try to pursue a mixed strategy of producing branded products and own label products using the same facilities. If this is attempted it requires a very clearly defined financial control system and extremely careful expense allocations and apportionments so that the real profitability of each segment of the business is revealed. Some companies have avoided this problem, to some extent, by using separate physical assets specifically and exclusively for each business segment but this may not resolve the problem of indirect and shared expenses (such as distribution, sales force and order processing, etc.).

Contribution analysis and transfer pricing

One company in the tissue industry solved major portions of this problem and had a strategy of concentrating on own label product production, so that its financial analysis was geared very strongly to cost reduction. (One aspect of this strategy is that it simplifies the financial analysis required by segments because the product and customer profitability analyses are very closely linked.)

In order to understand the product costs it was necessary, since the company was vertically integrated and produced its own bulk tissue, to have a good estimate of the total cost for each different type of tissue produced. If we simplify the example to consider only two grades of tissue with significant differences – facial tissue and kitchen towel – we can examine the problem faced by the company. With a good costing system it is not difficult to calculate the variable cost of each tonne of each grade of tissue produced but, as in many highly automated process industries, the indirect costs of the process are highly significant in assessing the total cost. Also the tissue mill has an opportunity to sell its production in bulk on the open market and the converting factory (the finishing, packaging and marketing unit) could buy in supplies from the same open market (there is an active global trading market in bulk supplies of tissue).

Consequently we have an opportunity cost problem which requires the tissue mill manager to establish a transfer price to the converting plant, whereby an appropriate contribution is made to compensate for the lost opportunity to sell an alternative product on the open market. The converting plant manager can decide whether to buy from within the group or to source externally by comparing the alternative prices quoted. This system enables both managers to make economically sound decisions which are in the best interests of the group (in other words goal congruence is achieved as per Chapter 10) provided that the methods of arriving at the indirect cost recovery and contribution rates are appropriate.

Originally the group was using a per tonne method of apportionment for both contribution and indirect cost recovery on the basis that the product was sold in tonnes and this therefore matched the indirect cost and contribution recovery to the sales units. However, as indicated in Figure 12.1 this was resulting in the group manufacturing a lot of facial tissue for sale externally and buying in for conversion a lot of bulk kitchen towel, because the transfer price from the tissue mill was above the market price for kitchen towel and vice versa for facial tissue. It was also illogical that under this system the tissue mill was given an incentive to act against the best interests of the group because, if it made the product heavier (as with most processes the product can be made within a specified range of parameters and for tissue this is defined in a weight range expressed in grammes per square metre (g/m^2) of product), the mill could produce more tonnage in the same production time. Therefore it

Transfer pricing – tissues example

Base data	*Facial tissue*	*Kitchen towel*
Base weight (g/m^2)	16	24
Output per machine-hour in tonnes	1.54	3.2
Direct variable cost per tonne	£250	£200

Tissue mill: Budget totals		
Indirect and fixed costs –	£12 m	
Profit target based on return on assets	£4 m	
Total contribution	£16 m	

Forecast output per annum:		
Facial tissue	–	45 000 tonnes
Kitchen towel	–	35 000 tonnes
		80 000 tonnes

Open market pricing data	*Sales opportunities*	*Purchase opportunities*
Facial tissue	£460 per tonne	£500 per tonne
Kitchen towel	£375 per tonne	£380 per tonne

Financial analysis based on contribution per tonne
Contribution required to achieve target profit
and recover fixed costs = $\dfrac{£16\ m}{80\ 000\ tonnes}$ = £200 per tonne

Thus transfer prices are:

	Facial tissue	*Kitchen towel*
Variable cost per tonne	250	200
Contribution per tonne	200	200
Transfer price per tonne	£450	£400

Open market deals taken based on these prices		
Sell facial tissue at	£460	
Buy kitchen towel at		£380

Figure 12.1

could generate more total contribution and more profit for the mill. Clearly the mill should be motivated to use the lowest amount of raw material possible to make the acceptable quality of product and this would mean a lighter not heavier weight product.

This problem highlighted that the tissue mill was using an incorrect basis for apportionment as its output was not, in fact, constrained by tonnage; the total tonnage produced was dictated by the sales mix (if only kitchen towel was produced the total tonnage would be 3.2 tonnes/hour × 40 000 hours or 128 000 tonnes of tissue). The limiting factor for tissue production was the availability of machine hours because the five tissue machines were already running 24 hours per day, seven days per week, 47.62 weeks per year (that is, only stopping for major maintenance work). Thus if the tissue mill maximized the contribution rate per machine hour, they would generate the maximum profit. This requires that the contribution per machine hour (not per tonne) is equal across all products because, if this is not true, the profits can be increased by reallocating machine time to the product with the higher contribution rate per machine hour.

As the outputs per machine hour differed considerably by product, principally because a heavier product is easier to produce and the machine can be run faster, this new basis changes the transfer prices per tonne of product as shown in Figure 12.2 and reverses the previous trends in buying in and selling out product. This illustrates the importance of identifying the limiting factor in any contribution analysis and of having a sound transfer pricing system.

Impact of vertical integration on product

This analysis was relevant to our tissue company because of its vertically integrated position in the industry and the need to establish transfer pricing. The degree of vertical integration can affect many businesses in varying ways and the problems of oil companies in this area were mentioned in Chapter 3 when we were considering value added statements (page 79).

For a major oil company, like BP, which is very vertically integrated, there is a large problem in determining whether each area of the business is making an adequate contribution to justify the resources involved. It may be more profitable for BP to concentrate on oil exploration and not be involved in the downstream marketing of the refined product particularly if this is an area where it has no competitive advantage. In an effort to analyse this issue BP has publicly separated out the financial results of its downstream marketing business in the United Kingdom (BP Oil Ltd). This business has external sales revenues from the finished products it sells to distributors, retailers and consumers, but it requires a transfer price system in order to assess the cost of the product transferred in as raw materials from elsewhere within the group. An apparently logical transfer price would seem to be the external market price if available and a market price for crude oil can be obtained through the quotations on what is known as the Rotterdam spot oil market (where oil cargoes are bought and sold on a spot and futures basis). The spot market deals with

Limiting factor analysis: tissues example

Five machines are running for 24 hours per day, seven days per week and 47.62 weeks per year; that is, 8000 hours per machine × five machines, or 40 000 total hours; total hours cannot be increased and are the *limiting factor*.

Therefore the true opportunity cost of using a machine for any particular product is the lost production which could have been achieved of another product. Thus contributions per machine hour should be equalized across all products for the maximum profit level to result.

$$Contribution\ per\ machine\ hour = \frac{£16\ m}{40\ 000\ hours} = £400\ per\ hour$$

This has to be translated into a contribution per tonne for pricing purposes:

	Output per hour	Contribution per tonne (that is, = £400 per machine hour)	Variable cost per tonne	Transfer price per tonne
Facial tissue	1.54 tonnes	£260	£250	£510
Kitchen towel	3.2 tonnes	£125	£200	£325

At these adjusted transfer prices, it becomes attractive to reverse the previous decisions (Figure 12.1) and buy in facial tissue at £500 per tonne (transfer price required of £510) and use the freed-up capacity to produce kitchen towel for sale on the open market at £375 per tonne (transfer price required of £325).

Figure 12.2

excess cargoes available for sale in the market and the prevailing price reflects this degree of excess or shortage of physical supplies in the market. It is consequently volatile and the fluctuations in quoted prices from period to period can have dramatic impacts on the perceived profitability of the BP downstream marketing activity.

Such violent and rapid apparent fluctuations in profitability do not help long-term planning decisions including the level of involvement, if any, in downstream marketing which is appropriate for the group. The decision process could be further clouded by the use of an irrelevant measure for the transfer price. The decision regarding involvement in downstream oil product marketing is a long-term strategic decision and should be made by reference to the long-term financial return on the required investment which can most suitably be calculated by using discounted cash flows. Using a very short-term spot market price which is extremely volatile as the base for such a decision would be very dangerous as any extrapolations from any particular position may prove to be disastrously wrong. The transfer price is relevant for short-term trading decisions, but not for strategic long-term planning, and it is important that the financial control system ensures that the 'right information' is used for the particular decision being considered.

Make or buy

A similar type of decision regarding products, and one that is often related to the degree of vertical integration, is that of whether a company should manufacture the product, or a component of the product, in-house or buy in from an outside supplier. This can be illustrated by a small packaging machinery company which was bought out from a publicly quoted group by its management team (that is, a management buy out) and consequently had a fundamental review of its business strategy. Under the previous owners the company had manufactured most of the machines itself, buying in basic raw materials such as sheet metal, and had also carried a full product range so that it could service almost any customer demand.

The new company had a restricted capital base and therefore wished to concentrate its limited financing resources on those areas where the greatest returns could be made, that is, the large value added areas of the business. The accounting system was set up on a fully absorbed cost basis for all indirect expenses and this was clearly irrelevant to the decisions regarding product range and level of own manufacture. What was required was an analysis of the differential cash flows caused by any particular decision, which for product deletion decisions meant the avoidable costs of the particular product (in other words, those costs which would be avoided, no longer incurred, if the product was dropped). These avoidable costs excluded any indirect costs which would not, in reality, be saved but would be reapportioned across the remaining products. This analysis also included the saving represented by the opportunity cost of funds released from stocks and debtors of the potential deleted products so that a full picture of the impact of the deletion decisions on the business was built up. As a result of this analysis the product range was rationalized considerably and particular segments of the market were selected for focused attention.

A similar analysis was carried out on the manufacturing process carried out by the business to identify where the profits of the business were generated, and which elements merely served to add cost. The basis of the analysis was again to build up the avoidable costs of each area rather than the total apportioned costs highlighted by the old system but, this time, these costs were compared with the price at which the component or processed material could be purchased from an external supplier. If the purchased cost was lower and the quality, reliability, etc.

were acceptable, the company phased out its own production and switched to buying in.

Not surprisingly the company found that it could buy in more cheaply a wide range of standard components and prefabricated metal parts, for example, machine body panels, and this enabled it to concentrate its resources, both financial and in terms of skilled labour, on the critical areas of the machine where the greatest value could be added.

One segment of the market which was identified as high growth was in the area of carton and case folding and erecting machinery (that is, machines which take flat packaging and turn it into a usable box) but this type of machine was becoming more specialized as packaging became more differentiated. Another growth segment was in packaging printing and cutting machines which had very fast changeover facilities so that products could be changed quickly and frequently. This was to satisfy the demand from a growing number of very small packaging suppliers who were offering their customers a service of very short packaging print runs as a way of differentiating themselves from the major suppliers who were low cost but who had high order volume requirements to ease the disruption to production.

Both of these areas were potentially highly profitable and could also generate considerable growth, but neither was likely to produce steady order levels on a repeat basis. Almost by definition, the needs of each customer were slightly different and although the basic machines were substantially the same, a system for controlling the cost of each 'special order' was required. If special orders were likely to form a substantial portion of the future sales revenue of the business, it was also important that all the relevant costs were included in the analysis and not simply the directly variable costs of any extra work. Thus a proportion of the design department had to be included if modifications were needed, and other indirect expense areas of the company had to be included as well. The company developed a job costing system for all special orders whereby the particular costs of any such order were recorded (for example, time worked in the design department on modifications was recorded against the order and valued at an hourly rate which reflected the total costs of the department and not just the directly variable cost of the individual doing the work) and a review of the job cost against the selling price was carried out at the end of the job. It was not possible to alter the price which had already been quoted for that particular job but the estimating department very rapidly acquired a database of actual costs for particular types of orders which enabled much more accurate future forecasting – in other words, they were using their historic financial control system as a learning process to improve future decisions (as discussed in Chapter 10).

Product life cycle

One of the problems faced by the company was that the changing nature of its customer base meant that its products were also changing more rapidly and thus the product life cycle was shortening. This created difficulties in financially justifying research and development activities into new products because the period of potential recovery through product sales was becoming far less predictable. One way of easing the problem was by minimizing the investment in plant and machinery which was too product specific (and by buying in a wider range of components as previously mentioned). Although the company had to pay an initial premium for the flexible machining systems (fms) which it purchased, the reduction in the risk of obsolescence if the products changed was considered a good financial justification for the higher cost. By focusing its investment on critical production areas, the company could afford to fund this higher investment cost.

Another example of problems caused by uncertainties regarding the product life cycle can be illustrated by a very different type of company starting out in an embryonic market. For some years a lift-off in demand for computer based training (CBT) has been forecast but has never really arrived, possibly due to the lack of good products (that is, courseware) available in the market. This was the argument of a new company formed to develop and launch CBT courseware in the corporate market and to provide consultancy services for companies which wished to have tailormade products for their in-house use or for onward sale to other companies. The company required initial funding to recruit the skilled personnel which would enable the new products to be developed and it also required funding to launch these products in an as yet undeveloped market. Clearly this business was high risk and therefore it would be sensible (as per Chapter 9) to raise low risk financing and venture capital was injected in the form of shareholders' funds (that is, outside investors bought a minority stake in the company).

The cash flow projections for the company were very good on the assumptions used, as was the internal rate of return (IRR), but the problem was how to take account of the risk of the market being later in developing (if it never developed, the company would, of course, fail), or developing at a slower rate than forecast. By using sensitivity analysis, the impact of different assumptions regarding the timing and rate of market growth were incorporated and the additional funding needs identified. The plan also highlighted the possibility of bringing in additional funds at a later stage if the market had still not developed and a further set of contingency plans were also developed. These looked at ways of reducing the cost base of the business, if necessary, so that the funding requirement was reduced if cash generated by sales revenue was substantially below expectations. Thus a wide range of alternatives were evaluated and plans made to take account of potential problems. Unfortunately the market did not develop and despite all these plans, the company ran out of cash and went into liquidation.

13

Price

Introduction

Setting a pricing strategy for a particular product in any specific market is a critical marketing decision for any company and depends upon many factors, but most importantly the pricing strategy must be linked to the corporate objectives. These corporate objectives should, as mentioned in Chapters 6 and 7, be as specific as possible and are required for each product and each market if *specific* and relevant pricing strategies are to be developed. Generically pricing strategies, particularly for new products, can be described as 'penetration pricing' or 'skimming pricing' but these generic labels hide a multitude of possible alternatives. Penetration pricing is a strategy of low pricing as a means of developing market share and is therefore most appropriate during the growth phases of the product life cycle when it is important for a company to maximize its share in readiness for the period of maturity when profits and cash inflows will be the more important objectives. Skimming pricing is a strategy of extracting profit from the product, even at the expense of market share, and can therefore logically be applied during the latter stages of the maturity phase of the product life cycle, although strangely it is also advocated as a launch strategy prior to competitors entering the market.

These strategies and their appropriate timings indicate that a pricing strategy should be decided in the context of the particular stage of development of the product and the corporate objectives for that product in that market. As any one product may be at very different stages of development in various markets the pricing strategies may need to be correspondingly different; ideally the financial control system should enable the company to learn from its experiences in the more developed markets.

Learning curves – cost-based pricing

A good illustration of the problems of setting pricing strategies is given by a product which is subject to a significant learning curve or experience factors, whereby the unit costs of the product reduce as the cumulative volume increases. A learning curve is normally shown graphically, as in Figure 13.1, and is of particular significance in low volume large value capital goods industries such as aeroplane manufacture.

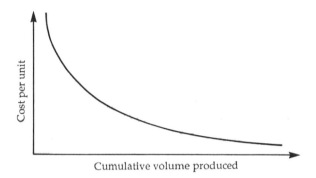

Figure 13.1 *Learning/experience curve*

In the aeroplane industry the cost reduction in per unit costs as the cumulative number of a particular model of aeroplane produced increases is well known because of historical financial analysis. Therefore the long-term cost structure will depend on the number of aeroplanes produced and this will depend, among other things, on the selling price established in the pricing strategy. Thus we now have a circular argument because the required selling price is conditioned by the cost per unit, which is conditioned by the volume sold, which is conditioned by the selling price as shown in Figure 13.2. We can develop a model which, given a forecast for the relationship between selling price per unit and sales volume, can be solved to show the best solution in terms of selling price in the light of the assumptions made by the company.

This use of long-run cost levels as a basis for pricing strategies means that the early sales of a new product may be made at an accounting loss. Unless these sales are priced appropriately the market will not achieve the sales volumes needed to reduce cost levels to their long-term forecast base. Therefore attempting to recover high development and launch marketing costs over a low volume of sales in the early high growth period of the product life cycle may cause price levels to be set too high to create adequate demand for the product, and so volumes never properly

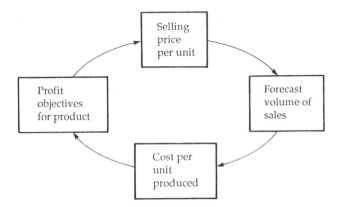

Figure 13.2   *Pricing strategy in a learning curve environment*

develop. Equally setting prices at very low levels on the assumption of achieving very high levels of sales may never recover the original investment in the project. The company must base its pricing decisions on the best assessment of price elasticity of the product (in other words, how does sales volume move when selling prices are changed) and the appropriate long-run cost structure of the product.

Therefore when a company is considering the development or launch of a new product and how to set its pricing level all the projected costs for that product are very important. This is because no costs have yet been incurred and any future cash flows are relevant to financial decisions. It is also important to remember, as discussed in Chapter 6, that the total costs over the life cycle of the project should be included, and adjusted where appropriate to take account of the effect of time on the value of money by using the discounting techniques explained in the chapter. However, when a company has already made the investment in product development and manufacturing facilities, etc., the financial decisions regarding pricing must also still consider the future cash flows, which now do not include these historic or sunk costs.

This can be particularly relevant when a company suddenly faces severe price pressure from a new competitor, possibly with an overseas sourcing base. A good example can be taken from the machine tool industry where major manufacturers in both western Europe and the United States had made substantial investments in new technology (for example, computer-controlled machines) and in productive capacity to supply the predicted demand from other sectors of manufacturing industry (such as car component and aeroplane component companies). These companies had set price levels on a cost build-up basis so that the variable costs of production and other direct costs were covered, and indirect costs were apportioned across the various products on suitable bases (these costs included a recovery of research and development costs) before an acceptable profit margin was added. Not surprisingly, as illustrated in Figure 13.3 the indirect costs and profit margin were often dramatically greater than the direct costs. This situation was further complicated in some large companies due to the components being produced in separate operating divisions of the group which were run as profit centres; in our example, the foundry and electronic control systems were separate divisions, and they both used the full costing build-up plus profit margins to set the transfer prices charged within the group.

Price analysis for illustrative machine

		£
Material and direct cost		15 000
Transfer price*	Foundry	9000
	Electronic control system	13 000
		37 000
Direct labour	Machining	5000
	Assembly	6000
		48 000
Indirect labour @ 100% of direct labour		11 000
Other indirect expenses @ 20% of other costs		12 000
Profit margin (approximately 20% of selling price)		18 000
	Selling price	89 000

*These transfer prices were made up:	*Electronics*	*Foundry*
Direct costs	£4000	£3000
Indirect costs	£6000	£4000
	£10 000	£7000
Profit	3000	2000
	£13 000	£9000

Figure 13.3

The particular company producing the product in Figure 13.3 suddenly found itself subjected to very severe competitive pricing pressure because eastern European manufacturers were offering the equivalent product at a price of £50 000 per machine, and this included their freight costs of shipping to the UK market. The established brand image of our company and its image of quality and reliability could sustain a small price premium against such overseas competition, but nothing as large as

£39 000 on a £50 000 machine. At first the company did not know how to respond but, after a major cost analysis exercise, carried out by a firm of consultants, it became clear that the company could reduce its selling prices in the short term so as to provide time for it to improve the efficiency of its manufacturing base and reduce its direct costs of production.

The revised cost build-up is shown below where all indirect costs and profit mark-ups are removed, so that the total group costs incurred in producing the machine are shown and the contribution achieved is highlighted.

	£
Material cost	15 000
Foundry direct cost	3000
Electronic division direct cost	4000
	22 000
Direct labour cost	11 000
	33 000
Contribution (34%)	17 000
Selling price of competitor	50 000

The £17 000 potential contribution revealed is considerably lower than the previous level achieved, but it indicates that in the short term it may be worthwhile reducing selling prices to maintain market share, if long-term cost reductions are possible or if it is expected that competitive selling prices will rise in the medium term (that is, if competitors are selling below their full costs, and are consequently pricing on a contribution basis only).

Several industries (such as motorcars, electrical goods, cameras, watches, etc.) believed this to be the case for many Japanese manufacturers when they started to take increasingly large market shares by offering substantially lower selling prices. They argued that the Japanese companies may have a small competitive advantage through lower direct costs of production but that the shipment costs to European or North American markets would restore the balance in long-term pricing. It has subsequently become apparent that any cost advantage in manufacturing is dramatically increased by a greater cost advantage in indirect costs and by a willingness to set prices according to a long-term expectation of costs, rather than requiring to recover all costs in the short term at today's lower sales volumes. Thus growth industries, which have large learning curve cost reductions, have been selected as major investment targets for these companies, because their selection of long-term costs as a pricing mechanism (and the consequent acceptance of accounting losses in the early years) gives a considerable competitive edge in establishing market share.

Special product pricing

Another area where establishing costs can be important for pricing is that of special products, particularly where the special products are produced as part of the normal process or use common resources. An example of this can be taken from the oil industry where the refining process separates the crude oil into a range of differentiated products, but the total costs of refining are incurred by the process and not by any particular product. Thus a specialized product which has specific performance requirements, such as aviation fuel or specialized lubricants, can only be produced along with the range of other products as part of the refining process. Some industries use very complex and sophisticated 'byproduct' and 'joint-product' costing systems in attempts to apportion the costs of the process across the various products produced; but these can create problems if the potential market price for one product increases or the demand changes dramatically. For example, if a minor byproduct of the oil refining process has a particular application as a specialized lubricant it may be possible to sell the product at very high unit prices (for example, lubricants for high speed drilling and cutting, and for specialized high performance engines) even though its specific costs can be regarded as very low. This product would appear very attractive and would show a very high product contribution due to the high selling price and low direct costs and may have good growth potential. However, it may be difficult for the company to increase its output of this particular product because it can only be produced in conjunction with a range of other products for which the prices and volumes may be moving in the opposite direction. Therefore pricing strategies for mixed products should be considered as a total so that the business produces a satisfactory return from the full product range, rather than trying to look at one product in isolation.

Aviation fuel, for example, forms a major part of the cost structure of airlines and any general change in the level of oil prices will have a significant impact on overall airline costs. This change could lead to a corresponding change in the demand for fuel by airlines; and if this volume change is greater than the volume effect on other elements of the product mix produced by the oil companies, the production and sales capabilities of the oil companies could become unbalanced. This might mean that the oil companies would want to alter the pricing levels of different product groups by different proportions depending upon the forecast price elasticity of demand in each area.

Segmentation pricing

Airlines, which were discussed in Chapter 8, are a good example of special product pricing where the cost base of the business is largely fixed. In any business with high fixed costs the pricing strategy should be set to maximize the total contribution achieved, and the success of this strategy is quite easily viewed in the case of airline flights because we have an instantly perishable product (that is, we can measure the total contribution achieved for the individual product, a flight, by any particular pricing strategy). The airline could use a marketing strategy of very low seat prices and very high volumes (that is, high occupancy rates per flight) or it could charge high prices and sell fewer seats per flight. This second strategy would require a higher level of service (that is, a differentiation of the product) to be provided to justify the higher price, but the actual risk is similar to the low price strategy: if insufficient seats are sold to cover the fixed costs, the airline makes a loss on the particular flight. What the airlines really need is a way of segmenting the market for the product (the basic product offered, that is, transportation from one place to another, is the same) by giving different levels of service (in the form of variable cost changes) for different price levels so as to attract as many customers as possible and hence maximize the total contribution achieved from the given level of fixed cost. This segmentation need explains the vast range of pricing levels used by airlines and why new ideas and experiments are constantly being introduced in a very competitive market.

Project pricing

Another service industry can be used to illustrate a further problem of setting prices and this is in regard to pricing projects, which are a form of the special (one-off) product pricing issue. In the computer software and consultancy industry, many systems solutions are major projects for which systems companies have to establish pricing strategies. From the selling company's perspective the low-risk pricing policy would be to price on a 'time and materials' basis, whereby the time taken to solve the problem is charged to the client at an agreed daily rate together with any materials used on the project (for example, computer development time as mentioned in Chapter 3). However, this low risk on the part of the selling company means that the customer has the high risk and is potentially signing a blank cheque to the supplier. Therefore as a way of differentiating themselves from competition, some companies started to quote fixed prices for computer solutions to client problems. This transferred the risk to the systems company because now the selling price is fixed in advance of the project being started, and thus the costs involved are not known.

For this pricing strategy to be successful, the company needs to have a very good financial control system which should be organized to provide accurate information on a project basis. The control system should allow the managers to learn about past project costs and hence to be able to forecast more accurately in the future. The system should also produce timely reports on current projects compared to plan so that managers can make decisions and take action on any projects which show signs of overrunning. This means that the plans and actual costs have to be capable of being compared against achievement milestones, not just expenditure levels. The rapid growth of fixed price software development contracts as a proportion of the total market means that a critical success factor for these companies is now the quality of their project management expertise, and this depends to a great degree on the quality of the financial information with which the project managers are provided.

In the construction industry this problem of pricing and cost control is also a major concern to customers and it is particularly so when a number of different suppliers (for example, the actual building company, architects, quantity surveyors, specialist contractors) are involved in any major contract. Out of this complexity, a new service has been developed, particularly by quantity surveyors who are expert in construction cost measurement, which provides the client with 'total project management'. This service should ensure that the client gets what was wanted for the fixed cost which was agreed at the start of the project, and thus the project manager resolves any cost overruns and frees the client from any detailed involvement in the project. Clearly the client pays a fee for the service provided, but it is a good example of the complexity of pricing leading to a marketing opportunity for a new product.

Transfer pricing

So far we have been considering pricing in the external environment but, as discussed in Chapter 10, for many organizations there is a need to establish internal pricing policies for the transfer of goods and services within the organization. The problems of transfer pricing have already been outlined and illustrated in Chapter 12, but in many cases it is very important that some form of pricing is charged because, if a service is free, other parts of the group may use it extravagantly and without regard to the cost and value of the service. This problem is frequently encountered in the field of computer systems, both development and operations, which can be provided by a centralized systems department or spread throughout the organization and controlled directly by the operational managers. It is important that the transfer pricing system is designed appropriately to its objectives as it should be used primarily to allocate resources and not as a means of apportioning the costs of one department (cost object) across the other areas of the business, as pointed out in Chapter 8. If the pricing system is designed with this objective, then transfer prices used should be based on the logic of opportunity costs to the group and not simply the costs incurred in the area.

Thus if an equivalent service can be obtained on the outside market, for example, from a computer bureau, or provided by the user department, such as through microcomputers, the costs of the alternatives should be used to decide if the centralized systems department is appropriate for the type of service. The transfer price could be set at the opportunity cost and the level of cost recovery of the systems department considered as a measure of efficiency in its operations. This does not measure the effectiveness of the systems operations and it may be that, by providing integrated systems for the company as a whole, a uniform database can be established. Unfortunately, as discussed in Chapters 10 and 11, it is commonly the case that the areas required to input the data are not the areas which will benefit from the information generated from a database. This makes it even more important that a transfer pricing system does not penalize areas of the business for using a centralized systems facility, if other areas will obtain great value from the information thereby generated. Indeed the ideal transfer pricing system should compensate the area for any additional work involved in inputting any extra data, which has no relevance to them but great value to other areas of the business.

This can be achieved if externally monitored opportunity cost transfer pricing is used, because a user with relatively simple processing and analytical needs (for example, the sales invoicing function) would be charged a low computer bureau equivalent price for a standard service, whereas the sophisticated requirements for a comprehensive sales analysis system for the marketing area would attract a higher transfer price. Thus the marketing area is effectively paying (through the transfer pricing system) for the sales invoicing function to input the required data, and this type of pricing system can ensure the effective allocation of resources. Whether the systems department recovers its costs through the transfer pricing process is then a measure of its efficiency and the effectiveness is created by the proper allocation of resources. In some companies this financial analysis of internal services has been developed to the level of using discounted cash flow techniques to justify investment in new computer systems, where the benefits clearly have to be financially quantified as well as the costs involved.

Foreign exchange

Transfer pricing also needs to be developed in multistage products, as illustrated in Chapter 12 and this can become extremely complicated in some industries, such as car manufacturing. Ford Motor Company manufactures vehicles and components in five countries across Europe and sells in 15 countries, with any vehicle potentially having component parts of it produced in each of the five countries. Not only is a transfer pricing system needed to ensure resources are allocated economically but the group has also to cope with the impact of fluctuating exchange rates. If the company produces a vehicle in Germany it will have costs denoted in deutschmarks but if it sells that vehicle to a customer in the United Kingdom it will have sales revenues in pounds sterling; just to complicate matters further, being a US-owned company it actually desires to generate profits in US dollars.

In some industries it is possible to set prices in the foreign currency where costs are incurred, but this normally makes the product unattractive to the customer, since the foreign exchange risk has been passed on to the customer. It is also not practical where competitors do not have the same production base and hence are not exposed to the same foreign exchange fluctuations (for example, UK-based manufacturers or even Fiat which, being based in Italy, is subjected to fluctuations in the lira exchange rate to the £ not the deutschmark rate). Thus Fords have to establish their pricing strategy in the United Kingdom in £s and try to limit their risks by fixing their costs in £s as well. This could be done by taking out forward exchange contracts whereby the company buys in advance the deutschmarks it requires so that it fixes the costs in £s; thus enabling prices in the United Kingdom to be calculated and a marketing strategy developed. As with most risk reduction exercises there is a cost involved of taking out a forward exchange contract and the company has to balance this cost against the benefit of having a known local currency cost base.

It is important to realize that this guaranteed local currency cost does not guarantee a profit in local currency because this will be determined by the actual selling prices achieved in the market place. If competitors reduce their selling prices, it is irrelevant what the exchange rate obtained by our company was or how prudent the managers were in hedging (for example, buying forward) their foreign currency exposures. In a fiercely competitive market where relative pricing is very important, the company has to set its prices by the market levels and not by its cost base, and this is true for cars and for electrical retailing, which is more heavily dependent on imported products. For example Dixons Group, the market leader in electrical retailing, may have very sophisticated financial managers who can expertly hedge their foreign currency exposures but they cannot use this argument to justify why a customer should pay £10 more for a television set or stereo from Dixons compared to a competitive retailer, such as Comet. They have to be price competitive in the high street so that the cost base is the ultimate determinant of profitability and long-term survival and growth.

Credit as part of marketing strategy

In a very price-competitive market for high value items, it may be desirable to achieve some level of differentiation and one potential development would be to make it easier for the company to buy the product from your company than from a competitor. We have already mentioned that extended credit can be used as part of a marketing differentiation strategy (Chapter 4) and looked at the specific use of financing in the motor industry (Chapter 9), but particular strategies can be developed for market needs. If, for example, market research indicates that many customers will make a decision to buy a major electrical appliance on the same day as they see the appliance, it becomes important to make that purchase as easy as possible. One way of doing this is by offering a level of 'instant credit' which is adequate for the normal purchase value, and many electrical retailers, etc. now do this.

Effectively the retailer is increasing the credit risk (that is, risk of non-payment by the customer) by making an instant decision, but the argument is that if customers are forced to wait a few days while the credit applications are processed they may not purchase the goods at that later time and the sale may be lost. Thus the financial analysis can be quite straightforward; we need an estimate of the risk of nonpayment and of the increase in sales revenue caused by adding 'instant credit' to the marketing mix (each of these can be monitored by the financial control system to see what the actual figures are and the analysis updated accordingly). An illustrative calculation is shown in Figure 13.4 which also shows why a retailer can take a larger credit risk than a bank or other lender of money. A bank only earns a spread (the gap between the rate of interest charged to borrowers and rate of interest paid to depositors) on the cash lent but the retailer earns a contribution on the product sale which is being financed, and should the debt not be paid this reduces the additional sales revenue needed to recoup the loss from the bad debt.

In Figure 13.4 we assumed the worst position for a retailer in that the whole balance of the selling price was lent and no interest charges were

Credit as part of marketing strategy

	£	
Selling price of television	300	
Cost price to retailer	225	
Contribution to retailer	£75	(25%)

Assumption: Sales increase by 1000 sets as a result of instant credit.
Gain to company = £75 × 1000
                  = £75 000

1   Credit risk per sale: assume 100% of selling price, that is, £300 per sale
    *If less than 250 customers fail to pay, that is more than 75% do pay the deal increases
    profits.*
    –   Bad debt loss = £300 × 250 = £75 000

2   Assume finance granted by bank on contribution of 5%.
    *If more than 50 customers fail to pay, the deal reduces profits,
    that is, contribution on total credit sales* = £300 × 1000 × 5%
                                                  = £15 000

    Bad debt loss = *loan amount* × *non payers*
                    = £300 × 50 = £15 000

Figure 13.4

made. In practice these would be used to make the position even more
financially attractive to *the retailer* by insisting on some initial payment
and charging a rate of interest on the outstanding balance (sometimes a
surprisingly high rate of interest is charged which should make the
retailer's financing unattractive to the customer!).

An alternative way of using credit as part of the marketing strategy is to
offer a discount for prompt payment (that is, payment by the customer
sooner than is normal for the industry or than is specified by the
company's trading conditions). Settlement discounts, as they are known,
are very common in some industries and therefore a company does not
differentiate itself by offering one but it can still achieve this differentiation by offering a higher rate of discount than the other companies in the
industry. It is interesting to note that as settlement discounts are
effectively a means of *paying* our customer to *pay us* earlier than they
would otherwise, the rate of discount should be calculated by reference
to interest rates prevailing in the market. This is illustrated in the example
below but it is virtually unknown for a company to adjust the rate of its
settlement discount when interest rates move; however, it is not unheard
of for customers to calculate which suppliers' settlement discounts are
financially worth taking.

Example: Settlement Discounts

The assumption is that normal payment terms are 30 days from date of invoice. Our company offers $1\frac{1}{2}$ per cent discount for payment within seven days. Effectively our company is paying $1\frac{1}{2}$ per cent to receive the cash from the sales revenue 23 days earlier (30 minus seven days).

Ignoring the compounding factor this is equivalent to an annualized cost of funds of

$$\frac{365}{23} \times 1\frac{1}{2}\%$$

or   23.8%

Customers will therefore decide whether it is worth paying earlier than required in exchange for a return of 23.8 per cent per annum. If the customer could borrow additional funds at less than this cost it could improve its profits by doing so and using the funds to take advantage of the settlement discount offered.

Note   In practice the customer should base its calculations not on the stated terms of trade (30 days) but on the actual payment period which is normal for the industry and for this supplier in particular.

Some suppliers can argue that offering a settlement discount can reduce the risk of non-payment by their customers (that is, credit risk) and it may therefore be worth paying a higher cost than is warranted by an interest rate-based calculation. If the settlement discount is offered for payment within seven days rather than the normal 30 days, this only reduces the risk of the customer going bust in the 23 days between when payment is made and was due anyway. If credit risk is seen as significant for a particular customer or segment of the market, it is preferable to offer even greater discounts for payment in advance or at the time of the sale (that is, cash on delivery, COD) so as to remove the credit risk altogether.

Our entrepreneur, George Taylor, was trying to expand his newly established wholesale business and decided that selling on credit to his larger customers would be one good way of achieving this. He was only making a contribution of 8 per cent on his wholesale sales revenue and so he wanted to maximize the volume achieved so as to cover the largely fixed operating costs. Unfortunately for George one of the larger customers, which he attracted with this new marketing strategy, went into liquidation owing George £20 000 which was never repaid. As shown below, George has to generate additional sales of £250 000 in order to recover the lost £20 000, which indicates that extending credit in such a low margin business is not a particularly sensible strategy and so George stopped extending credit to his wholesale customers.

Sales revenue	100%
Cost of goods sold	92%
Contribution	8%
Bad debt suffered	£20 000
Additional sales needed at 8% contribution	£250 000

(£250 000 × 8% contribution = additional contribution of £20 000)

Discount structures

He still wanted to generate some sales revenue growth and was well aware that the wholesale trade was fiercely price competitive. The idea of a price discount for all major customers therefore seemed attractive and he developed a proposal for a 2 per cent discount on all sales revenue for customers who spent more than £100 000 in a calendar year. This level of discount was not excessively exciting, but could be attractive to a retailer and George thought it might build some customer loyalty. As shown in Figure 13.5, which uses the formula developed in the appendix to Chapter 8, the increase in sales needed to break-even on this pricing change is a substantial 33⅓ per cent which for such a small price discount requires a massive degree of price elasticity in this wholesale market.

Price discounts

George Taylor is considering a 2% price discount for major customers.

	Before discount	*After discount*
Sales revenue	100%	98%
Cost of goods sold	92%	92%
Contribution	8%	6%

Sales revenue per major customer £100 000
∴ contribution is £8000
New sales revenue needed to generate the same contribution

$$= \frac{£8000}{6\%} = £133\ 333$$

Using Chapter 8 formula:

$$\text{Volume increase} = \frac{\text{Contribution given up}}{\text{Contribution retained}} \times 100\%$$

$$= \frac{2\%}{6\%} \times 100\% = 33.3\%$$

Figure 13.5

This type of price discount is very common and can be financially evaluated using this type of contribution analysis, but the actual response to different levels of pricing must be monitored to enable future forecasts of likely outcome to be more accurately made (that is, treating the financial control system as a learning process). Price discounts can be given on the basis of total sales values, as in George's case, or sales volumes which is very common in fmcg industries, where large volume orders attract lower selling prices. This latter type of discount is based on the argument that large volume orders reduce the costs of the selling company because several of the costs associated with processing any order (for example, clerical effort and physically picking the goods) are largely fixed and therefore a large volume order is more cost-effective than a small order. Some companies have implemented this pricing policy in the opposite manner by making a surcharge for small orders, which has the same financial effect but is often regarded as less motivational to the customers.

The logic of passing on cost savings to customers in the form of price discounts is, of course, not new and many companies built their original success by differentiating themselves as low price and low service businesses (for example, discount supermarkets and self-service petrol stations). In fmcg industries this has now become quite sophisticated with companies giving price discounts to retailers for ordering in full pallet quantities (as this saves distribution cost incurred in splitting pallets and restacking the product for delivery), and for deliveries to the retailers' warehouses rather than shops (as this saves delivery cost incurred in delivering smaller order quantities to individual shops). Thus price discounts can represent a genuine saving, some of which is passed on to the customer, or can really be a transfer of cost to the customer, as in the last example where the retailer still has to deliver the product to the stores.

Price discounts can also be used to segment the market and to encourage customers to increase their purchases, even without volume savings being easy to establish. This can be illustrated by considering the case of a sports and leisure complex where a range of sporting facilities is offered as well as bars and restaurants. Membership is often offered on a sport-by-sport basis so that members pay to join the squash or tennis sections etc. and then normally pay for their usage of the facilities in addition. A more sophisticated mechanism of pricing is to allow this type of single sport membership but to offer extra sports at increasing levels of discount from the combined membership fees, thus encouraging members to increase their participation in the complex and adding to total sales revenues. Even more powerful is a membership level where the annual fee includes the cost of usage of the relevant sports facilities and this can be offered on a restricted (for example, excluding evenings and weekends) or open basis. This highest level of membership (sometimes deliberately titled 'silver star' and 'gold star' members) can provide a guaranteed level of income to the leisure company and since the majority of operating expenses involved in such a complex are relatively fixed, this can dramatically reduce the financial risks associated with the business. The relative discounts must be carefully calculated to be of interest to the members, while still providing the complex with adequate total income, but the financial evaluation techniques are quite straightforward and the pricing structure can always be adjusted when actual membership profiles and usage levels are established.

Some leisure complex developments are even raising some of the initial development funding by selling lifetime founder memberships at quite high prices, but which for a one-time payment guarantee the member usage of the facilities with a varying level of additional founder member privileges.

Special offers, deals and allowances

This is one type of special offer pricing but there are several other ways in which this can be used. (We are not intending to deal with promotional activities here as they are considered in Chapter 14.) Special offer pricing is important in seasonal businesses in order to try to stimulate sales activities in the off-season period; for example, squash court hire charges will often be lower in the summer than during the normal squash season (summer leagues and tournaments are classed as promotional ways of stimulating demand).

Another good example of this type of very selective pricing is the holiday industry where the price range between the peak season and other parts of the year can be dramatic. Also the holiday company should understand its particular customer base and set its prices accordingly so that if, for example, it is aiming at the family holiday market it will normally charge premium prices for the school holiday weeks, whenever they fall. If its target market is young singles such a pricing policy may leave it with unsold accommodation during the peak season due to the seemingly excessive pricing increases. It may have massive demand which it is unable to satisfy for the weeks on both sides of the school holidays when its significantly lower prices will make it much more attractive to its particular customers, who are not so restricted in when they go on holiday.

Pricing policy must therefore be carefully and specifically directed at the target market and be designed for the product's particular stage of development, as was stated at the beginning of the chapter.

14
—

Promotion

Introduction

The promotion element of the marketing mix concerns all forms of promotional activity, including both advertising and more direct sales promotions such as personal selling. It may be useful therefore to start this chapter by considering some of the differences between advertising and sales promotions from a financial standpoint before illustrating the financial impact of each by a series of examples, but it should be remembered that the distinctions are becoming increasingly blurred and the two activities are frequently used together.

Advertising versus sales promotion

The first and most obvious general financial difference between advertising and sales promotion is that the cost of any advertising campaign is fixed and determined by the media selected and the scale and frequency of the campaign. Thus the cost is not dependent upon the success in terms of increasing sales volumes or revenues, whereas a large part of the cost of a typical sales promotion will be determined by the sales activity during the promotional period, even though this sales activity may not directly result from the promotion.

Any fixed cost expenditure with an uncertain financial return must be regarded as a quite high risk activity and where the expenditure may have to take place some time before any benefit is expected to be seen the risk should be regarded as even higher. Since this is often true of advertising expenditure the risk should be justified by a compensatingly high level of financial return, but it is often argued that it is impossible to measure the return from advertising. By contrast if the expenditure is variable and is automatically controlled by the success of the activity (that is, low success leads to low cost, whereas high success increases the cost proportionately) the risk is lower and the level of financial return can be commensurately reduced. When this level of return can be immediately and accurately determined, as is sometimes argued for sales promotions, the degree of financial control which can be exercised is very high.

In this chapter it will be argued that both these views overstate their respective cases and that financial control of advertising is achievable and that the level of control which can be achieved over sales promotions is not much greater. It is also frequently true that advertising has an impact over a longer time-scale than sales promotions and while this makes the evaluation process more difficult, it may make the expenditure considerably more valuable. In order to exercise control we have already emphasized, in Chapters 10 and 11, that we may need to use physical comparisons, rather than just financial measurements, whenever possible, and it can be argued that this type of physical measurement is particularly relevant to the control of advertising and sales promotions.

Advertising: efficiency versus effectiveness

Advertising is a perfect example of the situation where many companies spend most of their financial analysis, planning and control effort on the efficiency of the activity rather than the effectiveness. In measuring the efficiency of advertising we can calculate the actual cost of an advertising campaign in terms of £s per thousand prospective customers and compare this to the budgeted costs (this clearly is a far superior measure to simply controlling actual expenditure against the budget). However, this comparison only measures the buying efficiency of the organization and some companies have recognized this by taking the media buying out of the marketing area and locating it along with all other purchasing so that expert buyers conduct the negotiations and structure the contracts.

The real measure of marketing performance is the effectiveness of the advertising activity carried out and this has little to do with the efficiency of buying. Buying the wrong campaign very efficiently is still a totally wasted expenditure, you may simply have wasted slightly less cash! Effectiveness is, as was discussed in Chapter 10, the measurement of how well the stated objectives were achieved, and this requires that the overall corporate objectives are broken down so that compatible objectives can be established for each area of the business including marketing, and for each element of marketing, such as advertising.

This should not be a problem because without clearly defined objectives it would be financially irresponsible for managers to spend large amounts on advertising. These objectives have to be more specifically identified than the statement that 'advertising is designed to increase sales revenue', because advertising is one element of the marketing mix, and we need to establish why advertising is more effective than, say, decreasing the price by the equivalent amount. Advertising can be designed for very different purposes and can be, among other things, image building (for the company and the brand), attribute communicating (simply giving factual information), comparative (establishing competitive advantages on a selective basis) or straightforwardly persuasive (turning a perceived need into a purchase decision).

The design of the advertising message and the choice of the appropriate media will all be made with the specific principal aim of the campaign in mind and this should enable well-defined objectives to be established. If we can define objectives, we can try to establish measurement standards by which we can judge the effectiveness of the advertising, and if we conduct pre and post campaign testing of these measures we can check the actual effectiveness against the forecast. In the more sophisticated high-spending advertising companies most of these measures exist and are monitored by regular tracking and market research studies, which can test the recall of consumers regarding the product and its attributes, their attitudes to the product and company, and their relative attitudes compared to competitors, as well as changes in their level of usage over time. Thus the physical controls are often in place, but what is frequently not done is to make the linkage between the physical controls and the expenditure on advertising.

This linkage should not be difficult as long as managers do not expect excessive precision and accuracy from the process. They should not expect too much accuracy in this area because it is not achieved in any other area of financial planning and forecasting involvement in the business, as has been demonstrated throughout the book. The process should aid decision-making and improve the allocation of resources in the future by enabling managers to learn from the intelligent analysis of the past and the comparison of actual events to those expected and included in plans. If the individual objectives for any element of advertising are understood, it is possible to incorporate these objectives (such as to improve consumer awareness of a new recently launched financial service product) into a model of how improving awareness will increase sales of the product in the future. This model can be tested and updated over time by comparing it to the actual events so that future decisions can be improved. In the short-term, evaluation of the current activity should be done against the best information which is available, as is the case for all financial evaluations, and this will normally be the model which was used for the original justification. Thus if our advertising campaign *did* increase awareness of the new product as predicted it should be considered an effective use of resources. Whether the increased awareness leads to higher sales levels should be monitored so as to enable the relationships in the model to be more accurately defined in the future.

We are therefore using physical measures as far as possible to judge the effectiveness of expenditure, and updating our planning models when more information on the linkage between awareness and product sales is obtained. This acknowledges that advertising is a long-term activity and in many cases should be regarded as an investment.

Advertising as investment expenditure

We have, at many stages through the book, referred to a company investing in marketing expenditure because cash is paid out in advance of any financial return being obtained by the business. We have also argued that the company should regard this marketing expenditure as an investment for its internal decision-making, even though it will have been written off in the published profit and loss account and thus will not be included on the published balance sheet as an asset at the end of the period. However, it should be made clear that not all advertising expenditure can be regarded as an investment, and this should be established by the specific objectives of the particular activity. If an advertising campaign is designed to maintain the existing level of awareness or knowledge of the product then it clearly is maintaining an existing asset (the brand franchise) and should be treated accordingly, that is, it should be written off in the period in which it is spent.

This is not different to how we treat more tangible assets such as plant and machinery where companies can differentiate without major problems between development, which increases the value of the asset to the business, and maintenance, which simply maintains it at the existing value to the business. For decision-making purposes the company should try to split its advertising expenditure into the same categories so that true investment in marketing can be identified. It is also clear that intangible marketing assets decline over time unless maintained properly and the company should attempt to compare the different ways in which the brand asset can be maintained, or developed where appropriate. This may be a question of the rate of decay, for example how quickly does the customer forget about the product, as it may be possible to maintain a particular product by relatively small bursts of advertising on a very frequent basis or to allow the decay to go further but then to inject a more sustained burst of advertising to redress the position. Some sophisticated models have been developed to try to evaluate this problem, such as using the net accumulated weight of advertising which measures the cumulative build-up in advertising but allows for a decay in effectiveness over time. This technique does not really take account of any qualitative weighting for the advertising concerned, but this factor can be included by using more specific monitoring techniques, such as tracking studies and other direct market research on the target of the advertising.

It is now quite widely agreed by marketing managers that a marketing asset must be measurable in some way if it really exists, and the financial challenge is to turn that measurement into a valid system of valuation. As mentioned in Chapter 12, we can value marketing assets when an acquisition involving brands etc. is made from another company (for example, IDV buying Smirnoff), and consequently similar analytical techniques should be used on internal marketing asset development and maintenance.

This analysis of advertising between development and maintenance also indicates a difference in the time-scale of each style of advertising. Some expenditure may be structured to achieve a long-term impact by building on a theme or developing a particular image for the organization (for example, developing the image of a financial services company as innovative, progressive and professional), while other expenditure will be on instantly relevant information (for example, if the rate of interest paid on deposits has changed) but will have no long-term significance.

Advertising agencies

This requires different financial justifications to be used for different types of advertising and may complicate the way in which the relative success of the current advertising agency can be judged. From a company perspective, advertising expenditure is incurred to achieve specific objectives which should enhance the long-term financial performance of the business (that is, show a satisfactory financial return on the investment made). These objectives do not include winning advertising awards and should be achieved as cost-effectively as possible. The reduction in total cost may be achieved by reducing the costs of producing any particular series of advertisements so that the vast majority of the expenditure is spent on media time, and if media time is bought *efficiently* the value achieved can again be increased.

Unfortunately, if advertising agencies are paid a commission which is based on the total advertising expenditure handled by them, any major gains in the efficiency of buying advertising which could be generated by their efforts result in their total commission income being reduced. This is clearly illogical but again any overemphasis on measures of efficiency is likely to be counterproductive; for example, it is more profitable for a commission-based agency if one advertisement is used in a large number of advertising bursts as they can get paid commission on the total media expenditure for relatively little effort. This also helps the company's advertising efficiency ratio, but the advertising may be more effective if a series of messages are communicated over the same period, and the advertising agency's measure of success should be linked to the effectiveness not efficiency of the expenditure.

One way of achieving this is for the advertising agency to be paid a fee for their services (in the same way as other expert consultancies are paid fees) rather than receiving a percentage commission on the expenditures made. In this way three benefits can be achieved:

1 The income of the advertising agency can be specifically linked to their contribution towards achieving the marketing objectives of the client company.
2 If more efficient means of achieving these objectives can be found, the advertising agency should receive part of the saving to the client rather than being penalized as they would be if they were paid on a commission basis.
3 The company is made more explicitly aware of where their advertising expenditure is going and may look for more specific value from their advertising consultants than simply buying media time.

Sales promotions

The complexity and specialist skills required in the field of advertising led to the development of specialized advertising agencies, but many companies have tended to produce all the other elements of the promotional mix in-house. This has started to change with the increasing development of specialist sales promotion companies who provide a comparative input in the field of promotions to that provided by advertising agencies in their field.

Some of this specialist work is paid for on a commission basis but an increasing proportion is fee-based, and again this highlights for the client what is being paid for. The major benefits for the client are that specific expertise can be employed on any particular promotion and that the costs involved are now variable rather than being a fixed cost of the business. This use of outside specialist companies means that different companies can be used for promotions with different objectives where the skills and expertise required may vary substantially.

Different objectives for sales promotions

It is clear that sales promotions can have a wide range of specific objectives and the nature of the promotion will normally be selected to suit the specific objectives (for example, encouraging trial of the product, encouraging repeat purchase, increasing the rate of purchase, etc.). There are other ways in which the promotion may vary in that it may be aimed at a segment of the market and cover a range of products or be single-product specific but be used in all the market segments. The promotion could be aimed directly at the end consumer of the product or at the intermediate customer of the company (that is the channel), and it could be part of the long-term development of the product or a short-term competitive tactic with almost no long-term strategic value. The financial evaluation of the promotional expenditure should be carried out in the context of the particular objectives and the relevant time-scale.

This financial analysis should be done before the expenditure is committed so that the decision is made in the knowledge of the financial justification, and the actual outcome should be financially analysed at the end of the activity. The post-events analysis should not be done as an apportionment of blame exercise if the promotion did not appear to be successful, but as part of the continuous process of updating our understanding of the business interrelationships so that better forecasts can be made in the future.

The pre-expenditure financial analysis should use the output of the process of setting the promotional budgets. This setting of the budget should be done by reference to the analysed marketing objectives which are developed from the corporate objectives, as illustrated in Chapters 6 and 7. Thus the promotional objectives should be as specific as possible, and the budget should be developed to achieve those objectives subject to the normal process of 'affordability' checking as mentioned in Chapters 8 and 9. If the promotional budget has been broken down, the specific proposals for promotions can be evaluated against the objectives identified in the budget and decisions made accordingly.

However, we have throughout the book emphasized that any plans will inevitably be wrong due, among other things, to changes in the external environment and this is particularly true of promotional activity, because of potentially rapid and large changes in competitive expenditure. A budget should never be regarded as a static plan or a 'tablet in stone' which cannot be altered and the company will need to 'flex the budget', as discussed in Chapters 8 and 11, to take account of such changes in the environment. The changes may be so dramatic that the planned objectives are no longer achievable or relevant and the revised promotional forecast should be established in the context of the new objectives.

Having established objectives for promotional activity we have to consider the evaluation of the specific proposals for each promotion and this should be done using the opportunity cost logic that there are normally several alternative ways of achieving any promotional objective and we are trying to select the best alternative.

Evaluating sales promotions

As a simple example of a sales promotion we will consider a money-off flash pack promotion for a convenience food product, using very simplified numbers. This promotion is aimed at the ultimate consumer as the flash pack (where the price reduction is clearly stated) is designed to ensure the benefit is both visible and passed on by the retailer. If this promotion is to run for a period of two months we need to know the sales forecasts for the company for at least the six months period starting two months before the promotion and ending two months after the promotion so that the 'steal' factor can be included. The steal factor represents those purchases which will be affected by the promotion as retailers, when they know a promotion is forthcoming, will logically defer purchases of the standard product prior to the promotion and buy heavily during the promotion period which will reduce their purchases in the immediate period following the promotion. Thus the sales forecast is required both with and without the promotional activity, and we also need an estimate of the costs of the promotion.

These costs should include not only the marketing costs of communicating the promotion (that is, linked advertising expenditure) but the increased product costs such as new packaging materials required (the flash pack carton, etc.) and any manufacturing inefficiencies caused by changing the product for the promotional period (not likely to be significant for this type of promotion). We should also include the increased distribution and stockholding costs which result from increasing the product range (we are adding a new temporary product), and this can be particularly expensive if not all customers take the promotional product so that the normal product has to be manufactured and distributed during the promotional period (some retailers do not accept 'flash pack' promotions preferring to negotiate a lower price throughout the year, which meets their corporate marketing strategy of discount pricing).

The base information for our promotion is shown in Figure 14.1 and the financial evaluation of the promotional proposal is illustrated in Figure 14.2 which shows how important the steal factor can be and why the financial evaluation needs to be done carefully.

If the objectives of the promotion are clearly stated it should be possible to carry out a post-completion financial analysis of the promotion even though the situation may have changed considerably since the original justification was carried out. What is needed is some form of model

Sales promotion for a canned meat product

Base data

The existing retail price per can is 80p and the product is sold in cases containing 24 cans. The average retail margin is 25% which leaves the manufacturer with a gross selling price per can of 60p, or per case of £14.40. The proposed promotion is to reduce the on-pack price to 70p, that is a 10p reduction for the customer, and for this illustration we are assuming that all the costs of the promotion are borne by the manufacturer and that the retailer's margin is maintained at 20p per can sold.

Cost structure

	£s per case
Selling price	14.40
Direct costs	7.20
Contribution per case	£7.20

Sales forecast   *'000 cases*

Month	1	2	3	4	5	6
Without promotion	20	20	20	20	20	20
With promotion	15	10	55	45	10	15
Gain/(loss)	(5)	(10)	35	25	(10)	(5)

The promotion is forecast to result in the sale of an additional 30 000 cases of product which appears to be financially attractive.

Figure 14.1

which can show what the sales achievement would have been without the promotion because the only actual data available will include the impact of the promotion. This analysis is important as part of the learning process so that better forecasts of the impact of different types of promotional activity can be made in the future.

Sales-force controls

Another area of the promotional mix which requires careful financial justification is the sales-force because in many companies the sales force is a major element in the total marketing expenditure. We have already considered, in Chapter 8, the role of physical standards in trying to determine the optimum size of a field sales-force, and this evaluation can also be used to compare the costs and benefits of alternative types of sales activities, for example, a telephone selling team or a third party sales-force. If standards are to be properly developed in this area the company needs a model of a sales process from which the role of the sales-force can be extracted and financially evaluated. Thus if the primary role of a field sales-force is to call on customers and to take orders, this can be

Analysis of sales promotion

	£ Normal	£ Flashpack	
Selling price	14.40	14.40	
Direct cost	7.20	7.20	
	7.20	7.20	
Additional direct costs	–	0.30	
Promotional allowance	–	2.40	(10p per can ×
			24 cans per case)
Contribution	£7.20	£4.50	

Total contribution without promotion = £7.20 × 120 000 cases
$$= £864\ 000$$

Total contribution with promotion = contribution/case × cases
= £4.50 × 100 000 cases sold during promotion
+ £7.20 × 50 000 cases sold before and after promotion
= £810 000

The net contribution with the promotion is lower by £54 000 and the promotion should not therefore be done.
Reasons for decrease:

	Increased volume during total period of effect of promotion is at lower contribution per unit – gain is 30 000 @ £4.50	= £135 000
but	Base volume during specific period of promotion is also sold at lower contribution per unit – that is, *loss* of 40 000 × (7.20 – £4.50)	= (£108 000)
	Subtotal	£27 000
and	Steal factor: transfer of volume from outside promotion means these sales are actually made at a lower contribution per unit – that is, loss is 30 000 × £2.70	= (£81 000)
	Net gain/(loss)	(54 000)

Figure 14.2

evaluated to establish the frequency with which various categories of customer should be visited, as shown in Figure 14.3.

This type of evaluation which uses a breakdown of specific objectives is even more important when the sales-force can only influence the customer but not directly take an order. This can be the case in several industries, but a good example is of wines and spirits companies some of which have a sales-force 'selling' to pubs but the publican will actually buy his wines and spirits from a wholesaler not from the salesperson, thus making the linkage indirect. In this case it is very difficult to try to control the effectiveness of the sales-force by the level of sales achieved, but if the particular objectives of employing such an indirect sales-force

---

Standards for sales force activities

Primary role for sales force: call on customers and take orders.

Costs	*Versus*	*Benefits*
Sales force total costs		Contribution generated from sales made

This can be evaluated by establishing a model for the cost effectiveness of the sales force in achieving their sales objectives, a simplified version of which is shown below which shows the contribution generated per sales person:

Effective selling days per year	× Calls made per day	× Probability of achieving an order on any call (hit rate)	× Average contribution per order	= Total contribution generated per sales person

---

Notes
1 Each element in this model is affected by changes in the total size of the sales force and the customer and product mix, so that it needs to be monitored continuously.
2 Using such a formula not only helps in budgeting and planning but when analysing the over or under performance of the sales force the process highlights which factor is not as forecast (for example, if the correct calls per day are being made but the hit rate is too low, this could indicate that the call frequency is too high for certain customers).

Figure 14.3

are identified it becomes possible to monitor the effectiveness of performance against measurable objectives.

Sales-force compensation

A very closely related problem is the question of sales-force compensation and how incentive schemes should be established. The company should try to ensure goal congruence between the interests of the salesperson and the company, because if this is not achieved the sales-force may concentrate their efforts on products which are less profitable than those where the company wishes to concentrate its resources. Most sales-force incentive schemes are based on sales revenue targets with some using volume measures as well, but where a salesperson has the job of selling a mix of products this may not lead to goal congruence as illustrated in Figure 14.4. The more logical financial incentive scheme would be based on the contribution of the various products rather than the absolute selling prices or volumes; if we want the sales-force to generate profit, we should motivate them to do so.

Some companies argue that to do this involves giving the sales-force information on the contributions of the various products, but this incentive can be implemented by using a weighting factor for the products based on their relative contribution, or setting specific volume objectives by products rather than globally. This reluctance to give to the

Sales incentive schemes

Individual targets for the sales force are £250 000 sales revenue and a sales volume of 20 000 cases.

Product range	A	B	C
Selling price per case	£10	£12	£15
Direct cost per case	£8	£4	£8
Contribution per case	£2	£8	£7

Salesperson X overachieves these targets by selling the following combinations of products:

	A	B	C	Total
Sales volumes	16 000	2000	5000	23 000
Sales revenues	£160 000	£24 000	£75 000	£259 000
Contribution achieved	£32 000	£16 000	£35 000	£83 000

According to our sales incentive scheme this salesperson has done well but another salesperson Y is judged a failure because of a shortfall in achieving the objectives.

Salesperson Y	A	B	C	Total
Sales volumes	3000	5000	10 000	18 000
Sales revenues	£30 000	£60 000	£150 000	£240 000
Contributions achieved	£6000	£40 000	£70 000	£116 000

If we compare the contributions to the company it is clear that Y has contributed £33 000 more than X and to pay X a substantial bonus for overachieving and to give Y nothing means we may be encouraging our sales force to focus on the wrong objectives.

Figure 14.4

sales-force financial information which may very well help them to do their job better is another illustration of the organizational structure problems referred to in Chapter 5, and these types of internal problems should not be allowed to interfere with the effectiveness of the business in achieving its objectives. All promotional activities must be aimed at achieving specific objectives which help in the achievement of the overall corporate objectives and the financial analysis, planning and control systems must aid this process.

Place

Introduction

One of the most important marketing strategy decisions for a business is which channel it should use to access its market and how far down that channel it should be. For example, should a clothes company sell to retailers, wholesalers, or through mail order catalogues, or all three; or should it go into retailing itself so that it has more direct control over the way in which the product is offered to the end consumer? Clearly different companies in the clothing industry have chosen different strategies and some businesses which started out as predominantly manufacturers have, over time, become exclusively retailers (for example, the Burton Group).

In this chapter we shall consider some of the financial issues regarding these major decisions and other aspects of the 'place' part of the marketing mix.

Channel choice

For some industries the right choice of physical location can be a primary reason for success (for example, retailing) but, as the environment changes, the right physical location may also change (for example, the growth of out-of-town shopping centres compared to the local high street). Therefore the choice of the place in which to do business should not be regarded as a static decision, but the effectiveness of the current channel should be monitored.

If a major investment has been made in specialized assets, such as freehold retail premises, this change in desired location may have severe financial consequences for the business. Therefore it may be preferable to reduce the financial risk by reducing the scale of the investment and renting premises rather than purchasing them. The contradiction is that if location is critical to a retailer, it would appear to make sound business sense to guarantee the continued use of this critical asset, and that is most securely achieved by acquiring either a freehold or long leasehold interest in the property. The final decision should be based on the forecast likelihood of a major change in the external environment which would mean that existing properties become more liabilities than assets.

Sometimes changes may be dramatic and lead the company to develop new channels of distribution which may, in themselves, be sizeable business. For example, the dynamic changes and increasing competitiveness in the financial services industry has led major companies to seek new methods of accessing customers, particularly at a time when they require financial services. Such an occasion arises when individuals buy houses, and this analysis has led both banks and insurance companies to build up, through acquisition, very sizeable chains of estate agents whereby access is gained at an early stage to a potential customer for financial services. A similar logic was perceived for both personal and institutional investment services, and major banks invested vast sums in acquiring a complete range of investment services so that they could offer 'one-stop shopping' to their customers. Both these industries had decided that these investments were justified because of the better channel of distribution which was gained to their customers, and not from any possibility of economies of scale between their existing businesses and the new ones into which they were moving.

The financial justification for the acquisition should not therefore be based on any improvement in the profit levels which could be achieved from the actual businesses acquired, and it is likely that the net present value of these future expected profits would be fully valued in their purchase costs. The profit improvements should be generated by the additional business opportunities which are created by access to this new channel of distribution, and the value will be determined by the ability of the combined businesses to pass business through from the initiating channel to the other areas. Indeed the lack of expertise of some of these large businesses in managing their newly acquired enterprises has made the acquisitions look very expensive, but it has probably proved that they could not have developed the new channel of distribution by themselves.

Wholesaling and retailing are the classic examples of where the choice of distribution channel can affect the success of the company, and a supplier should choose the channel which is most appropriate to the current stage of development of their product as discussed in Chapter 2. However, some companies decide very deliberately to bypass the traditional means of accessing the customer and to set up their own channel of distribution. This may mean establishing direct consumer outlets, such as a chain of retail shops, and where the business is growing rapidly anyway such a development could place an intolerable strain on the financial resources of the business.

One means of reducing the funding requirement but effectively maintaining control of the channel of distribution is by franchising the concept to other independent businesses, who can use their own financing to develop *their* business. Franchising works best when a specific concept has been developed by the originator (franchisor) which can be exactly replicated by independent small businesses (franchisees) so that a consistent image and quality of product is delivered to the customer, who may not know that the particular outlet being used is a franchised business. Some franchise businesses, such as McDonalds, have developed very sophisticated and exhaustive training and control procedures in order to ensure that the consistent level of quality and service on which they built their originally successful business is maintained in each branch. Franchising allows the business to grow very much faster than it could on its own and should also ensure goal congruence at the individual outlet level because the franchisees are motivated to develop their own businesses. The franchisor normally charges a royalty on sales or supplies all the product sold on which a margin is earned, or both, as well as requiring a sizeable initial payment from the franchisee to acquire the product rights.

In exchange for these payments, the franchisee is normally granted an exclusive area in which to trade and will be supported by training, management assistance where necessary and, most importantly, overall marketing support for the total business. Thus a national, and even international, image can be developed and a McDonalds franchisee in (say) Cologne, Germany will benefit from custom from overseas visitors who know and trust the name and image, even though they may never have visited the particular outlet before. This means that franchising is attractive to many businesses which require a high level of national marketing support in order to establish an image but where a high degree of personal service is required with strong local management motivation. Consequently franchising is now well established in such areas as fast food, clothes retailing, speciality retailing, car parts and specialist repairs, photocopying and printing services, and even such businesses as picture framing, plumbing and drain clearing.

However, several very large companies have been using a form of franchising for many years but possibly with less emphasis on controlling the quality of service delivered to their ultimate customers, with a consequent lessening in overall customer satisfaction. This occurs where a company sells and distributes its product through exclusively appointed agents, who are supposed to be experts at providing direct consumer support to the overall marketing efforts of the company. An example of this is the distribution of motor cars which are sold by the manufacturers to dealers who have an exclusive right to sell that manufacturer's vehicles to the public in a specified area. The product and the image of the producing company is controlled on an overall basis but the local dealer is expected to develop his customer base and effectively build a local franchise of his own. The dealers also normally ensure the quality of the product before onward delivery to *their* customers and also carry out the post-sales repair work for the customer, including any required warranty work (for which they are reimbursed by the manufacturer). If it works well the customers develop a closer relationship with the local business, the dealer, than they are likely to with a major multinational business producing possibly several million vehicles across Europe.

There should be a financial attraction to the major car manufacturer of introducing specialist dealers because they could control the entire distribution network directly, selling through their own retail outlets. The required investment in retail locations and stocks of vehicles and spare parts would be immense if it was to be done on a national or international scale, and the argument is that the removal of the local entrepreneurial motivation might result in less sales revenue being generated than at present. This is particularly true where, despite exclusive dealership areas, one car company's dealers are actively competing with each other as well as with dealers for other motor manufacturers. If this level of competition increases the total market share achieved, the manufacturer sells more cars without having had to invest in increased marketing activity. The risk of this strategy is that local dealers may build very strong local brand franchises for themselves. If they decide to change their allegiance and become dealers for a different manufacturer, they may be able to maintain a high proportion of *their* previous customers (that is, consumers) because the consumer identifies with the dealer and not the distant manufacturer. Thus there may be some financial benefits of maintaining some distance from ultimate customers but there are also risks involved which may be more harmful in the long term than the benefits in the short term of reduced costs and investments.

Market segments

This use of local smaller businesses to access the end customer can be taken to even greater levels of sophistication by some companies because different channels of distribution can be used for different customers, depending on cost effectiveness or selective branding.

Some fmcg manufacturing companies will only sell directly to major

412   *Applications and Examples*

chains of supermarkets or other such large retailers, and will distribute their products through wholesalers to the remainder of the retail market, on the basis of cost effectiveness in distribution and selling. In financial services the same arguments have been applied with companies only employing their own salesforces for certain segments of the market and also paying independent brokers to sell their products on a commission basis in the other market segments.

It can be possible to create a strong marketing strategy by deliberately using a different channel of distribution to access the market and this could be done by only selling direct to the consumer and not paying brokerage commissions (for example, The Equitable Life Assurance Co.). In the travel industry, for example, Tjaereborg do not pay travel agents commissions and therefore sell their holidays direct to the public on the platform of passing on the saving in commission and being consequently better value. Some other tour companies are now also large-scale travel agents and provide additional financial services such as their own travellers cheques as well (for example, Thomas Cook, which is owned by Midland Bank Group). The use of different channels can therefore change the positioning of the business and attract customers from particular market segments.

This can also be used to remove major growth constraints on the business by opening up new channels to attract additional customers. For example, a fast-growing retailer, such as Next plc, may find its sales growth rate restricted by its ability to find good retail locations which are suitable for its particular merchandise. If a new channel of distribution can be found this may alleviate not only this problem but could also provide a means of servicing additional customers, to whom the existing products are attractive but who cannot physically visit the shops during normal business hours. By moving into mail order and launching a suitably upmarket catalogue to match the existing brand image, Next has opened up a major new channel of distribution which builds on the existing market image which has been established. In order to minimize the risk created by its lack of experience and management expertise in the business of mail order, Next based the move around its merger with/ acquisition of Grattans, a well-established mail order business. As well as gaining expertise, Next can add its own retailing expertise (for example, in inventory management) potentially to improve the asset utilization of Grattans and a new national distribution centre was constructed for Grattans very shortly after the businesses merged. Thus the combination of some businesses can add value to both, and consequently create an increased combined value for the shareholders.

If the growth of a business is constrained not so much by access to physical locations but by its existing dominant market share, it may be logical to seek to use its management expertise and product knowledge in a different segment of the market. Hence a move into a new geographical segment could be a strategic decision which utilizes the strengths of the business and opens up new growth opportunities (for example, as Dixons Group plc has done with its move into the United States, again minimizing the lack of local knowledge by initially entering the market by acquisition and thus buying in experienced local managers). Alternatively, a company could decide that its customer base is its most important marketing asset and decide to sell more products to these customers by expanding its range of products, thus moving the opposite way within the Ansoff matrix considered in Chapter 6 (page 171). Companies using either of these strategies are trying to improve the financial return by increasing the utilisation of their principal marketing assets, which of course are frequently excluded from the calculation of return on assets or investment, but which can have significant impacts on the correct decision and should consequently be included in any internal financial evaluations.

Service levels

Another way in which place can be used to affect the financial return achieved by a business is by differentiating the level of service offered to the customer away from the normal level supplied by the industry. The change may be relatively small or it can be quite dramatic and have very far-reaching implications for the competitors.

For example, furniture retailing used to be based on a strategy of holding display stocks only and taking orders from customers which were passed on to manufacturers. This could cause considerable delay in the delivery of the furniture to the customer depending on the supply position from the manufacturer to retailer. This strategy minimized the financing cost of holding stock for the retailer and also reduced the risk of stock obsolescence when new ranges were introduced, because only one display range was held and this was normally sold at a discount in 'the sales'. However, if there was a segment of the market which preferred to take home the furniture as soon as it was purchased, there was potential for a different service level approach to furniture retailing. MFI developed this market segment by holding considerable stocks of flat pack furniture for self-assembly by the customer and allowing the customer to collect the purchases immediately, rather than even waiting for delivery. This meant that car parking space was essential and to achieve this, most store locations were out of town and many were not even located among other retailers. Sites were chosen for good, cost-effective space where products could be displayed and also stored in volume, as well as for good road access on the basis that all customers would be coming by car.

This trend in segmenting retailing by service level has spread to the do-it-yourself sector where similarly large out-of-town superstores are being developed which carry a very wide range of instantly available merchandise at competitive prices, but where the product knowledge of the average staff member may be lower than the more established small DIY store, many of which personally served customers rather than requiring them to self-select their purchases using a supermarket-style trolley. The financial strategy for the large chains of such retailers is to use their bulk buying power to obtain the lowest possible costs and to accept a lower contribution level in order to achieve very high sales volumes which can generate a satisfactory return on the often high investment in fixed assets. Their buying power can also be used to minimize their investment in stocks, even while holding an extensive range in the shops, by negotiating (or simply taking) extended credit from their suppliers. This facility is normally unavailable to other smaller retailers and thus a significant competitive advantage has been obtained.

It is possible to use similar strategies to sell other products where service can be made an optional part of the offering, and the lack of service may be compensated by a lower price level. A good example here is electrical retailing where some retailers, such as Comet, hold high stock levels, which are principally financed by suppliers, in out-of-town locations and so keep their cost base to a minimum which enables them to sell at discount prices. Other electrical retailers, generally stocking a more upmarket product range, rely not on discount pricing but on the customer being able to see or hear the comparable products in a pleasant setting and on the technical knowledge of their sales staff to add value to the sale. The critical point for both is that their selling price is related to the cost base of the business and to the investment in assets, so that a satisfactory return is achieved.

Stockholding costs

If a business decides to differentiate its service level by holding high inventory levels near to its customers so that very quick delivery times can be achieved, it is essential that the full costs of stockholding are included in the financial justification for this strategy to ensure that the pricing level fully recovers this total cost. The total cost of stockholding can be extremely high, particularly where the products require special handling or storage conditions (for example, frozen or chilled storage).

Stockholding costs can increase due to deterioration and shrinkage (especially due to theft) and stocks may become obsolete and unsaleable.

These are in addition to the costs involved in physically storing the inventory (for example, rent of warehousing, use of equipment, labour, lighting and heating and transport) and in financing the inventory as well as insuring the stocks. Some estimates of the stockholding costs are as high as 25–30 per cent of the total value of the stocks and so any ways in which stockholdings can be reduced without affecting the ability of the company to service orders should be investigated thoroughly. Not surprisingly therefore inventory management is now very sophisticated and required stockholding levels are often calculated by computerized models which take account of the wide range of factors which affect the optimum stockholding level. Most of these models are based on the classic economic ordering quantity (EOQ) which shows the volume of any stock item which it is most economical to purchase using the factors included. The formula is generally used is:

$$EOQ = \sqrt{\frac{2 \times S \times F}{V \times I}}$$

where S = annual sales volume
   F = fixed costs incurred by placing one order
   V = cost per unit of product
   I = inventory holding cost – that is, the cost of
      holding one unit in stock

Because of the specialist skills required for many areas of inventory and distribution management, many companies are subcontracting these functions to third party specialists, who may provide a complete facilities management service for many similar companies and hence achieve economies of scale.

Exporting

Companies also differ in the way they pass on to their customers the costs of distribution which in the case of exporting can be considerable. There are several different ways that an exporter can quote selling prices which indicate the degree to which if any, the price includes the distribution costs. These include:

1	Ex-factory gate	goods are sold at prices which do not include any allowance for distribution
2	Free alongside ship (FAS)	goods are delivered to the port but not loaded onto the ship
3	Free on board (FOB)	the goods are delivered and loaded on the ship but not transported to the destination port

4   Cost, insurance, freight (CIF)   the goods are delivered to the
                                     customer with the costs reflected in
                                     the price.

In many cases this level of pricing is not really part of the marketing mix as it represents different ways of the distribution costs being passed to the customer, and how visible these costs are made as part of the total selling price.

As well as increasing the distribution costs involved, exporting often increases the credit risk involved in the sale because, as well as potentially introducing the risk of movements in foreign currencies (mentioned in Chapter 13), the level of control over and contact with the foreign customer may be lower. If the selling company has no operation in the country concerned it may not have a great deal of knowledge of the local environment and the creditworthiness of its potential customers. In order to encourage exporting, which is vitally important to a trading nation such as Great Britain, the government has set up an export financing institution which for a fee will insure a proportion of the sale proceeds on export deals. The Export Credit Guarantee Department (ECGD) has very good information on the country's major trading partners and can offer advice on how to do business overseas as well as providing a guarantee of the company receiving up to 90 per cent of the sales proceeds if the customer eventually fails to pay. The idea is that the supplier should be able to recover its costs from the ECGD and only be at risk for the profit margin on the sale. As mentioned the ECGD charges a fee for its services and it is supposed to be a self-financing organization in the same way as privately owned credit insurance companies are. However, economic disruptions in particular countries (such as Nigeria), which interrupt almost all payment flows from that country, can create severe pressures on an organization like the ECGD if it is supporting a large volume of outstanding exports to that country.

If a company wishes to develop its trading in a particular country but does not believe that the ultimate sales volume will justify setting up a fully fledged overseas company it may consider appointing an overseas agent to handle its affairs. By definition agents act on behalf of the company and do not therefore buy the product themselves to sell on to their own customers; this role would be fulfilled by an independent distributor, possibly under a franchise agreement as mentioned earlier in the chapter. The ideal overseas agents should have good knowledge of the relevant local market and the appropriate channels of distribution, as well as having sales and marketing expertise. If the exporting company's range of product is insufficient to support a viable agency business, the agents should be handling other complementary but not competitive products so that their businesses are financially sound and the overall product range is strong enough to establish a good negotiating position with local customers. It should be remembered that the agent is selling on the exporter's behalf and is normally paid on a sales commission basis, so that although the agent is the local representative of the company the credit risk on the exported sales normally remains with the exporter.

When export sales expand sufficiently the company may decide to set up its own sales and marketing company in the country and, depending on the relative distribution costs involved, it may become worthwhile to set up a separate production or operations business locally as well. The company could do this by 'going international' itself and form an overseas subsidiary or division or, increasingly due to local regulations and the need for local market knowledge, it could license another company to produce and market the product on a local basis. Licensing arrangement are now quite common even for very major global brands (such as Coca-Cola) where the problems and costs of distribution outweigh the advantages of maintaining direct control over the product quality and the implementation of the marketing strategy. Licensees normally pay a royalty on sales revenues and may pay a fee to purchase the licence and so, in several ways, a licence is similar to a franchise arrangement. However, generally the freedom is greater for licensees to manage and develop the business in accordance with their own objectives and often licences for overseas-based products form only one element in the total product range of the licensee (for example, IDV and its licence for Smirnoff mentioned in Chapter 12) whereas for a franchisee the franchise is normally the only business segment.

Thus if exports are successful, there are several ways in which a company can develop its presence in these overseas markets, but the initial marketing strategy may be critically important to this and other new market segments. One problem which many companies face is how to deal with small orders because in a new market segment the initial orders are likely to be small but, if successfully handled, can develop into a major part of the company's future business. For most companies there is a cost penalty of accepting small orders, not least because a large part of the order processing and delivery costs are incurred by each physical order and are not proportional to the order value. Therefore there is a financial argument for putting a surcharge on small orders (this could be effectively achieved by giving a discount on large orders as discussed in Chapter 12) to compensate for the increased costs involved, and some businesses have implemented this concept by establishing a minimum order value which they will accept. However, charging a surcharge on small orders puts these customers at a competitive disadvantage and if the marketing objective is to develop these market segments the surcharge may make it more difficult to achieve this objective. Indeed in order to stimulate growth in these segments it may be advisable to sell at lower prices than normal, not higher.

It is important that the company does not achieve this lower price level during the launch and growth phases by apparently granting a discount for small orders, because there is no incentive for a customer to increase its individual order size even as its total purchase volume grows and the company may find itself processing a vast number of small orders. If the financial analysis is properly carried out, the company should be able to calculate a reasonable surcharge for small orders, which reimburses the additional costs which it incurs, and to make a separate promotional allowance in some form so as to reduce the effective selling price in a potential growth market segment. By doing this, the promotional marketing activity is focused according to the marketing objectives and other small orders are charged an extra cost as an effective disincentive.

Marketing strategy issues

Product versus customer emphasis

We have regularly referred to the need for financial information to be analysed into the appropriate segments for decision-making and this often can be reduced to a product and customer matrix. One marketing strategy issue which can be important is which element, product or customer, is seen to be dominant as this will tend to control how the marketing image is developed. If the company consider the customer as the critical marketing asset, then it will probably wish to generate the maximum level of company association in the customer's mind across the whole product range. This may lead to the company name being the brand name or being closely associated with each product. For single product companies this may not be a problem but even here some businesses have decided to retain a number of distinct brand images whereas others have only one profile in the market place (for example, in the car industry Ford, Mercedes, BMW have only one brand but Rover Group until recently had several different names and General Motors maintains Vauxhall in the United Kingdom and Opel in Germany and several distinct images in the United States).

Even for multiproduct companies, having a single identity can be argued to be cheaper in terms of advertising because only one message has to be communicated, and there is a higher probability of spinoff sales from one product group to another. For example if a customer buys a Sony television which they like, they may be more willing to buy a Sony video recorder, because they recognize and trust the brand name, but Sony's very much larger competitor Matsushita (the world's largest electrical manufacturer) does not have such a single image since it produces a number of competing brands. One argument for this proliferation of branding has already been illustrated in Chapter 12 as erecting an effective barrier to entry. Another is to minimize the risk of damaging the image or reputation of all of the business if a problem is encountered with one specific product or brand name, and thus each brand is given an identity of its own and the corporate name is not used as a major product marketing platform.

This may be relevant where there is a high risk of failure in new products due to their using new technologies and the company does not want to damage the reputation for quality of existing products, but it can also be appropriate where joining two products together in the consumer's mind may be detrimental. For example, the major companies in the petfood market also produce canned food for people, using related technologies to that used to process petfood, but they may not consider it appropriate to highlight their linkage. Also the major banks all have very strong corporate brands but they do not incorporate some of their operations (for example, debt factoring), under these corporate brands, presumably because they are seen in a less favourable light by some of their customers and could damage the overall image built up on the other product areas.

New customers versus new products

Another aspect of the relative emphasis between products and customers is whether the major investments are made in launching new products which are aimed at existing customers, or in finding new customers for the existing products. Clearly companies can do both, and sometimes do, but with limited marketing resources the company should select which of these growth strategies is seen as more appropriate. If a company wishes to achieve sales of additional products to its existing customer base it can build on the corporate brand which it has developed and this has been very successfully achieved by major retailers with their private label products, which are very strong corporate brands (for example, St Michael and Sainsbury's).

However, this strategy means that all new products must be attractive to the specific customer profile which has already been selected and should build on the brand attributes which have been invested in and developed over time. Thus if the external environment should change substantially and the relative customer power base change significantly, this type of company could find it more difficult to adjust its market positioning quickly than a business with no corporate image but a series of strong individual brands.

If it is desired to expand the range of existing customers and sell similar products to new customers, the establishment of a strong corporate brand may make this difficult, and may force the company to develop or acquire a second, or several, other franchises which can be used for other market segments. Thus in our car industry example Volkswagen with

Audi and Fiat with Alfa Romeo can attack two segments of the market in a very focused way, while the very strong single franchise of Ford is more restricted. The ability to increase the utilization of very high investments in fixed assets by selling in more than one segment of the market can improve the financial return substantially.

Segmentation strategies

This segmentation strategy has been adopted by some airlines both in terms of following a focused strategy of low price and low service levels (for example, People Express and Virgin Atlantic) and also by major airlines which have provided very high price and high service levels on some products while also running low price, low service operations as well. This strategy can be successful provided the customer expectation is correctly conditioned by the price and overall package presented, so that the business traveller on Concorde does not expect the same level of service when flying on a British Airtours package holiday to Spain.

The usage of the marketing mix is another way of achieving differentiated products aimed at different segments of the market so that a basically generic product can be positioned in several ways to appeal to specific categories of customers. Thus a company can produce a 'value brand' which is low priced and has the minimum marketing support to create awareness of the value message. The company could also have a 'premium brand' which is high priced but very glossily presented in terms of packaging and overall marketing support. In between the same company could have one or more tactical fighting brands which can be used against competitors, and whose exact market positioning can be made moderately flexible when necessary. By doing this the company can generate sales from all segments of the market and can also respond rapidly to competitive moves in any sector. Also if one segment shows unexpected growth or decline, the company can use its existing presence as a base from which to develop the appropriate marketing strategy. This type of multilayered product strategy can be particularly relevant where the investment in fixed and current assets is very high and a large proportion of costs are fixed so that maintaining volume of activity can be critically important.

Pre-emptive positioning

We have already seen in Chapter 13 how the use of the long-run cost curve as a pricing strategy in a experience-based industry can be extremely useful as a competitive measure and it may deter new competitors from entering the industry if they see existing prices as unattractive. We have also seen, in Chapter 12, brand proliferation as another potential barrier to entry and these are two examples of market positioning being used pre-emptively. If a strong competitive advantage can be established this can be used to forestall any aggressive moves by competitors and may stop serious competition developing if used early and strongly enough.

However, if the market is already developed with established competitors when a competitive advantage becomes available the sensible strategy may be different. When competitors are considering entering a market they should logically include all the costs incurred in producing and launching the product, and these costs may be sufficiently great to deter them from doing so, if we use our pre-emptive positioning strategy. Once they are in the market, their options are different; they either stay in or leave (that is they have a possible exit strategy if we make it too costly for them to remain). The financial evaluation of an exit strategy is based on the costs saved by leaving and the opportunity cost of the realizable value of the assets employed in the business (the investment which could be taken out of the industry). Normally this is significantly less than the original cost of the assets invested and so it may be more difficult to force competitors out of the market than it is to stop them entering in the first place. This is illustrated in Figure 16.1 which shows that if the assets only have scrap value if sold on exiting from the industry then the competitor may well stay in the market even when making a very small contribution over variable costs. In some industries there is a sizeable cost to be incurred in closing down certain facilities (such as mining, as the mines have to be made safe) and so it may be financially worthwhile staying in the industry even if a small accounting loss is being incurred.

Changing technology

Therefore to force a company out of an industry the competitive advantage has to be very great and this is often caused by changing technology. Consequently it may be possible for a company to use a breakthrough in technology to force competitors out of the industry and, if this is done, it becomes very difficult for them to justify re-entering the industry even when they have developed comparable technology. If our pre-empting company plans ahead it will try to ensure that the market price level is maintained just below the level at which competitors can financially justify investing in new plant and equipment. Once competitors have left the industry they should justify any new investment as exactly that: a new investment on which a satisfactory financial return

Entry and exit decisions

Opportunity cost of capital	= 15%
Investment required in fixed assets	= £4 m
Investment in working capital	= £1 m
Total investment	£5 m
Estimated realizable value of assets	= £100 000

Cost structure of product	*£/unit*
Direct variable costs	5
Indirect costs	10
	15
Fixed cost	10
Total costs	£25

Notes
1 Costs per unit based on output of 100 000 units per year, which is best forecast of sales activity
2 If production ceased, the indirect costs and fixed costs would still be incurred once taken on for this product because of their requirement for other products, which are also being produced at this time.

Selling price required for:	*Entry*	*Exit*
Cost base	£25	£5
add Return on investment needed using 15%		
and assumed 100 000 units per year	7.50	0.15
Price	£32.50	£5.15

Conclusion
1 In order to enter the market, the company has to be confident that a price level of £32.50 can be advised.
2 Once in the market, the fixed and indirect costs can be ignored and the only cost saving is £5 per unit plus the opportunity cost volume at 15% on the salvage value of the investment. Thus if the selling price is above £5.15 the company will stay in.

Figure 16.1

should be made, that is, by using the cost of the investment in the computation.

What is happening is that the technology breakthrough is significantly reducing the value of the existing assets owned by the companies in the industry because, if price levels are effectively reduced for the current range of products in the market, the future profits will be lower and so the asset values should accordingly be reduced. If the company developing the new technology does not have any existing investment in the market, they do not suffer any of this decrease in value, and so can attempt to force out competitors at no cost to itself.

However, if the company developing the new technology is already dominant in the existing market (for example, IBM), it would face the largest asset value writedown because of the launch of the new technology. It may therefore not be in its financial interest to announce the breakthrough if it will not increase its overall profitability due to the impact on its *existing* profit stream. It may wait to make the announcement until it feels that its dominant position is under threat by a competitor or some other possible new technology which it feels could be launched in the market. If this is so it would be best to pre-empt their announcement and ideally to stop their product from being launched. This might be achieved by demonstrating that there is a better new technology which will place the competitor at a severe competitive disadvantage should it decide to go ahead with the new investment.

Information as a marketing advantage

This places an immense value on the information regarding forthcoming new product announcements, but information is also frequently capable of generating other marketing advantages. Consequently where information is a critical factor some companies have invested heavily in building management information systems which can give faster, more usable marketing information so as to enable better decisions to be made and actions taken to produce improved financial results. A very clear example can be taken from the area of very perishable products where fruit and vegetable market traders will adjust their selling prices according to the rate of sales and the level of stocks remaining, on the basis that the stock may be worthless if not sold in a very limited period. In this case the marketing information system may be in the trader's head but airlines and some hotel groups have developed very much more sophisticated versions of the same idea. Aeroplane flight tickets and hotel beds for a specific night have no value after the event and so it is vitally important that all possible efforts are made to sell each one. This requires the best information regarding not only how sales are going but how they *should* be going if everything is to be sold. Thus a predictive model based on the historical analysis can be developed which can generate early warnings if sales are falling behind the required rate. The earlier the warning can be given, the more time is available for a change in the marketing activity to stimulate demand so as to increase the overall contribution (for example, increase advertising, reduce prices, offer special promotions, etc.). This is a classic illustration of financial analysis, planning and control interacting with the marketing mix to improve the performance of the business – which is how we started the book.

Appendix 1: Discount factors – present value tables

Present value of £1 received *n* years hence, at a discount rate of *x*% per year

Years (n)	1%	2%	3%	4%	5%	6%	7%	8%	10%	12%	14%	15%	16%	18%	20%	22%	25%	28%	30%	35%	40%	50%
1	0.990	0.980	0.971	0.962	0.952	0.943	0.935	0.926	0.909	0.893	0.877	0.870	0.862	0.847	0.833	0.820	0.800	0.781	0.769	0.741	0.714	0.667
2	0.980	0.961	0.943	0.925	0.907	0.890	0.873	0.857	0.826	0.797	0.769	0.756	0.743	0.718	0.694	0.672	0.640	0.610	0.592	0.549	0.510	0.444
3	0.971	0.942	0.915	0.889	0.864	0.840	0.816	0.794	0.751	0.712	0.675	0.658	0.641	0.609	0.579	0.551	0.512	0.477	0.455	0.406	0.364	0.296
4	0.961	0.924	0.888	0.855	0.823	0.792	0.763	0.735	0.683	0.636	0.592	0.572	0.552	0.516	0.482	0.451	0.410	0.373	0.350	0.301	0.260	0.198
5	0.951	0.906	0.863	0.822	0.784	0.747	0.713	0.681	0.621	0.567	0.519	0.497	0.476	0.437	0.402	0.370	0.328	0.291	0.269	0.223	0.186	0.132
6	0.942	0.888	0.837	0.790	0.746	0.705	0.666	0.630	0.564	0.507	0.456	0.432	0.410	0.370	0.335	0.303	0.262	0.227	0.207	0.165	0.133	0.088
7	0.933	0.871	0.813	0.760	0.711	0.665	0.623	0.583	0.513	0.452	0.400	0.376	0.354	0.314	0.279	0.249	0.210	0.178	0.159	0.122	0.095	0.059
8	0.923	0.853	0.789	0.731	0.677	0.627	0.582	0.540	0.467	0.404	0.351	0.327	0.305	0.266	0.233	0.204	0.168	0.139	0.123	0.091	0.068	0.039
9	0.914	0.837	0.766	0.703	0.645	0.592	0.544	0.500	0.424	0.361	0.308	0.284	0.263	0.225	0.194	0.167	0.134	0.108	0.094	0.067	0.048	0.026
10	0.905	0.820	0.744	0.676	0.614	0.558	0.508	0.463	0.386	0.322	0.270	0.247	0.227	0.191	0.162	0.137	0.107	0.085	0.073	0.050	0.035	0.017
11	0.896	0.804	0.722	0.650	0.585	0.527	0.475	0.429	0.350	0.287	0.237	0.215	0.195	0.162	0.135	0.112	0.086	0.066	0.056	0.037	0.025	0.012
12	0.887	0.788	0.701	0.625	0.557	0.497	0.444	0.397	0.319	0.257	0.208	0.187	0.168	0.137	0.112	0.092	0.069	0.052	0.043	0.027	0.018	0.008
13	0.879	0.773	0.681	0.601	0.530	0.469	0.415	0.368	0.290	0.229	0.182	0.163	0.145	0.116	0.093	0.075	0.055	0.040	0.033	0.020	0.013	0.005
14	0.870	0.758	0.661	0.577	0.505	0.442	0.388	0.340	0.263	0.205	0.160	0.141	0.125	0.099	0.078	0.062	0.044	0.032	0.025	0.015	0.009	0.003
15	0.861	0.743	0.642	0.555	0.481	0.417	0.362	0.315	0.239	0.183	0.140	0.123	0.108	0.084	0.065	0.051	0.035	0.025	0.020	0.011	0.006	0.002
16	0.853	0.728	0.623	0.534	0.458	0.394	0.339	0.292	0.218	0.163	0.123	0.107	0.093	0.071	0.054	0.042	0.028	0.019	0.015	0.008	0.005	0.002
17	0.844	0.714	0.605	0.513	0.436	0.371	0.317	0.270	0.198	0.146	0.108	0.093	0.080	0.060	0.045	0.034	0.023	0.015	0.012	0.006	0.003	0.001
18	0.836	0.700	0.587	0.494	0.416	0.350	0.296	0.250	0.180	0.130	0.095	0.081	0.069	0.051	0.038	0.028	0.018	0.012	0.009	0.005	0.002	0.001
19	0.828	0.686	0.570	0.475	0.396	0.331	0.277	0.232	0.164	0.116	0.083	0.070	0.060	0.043	0.031	0.023	0.014	0.009	0.007	0.003	0.002	0.001
20	0.820	0.673	0.554	0.456	0.377	0.312	0.258	0.215	0.149	0.104	0.073	0.061	0.051	0.037	0.026	0.019	0.012	0.007	0.005	0.002	0.001	
21	0.811	0.660	0.538	0.439	0.359	0.294	0.242	0.199	0.135	0.093	0.064	0.053	0.044	0.031	0.022	0.015	0.009	0.006	0.004	0.002	0.001	
22	0.803	0.647	0.522	0.422	0.342	0.278	0.226	0.184	0.123	0.083	0.056	0.046	0.038	0.026	0.018	0.013	0.007	0.004	0.003	0.001	0.001	
23	0.795	0.634	0.507	0.406	0.326	0.262	0.211	0.170	0.112	0.074	0.049	0.040	0.033	0.022	0.015	0.010	0.006	0.003	0.002	0.001		
24	0.788	0.622	0.492	0.390	0.310	0.247	0.197	0.158	0.102	0.066	0.043	0.035	0.028	0.019	0.013	0.008	0.005	0.003	0.002	0.001		
25	0.780	0.610	0.478	0.375	0.295	0.233	0.184	0.146	0.092	0.059	0.038	0.030	0.024	0.016	0.010	0.007	0.004	0.002	0.001	0.001		
26	0.772	0.598	0.464	0.361	0.281	0.220	0.172	0.135	0.084	0.053	0.033	0.026	0.021	0.014	0.009	0.006	0.003	0.002	0.001			
27	0.764	0.586	0.450	0.347	0.268	0.207	0.161	0.125	0.076	0.047	0.029	0.023	0.018	0.011	0.007	0.005	0.002	0.001	0.001			
28	0.757	0.574	0.437	0.333	0.255	0.196	0.150	0.116	0.069	0.042	0.026	0.020	0.016	0.010	0.006	0.004	0.002	0.001	0.001			
29	0.749	0.563	0.424	0.321	0.243	0.185	0.141	0.107	0.063	0.037	0.022	0.017	0.014	0.008	0.005	0.003	0.002	0.001	0.001			
30	0.742	0.552	0.412	0.308	0.231	0.174	0.131	0.099	0.057	0.033	0.020	0.015	0.012	0.007	0.004	0.003	0.001	0.001	0.001			
40	0.672	0.453	0.307	0.208	0.142	0.097	0.067	0.046	0.022	0.011	0.005	0.004	0.003	0.001	0.001							
50	0.608	0.372	0.228	0.141	0.087	0.054	0.034	0.021	0.009	0.003	0.001	0.001	0.001									

Appendix 2: Cumulative discount factors – annuity tables

Present value of £1 received each year for *n* years

Years (n)	1%	2%	3%	4%	5%	6%	7%	8%	10%	12%	14%	15%	16%	18%	20%	22%	25%	28%	30%	35%	40%	50%
1	0.990	0.980	0.971	0.962	0.952	0.943	0.935	0.926	0.909	0.893	0.877	0.870	0.862	0.847	0.833	0.820	0.800	0.781	0.769	0.741	0.714	0.667
2	1.970	1.942	1.914	1.886	1.859	1.833	1.808	1.783	1.736	1.690	1.647	1.626	1.605	1.566	1.528	1.492	1.440	1.392	1.361	1.289	1.224	1.111
3	2.941	2.884	2.829	2.775	2.723	2.673	2.624	2.577	2.487	2.402	2.322	2.283	2.246	2.174	2.106	2.043	1.952	1.868	1.816	1.696	1.589	1.407
4	3.902	3.808	3.717	3.630	3.546	3.465	3.387	3.312	3.170	3.037	2.914	2.855	2.798	2.690	2.589	2.494	2.362	2.241	2.166	1.997	1.849	1.605
5	4.853	4.713	4.580	4.452	4.329	4.212	4.100	3.993	3.791	3.605	3.433	3.352	3.274	3.127	2.991	2.864	2.689	2.532	2.436	2.220	2.035	1.737
6	5.795	5.601	5.417	5.242	5.076	4.917	4.767	4.623	4.355	4.111	3.889	3.784	3.685	3.498	3.326	3.167	2.951	2.759	2.643	2.385	2.168	1.824
7	6.728	6.472	6.230	6.002	5.786	5.582	5.389	5.206	4.868	4.564	4.288	4.160	4.039	3.812	3.605	3.416	3.161	2.937	2.802	2.508	2.263	1.883
8	7.652	7.325	7.020	6.733	6.463	6.210	5.971	5.747	5.335	4.968	4.639	4.487	4.344	4.078	3.837	3.619	3.329	3.076	2.925	2.598	2.331	1.922
9	8.566	8.162	7.786	7.435	7.108	6.802	6.515	6.247	5.759	5.328	4.946	4.772	4.607	4.303	4.031	3.786	3.463	3.184	3.019	2.665	2.379	1.948
10	9.471	8.983	8.530	8.111	7.722	7.360	7.023	6.710	6.145	5.650	5.216	5.019	4.833	4.494	4.192	3.923	3.571	3.269	3.092	2.715	2.414	1.965
11	10.368	9.787	9.253	8.760	8.306	7.887	7.499	7.139	6.495	5.938	5.453	5.234	5.029	4.656	4.327	4.035	3.656	3.335	3.147	2.757	2.438	1.977
12	11.255	10.575	9.954	9.385	8.863	8.384	7.943	7.536	6.814	6.194	5.660	5.421	5.197	4.793	4.439	4.127	3.725	3.387	3.190	2.779	2.456	1.985
13	12.134	11.348	10.635	9.986	9.393	8.853	8.358	7.904	7.103	6.424	5.842	5.583	5.342	4.910	4.533	4.203	3.780	3.427	3.223	2.799	2.469	1.990
14	13.004	12.106	11.296	10.563	9.899	9.295	8.745	8.244	7.367	6.628	6.002	5.724	5.468	5.008	4.611	4.265	3.824	3.459	3.249	2.814	2.478	1.993
15	13.865	12.849	11.938	11.118	10.380	9.712	9.108	8.559	7.606	6.811	6.142	5.847	5.575	5.092	4.675	4.315	3.859	3.483	3.268	2.825	2.484	1.995
16	14.718	13.578	12.561	11.652	10.838	10.106	9.446	8.851	7.824	6.974	6.265	5.954	5.669	5.162	4.730	4.357	3.887	3.503	3.283	2.834	2.489	1.997
17	15.562	14.292	13.166	12.166	11.274	10.477	9.763	9.122	8.022	7.120	6.373	6.047	5.749	5.222	4.775	4.391	3.910	3.518	3.295	2.840	2.492	1.998
18	16.398	14.992	13.754	12.659	11.689	10.828	10.059	9.372	8.201	7.250	6.467	6.128	5.818	5.273	4.812	4.419	3.928	3.529	3.304	2.844	2.494	1.999
19	17.226	15.678	14.324	13.134	12.085	11.158	10.335	9.604	8.365	7.366	6.550	6.198	5.877	5.316	4.843	4.442	3.942	3.539	3.311	2.848	2.496	1.999
20	18.046	16.351	14.878	13.590	12.462	11.470	10.594	9.818	8.514	7.469	6.623	6.259	5.929	5.353	4.870	4.460	3.954	3.546	3.316	2.850	2.497	1.999
21	18.857	17.011	15.415	14.029	12.821	11.764	10.835	10.017	8.649	7.562	6.687	6.312	5.973	5.384	4.891	4.476	3.963	3.551	3.320	2.852	2.498	2.000
22	19.660	17.658	15.937	14.451	13.163	12.042	11.061	10.201	8.772	7.645	6.743	6.359	6.011	5.410	4.909	4.488	3.970	3.556	3.323	2.853	2.498	2.000
23	20.456	18.292	16.444	14.857	13.488	12.303	11.272	10.371	8.883	7.718	6.792	6.399	6.044	5.432	4.925	4.499	3.976	3.559	3.325	2.854	2.499	2.000
24	21.243	18.914	16.936	15.247	13.798	12.550	11.469	10.529	8.985	7.784	6.835	6.434	6.073	5.451	4.937	4.507	3.981	3.562	3.327	2.855	2.499	2.000
25	22.023	19.523	17.413	15.622	14.094	12.783	11.653	10.675	9.077	7.843	6.873	6.464	6.097	5.467	4.948	4.514	3.985	3.564	3.329	2.856	2.499	2.000
26	22.795	20.121	17.877	15.983	14.375	13.003	11.825	10.810	9.161	7.896	6.906	6.491	6.118	5.480	4.956	4.520	3.988	3.566	3.330	2.856	2.500	2.000
27	23.560	20.707	18.327	16.330	14.643	13.211	11.986	10.935	9.237	7.943	6.935	6.514	6.136	5.492	4.964	4.524	3.990	3.567	3.331	2.856	2.500	2.000
28	24.316	21.281	18.764	16.663	14.898	13.406	12.137	11.051	9.307	7.984	6.961	6.534	6.152	5.502	4.970	4.528	3.992	3.568	3.331	2.857	2.500	2.000
29	25.066	21.844	19.188	16.984	15.141	13.591	12.277	11.158	9.370	8.022	6.983	6.551	6.166	5.510	4.975	4.531	3.994	3.569	3.332	2.857	2.500	2.000
30	25.808	22.396	19.600	17.292	15.372	13.765	12.409	11.258	9.427	8.055	7.003	6.566	6.177	5.517	4.979	4.534	3.995	3.569	3.332	2.857	2.500	2.000
40	32.835	27.355	23.115	19.793	17.159	15.046	13.331	11.925	9.779	8.244	7.105	6.642	6.233	5.548	4.997	4.544	3.999	3.571	3.333	2.857	2.500	2.000
50	39.196	31.424	25.730	21.482	18.256	15.762	13.800	12.233	9.915	8.304	7.133	6.661	6.246	5.554	4.999	4.545	4.000	3.571	3.333	2.857	2.500	2.000

Recommended further reading

Financial Accounting/Analysis

Reid, W. P. and Myddelton, D. R. *Meaning of Company Accounts*, Gower

Management Accounting/Planning

Drury, Colin *Management and Cost Accounting*, Van Nostrand Reinhold (UK)

Myddelton, D. R. and Corbett, P. *Accounting and Decision Making*, Longman

Allen, Michael and Myddelton, D. R. *Essential Management Accounting*, Prentice-Hall

Control Systems

Wilson, R. M. S. *Management Controls and Marketing Planning*, Heinemann

Simon, Sanford R. *Managing Marketing Profitability*, American Management Association

Donaldson, Gordon *Managing Corporate Wealth*, Praeger

General Texts

Myddelton, D. R. *Financial Decisions*, Longman

Robson, A. P. *Essential Accounting for Managers*, Cassell

Wilson, Brian (ed.) *The Small Business Handbook*, Blackwell

Index